"Michael Woods's exploration of the theological, liturgical, and practical relationships between the American liturgical movement and the National Catholic Rural Life Conference is an historical study of these movements and their leadership—and so much more. *Cultivating Soil and Soul* addresses the sacramental quality of agrarian life, of the soil and the turning of the seasons. In an age when environmental consciousness is strong and when consumers are making deliberate choices about buying food which is locally produced, Woods provides the sacramental underpinnings of those choices and promotes the reestablishment of the liturgy-life-justice connection so obvious to the early reformers."

Kathleen Hughes, RSCJ
Author of *Finding Voice to Give God Praise:*
*Essays in the Many Languages of the Liturgy*

"Michael Woods's book is a timely story of the holistic vision of the National Catholic Rural Life Conference and liturgical renewal before Vatican II. The agricultural vision was one of sustainability before that word became popular; the liturgical vision was unifying and inclusive, linking sustainability with sacramentality. Here a deepening spirituality is seen in its historical context. Woods's telling of the story of these two linked movements is vital to the contemporary church's self understanding. I heartily recommend it."

Brother David Andrews, CSC
Senior Representative, Food & Water Watch

*Michael J. Woods, SJ*

# CULTIVATING
# SOIL AND SOUL

Twentieth-Century Catholic Agrarians
Embrace the Liturgical Movement

**A PUEBLO BOOK**

Liturgical Press   Collegeville, Minnesota
www.litpress.org

A Pueblo Book published by Liturgical Press

Cover design by David Manahan, OSB. Illustration and logo © National Catholic Rural Life Conference. Used with permission.

Excerpts from documents of the Second Vatican Council are from *Vatican Council II: The Conciliar and Post Conciliar Documents*, by Austin Flannery, OP © 1992 (Costello Publishing Company, Inc.). Used with permission.

Scripture texts in this work are taken from the *New American Bible with Revised New Testament and Revised Psalms* © 1991, 1986, 1970 Confraternity of Christian Doctrine, Washington, DC, and are used by permission of the copyright owner. All Rights Reserved. No part of the *New American Bible* may be reproduced in any form without permission in writing from the copyright owner.

Library of Congress Cataloging-in-Publication Data

Woods, Michael J., SJ.
    Cultivating soil and soul : twentieth-century Catholic agrarians embrace the liturgical movement / Michael J. Woods.
        p.   cm.
    "A Pueblo book."
    Includes bibliographical references and index.
    ISBN 978-0-8146-6224-3
        1. Liturgical movement—Catholic Church—History—20th century.
    2. National Catholic Rural Life Conference (U.S.)—History.   3. Sociology, Rural—Religious aspects—Catholic Church.   I. Title.

BX1975.W65  2010
264'.02009730917340904—dc22

                                                            2009027691

*To my mother and father, Ellie and Jack,*
and the graced good sense they had in raising
John, Michelle, Christine, myself, and Douglas

# Contents

# Abbreviations

| | |
|---|---|
| ACLA | American Country Life Association |
| *AG* | *Ad Gentes* |
| CA | Catholic Action |
| CCD | Confraternity of Christian Doctrine |
| *CRL* | *Catholic Rural Life* |
| *CRLB* | *Catholic Rural Life Bulletin* |
| CUAA/SAD | The Catholic University of America Archives, National Catholic Welfare Conference/United States Catholic Conference, Social Action Department |
| DCA | Diocese of Covington, Kentucky Archives |
| DSA | Diocese of Springfield, Illinois Archives |
| *GS* | *Gaudium et Spes* |
| GUA/JLF | Georgetown University Archives, The John L. LaFarge Papers |
| *L&H* | *Land and Home* |
| MUA/LGL | Marquette University Archives, The Monsignor Luigi G. Ligutti Papers |
| MUA/NCRLC | Marquette University Archives, The National Catholic Rural Life Conference Records |
| MUA/SCA | Marquette University Archives, The Seminarians' Catholic Action Collection |
| NCRLC | National Catholic Rural Life Conference |
| NCWC | Nation Catholic Welfare Conference |
| *OF* | *Orate Fratres* |

| | |
|---|---|
| RLB | Rural Life Bureau |
| *RLC* | *Rural Life Column* |
| SAD | Social Action Department |
| *SC* | *Sacrosanctum Concilium* |
| SJAA | St. John's Abbey Archives, The Vigil Michel Papers |
| SJUA | St. John's University Archives, The Rural Life Collection |
| UNDA/GRM | University of Notre Dame Archives, Joseph Gremillion Papers |
| UNDA/PKNA | University of Notre Dame Archives, Frederick P. Kenkel Papers |
| *WBC* | *With the Blessing of the Church* |

# Preface

Under the leadership of Virgil Michel, OSB, the American liturgical movement had at least two central goals in the period prior to Vatican II: to restore to the faithful a participative role in the liturgy and to make a clearer connection between liturgy and life. The latter aim indicated that a rupture had taken place between the two, a problem that endures to the present day. To realize these goals, the liturgical movement collaborated with various Catholic social movements. The National Catholic Rural Life Conference (NCRLC) was one of them that made the liturgy the spiritual foundation of its social program for Catholic agrarians. During the eucharistic liturgy, bread and wine were offered that the farmers themselves grew. The agricultural blessings found in the *Roman Ritual* also joined liturgy and life. The liturgical year, so closely allied to nature's cycles, afforded farmers further opportunity to meld liturgy and life. In other NCRLC programs—religious schools, farmers retreats, study clubs—liturgical catechesis that employed agrarian imagery was constitutive of its overall program. The NCRLC maintained that there was a sacramental quality to rural culture as a whole. Soil, especially, had this quality, in that it brought forth both the material elements of sacramental liturgy (and other sacramentals) and food to feed a family, nation, and world. Soil conservation was a matter of justice. Rural arts and handcrafts also manifested this sacramental trait—things of the earth combined with human ingenuity. This study demonstrates that the NCRLC fostered a thoroughly sacramental worldview that joined land, liturgy, and life. In doing so, and in light of Catholic social teaching, a just social order was achieved. The research, primarily archival in nature, brought to light the close relationship shared between the liturgical movement and the NCRLC. This study demonstrates that in the preconciliar period rural Catholics did a fair job of trying to integrate their agrarian lives with the mysteries celebrated in the liturgy.

Saint Ignatius of Loyola once said that the source of all sin was *ingratitude*. I owe a debt of gratitude to many people. Thanks to the Society of Jesus and two provincials who trusted my discernment to do doctoral studies in liturgy and supported me all along the way, especially Fr. Tim Brown, SJ; to the parishioners at St. Alphonsus Church in Woodstock, Maryland, for their prayers, support, and for teaching a newly ordained priest much about what it means to be a minister in the church; to my dissertation committee of Msgr. Kevin Irwin, Sr. Margaret Mary Kelleher, OSU, and Christopher Kaufmann for their timely return of materials, questions that pressed for greater clarity, and their good scholarly example. Thanks also goes to Keith Pecklers, SJ, who, knowing my interests in rural life issues suggested that I explore the NCRLC archives. I discovered a wealth of material, and this obviously became my dissertation topic and thus, this book. One never forgets "where" one writes a dissertation, so much thanks goes to the Marquette University Jesuit Community where I lived during much of the research and writing. Marquette was chosen because the National Catholic Rural Life Conference archives are housed there in Raynor Library. Anyone who has worked in the area of Catholic Social Action inevitably mentions the name of Phil Runkle, the archivist in charge of that collection—thank you, Phil; additionally at Marquette, Matt Blessing, director of special collections, has helped to make those archives a destination for many a researcher; and thanks to Susan Stawicki-Vrobel and other staff for their assistance and encouragement. To David Klingeman, OSB, archivist at St. John's Abbey and University in Collegeville, Minnesota, for his assistance and hospitality, and where I found the pattern of praying *and* working an indictment of my own tendency to overwork. To Sharon Sumpter, archivist at the University of Notre Dame; Heidi Rubenstein at Georgetown University; W. John Shepherd, Associate Archivist, and Jane Stoeffler, Administrative Assistant at The Catholic University of America Archives; Mary Struckel at the Midwest Jesuit Archives in St. Louis; Audrey P. Newcomer, archivist for the Archdiocese of St. Louis; Sr. Mary Joan Dyer and Sr. Virginia Volkerding, Precious Blood Sisters of O'Fallon, Missouri; Christine Rivers, Chancellor, Diocese of Shreveport, Louisiana; Peter Ueberroth, archivist, Diocese of Toledo; Tom Ward, archivist, Diocese of Covington, Kentucky; to Sr. Susan Karina Dickey, OP, archivist and historian, Diocese of Spring-field, Illinois, for her assistance and wonderful hospitality at the Spring-field Dominican House. Thanks to my colleagues at The Catholic

University of America, for meals out and the necessary encouragement needed for the labor of doctoral work—Steve Wilbricht, CSC, Jim Sabak, OFM, Miriam Perkins, Trish Panganiban, Katie Mitnaul, Gabriel Pivarnik, OP, Stephen Sauer, SJ, Cristobal Fones, SJ, and Fr. Ted Kazanecki of the Diocese of Brooklyn (d. October 18, 2004), probably the smartest of us all, but who, in God's challenging providence, was taken from us all too soon; thanks to Jim Greenfield, OSFS, and all the Oblates at De Sales Hall for their gracious hospitality. Special thanks must go to Father Francis "Paul" Prucha, SJ, of the Marquette Jesuit community for his editorial assistance. I was warned when I submitted my manuscript to Fr. Prucha for editing and feedback; his honest critique of my writing was invaluable and I have tried to follow Paul's good counsel. Many thanks, too, must go to those at Liturgical Press who took on this project and brought it to completion: Hans Christoffersen; Aaron Raverty, OSB; David Manahan, OSB; Mary Stommes; and Colleen Stiller.

Finally, special gratitude is owed to my great friend Father Raymond Michael Utz, retired priest of the Diocese of Pittsburgh, who also read the dissertation and gave me much valuable feedback and encouragement. It was also Ray who opened my eyes to the power of liturgy well done. *Omnia Ad Maiorem Dei Gloriam!*

# Introduction

In a 1960 interview, Msgr. George "Alfalfa" Hildner, a priest of the St. Louis archdiocese, was quoted as saying: "Plowing straight up and down the hills is like stabbing into the back of the soil. I told the farmers they would receive absolution for any sin they confessed, but God help them if they confessed plowing straight up and down the hills."[1] This beloved pastor of St. John Church (Gildehaus, Missouri) articulated (albeit in language that strikes one today as pastorally insensitive) an insight which the National Catholic Rural Life Conference (NCRLC) promoted from its earliest days.[2] That is to say, soil and souls possess a unique affinity through which Christ's redemptive mission is expressed and lived out according to the church's liturgical and sacramental life. The NCRLC asserted that Christ's redemption was experienced in the working of the fields as well as through the celebration of the church's liturgy. God's salvific plan must always unfold and be realized in particular cultural contexts, in actual places involving real persons. The NCRLC believed that the rural-agricultural context provided an optimal environment for Christ's salvific mission to take root and to be lived out most fully. The liturgical-sacramental practices of the church provided one of the essential means to realize this goal.

In the early twentieth century, Virgil Michel, OSB, a monk of St. John's Abbey in Collegeville, Minnesota, judged that it was opportune to give new emphasis to the relationship between Christian worship and the living out in daily life of what that worship expresses. Among other possible sources, he combined two insights from contemporary papal teaching and made them integral to the agenda of the then

---

[1] "Alfalfa George: A Pastor Talks about God, the Land, and his People," *Jubilee* (August 1960): 14. Copy in Marquette University Archives, Monsignor Luigi G. Ligutti Collection, box F-2, folder "Correspondence H."

[2] The word "Conference" will be used interchangeably with NCRLC.

burgeoning American liturgical movement: "Pius X tells us that the liturgy is the indispensable source of the true Christian spirit; Pius XI says that the true Christian spirit is indispensable for social regeneration. Hence the conclusion: The liturgy is the indispensable basis of social regeneration."[3] Michel argued that the Mystical Body of Christ, shaped and sustained by the church's worship, was to be the animating force behind a more just social order. Despite the movement's efforts to bring the worshiping life of the church into closer alignment with her social teaching, it was often the case that these remained separate, and their intrinsic interrelationship was not always understood.

In essence, founders and leaders of the American liturgical movement were not attempting to initiate anything radically new. Rather, through their study of the church's liturgical history they wanted the Catholic Church "to return to its roots in the early Church where the lives of Christians, both individually and corporately, were formed and shaped by the worship in which they participated, living their baptismal dignity as partners in Christ's Mystical Body."[4] Clearly, the most distinguishing characteristic of the movement was its fostering among the faithful a more intelligent and active participation in the church's liturgy. The work of these leaders bore its fruit at the Second Vatican Council (1962–65) with the promulgation of *Sacrosanctum Concilium*. The postconciliar period witnessed the founding of numerous academic programs and liturgical institutes that further deepened reflection on liturgical praxis. Active participation in the liturgy would impact a wide array of other renewal movements in the church—liturgical arts, music, education, and social justice. The American component of the movement (compared to the European) made the liturgy's relationship to social justice a distinctive trademark of its efforts.[5]

[3] Virgil Michel, "The Basis of Social Regeneration," *Orate Fratres* (hereafter *OF*) 9 (1935): 545; Pius X, *Motu proprio Tra le sollecitudini*, November 22, 1903. Vatican City: *Acta Sancta Sedis*.

[4] Keith Pecklers, *The Unread Vision: The Liturgical Movement in the United States of America, 1926–1955* (Collegeville, MN: Liturgical Press, 1998), 44–45. Pecklers' work has become a standard reference for anyone working on the American liturgical movement. He has uncovered the extensive network of relationships established between the liturgical movement and many mid-twentieth century Catholic social movements in the church. One of those organizations (movements) was the NCRLC.

[5] Pecklers, *Unread Vision*, 81–150.

One way the liturgical movement tried to reestablish the liturgy-life-justice relationship was through the retrieval of the seminal insight attributed to Prosper of Aquitaine (ca. fifth century). As personal secretary to Pope St. Leo the Great, Prosper put forth the maxim *ut legem credendi lex statuat supplicandi*, often recognized by its shortened version *lex orandi lex credendi*—the law of prayer grounds the law of belief.[6] Contemporary liturgical scholarship verifies that during the Middle Ages, the church experienced a break in this fundamental relationship between liturgy and theology, which had implications for the living out of the Christian faith. Thus, in light of Prosper's basic insight, the maxim *lex orandi lex credendi* requires the addition of the *lex vivendi* (or *lex agendi*).[7] The *lex vivendi* further helps to illuminate what the *lex orandi lex credendi* entails for the daily spiritual and moral existence of the Christian. The liturgy is comprised of many facets that come together to form a rather complex event (or *actio*) of "word, prayers, symbol, ritual, and the arts."[8] Such elements do not arise in a vacuum, but find their source and expression within a particular cultural context, something leaders in the liturgical movement realized. Central to how the law of Christian living plays out is the liturgy's interface with culture and culture's role in contributing to a just society.

In spite of the liturgical movement's efforts to make the liturgy and life connection clearer, the connection was missed at Vatican II. Margaret Mary Kelleher has identified several possible reasons. The relationship between liturgy and social reform was simply not a part of the American bishop's preparatory discussions in spite of the above-noted efforts in the United States. Twenty years after the Council, Msgr. John Egan, a priest of the Archdiocese of Chicago, declared that the relationship between liturgy and justice remained the "unfinished agenda" and added that there were simply "too few people" who saw the connection between the two. In addition, Kelleher

---

[6] Kevin Irwin, *Context and Text: Method in Liturgical Theology* (Collegeville, MN: Liturgical Press, 1994), 4, 44–45. In addition, contemporary liturgical theology has recovered the patristic terms *theologia prima* and *theologia secunda*. *Theologia prima* represented the liturgy as the church celebrated it (the act or event). *Theologia secunda* was the church's reflection on that theological event, and at times it served as a corrective to the first. *Theologia prima* and *theologia secunda* correspond to, but are not to be narrowly equated with, the *lex orandi* and the *lex credendi*.

[7] Ibid., 46; and Kevin Irwin, *Models of the Eucharist* (Mahwah, NJ: Paulist Press, 2005), 29–30.

[8] Irwin, *Models of the Eucharist*, 21.

considers the work of historian Eugene McCarraher, who labeled people such as Virgil Michel, Dorothy Day, Gerald Ellard, and Paul Hanley Furfey as "sacramental radicals." These were people who combined "neo-medievalist religious ideas with American republicanism to create a social gospel." This vision for social change was distinct from and likely "eclipsed by a Catholic social action more accommodating to the managerial interests of corporate capital and the New Deal." The latter was the position advanced by Msgr. John A. Ryan and the National Catholic Welfare Conference. McCarraher asserted that the sacramental radicals were unable to make their cause palatable to common working folk; and they "tended to advocate an alternative culture, a strategy of separation."[9] Forty-plus years after Vatican II the church has yet to make a clearer connection between liturgy and life (social justice), but some good strides have been made.

The National Catholic Rural Life Conference, founded by Father Edwin Vincent O'Hara in 1923, put forth a rather sweeping vision of how it would minister to the faithful in the countryside, a marginalized population. The Conference insisted that the spiritual dimension of life always remain at the basis of its social agenda; the primary means for doing so would be the church's liturgical and sacramental life.

---

[9] Kelleher, "Liturgy and Social Transformation," 64–65. For the missed connection at Vatican II see Joseph Komonchak, "U.S. Bishops' Suggestions for Vatican II," *Cristianismo nella storia* 15 (1994): 313–71; John J. Egan, "Twenty Years after the Council: Liturgy and Justice: An Unfinished Agenda," *Origins* 13 (September 22, 1983): 247. Egan challenged the contemporary church to recover three basic principles which were central to Virgil Michel's vision for the liturgical movement: awareness of the church as the Mystical Body of Christ, the conviction that salvation is addressed to the "whole" person, and reconstruction of the social order. All three, it will be shown, formed part of the NCRLC's program. See also Eugene McCarraher, "American Gothic: Sacramental Radicalism and the Neo-Medievalist Cultural Gospel, 1928–48," *Records of American Catholic Historical Society Philadelphia* 106, nos. 1–2 (Spring–Summer 1995): 3–23; *idem*, "The Church Irrelevant: Paul Hanley Furfey and the Fortunes of American Catholic Radicalism," *Religion and American Culture* 7, no. 2 (Summer 1997): 163–94. McCarraher's thesis has some value, but there are limits. He and other American church historians have seriously neglected the field of American rural Catholicism. His contention that the sacramental radicals did not give sufficient attention to the material welfare of working class Catholics may be true. I would, however, with some nuance, label some of the NCRLC's leaders as "sacramental radicals" who in fact did speak to farm laborers and sought their material betterment. Most of the chapters in this book will provide evidence that contests McCarraher's position.

From their inceptions, both movements—the American liturgical movement and the Catholic rural life movement (as embodied by the NCRLC)—saw that a natural kinship existed between the liturgy and the people who worked the land. Employing insights gleaned from the liturgical movement, the NCRLC made a concerted and conscious attempt to integrate the church's official worship with the lived experience of rural people, making the relationship between liturgy and life more explicit.

In 1923, at the first NCRLC convention in St. Louis, Vincent Wehrle, OSB, bishop of Bismarck, North Dakota, declared: "There is something almost sacramental about the life of the rural family."[10] That is, the rural family was positioned to foster an organic and holistic way of living. The Conference maintained that land (especially soil) was "the greatest material gift from God" and possessed a sacramental quality to it. The NCRLC later declared soil stewardship the "11th Commandment."[11] God's gift of material creation coupled with human reception, cooperation, and stewardship constituted this fundamental theological relationship between liturgy and rural culture. Liturgy and the agricultural life made for a natural connection, with the farmer situated so close to what the church utilized in her worship—the fruits of the earth and vine, the work of human hands. There was too the obvious connection between the annual cycles of nature and the liturgical year. Thus, at a minimum, the rural church's closeness to the raw materials of the liturgical and sacramental celebration and to the annual cycles of nature provided a theological and liturgical basis for the manner in which the two movements intersected.

Because of the close association of the liturgical and rural life movements, the rural areas became fertile grounds for what was then regarded as liturgical experimentation. Active participation in the liturgy was deemed essential to worship. Some rural pastors integrated as much of the agricultural life with the liturgy as was possible and allowable by the church. In 1946 thirty-two blessings particular to the agricultural life, and found in the Roman Ritual, were translated into English by Bishop Joseph Schlarman of Peoria. These were published

---

[10] Timothy Dolan, *Some Seed Fell on Good Ground: The Life of Edwin V. O'Hara* (Washington, DC: The Catholic University of America Press, 1992), 58.

[11] Walter C. Lowdermilk, "The 11th Commandment," *American Forests* 46 (January 1940): 12–15.

by the NCRLC under the title *With the Blessing of the Church*.[12] This book formed part of a larger effort that pressed for greater use of the vernacular in the liturgy. It represented a worthy attempt to relate the church's liturgy to the farmer's daily life. Martin Hellriegel, a founding editor and frequent contributor to *Orate Fratres*, wrote the foreword to the book. He made explicit the central role that "sacramentals" play within the liturgical life of the Mystical Body of Christ, serving as a vital connection between "altar and home," between liturgy and life, a connection Hellriegel declared the church had lost.

The NCRLC also made a consistent effort to assure that devotions and the use of sacramentals were more clearly connected to the official worship of the Catholic Church. This was another contribution of the liturgical movement. In 1947 St. Isidore the Husbandman (Farmer) was declared the patron saint of the NCRLC and a Mass Proper was created for the feast.[13] The *Novena of St. Isidore* was published with the help of the monks of St. John's Abbey in Collegeville, Minnesota. It was a thoroughly "liturgical" novena and not the stereotypical rote repetition of prayers. Having a patron saint bestowed a newfound dignity upon the vocation of farmers whose way of life was often looked down upon by their urban counterparts. More generally, the relationship between the liturgy and human dignity (principally affirmed in baptism) forms a consistent dimension to this study. That is to say, when a marginalized population (here Catholic agrarians) and its way of life was recognized and affirmed by popes, especially through the official liturgy of the church, a deeper awareness of one's Christian dignity was realized. This strengthened the farmers' commitment and action as members of the Mystical Body of Christ.

In light of the above historical, liturgical, and theological explorations, a concluding chapter considers what the intersection of the American liturgical movement and the NCRLC might offer to the contemporary study of liturgical inculturation and the liturgy's role in promoting a more just social order. The NCRLC dealt with rural issues in a thoroughly *catholic* way looking to invigorate every dimension of life—social, economic, educational, cultural, and religious (liturgical)—

---

[12] NCRLC, *With the Blessing of the Church* (Des Moines, IA: National Catholic Rural Life Conference, 1947).

[13] Saint Isidore was canonized March 22, 1622, along with Ignatius of Loyola, Francis Xavier, Philip Neri, and Theresa of Avila. Isidore and his wife Santa Maria de la Cabeza (canonized in 1697) were the first husband and wife to be canonized.

for those working on the land, as well as a world that depended on the agricultural community. This purview will be approached by taking up the thought (and praxis) of the noted author and agrarian Wendell Berry, who, it will be argued, possesses a profound sacramental view of the world. There is a unifying thread that runs through this entire study—the principle of sacramentality. This rather traditional precept of the church has not received much attention from scholars in the post–Vatican II era. It will be argued that this principle may help to bring the worship life of the church into a closer relationship with her daily life. The confluence of liturgy, culture, and social concern (for the rural context in particular) did in fact contribute to the "reconstruction of the social order." The principle of sacramentality carries the potential to draw the liturgy into a closer relationship with life.

# Chapter 1

# Christ to the Country, the Country to Christ!

## EDWIN V. O'HARA AND THE NATIONAL CATHOLIC RURAL LIFE CONFERENCE

To be born on a farm hardly qualifies one to undertake what Edwin Vincent O'Hara set out to do in ministering to America's rural Catholics. But his early experiences must have sensitized him to the plight of his rural parishioners when he became pastor of St. Mary's Church in Eugene, Oregon (1920). O'Hara was influenced by some of the great promoters of the church's social teaching. While he was a pragmatist at heart, his endeavors were formed by his role as a priest ordained to serve God's people. He viewed his mission and ministry as being primarily of a spiritual nature. Thus it will be germane to explore some of the more significant social justice and liturgically formative experiences of Edwin O'Hara.[1]

Edwin Vincent O'Hara, the last of eight children, was born in 1881 on a farm near Lanesboro, Minnesota. His parents, Owen and Margaret,

---

[1] Histories have already been written on both O'Hara and the NCRLC; they will be relied upon significantly to develop this brief historical sketch. See Timothy Dolan, *Some Seed Fell on Good Ground: The Life of Edwin V. O'Hara* (Washington, DC: The Catholic University of America Press, 1992); *idem*, "The Rural Ideology of Edwin O'Hara," *U.S. Catholic Historian* 8 (Fall 1989): 117–29. This entire issue was devoted to Catholic rural life in America. On the NCRLC, see Raymond P. Witte, *Twenty-Five Years of Crusading: A History of the National Catholic Rural Life Conference* (Des Moines, IA: National Catholic Rural Life Conference, 1948). This was the only history of the NCRLC until David Bovée's in 1985. See David Bovée, "The Church and the Land: The National Catholic Rural Life Conference and American Society, 1923–1985," (PhD diss., University of Chicago, 1986). Bovée has recently updated this history. See bibliography.

were natives of Ireland who fled the famine of the 1840s. As their respective families made their way across the new land, each independently settled near Plymouth, Indiana. It was here that the couple met and then married in April 1865. At the encouragement of Bishop Mathias Loras of Dubuque, Iowa, the couple and their two children headed west in search of more fertile land on which to settle and farm. While passing through Illinois they heard about the better farming opportunities in Minnesota and continued on to Lanesboro. It was there that Owen purchased the 320-acre Harriet Miller farm where the family settled. Theirs was that pioneer spirit that came to be identified with nineteenth-century America. Owen, in fact, was known to be somewhat of a "scientific farmer," unafraid of exploring and testing new methods of farming to enhance soil productivity. As a family, the O'Haras were self-sufficient, not only with farm and home, but in regard to education and religion as well.[2]

It would be difficult though to characterize the O'Haras as a typical frontier family. Certainly, as a farming family living in post–Civil War America, they were quite familiar with all the hardships associated with such a life. All the O'Hara children shared the difficult work involved in operating a rural homestead. This, no doubt, helped to forge Edwin's work ethic, which enabled him to accomplish many great things for the nation and the church. His mother Margaret was educated through the local missionary efforts of the Holy Cross priests and brothers of South Bend, Indiana. She was trained as a catechist by Holy Cross Father Edward Sorin himself, the founder of that Holy Cross community. Margaret eventually worked as a teacher in Elkhart, Indiana. Owen, while having little formal education, was known to have quoted from the *Iliad* and other classics. Education always held a privileged place in the family. Since no school system yet existed when the family arrived in Lanesboro, Owen donated an acre in the corner of the farm and built a one-room schoolhouse called the "O'Hara School, in District 29."[3] All the O'Hara children attended this school, which provided the rudiments of education. The schooling received during the day was augmented by evening study sessions conducted by Owen and Margaret. Eventually Lanesboro High School was built, and all the O'Hara children graduated from there. Several of the older

[2] Dolan, *Some Seed*, 1–3.
[3] Ibid., 4.

boys went to college and had well-established careers, traveling abroad for work and study. Edwin's sister, Mary Genevieve, entered the Poor Clares of Omaha, Nebraska.

Naturally, the family took their religion as seriously as they did their education. Because Minnesota was a true frontier, there was no established parish in the area. The Catholic population was scattered and unorganized. Priests from nearby Winona or from across the state line in Illinois ministered in this remote area. The family had to adapt by practicing devotions, saying common prayers, and reading from the bible in the evenings. Margaret, the trained catechist, made certain that the fundamentals of the faith were taught. When a parish was established in 1871, Father William Riordan utilized the family school house for liturgy while the first church was being built. Saint Patrick's parish was formally established in 1875, and Edwin was baptized there in 1881 by Father James Coyne. Coyne, who was pastor of the parish for forty-one years, exerted a good influence on Edwin. Because of the great difficulty families faced in getting to church, Coyne insisted that at least one family member attend Sunday Mass. For the O'Haras, this was a nine-mile journey by horse-drawn wagon.[4]

In 1897 Edwin finished his high school coursework early and began taking classes at the recently founded diocesan College of St. Thomas in St. Paul, Minnesota. In 1900 Edwin entered St. Paul Seminary to begin his formal study for the priesthood. His years in the seminary were formative in many ways. In addition to his family upbringing, two people in particular greatly colored his outlook on church and world; these were Archbishop John Ireland and Father John A. Ryan. As Dolan pointed out, there was good reason why Ireland was known as the "consecrated blizzard of the northwest." His leadership style was aggressive and often controversial. Archbishop Ireland was both hailed and scorned as one of the great progressives among the American hierarchy. He promoted a broad liberal education that did not back down from the modern age. Faithful to Leo XIII's *Rerum Novarum* (1891), he led the way in advancing the church's socioeconomic agenda, making it integral to the seminary's formation program. He

---

[4] Ibid., 6–7. This "frontier" situation points to the contemporary church's problem in which parishes lack resident pastors. This led, in 1994, to the creation and publication (for use in the United States) of *Sunday Celebrations in the Absence of a Priest*, a ritual book that allows for a lay person to preside over a Communion service.

lectured on such "delicate" topics as labor unions, race, urban affairs, education, science, and other topics usually the domain of secular experts. Archbishop Ireland ordained Edwin in December 1905 for the diocese of Oregon City, Oregon, in response to the great pastoral needs in the Western United States.[5]

In Oregon, O'Hara immediately assumed some teaching duties, not only in the parish school but at the all-girls' St. Mary's Academy and College, where he lectured on Scripture and apologetics. So well was he received that teachers asked him to conduct some additional classes for themselves as a way of staying up-to-date. He did likewise at the Blanchet School for boys run by the Christian Brothers. As he became more aware of the widespread ignorance among Catholics regarding the faith, he founded the Catholic Educational Association of Oregon in 1907. He conducted the first Diocesan Teachers Institute and served as school superintendent for the diocese. O'Hara saw a constant need to organize Catholics, which he felt would allow them to develop a stronger Catholic identity, the ultimate end being a more vigorous living out of the Christian life. Behind such work was also the goal of making the Catholic Church more acceptable to the American public.

In Oregon he had to contend with considerable anti-Catholic bias not only from certain Protestant groups but more so from the well-organized Masons and the Ku Klux Klan. O'Hara sought to make the Catholic faith both public and palatable by dispelling erroneous notions of what the church believed. He formed the Dante Club that met in the art room of the Portland Public Library. There he delivered erudite lectures on the classics and history. Lastly, among the few things mentioned here, he followed in Archbishop Ireland's footsteps by promoting temperance. This gained him the trust and acceptance of many local Protestant pastors. O'Hara became one of the most popular figures in the city of Portland.

Involvement in so many projects eventually caught up with O'Hara in March of 1910, and he developed bronchitis. Archbishop Christie ordered rest for the young priest, and so in August he traveled with his sister Anna to Europe for six weeks. When he returned, he spent a

---

[5] Archbishop Ireland played a significant role in the Irish Catholic Colonization Association. See *New Catholic Encyclopedia*, 2nd ed., "Ireland, John," 549–52. See also New Catholic Encyclopedia, 2nd ed., "Irish Catholic Colonization Association of the U.S.," 573.

semester in Washington, DC, taking classes at The Catholic University of America and finishing research for his first book, *A Pioneer Catholic History of Oregon*.[6] Rejuvenated, he returned to Portland in early 1911. The time away allowed O'Hara to gain some perspective on his work, especially that which focused on the social needs of the people. He realized that he could not continue only to provide immediate material relief for Oregon's poor. Rather, faithful to *Rerum Novarum*, there were structures in society that had to change. One project among many deserves special mention, for it demonstrated how O'Hara often worked.

O'Hara's investigation into the deplorable urban housing conditions in Portland led him to discover the very low wages that factory workers received, particularly women. In cooperation with the Oregon Consumer League (a group that promoted pro-labor reform), he took the lead in 1912 to begin a campaign that would secure a minimum-wage law for Oregon's working women; O'Hara was made the chairman of the committee to study the issue. Meanwhile, another committee member, Carolyn Gleason (who became a Sister of the Holy Names of Jesus and Mary), began to infiltrate factories and stores to assess the working conditions of women. As one could expect, conditions were appalling. Gleason spent ten hours a day gluing boxes together in an unsanitary shop, and was paid fifty-two cents per day. Gleason also interviewed the women themselves. O'Hara published the findings in a book and disseminated it to public officials, leaders, and editors of newspapers. Naturally, all this made local business leaders nervous, especially those who were Catholic. Moreover, he did not always receive the support of his brother priests, who often thought that O'Hara was involved in too many projects outside the typical boundaries of a clergyman.

On June 3, 1913, Governor Oswald West signed "The Minimum Wage Law," essentially authored by O'Hara. It required, among other things, the establishment of the Industrial Welfare Commission. The governor appointed O'Hara the first chairman of that commission, which was represented by both labor and management, something O'Hara insisted upon in order to foster collaboration and understanding. The new law's signing would not be the end of the debate.

---

[6] Dolan, *Some Seed*, 58–61. See Jeffery Marlett, *Saving the Heartland: Catholic Missionaries in Rural America, 1920–1960* (DeKalb: Northern Illinois University Press, 2002), 20–23 (hereafter, Marlett, *Saving the Heartland*).

In 1914 Frank Settler, a local businessman, filed a suit to challenge the law. The Oregon Supreme Court upheld the law in *Settler v. O'Hara*. Undaunted, Settler took it to the U.S. Supreme Court, where on April 9, 1917, the high court ruled to uphold the Oregon court's decision. O'Hara's leadership on this project brought him to national prominence, and the experience would bode well for the future NCRLC.[7]

Around the same time, two experiences reawakened O'Hara's interest in rural life. First, he served an eight-month tour as a Knights of Columbus chaplain in France during World War I. This experience permitted him to see the vast destruction of farms and livelihoods, and it renewed in him the desire to return to his rural roots. Second, upon his return to the United States in 1918, he spent several months on the East Coast speaking with religious organizations. One of them was the National Catholic Education Association, which voiced its concern for Catholics living in the countryside and the lack of educational resources available for them.

Based on these two encounters, O'Hara would later cite a couple of reasons that compelled him to move on to new apostolic endeavors; they speak volumes about what would occupy much of his life's work. The first reason involved his concern for the students he encountered at the University of Oregon in Eugene (all students, not only the Catholic ones), where he wanted to expound "the Catholic philosophy of life." Eugene, Oregon, was a university town and O'Hara relished the opportunity to engage the academic culture. O'Hara became one of the most familiar faces on the University of Oregon campus— attending lectures, using the library, and reinvigorating the Newman Club begun by his brother John who taught there. Education formed the thrust of his apostolic activities. The second reason was more pointed: "I have long been interested in the rural social problem. The conviction had grown upon me that the most important and most neglected single problem in the United States is the rural social problem." He referred to the paper he was preparing on rural Catholic

---

[7] Dolan, *Some Seed*, 21, 32, 34. This initiative moved the city of Portland to adopt his considerations for a more rigorous housing code, and the city appointed O'Hara to the inspection committee for three years. He also played a leading role in the famous "Oregon School Case," which serves as another example of his defense of civil and religious freedoms. Concerning the latter issue see Dolan, *Some Seed*, 41–49. The University of Notre Dame gave him an honorary doctorate for his work on the Oregon Minimum Wage Law.

education and how he deemed it crucial for the well-being of the church to "maintain on the land a population which will be prosperous, contented and cultured."[8]

In the spring of 1920, after fifteen years of urban ministry, O'Hara was appointed pastor of St. Mary's parish in rural Eugene, Oregon. He immersed himself fully in the ministry, placing education and social welfare at the forefront. He realized that many of the parishioners in Portland had originally been settled on land outside the city but left in order to be closer to church and school. It became evident that many of the children (not to mention the adults) in his extensive new parish were not receiving even a basic religious education. He initiated three programs: a Sunday school, a religious vacation school, and a religious correspondence course. (The latter was the inspiration of Monsignor Victor Day of Helena, Montana.)

O'Hara began at once an ambitious social program for his rural parishioners. He organized a "Clinic on Wheels" to serve the county's health needs, and it reached some three hundred people in the first year. O'Hara never lost his farming roots and readily realized how ignorant his farmer-parishioners were of sound farming techniques. He utilized every means available to educate the people—flyers, expert speakers, and radio programs. "Farm day" programs sponsored by St. Mary's helped the farmers adopt sound methods of crop rotation, soil conservation, home modernization, and efficient farm management. He recruited experts from the Oregon Agricultural College to come and give "Farmer's Short Courses." He promoted parish credit unions and cooperatives—endeavors that would hold a central place in the philosophies of both the NCRLC and the liturgical movement. He also recruited women religious and laywomen to serve as catechists. He did all this while keeping up with the usual "pastoral" responsibilities of parish life. In sum, O'Hara constantly promoted a Catholic lifestyle that always attended to the spiritual and material welfare of the people.[9]

O'Hara had a deep love for the church's liturgical and sacramental life, believing the liturgy to be something very formative for the

[8] In the *Oregon Sunday Journal*, May 30, 1920, p. 6, as quoted in Dolan, *Some Seed*, 51.

[9] Dolan, *Some Seed*, 55. O'Hara's valuable pastoral experience at St. Mary's in Eugene, Oregon (1920–30) was expressed in book form; see Edwin V. O'Hara, *The Church and the Country Community* (New York: Macmillan, 1927).

church as the Mystical Body of Christ. In the late 1920s O'Hara initiated some conversations with liturgical leaders Virgil Michel and Bill Busch, wishing to collaborate more closely. Dolan credited "Catholic ruralism" as giving birth to two other movements—the Confraternity of Christian Doctrine and the liturgical movement. There can be no doubt that from their earliest days there was close collaboration between the liturgical and rural life movements, both of which had the renewal of the church at the forefront of their agendas. A deeper mutual philosophical basis existed between the two movements that would take a couple of decades to manifest itself practically.[10]

Both Virgil Michel and O'Hara held catechesis to be central to their apostolates. Because the CCD shared wider support among most of the hierarchy, O'Hara utilized it as a platform for other programs that were not so readily embraced by the bishops. Two such organizations were the NCRLC and the liturgical movement. Cooperation between the NCRLC and the CCD also proved to be a point of contention. At conjointly held meetings in the mid-1930s, the NCRLC leadership felt that the CCD began to overshadow the rural life meetings.[11] Around the same time, O'Hara was updating the *Catechism* and pressed for its use as the national text for all Catholics. Virgil Michel too had been preparing a catechism based on the liturgy. Correspondence between the two revealed Michel's concern that the liturgical and sacramental life would not receive the treatment it deserved in a more general catechism.[12]

O'Hara embraced the liturgical renewal from the beginning, viewing the liturgy as yet another tool to form people in the faith and, thereby, renewing the Christian spirit as Pius X had urged. O'Hara wrote the foreword to Father Gerald Ellard's *Participation of the Faithful in the Priesthood*, in which he claimed: "If one is looking for radicalism in Fr. Ellard's volume, it is but the radicalism stated by Pope Pius X years ago, and now continued by Pius XII, of making every single Catholic

[10] Dolan, *Some Seed*, 98–99, 106–7. The correspondence between Michel, O'Hara and Busch will be considered below. It may be a slight overstatement to say that Catholic ruralism gave birth to the liturgical movement per se as Dolan claims, but ruralism did offer fertile ground for the liturgical movement to implement its agenda.

[11] Raymond P. Witte, *Twenty-Five Years of Crusading: A History of the National Catholic Rural Life Conference* (Des Moines, IA: National Catholic Rural Life Conference, 1948), 95 (hereafter, Witte, *Crusading*).

[12] Dolan, *Some Seed*, 150–51, 156.

an active officer of Sunday Mass." As bishop of Kansas City, he worked with Ellard on incorporating the dialogue Mass, knowing the impact a participative liturgy could have on the faithful. This was based in part on his experiences of celebrating liturgy in German prisoner-of-war camps where they employed vernacular prayers and hymns. When O'Hara visited Bishop Aloisius Muench, the papal nuncio to Germany, the bishop gave him a copy of the German-language *Ritual*. This set in motion the eventual English translation of the *Collectio Rituum*, and O'Hara was a principal force behind its publication. He also joined the English Liturgical Society, a group that advocated greater use of the vernacular in worship.[13]

O'Hara also promoted liturgical art and was patron to the artist Charlton Fortune. She was responsible for the renovation of Immaculate Conception Cathedral in Kansas City. The renovation project received high praise from Maurice Lavanoux of the Liturgical Arts Society. O'Hara also saw liturgical music's potential to enhance liturgical participation. In 1951, under the auspices of the CCD, he invited the Gregorian Institute of America to conduct a national survey to determine the feasibility of publishing a national hymnal. Not possessing any musical expertise, O'Hara offered episcopal and financial support while he left the details to professionals. The Hymnal Committee presented its results two weeks after O'Hara's unexpected death on September 11, 1956, en route to the International Congress of Pastoral Liturgy in Assisi, where he was slated to report on the renewal of the Holy Week liturgy and the further revision of the Roman Ritual.[14]

The founding of the National Catholic Rural Life Conference had a rather inauspicious start. In December 1918, upon returning from Europe (as a chaplain in World War I), O'Hara submitted a report that called for a National Catholic Resettlement Board as part of the newly formed National Catholic War Council (this became the National Catholic Welfare Conference—NCWC—in 1922). The Resettlement Board formed part of the Council's Committee on Reconstruction and After War Activities. As O'Hara ministered to the troops in France he was struck by the great number of soldiers, raised in the American countryside, who came to Europe to serve alongside the American

[13] Ibid., 177, 179, 181–83.
[14] Ibid., 180–84.

allies. He regularly and joyfully celebrated field Masses to which the soldiers flocked. He had great sympathy for the soldiers, realizing that many of them gave up school and jobs to serve in the military. This led him to undertake the resettlement initiative. Because of his greater involvement in these national issues, he was made a member of the executive committee of the NCWC in March 1920.

The year 1918 also marked O'Hara's important meeting with members of the Catholic Education Association who voiced its concern about the Catholics in the rural areas. In response to their concerns, O'Hara had agreed to conduct a thorough national study of the problem from Portland during the year 1919 and present the results of the study at the 1920 national meeting.[15] The survey questions dealt primarily with education as it pertained to the rural areas, but it also gave pastors an opportunity to express their general views toward the rural apostolate and suggest some solutions.[16] The pastors revealed some sensitivity to rural culture. Some of them thought that rural education should be more rural-oriented and should present the dignity of farming, the beauty of the country, and persuade children to stay on the farm. The pastors' suggestions included sodalities, sermons, hymns, devotions, and a greater emphasis on the celebration of certain feast days. Surprisingly, none of them proposed a national organization to advance the rural apostolate. In fact, the pastors expressed some resistance toward any top-down administrative program, thinking it best to work at the parish or diocesan level.[17] The results of the questionnaire provided O'Hara with the necessary data he needed to

[15] Bovée, "The Church and the Land," 81–101. He treats the foundational years of the Conference on 81–144.

[16] Witte, *Crusading*, 43–57. The survey questions can be found here, and they are followed by O'Hara's address to the NCEA entitled, "The Rural Problem and Its Bearing on Catholic Education."

[17] Bovée, "The Church and the Land," 99. Obviously, in spite of their suggestion about a national effort, O'Hara eventually organized the NCRLC anyway. Anything that came from the RLB must have been a welcome relief to these pastors, regardless of its effectiveness. The survey responses revealed exasperated priests who felt their work was greatly undervalued. The rural areas also tended to house "problem priests" (usually those with alcohol problems). Laypeople complained about lazy priests who seemed to be just "putting in their time" until a more prestigious city parish assignment opened. It was generally true at the time that being assigned to a rural parish was not considered ecclesiastical advancement. The pattern of a large city parish with church, school, convent, and social hall was a source of pride and prestige. See Bovée, 97–98.

persuade the bishops to establish a Rural Life Board (not yet the Rural Life Bureau), arguing that a more concerted ministerial effort had to be made on behalf of rural Catholics.

O'Hara's reputation surrounding national rural issues led Bishop Peter Muldoon (Rockford, Illinois) to place his name on a list of invitees to a Chicago meeting that would eventually form the Social Action Department (SAD) of the NCWC in February 1920. It was O'Hara's old seminary professor, John A. Ryan, who was named as the first director of SAD. In June of the same year O'Hara delivered his address to the NCEA entitled "The Rural Problem and Its Bearing on Catholic Education." His insistence that the rural question be given more of a hearing moved SAD to officially create the Rural Life Bureau (RLB) in May 1921. O'Hara was its first director, and he conducted all the Bureau's affairs from a small office in the Newman Club's house in Eugene, Oregon. The RLB's central purpose was to disseminate materials in the form of pamphlets, newspaper columns, and magazines in order to educate (and motivate) pastors and organizations working among the rural people.

Working from his office in Eugene, O'Hara quickly began forming an extensive network of contacts in order to acquaint people with the RLB. The list included the American Country Life Association, the American Farm Bureau Federation, various Protestant and Jewish groups, and agricultural colleges; the last one proved especially important. At these agricultural schools, O'Hara established state advisory councils made up of Catholic professors and students, encouraging them to take a more prominent role in reaching out to clergy and farmer alike.[18] These councils reported what activities they were involved in and this helped O'Hara get a more accurate picture of rural problems. He also edited and wrote most of the articles for *St. Isidore's Plow*, which became the primary organ for disseminating his philosophy of rural life. In the corner of each issue was a picture of Giotto's *Agriculture*, depicting a man plowing with two yoked oxen. It came from the base of the bell tower in Florence designed by the famous artist. Each issue carried a rural poem such as the following from Paisely Turner entitled *The Plowman*: "Plowman, as you turn sod, you are worker, with Mighty God. Think not, such task lowly, ground He made, still is holy." O'Hara had reason to be pleased with the first

---

[18] Dolan, *Some Seed*, 85.

year and a half of the RLB's existence. *St. Isidore's Plow* had reached a circulation of fifteen hundred. He had kept up an extensive correspondence with pastors, religious communities, Catholic colleges and seminaries, agricultural colleges, and representatives of rural life agencies that were concerned with health, education, cooperatives, and home life.[19]

In May 1923 Henry Israel of the American Country Life Association (ACLA) invited O'Hara to bring a delegation to its annual meeting in St. Louis. O'Hara, however, began to think more broadly. In July of the same year, he began issuing invitations to the first "National Catholic Rural Life Conference" to be held jointly with the ACLA in St. Louis that November; O'Hara's contingent of invitees was meeting under the auspices of the RLB. O'Hara recruited Frederick P. Kenkel of the German-American Catholic organization Central Verein, based in St. Louis, to plan the meeting. Kenkel was also a member of the Social Action Department of the NCWC. He was a well-known figure in the social apostolate, and he was familiar with rural issues. Archbishop John J. Glennon of St. Louis supported O'Hara's initiative and offered the services of Fr. George Hildner, a priest of the archdiocese, to assist with organizational responsibilities. The city-born Hildner became a stellar apostle of rural life in America. Father William Howard Bishop (Clarkesville, Maryland), also in attendance, went on to found the Glenmary Home Missioners in 1939.[20] On the morning of November 9, 1923, the first meeting of the National Catholic Rural Life Conference opened in the library auditorium of the Jesuit-run Saint Louis University. There were seventy-three registrants; most were priests and religious, but sixteen laypeople participated.

The meeting generated much enthusiasm among the participants. O'Hara, the consummate organizer, posed the obvious question: Where do we go from here? After some debate, the conference decided that it would be best to form a separate organization, and it drafted a one-page constitution for the new organization. The NCRLC, now somewhat independent of the RLB, would however remain connected to it, since the RLB's director was the *ex officio* executive director of the new organization. While no bold resolutions emerged, the meeting's

[19] Ibid., 89.
[20] Witte, *Crusading*, 65. See Christopher J. Kauffman, *Mission to Rural America: The Story of W. Howard Bishop, Founder of Glenmary* (New York: Paulist Press, 1991). On Hildner's work see the epilogue below entitled "Saints of the Soil."

participants articulated the simple goal of "promoting the spiritual, social, and economic welfare of the rural population."[21] Throughout its first decade, the NCRLC's fundamental task was to organize the rural apostolate and provide resources for those engaged in ministry and work in the rural areas. Annual meetings grew significantly; the 1929 Des Moines gathering drew over five hundred people.

Several key people joined the Conference the following year (1924), who went on to play significant and enduring roles in the Catholic rural life movement. Among those who became associated with the NCRLC were Luigi G. Ligutti, a priest of the Diocese of Des Moines, Iowa, Jesuit John LaFarge, Aloisius Muench (later bishop of Fargo, North Dakota), Lucille Reynolds of the Farm Credit Administration, and Margaret Lynch of the National Council of Catholic Women. Ligutti's name became synonymous with the NCRLC, especially after 1940 when he was named the executive secretary and eventually executive director. The following year (1925), Alphonsus Matt of the Minnesota League of the Central Verein and publisher of *Der Wanderer* joined.[22] Matt remained a close associate who helped to organize annual meetings and publish materials for the Conference.

In the summer of 1930 Edwin O'Hara was named bishop of Great Falls, Montana. NCRLC leaders knew that he would not be able to maintain his level of involvement with the organization. Besides, it was also obvious that he had begun to devote more time and energy to the Confraternity of Christian Doctrine. Education remained his most deeply held passion. O'Hara could truly be characterized as a Renaissance man who engaged life at every turn. He possessed an all-encompassing vision of church that must be labeled "catholic" in the fullest sense of the word—whole and organic—a vision that resonated deeply with the liturgical movement. O'Hara set the NCRLC on a course that consistently tackled all dimensions of rural life—social,

---

[21] Bovée, "The Church and the Land," 132–33. Brief mention should be made of the Extension Society, founded by Father Francis C. Kelley in 1905. Kelley's organization also played a part in the RLB's fundamental mission by providing financial support to build Catholic churches in the rural areas. While O'Hara and Kelley communicated and were cordial with one another, regrettably, they could never harness their energies for the benefit of a single rural organization. Kelley spoke at the first NCRLC meeting (1923) in St. Louis. See Witte, *Crusading*, 67; Bovée, "The Church and the Land," 100.

[22] Witte, *Crusading*, 78.

educational, economic, cultural, and religious—seeing all such endeavors as working to build the kingdom of God.

By the late 1920s, the Conference made liturgy, sacraments, and the sacramentals integral to its social and spiritual mission. The Conference recognized that if it was to authentically invigorate the many aspects of Catholic rural life it would have to maintain a sound spiritual base. It shared this goal with the liturgical movement and, as Vigil Michel believed, if a true regeneration of the social order was to occur, it would have to emanate from the church's principal spiritual source—the liturgy.

## TILLING THE SOIL—THE LITURGICAL AND RURAL LIFE MOVEMENTS, 1920–1930

There must have been something especially fertile about the Minnesota soil, since both Virgil Michel and Edwin O'Hara were natives of that state. Both the liturgical and Catholic rural life movements began about the same time, albeit in different places. By 1927 each man was aware of the other's nascent organization. Both men had sweeping visions for revitalizing the church; both believed that the liturgical and sacramental life should occupy a distinguished place in that mission. Each one, it can be said, being a faithful disciple of Pius X, firmly believed in the pope's motto *instaurare omnia in Christo*—to restore (reestablish) all things in Christ.[23] Each wished to inject new vigor in the Christian life so that people might live that life more authentically.

The liturgical movement's seminal meeting between Virgil Michel, Gerald Ellard, SJ, and Martin Hellriegel in 1925 took place in O'Fallon, Missouri, only two years after the inaugural NCRLC meeting in St. Louis. Michel and Ellard witnessed what Hellriegel was implementing liturgically for the Precious Blood Sisters, and this enabled them to give direction and scope to the liturgical movement in the United States.[24] William Busch, another Minnesota priest interested in

---

[23] Pius X, *E Supremi* (Vatican: *Acta Sancta Sedis*, 1903). Pius X says: "We proclaim that We have no other program in the Supreme Pontificate but that 'of restoring all things in Christ (Ephes. i., 10), so that 'Christ may be all in all' (Coloss. iii., 2)." In *The Papal Encyclicals: 1903–1939*, Claudia Carlen, IHM, ed. (Wilmington, NC: McGrath Publishing, 1981), #4; see also Jeremy Hall, *The Full Stature of Christ: The Ecclesiology of Virgil Michel, O.S.B.* (Collegeville, MN: Liturgical Press, 1976), 52; and Gerald Ellard, "A Papal Motto and Its Meaning," *OF* 1 (March 1927): 141–45.

[24] Keith Pecklers, *The Unread Vision: The Liturgical Movement in the United States of America, 1926–1955* (Collegeville, MN: Liturgical Press, 1998), 28.

liturgical renewal even before Michel, also figured significantly in the early years of both movements. Luigi Ligutti, who became the face of the NCRLC, and Virgil Michel lived next door to each other in Caldwell Hall at The Catholic University of America during the academic year 1917–18.[25] Fifteen years would go by before their paths crossed again. The NCRLC and the liturgical movement found each other to be a willing partner to carry out this vital renewal for the church.

In the years 1923–25, one finds little or no reference to the liturgy in *St. Isidore's Plow*, which became *Catholic Rural Life* in 1925, the primary means of communication for the RLB and then the NCRLC. *St. Isidore's Plow* and *Catholic Rural Life* put forth the Conference's rural philosophy as it tried to deal with social, economical, educational, and agricultural problems. Both publications were primarily educational in nature. In almost every article with a spiritual theme (usually written by O'Hara), the religious problem was framed in educational terms. The only concrete reference to liturgy and devotions was in relation to the "Catholic Vacation Schools," which espoused visits to the Blessed Sacrament and frequent Communion, but the children also learned sacred singing, Mass prayers, altar setting, and serving.[26]

O'Hara wrote several articles about rural priestly ministry that called pastors to a style of leadership not typical for that time, asserting that the priest must become knowledgeable in fields outside what was generally accepted priestly domain. It can be presumed that priests generally did what was expected of them liturgically at the time—Mass and sacraments. O'Hara had visited many seminaries and encouraged them to begin offering courses in rural and pastoral sociology.[27] By 1923 St. Paul Seminary in Minnesota had one hundred fourteen paid subscriptions to *St. Isidore's Plow*. Abbot Alcuin Deutsch, OSB, of St. John's Abbey in Collegeville, Minnesota, was one of several

[25] Vincent Yzermans, *The People I Love* (Collegeville, MN: Liturgical Press, 1976), 12–13. Michel's thesis at The Catholic University of America was entitled "The Critical Principles of Orestes A. Brownson."

[26] Edwin O'Hara, "Catholic Vacation Schools," *St. Isidore's Plow* 7 (May 1923): 1.

[27] Edwin O'Hara, "The Great Problem of the Rural Pastor," *St. Isidore's Plow* 2 (October 1923): 2; *idem*, "The Clergy and Rural Life," *St. Isidore's Plow* 2 (October 1923): 3; *idem*, "Missionary Work in Rural Parishes," *Catholic Rural Life* 3 (May 1925): 5.

Benedictine abbots O'Hara had approached and encouraged to offer agricultural courses at their schools.[28] Abbot Deutsch was also among a group of NCRLC "Founders," those who had paid one hundred dollars in support of the organization. Overall, the seminary visits stirred some enthusiasm and prepared a few future priests to respond to the great needs of rural Catholics.

Not until November 1925 did something explicitly liturgical and rural appear in print. A small blurb in *Catholic Rural Life* suggested celebrating a Mass on Thanksgiving Day (or the nearest Sunday) in gratitude for the harvest. H. F. Roney connected the religious ceremony held the previous March in which seed was blessed and the harvest reaped:

> It brought out the farm folks, the nearness of God in their profession and made religion vital to them. Now God has abundantly blessed the seeds sown and granted to us a bountiful harvest. . . . It [Mass] will complement the idea of the special service of blessing the seeds, and help bring into the farmer's life the fact of God and what we owe Him. . . . Let the sermon be a theme fitting for the intention and the choir music suitable to Thanksgiving. If the people could pay Church dues at that time as a return to God for the harvest given, it would be a religious act and make spiritual the offering.[29]

The blessing of seed and harvest started to become a regular practice among some Catholics in the countryside, a practice that declined through the centuries. This explicit blessing served to link the farmer's life more closely to God. Also, payment of "Church dues" made plain the notion that the "offering" was something religious and spiritually connected to the material bounty of God's creation and human labor.

Beginning in November 1927, liturgical and sacramental themes began to emerge more regularly in the pages of *Catholic Rural Life*. A monthly column appeared that was signed "By a Corpus Christi Sister." This sister belonged to the Carmelites from Duluth, Minnesota, living in Corpus Christi House. The Carmelites became associated

---

[28] O'Hara to Deutsch, April 6, 1923, cited in Dolan, *Some Seed*, 79.

[29] H. F. Roney, "A Thanksgiving Mass," *CRL* 3 (November 1925): 6. This simple seed, planted in 1925, was eventually harvested in the liturgical reform of Vatican II whose Sacramentary for the United States provides a Mass for Thanksgiving Day with proper prayers, prefaces, and readings.

with the NCRLC through O'Hara who requested that two sisters be sent every September to assist his rural mission in Oregon. In several articles she referred to some aspect of the liturgical and/or sacramental life and to the task of getting the people to participate more actively as Pius X urged. In these early years, at least as far as *St. Isidore's Plow* and *Catholic Rural Life* revealed, the sister's column was the only one that consistently treated liturgical and sacramental themes, but without connection to rural life proper.[30]

In one article, after noting that one does not need to go to Africa or Asia to be a missionary (since missionary places exist here in the United States), this Carmelite sister described a 1927 summer religious school that began each day with Mass in which the prayers were recited in English by both the sisters and children. Hymn singing was taught. The instructions and explanations that were given for the children moved some of the adults to join in the Mass prayers. The fact that many children were ignorant of the faith indicated, in part, that the parents themselves lacked basic religious formation. Many had been away from the church and sacraments for a long time. In most cases it was no fault of their own but was due partly to the isolated rural context. One adult remarked, "Sister, I learned things about the Mass this morning I never knew before."[31] Every night some of the sisters drove twelve miles into the countryside to give instruction. One of them gave the following account of a rural mission: "Made 254 visits; instructed 93 children for the Sacraments; brought 30 children to the priest for baptism, many over seven years of age; validated 4 marriages." Many lapsed Catholics came back to Mass and the sacraments during the five weeks the sisters were there.[32] The sisters assumed a proactive

---

[30] A Corpus Christi Sister, "The Corpus Christi Sisters," *CRL* 6 (November 1927): 13–14. (Hereafter she will be referred to as CCS.) The Carmelite sister's articles dealt with a variety of themes which described the order's diverse work; the columns were also written with a view to inspire vocations. Their apostolates included work with orphan girls, Native Americans, and migrant Mexican beet farmers; they were involved in census taking, education, hospital ministry, and work in the rural areas. Additionally, these sisters baked all the altar breads for the Diocese of Duluth. She spoke highly of the community's common prayer life and related with certain amazement that "the sisters were saying the Divine Office," and the Blessed Sacrament was "liturgically worshiped by the Divine Office," as part of their daily order of prayer.

[31] CCS, "A Corner of Our Lord's Vineyard," *CRL* 6 (February 1928): 10.

[32] Ibid., 11.

role in getting the children to participate in the liturgy, a founding principle of the liturgical movement.[33] The children's fine example encouraged the adults toward greater participation. Religious illiteracy existed among the rural faithful, even to the extent of not knowing basic prayers, which would have been said *during* the liturgy. One must also keep in mind that immigrants were at times quite self-conscious about publicly practicing some devotions that were common in their homeland. As far as can be determined, little of this instruction seemed to have a "rural" emphasis.[34]

The Carmelite sister's January 1929 column revealed the source of her thinking on the central role of the liturgy. She noted that in many small towns of Europe there remained a strong sense of feast days in which the entire town participated, culminating with a High Grand Mass and feast. She remarked with some nostalgia: "This goes with the Catholicity of centuries, and for these people the Church is the centre of their lives, and the Mass is in their bones."[35] Such beginnings were being made, she added, in the rural church in the United States through the efforts of the NCRLC. Father Philip Kiley of rural Atkins, Minnesota, promoted music in the liturgy with congregational singing. Explicit mention of the liturgical movement and its diffusion was made in connection to Gerald Ellard's article in a recent issue of *Orate Fratres*, "Liturgy for the Common Man in Austria." She noted the Jesuit's encounter with Pius Parsch at Klosterneuburg and how he (Parsch) was forming the people there for participation in, and understanding of, the liturgy.[36] She urged that the same be done in the rural parishes. Finally, after mentioning Nathaniel Hawthorne's *A Wonder Book for Boys and Girls*, she declared, "a Missal or Mass Book was put into my hands for the first time, and the first thought that

---

[33] Virgil Michel, "Participation in the Mass," *OF* 1 (1926–27): 17–20.

[34] The Conference wished to make rural Catholics aware of the resources available to them, thus, the Carmelite sister recommended several books—five of which were in the area of sacraments and liturgy: *Our Sacraments* by Wm. R. Kelly; *Assignments and Direction in the Study of Religion*; *The Sacraments* by Sister M. Mildred, OSF, PhD; *Thy Kingdom Come, Series V: Eucharistic Echoes*, by J. E. Moffatt, SJ. Sister M. Mildred also prepared a companion book to *Our Sacraments* designed for classroom use.

[35] CCS, "What in Life is Most Worth While?" *CRL* 7 (January 1929): 8.

[36] Gerald Ellard, "Liturgy for the Common Man in Austria," *OF* 3 (1928–29): 7–9. Two other articles appeared in the same issue, one was by William Busch called "The Mass—Principle Parts," and the other was by James E. O'Mahoney, OFM, Cap., entitled "The Sacramental Principle."

instantly flashed through my mind was: This is Almighty God's Wonder Book."[37] Thus, by the late 1920s, the NCRLC had begun to promote the liturgy in ways that were consistent with the liturgical movement.

At the 1929 NCRLC meeting in Des Moines, Fathers John LaFarge, Felix Pitt, and Philip Kiley were asked to draw up a series of objectives and resolutions. Indicative of the NCRLC's comprehensive vision, the authors stated:

> Our general objective is Rural Life. By "life" we mean a rounded Catholic life, with proper unity and proportion for its different factors. The most characteristic element of that life is Christian, supernatural *charity*, which should inspire and ennoble all its manifestations and activities.[38]

The "different factors" revealed an ambitious agenda for rural Catholics and included health care, economics (cooperatives and credit unions), family life, religious life (for the lay and religious state), education, community life (parish centered), civic life (including relations with non-Catholics), relations with wider life (mention is made of "negroes," no doubt the influence of LaFarge), and liturgy.[39] LaFarge, working among African Americans in rural southern Maryland and, closely aligned with the liturgical movement, had written to O'Hara in April 1929 and urged him to give the liturgy special emphasis in the Conference's plan of action.[40] While the liturgy had been a part of the NCRLC's mission, now it was officially designated as such.

---

[37] CCS, "What in Life Is Most Worth While?" 8. The use of the missal was one of the first ways the liturgical movement attempted to foster greater participation. Her next six columns were a sustained liturgical catechesis. The articles, however, made no explicit reference to the rural life proper. They were: "Words," CRL 7 (April 1929): 5, 8; "Lessons Given by God," CRL 7 (May 1929): 5–6; "Told Beforehand," CRL 7 (June 1929): 3, 8; "I Will Go Unto the Altar of God," CRL 8 (December 1929): 3, 8; "In Hebrew, Latin and Greek," CRL 8 (January 1930): 3; "God's Wonder Book IV," CRL 8 (February 1930): 3; "God's Wonder Book VI," CRL 8 (April 1930): 3; This last article was preceded by William Busch's seminal article "Liturgy and Farm Relief," which will be considered below.

[38] Witte, *Crusading*, 83.

[39] Ibid., 82–88.

[40] Dolan, *Some Seed*, 99n58.

The liturgical "objective" was titled, "Rogation Days: The Liturgy and Rural Life." The brief resolution explained that it had been the ancient tradition of the church to ask at all times for the blessing of God upon all things spiritual and temporal, but most especially during the days preceding Ascension. This often involved the blessings of crops for their protection. It went on to say, "we urge that the Fifth Sunday after Easter be nationally observed as Rural Life Sunday, and that the liturgical prayers and ceremonies of the ensuing Rogation Days be carried out . . . by the Catholics of this country."[41] The resolution also noted that the Conference would participate "in a movement already widespread amongst our fellow citizens in the United States." A 1929 letter from Harrison W. Foreman of the National Council of the Protestant Episcopal Church encouraged O'Hara and the NCRLC to join President Hoover, the Agriculture Secretary, and many other religious and civic groups in observing Rogation Days as well as the Fifth Sunday after Easter as "Rural Life Sunday." The accompanying letter made suggestions for hymns, Scripture, prayers, plays, pageants, and a bibliography.[42] Governmental, civic, and ecumenical cooperation were nothing new to O'Hara, but now he made such cooperation an explicit objective of the NCRLC's program for rural America. Liturgically speaking, the Conference took as its point of departure Rogation Days as the most logical means of connecting the liturgy to rural life.

O'Hara was deeply interested in the renewal of the liturgy for three reasons. First, he was a disciple of Pius X and shared the pontiff's wish for a revitalized Christian life by way of the liturgy. Second, he believed that the faithful of the countryside had high esteem for the liturgy, especially its communal dimension that helped to overcome the isolation they may have experienced. Third, he perceived that active participation in the liturgy was an attitude often transferred to the Christian life in general. He shared this sentiment in a letter to Virgil Michel:

> I am particularly interested in developing the sound basis for a discussion of the laity's position in the liturgy. It seems to me that we have sadly neglected the possibilities of the doctrine of the character

[41] Witte, *Crusading*, 87.

[42] H. W. Foreman to Edwin O'Hara, 2 July 1929, The Catholic University of America Archives, NCWC/USCC, Social Action Department, box 53, folder 25 "Rural Life Movement and Liturgical Movement" (hereafter, CUAA/SAD).

imprinted by the sacraments of confirmation and baptism. Just
recently, in going over the writings of some of the early Fathers . . .,
I found their teaching was that confirmation was in some way an
ordination to the priesthood of the laity.[43]

O'Hara expressed his affinity for one of the liturgical movement's core
principles, namely, a greater participative role for the laity in the
liturgy, and he wanted to make it central to the NCRLC's spiritual and
liturgical programs. While he would play several significant roles in
the liturgical movement, it was not "as an expert in liturgy, but as a
teacher." O'Hara cooperated with any group he felt could advance his
agenda for rural life and in particular the CCD, the work for which he
became most well known in Catholic circles. Quite simply, he saw the
liturgical movement and the renewal it promoted as one more "*means
of religious education.*"[44]

Meanwhile, Michel responded to O'Hara, thanking him for his kind
words in regard to a recent article of his in *Ecclesiastical Review*. Michel
promised to send him pamphlets from the Liturgical Press for a course
in "Parish Sociology" that O'Hara was to teach at The Catholic
University of America, a course that focused on the rural parish. He
taught a similar course at the University of Notre Dame during the
summers.[45] He related to Michel that, "we shall discuss the Liturgical
movement in a few weeks and I shall get the students acquainted
with your literature."[46] In the same letter, O'Hara mentioned that he
had expressed to Bill Busch his desire to spread interest in Rural Life
Sunday and the Rogation Days, seeking a deeper integration of
religion and rural life:

[43] O'Hara to Michel, 15 February 1930, quoted from Dolan, *Some Seed*, 177n70.

[44] Dolan, *Some Seed*, 178. In a personal conversation with me on February 2, 2006, Dolan was in complete agreement with my assessment of O'Hara's pragmatism with regard to the liturgy. Dolan added that it was also the case with his push to have the CCD translate the New Testament. Education drove nearly everything that O'Hara undertook. See Witte, *Crusading*, 95.

[45] Virgil Michel to Edwin O'Hara, 21 February 1930, CUAA/SAD, box 53, folder 25 "Liturgical Movement and Rural Life Movement." The article was "The True Christian Spirit," *Ecclesiastical Review* 82 (1930): 128–42.

[46] Edwin O'Hara to Virgil Michel, 25 February 1930, CUAA/SAD, box 53, folder 25 "Liturgical Movement and Rural Life Movement."

Such things as a sermon on the Catholic Church and the farmer and a procession blessing the fields are obvious enough but we desire to see in what way we can go further in interesting the farmer in the liturgy or interpret the liturgy to the farmer through his occupation.[47]

Michel replied to O'Hara:

It strikes me that there is a special chance to build the parish life of a rural community on the liturgy. It should be easy for the farmers to get consciousness of the Liturgical Year engrained in them, since the Liturgical Year has such a fine parallel with the natural year and since nature herself exemplifies so wonderfully the principle that the seed must die in order to live . . . I think this idea itself is full of many possibilities.[48]

Both O'Hara and Michel viewed the liturgy as an effective educational tool especially for the rural faithful. Each instinctively sensed the particular closeness between the liturgy and the life of the farmer and saw ample opportunity to develop it further.

The correspondence broadened to include Bill Busch. In October 1929, Busch wrote to Michel: "Father O'Hara of Oregon has suggested to me an article on a topic which may sound surprising to those who have not thought deeply about the liturgical movement. It is: The liturgy and farm relief."[49] The letter demonstrated a maturity in Busch's thought about the implications of a revitalized liturgical life. That he would have so easily seen such a natural connection between these two themes was impressive. Busch wrote again to Michel in March 1930 and enclosed a copy of the article that was intended to give its readers a "jolt." O'Hara had intimated to Busch that the U.S. bishops, as a body, would be willing to encourage the faithful to observe Catholic Rural Life Sunday. However, they needed to be

---

[47] Ibid.

[48] Virgil Michel to Rev. Frank O'Hara, 5 March 1930, CUAA/SAD, box 53, folder 25 "Liturgical Movement and Rural Life Movement." The correspondence seems to be a bit confused. The dates are consistent with the content of the letters, but the addressees are not. Michel addresses his letter to "Frank O'Hara" (Edwin's brother) who also taught at Catholic University, while Edwin writes to Fr. "Mitchel." However, the topic of his letter pertains to the correspondence with Edwin O'Hara.

[49] Bill Busch to Virgil Michel, 17 October 1929, St. John's Abbey Archives, Virgil Michel Papers, Box Z 23. (hereafter, SJAA) The letter will be examined more closely below. This collection is distinct from the St. John's University Archives (SJUA).

"strengthened in their attitude" with a short article that would make clearer the relationship between the liturgy and rural life.[50] In these early years, the liturgical and rural life movements did not as yet enjoy the full backing of the hierarchy, at times encountering resistance from clergy and bishops alike. The liturgical movement did not receive more official backing until the early 1940s.

Busch's article, "The Liturgy and Farm Relief," was provocative and perhaps a tad elitist, which may not have helped to produce its intended effect.[51] Yet the article stands as a seminal work, for it provided Catholic agrarianism, as embodied by the NCRLC, a more profound liturgical, theological, and social foundation. The context was the institution of Rural Life Sunday and the nationwide observance of the Rogation Days, not to mention the Great Depression. With regard to the Depression especially, the observance of Rogation Days could no longer be considered an interest of the agriculture sector alone but were meant to be relevant to an entire nation. Liturgy and farm relief should be a common concern for any Catholic. The liturgical movement, Busch believed, served as a rallying point that pressed for the general reform of modern life through the Catholic liturgy.

In good scholarly fashion Busch placed the question on a liturgical-historical foundation. Rogation Days originated in the fifth century and preceded the feast day of the Ascension. They were observed as days of prayer to avert plague and drought, as well as to implore the blessing of God for good harvests. There was a penitential dimension to them, but more important their observance was public, in which the whole community went in procession through the fields chanting the litanies and other prayers.[52] One of the *sine qua non* principles of the

---

[50] Bill Busch to Virgil Michel, 19 March 1930, SJAA, Virgil Michel Papers, Box Z 23. It was also around this time that Michel began to suffer fatigue and was plagued by several illnesses. Abbot Deutsch ordered Michel to rest, and this he did on the Chippewa reservation in northern Minnesota.

[51] William Busch, "Liturgy and Farm Relief," *CRL* 8 (April 1930): 2–3. This notion of elitism was a persistent and contentious issue with the NCRLC's publications. That is, articles were written in a language somewhat removed from the people they were supposed to help. See Witte, *Crusading*, 164–65. Similar criticism may be made of the liturgical movement. In 1934, the publication *Altar and Home* was begun by the Benedictines of Conception Abbey (Missouri) in order to make the movement more accessible to the laity.

[52] William Busch, "Liturgy and Farm Relief," *CRL* 8 (April 1930): 2. It was announced (but not published) in *Orate Fratres* that the article would appear in the

liturgical movement was the restoration of the social character of the Christian worship. The Rogation Days' present observance had become somewhat perfunctory and their wider social significance lost. They came to be celebrated as one of many common devotions that lacked a clear connection to liturgical prayer. Rogation Days produced their full effect when they were observed in the context of the church's overall liturgical life, especially in close conjunction with the liturgical and natural cycles of time. The NCRLC attempted to make the Rogation Days as fully participative as possible, restoring their proper place within the liturgical life of the church.

Busch had realized that the church had been caught for a very long time in a pattern of worship that reinforced an individualistic piety, and the liturgical movement had just begun to assist the faithful in breaking free of this pattern. Busch invoked Prosper of Aquitaine's ancient axiom in order to draw liturgy, theology, and life back into closer union:

> Prayer not only implores and honors God, it also educates mankind. This is especially true of liturgical prayer. The liturgy well understood will show us the meaning of the Christian religion in all its scope. The *lex orandi* will help us to know the *lex credendi* and the *lex agendi*. We shall be conscious once more of our social solidarity in Christ. We shall see a transformation of social life, agricultural, industrial and political. If this is too much to hope for Christian nations, then the outlook of the modern world is dark indeed.[53]

The liturgical movement maintained that regeneration of the social and economic spheres must begin with a renewal of authentic worship. Liturgy transformed the assembly first and heightened the Christian's awareness of the social ills endemic in society. By its own accord, the liturgy was insufficient to correct unjust social structures. Like the church's social teaching, the liturgy did not provide ready-made solutions to the world's problems. Rather, through worship and study, the

---

April 1930 issue of *CRL*. See "The Apostolate," *Orate Fratres* 4 (1929–30): 424. Busch also thought it might be published in the *NCWC Bulletin*, widening its readership, especially among the bishops. My perusal of the *NCWC Bulletin*, and later the *NCWC Review*, from 1929 to 1932 did not locate this article. The Rogation Days are treated more fully in chapter 5.

[53] Busch, "Liturgy and Farm Relief," 2. The *lex agendi* may be translated as the rule of right action, as in the contemporary use of *lex vivendi*.

Christian received the spiritual means to discern which course of action most benefited the common good.

Another key principle of the liturgical movement that had special resonance with Catholic rural life was the "sacramental principle." Throughout the first twenty-five years of *Orate Fratres*, numerous articles were written about this theme and its relationship to the church's official worship. Naturally, the retrieval of this principle found a welcome with the NCRLC. The relationship between the material and spiritual (a natural and supernatural sacramentality) dimensions of life formed one of the core theological pillars of both movements. The sacramental principle, and one of its corollaries—sacramentals—served as the crucial link between liturgy and daily life. Busch offered an eloquent statement that could have served as the Magna Carta for the manner in which the liturgical and rural life movements were theologically related, and more so, how liturgy and daily life were brought into closer relationship:

> The task should be all the easier in the case of agriculture. For the liturgy long antedates modern industrialism and speaks in a language of an age more closely in touch with nature and filled with references to rural life. Like the parables . . . and the . . . pastoral and nature imagery of all the Bible, the liturgy, true always to the sacramental principle, brings us through the things of nature to the things of grace. To the dwellers in the country the liturgy speaks in a familiar way, and to all of us in a way that tends to correct our modern life in which man is divorced from nature while nature is mechanized and divorced from God. The appeal to nature is, however, only the method by which the liturgy instructs us regarding human relationships and regarding the relation of man to God. Nor is it instruction only, for the liturgy imparts the power to do what it teaches. It brings social enlightenment, it instills a sense of social responsibility, it prompts to social action. The liturgy is indeed a cosmos in which the individual, the parish community, the diocese and the universal Church find their life ordered and ennobled in Christ.[54]

That Busch did not explicate what farm relief entails could be seen as a weakness of the article. However, he did not place any unrealistic burden on the liturgy, such as, "When one celebrates the liturgy in this fashion, it will yield these solutions to the farm problem." Rather, he

[54] Busch, "Liturgy and Farm Relief," 2–3.

affirmed that the liturgy inspired a deep "social solidarity in Christ" that enabled the Christian to discern the best course of action to pursue. The liturgy did not do this alone but in conjunction with a study of the church's teachings and other spiritual practices.

The rural life movement was aided substantially by Frederick Kenkel of the Central Verein (hereafter, Verein), many of whose constituents were farmer-immigrants from the German countryside. Kenkel was very well connected and had established Verein chapters around the country, predominantly in Missouri and Minnesota. It was he who helped organize the first NCRLC meeting in St. Louis. O'Hara utilized Kenkel's network to send lecturers from local Verein chapters to speak after Sunday High Masses, setting forth the Conference's rural program. One of the Verein's publications, *Central Blatt and Social Justice*, served to keep the social question at the fore, including the *Farmerfrage*. The Verein supported the cooperative movement, which was much valued by O'Hara and Michel. However, Kenkel shared the same hesitation as Michel toward uncritically embracing cooperatives, fearing that the cooperatives could be used as a screen for transferring ownership to the state. The two men also agreed that the cooperative spirit [*Genossenchaftsgeist*] should be stressed over merely employing cooperative techniques [*Genossenschaftswesen*]. Kenkel, of decentralist persuasion, saw the cooperatives as a means to a spiritual revolution, "quickening the social spirit," and able to build strong faith communities.[55]

Kenkel continually sought to strengthen the spiritual center of the Verein, and this created a natural link to O'Hara and Michel. All these men asserted that the modern industrial revolution (industrial farming operations included) carried with it negative spiritual side effects. The liturgy seemed to be the most logical means to foster the spiritual and social dimensions of Catholic life, while at the same time not turning completely away from modern American society. A strong spiritual base already existed among German Catholics, where an amalgamation of local traditions and popular liturgical practices were often observed. This was especially true in the rural areas. It should be no surprise that the American liturgical revival often seemed to flourish in German-American Catholic centers such as Minnesota and Missouri.

[55] Philip Gleason, *The Conservative Reformers: German-American Catholics and the Social Order* (Notre Dame, IN: University of Notre Dame Press, 1968), 186–87, 190.

Kenkel did not write extensively about the liturgy, but he believed in its central importance. Two years before Michel initiated the American liturgical movement, Kenkel published an article entitled "The Parish Church, A True Community Center," where he articulated what the implications of a reformed liturgy might mean for the total life of the parish community. In 1925 the *Central Blatt* published the seminal liturgical work by Anthony Jasper and Martin Hellriegel, *Der Schluessel zur Loesung der sozial Frage*, which Bill Busch translated in 1938 under the title *The True Basis of Christian Solidarity* (that basis being the liturgy). In the late 1930s, Kenkel and the Verein would play key roles in the Institutes of Social Study and Rural Life Schools held at St. John's in Collegeville.[56]

By the late 1920s, O'Hara had established a rather wide array of contacts for his burgeoning apostolate, and some of these persons were key figures in the liturgical movement. Initial, laudatory efforts were made to inculcate the people with a renewed liturgical spirituality, one that distanced itself from the individualistic piety that dominated church life. The social encyclicals of Leo XIII and Pius XI also began to play a role in stretching Catholic piety beyond the church doors on Sunday. Participation in the public worship of the church demanded a *public* living out of one's faith so as to regenerate the social order, an order that was about to be seriously disrupted.

## SOWING SEEDS—THE LITURGICAL AND RURAL LIFE MOVEMENTS, 1930–1940

The Great Depression and the Dust Bowl, both lasting throughout the decade of the 1930s, were defining moments in the history of the United States. The NCRLC was both affected by, and responded to, these events. Publication of *Catholic Rural Life* ceased during the years 1930–33, but was then resurrected by Conference president Father W. Howard Bishop in late 1933 under the title *Landward*. During these years one finds little of liturgical significance published in this journal. The topics addressed in the NCRLC's journals were often shaped by whoever was the current executive secretary. In the years 1931–34, this

---

[56] Ibid., 190. See Anthony Jasper and Martin Hellriegel, "Der Schluessel zur Loesung der sozial Frage," *Central Blatt and Social Justice* XVIII (July–August 1925): 122–24, 158–60; idem, *The True Basis of Christian Solidarity*, trans. William Busch (St. Louis: Central Bureau of the Central Verein, 1938). The institutes and rural life schools will be treated below.

was Edgar Schmiedeler, OSB, of St. Benedict's Abbey in Atchison, Kansas. The Depression caused *Landward* to focus on political and economic issues as they related to agrarians.[57] This does not mean, however, that the Conference failed to address the liturgical question.

In his 1930 presidential address, W. Howard Bishop noted the close relationship between rural life and religion, especially as it was expressed in the Scriptures. He exhorted the Conference to attend to both temporal and spiritual needs, and to support the "lay liturgical movement" as advancing the latter.[58] At the 1931 Wichita convention the principles of *Rerum Novarum* and *Quadragesimo Anno* were quoted in their bearing on cooperative farming. The spiritual ideal, the Conference argued, manifested itself when collaboration between priests and people, scholars and workers, harnessed their "spiritual and material" forces in order to overcome the menace of individualism. The NCRLC fostered the true spirit of Christian collaboration through retreats, confraternities, and the "cultivation of liturgy."[59]

Father Hubert Duren of Westphalia, Iowa, was introduced to the NCRLC at the 1932 Dubuque convention. He became one of the organization's many success stories. Duren took the "cooperative" principle quite seriously, making it operative in everything from liturgy to economic endeavors. On the morning of October 20, 1932,

---

[57] Witte, *Crusading*, 190–94. The publication addressed such national policies as the Bankhead Bill and the Agricultural Adjustment Act. Both formed part of New Deal legislation which attempted to give immediate relief to farmers while at the same time advocating more significant agricultural reform. The 1933 National Industry Recovery Act had set aside $25 million for the establishment of new homesteads. Perhaps one of the most successful homesteads created was that of the NCRLC's Luigi Ligutti in Granger, Iowa. The NCRLC supported the Roosevelt plans initially but realized in the late 1930s that the relief was only temporary and that the administration saw farming as one industry among many that needed help. For an interesting and related study from a different perspective see Edward Shapiro's, "The Catholic Rural Life Movement and the New Deal Farm Program," *American Benedictine Review* 28 (September 1977): 307–22. See also Witte, *Crusading*, 161; Dolan, *Some Seed*, 108–9.

[58] W. Howard Bishop, "Presidential Address: Eighth Annual Catholic Rural Conference," MUA/NCRLC, Series 8/1, box 1, folder "National Convention, Springfield, IL, August 26–28, 1930," 5.

[59] "Executive Committee Minutes, Witchita, KS, 1931," MUA/NCRLC, Series 8/1, box 1, binder, 73. In this box is a black binder that contains the Executive Meeting Minutes from 1923–1932 with pages marked consecutively. It will be referenced as "binder, page#."

there was a *Missa recitata* by the children of Nativity parish in Dubuque—a liturgical practice that was growing more common.[60] Executive committee members noted that "Rural Life Sundays are being observed."[61] Cultural (folk) arts and music were to be fostered in the rural community. Also at the Dubuque convention, John LaFarge declared: "The land is the Creator's gift for maintaining the existence of the Christian world." LaFarge upheld the rural Catholic parish as crucial in the fight against secular and Communistic forces that treated the land as one commodity among many. Communists often used the land as an "instrument of warfare." The parish, because of its local network of relationships, in addition to its material and spiritual resources, stood as a potential force of social change and cohesion. The parish's "territorial unity," and its "unity and definiteness of doctrine" (through preaching from the pulpit and its schools) was key to effecting such change. The sacramental life, and more specifically, the common liturgical life of the parish, provided the best means to unify all other aspects of the community.[62] Cooperation and common endeavors extended to include social, economic, and educational programs. Parishes that implemented, as fully as possible, the NCRLC's philosophy impacted not only the well-being if its own Catholic community but that of the town and sometimes the region.

The NCRLC made a resolution at the 1935 Rochester convention that stressed the role "economic cooperation" could play in promoting the common good. In the midst of the Depression, such an ethos of cooperation was crucial. The image of the Mystical Body of Christ was adopted as the best way of expressing such cooperation. The NCRLC embraced credit unions and cooperatives, naming the Antigonish Movement of St. Francis Xavier University in Nova Scotia as an outstanding example.[63] To anchor the cooperative Catholic rural life, the

---

[60] "Tenth Annual Convention, Dubuque Program," MUA/NCRLC, Series 8/1, box 1, binder, 77.

[61] "Executive Committee Minutes, Dubuque, IA, 1931," MUA/NCRLC, Series 8/1, box 1, binder, 82.

[62] John LaFarge, SJ, "Land the Hope of the Future," in *Catholic Rural Life Conference: Proceedings* (NCRLC, 1933), 71, 73–74, University of Notre Dame Archives, Frederick Kenkel Papers, Series Miscellaneous 1/17, 70–74; also in Georgetown University Archives, John L. LaFarge Collection, box 41, folder 9.

[63] The Antigonish Movement was the strongest Catholic Cooperative in North America. Father W. Howard Bishop was responsible for bringing its founder

Conference looked to the liturgical movement as a centralizing force: "We urge likewise the study of the liturgy of the Church and the participation of our rural people in the liturgy according to the mind of the Church as the spiritual basis of the communal spirit and the source of Christ-like living and apostolic social action." This may have prompted the Conference to invite Virgil Michel to the following year's Fargo convention, where he delivered his talk on the liturgical and cooperative movements.[64]

Amid the Great Depression and Dust Bowl, the NCRLC issued its most authoritative statement to date, the *Manifesto on Rural Life*. Approved at the Vincennes meeting in 1938 and published in 1939, the *Manifesto* stands as one of the more comprehensive social documents produced by a recognized Catholic organization. Bishop Aloisius Muench of Fargo wrote in the preface:

> In propounding social philosophy, the Catholic Church does not leave out the view of the spiritual nature of man. . . . Indeed, the salvation of souls must ever be her first concern. But so intimately are material things interwoven with man's daily conduct, its motives and deeds, that the Church cannot be unconcerned about what goes on in the material order of things.[65]

---

Fr. Coady and some co-op members to the 1934 St. Paul convention. After this meeting, a "cooperative committee" was formed as part of the NCRLC. See Witte, *Crusading*, 107, and Kauffman, *Mission to Rural America*, 92, 123.

[64] "Resolutions Thirteenth Annual Convention, Rochester, NY," MUA/NCRLC, Series 8/1, box 2, folder "Meetings and Conventions October 27, 1935–September 25, 1938," 159. N.B. Michel's talk was later published in *Catholic Rural Life Objectives* (1936) and in *Orate Fratres* (1939). Immediately following the NCRLC's 1936 Fargo convention, which Michel attended, he returned to St. John's where the first weekend of the Institute for Social Study was to be held October 17–18, 1936. The Institute for Social Study will be considered in the next chapter. It was one of the venues in which Michel specifically explored the agrarian question.

[65] NCRLC, *Manifesto on Rural Life* (Milwaukee: Bruce Publishing, 1939), vi. The chapters of the *Manifesto* reveal its breadth: "The Rural Catholic Family," "Farm Ownership and Tenancy," "Rural Settlement," "Catholic Rural Education," "Rural Catholic Youth," "Catholic Culture in Rural Society," "Rural Community," "The Rural Pastorate," "Rural Church Expansion," "Rural Health," "Rural Social Charity," "The Farm Laborers," "Farmer Cooperatives," "Rural Credit," "Agriculture in the Economic Organism," "Rural Taxation." Each chapter had an accompanying "Annotations" section in the back; it was made up mostly of quotes from popes, theologians, and social theorists.

The *Manifesto* situated the rural question in the context of the papal encyclicals of the day along with current socioeconomic research. The *Manifesto* did not, however, make a single reference to liturgy or much else of a spiritual nature. This was especially surprising since two years earlier Virgil Michel spoke at the Fargo convention about the cooperative and liturgical movements.

In the *Manifesto*, Michel collaborated with John LaFarge in writing the chapter that dealt with farmers' cooperatives, and made no mention of the liturgical movement. "Social charity," the most explicitly religious terminology used in the *Manifesto*, was to act as the primary animating force of the Christian cooperative.[66] This liturgical lacuna is interesting. In April 1937 the various committees responsible for producing the *Manifesto* met in St. Louis, and each one submitted a preliminary report in November of the same year. The third of these reports, "Christian Cooperatives," was prepared by LaFarge and Michel. The report made a direct connection between ethical relationships (here in the agrarian-economic sphere) and the Mystical Body of Christ. LaFarge and Michel suggested that the church's liturgy served as a sound "model" for cooperation. For some reason these insights did not make it into the final redaction.[67]

The liturgical and spiritual lacunae of the *Manifesto* did not escape the attention of Martin Schirber, OSB, a fellow monk from Michel's community.[68] Schirber's review of the *Manifesto* in *Orate Fratres*

---

[66] Ibid., 58.

[67] "Catholic Planning for Rural Social Welfare," NCRLC, Richmond, VA, November 7–10, 1937. See MUA/NCLRC, Series 12/1, box 1, "1937." Out of eight reports submitted, John LaFarge had a hand in five of them and submitted one on family life independently. There were many people involved in producing the *Manifesto*. This lack of more specific liturgical and spiritual matter in the document is interesting. In the final redaction, none other than Msgr. John A. Ryan (among others) was brought in for consultation. One wonders if the liturgical material had been originally included in an earlier version only to be excised based on the "Ryan" approach, which tended to rely too heavily on socioeconomic theory. See NCRLC, *Manifesto*, 73–74.

[68] Martin Schirber, OSB, "Manifesto on Rural Life," *OF* 14 (1939–40): 93–94. Schirber assumed leadership of the rural summer schools after Michel's death. He remained close to rural life but was critical of it in many ways. See Martin Schirber, "Catholic Rural Life," in *The American Apostolate*, Leo Ward, ed. (Westminster, MD: Newman Press, 1952), 133–48. Michel wrote to Schirber in 1935 when the latter was studying at The Catholic University of America and encouraged him to write his master's thesis on liturgy and sociology. He suggested working with Fr. Paul Hanley

praised the measured manner in which the document laid out its program for agrarian reform and that it offered no simplistic answers to the agricultural problems of the day. Faithful to Catholic social teaching, the document maintained that concrete solutions needed to develop from within a society, more organically. In spite of the *Manifesto*'s reliance on Catholic social principles, Schirber wondered if it had done so too narrowly and offered this pointed criticism:

> The *Manifesto* admittedly draws its principles from Catholic social philosophy, which even in its broad sense must be taken from reason guided by revelation and from empirical investigation; and even a cursory reading of the book reveals that the data of revelation are not explicitly woven into the finished fabric. It scarcely mentions grace, the supernatural life, the mystical body, life in Christ, the liturgy, sacraments, the Mass as community worship and sacrifice, and the Eucharist as the bond of social unity. Even the discussion of social charity leaves the impression that the writers have in mind merely a rural community chest campaign, whose purpose is to bolster up a faltering justice—with little to distinguish it from mere humanitarianism.[69]

Schirber was not too far off the mark and, as a liturgical disciple of Virgil Michel, he raised some of the very questions his mentor would have proffered. Schirber suggested that the supernatural realities may be presumed, and to have brought them out explicitly may have alienated the many non-Catholics with whom the NCRLC collaborated. He concluded by pondering whether "the *Manifesto* might not safely have been more radically Christian seems at least worthy of discussion."[70]

Liturgically speaking, there was little else that emerged directly from the Conference during this decade. Upon Virgil Michel's return from the Chippewa reservation (a four-year hiatus recovering from illness), he took up the agrarian question and made Collegeville a center for rural life study and action. He used St. John's reputation as

---

Furfey with whom Schirber had taken courses. See the following correspondence: Michel to Schirber, 27 November 1935, SJAA "Virgil Michel Papers," Z 27, folder 7. Other relevant correspondence from 18 October and 25 November 1935, and 26 April 1936, can be found in SJAA, "Virgil Michel Papers" Z 27, folder 8.

[69] Schirber, "Manifesto on Rural Life," 94.

[70] Ibid., 94. Bishop Aloisius Muench had final editing responsibilities. I have not been able to find anything in the correspondence on the *Manifesto* that would suggest concerns that Schirber addressed.

a locus of the liturgical movement and expanded its vision to include the rural apostolate. Michel (and others) made significant contributions to Catholic agrarianism and incorporated it into the larger project of reconstructing the social order, the liturgy occupying a key place in this enterprise.

Chapter 2

# Liturgy Is God-Conscious and Land-Conscious

During the 1940s the NCRLC witnessed a veritable explosion of programs and publications in general, but especially with regard to its liturgical and devotional life. Interestingly enough, this occurred in conjunction with similar stirrings of the Liturgical Conference and its annual Liturgical Weeks. Martin Hellriegel set the tone for collaboration between the two groups in the opening remarks of his talk at the 1941 National Liturgical Week in St. Paul, Minnesota. The new pastor commented on the makeup of his parish, Holy Cross, in O'Fallon, Missouri, which was about two-thirds urban and one-third rural. He cautioned the assembled group to not repeat the following oversight:

> Third, while speaking of rural life this pastor is going to raise a note of protest (please watch the smile) about the concurrence of the "National Liturgical Week" here at St. Paul and the "National Rural Life Conference" now convening in Jefferson City, Missouri. As a Missourian and as a lover of the Rural Life Conference I should this evening be in Jefferson City, and as a Catholic and a lover of the liturgical apostolate I am happy to spend these holy days here in St. Paul. But now I quit smiling as I say the following: In the future we should not permit such a simultaneousness. These two movements are like the two halves of a circle and the leaders of one should bring information and inspiration to the other. But that is impossible when the two are convening at the same time. The liturgical group is the "husband" and the rural life group is the "wife" and, what God has joined together, let no man put asunder. But right now they are "divorced."[1]

[1] Martin B. Hellriegel, "A Pastor's Description of Liturgical Participation in His Parish," *National Liturgical Week*, 1941 (Newark, NJ: The Benedictine Liturgical Conference, 1942), 82–83.

This liturgical leader's endorsement of the NCRLC would not be his last. Throughout the decade Hellriegel had his hand in several of the Conference's liturgical initiatives, spoke at its annual conventions, and served on its board of directors from 1947 to 1950. The close relationship that Hellriegel encouraged between the two groups can be seen in the NCRLC's executive committee meeting minutes and annual convention programs from this time period.

HARVESTING THE FIRST FRUITS: THE LITURGICAL AND RURAL LIFE MOVEMENTS, 1940–1950

The inaugural National Liturgical Week held in Chicago in 1940 stood as the first large-scale manifestation of the liturgical movement. It was the initiative of the Benedictine Liturgical Conference, later known simply as the Liturgical Conference. While many cities had already hosted single-day liturgical gatherings, the Chicago meeting gave the movement national status. Besides hearing talks from leaders in the movement, participants regularly celebrated the *Missa recitata*. After 1940, one finds that the "dialogue Mass" was a consistent feature at most of the NCRLC's annual gatherings. Not only did some of the NCRLC leaders attend the Nation Liturgical Weeks, some also gave talks.[2]

The NCRLC executive committee met two or three times a year to plan the annual gatherings and other projects. A few of these meetings were especially telling of the NCRLC's liturgical activities. For example, at the January 12, 1944, meeting in Chicago the executive secretary reported that a rural prayer book for the family would be edited and overseen by Bishop Joseph Schlarman (Peoria, Illinois) and the Jesuits of St. Mary's in Kansas; this became *With the Blessing of the Church*, not a prayer book proper. Alban Dachauer, SJ, was called upon to organize the project at St. Mary's. (It would take another decade to publish the actual prayer book.) Also present at this meeting was Msgr. Joseph Morrison, then president of the Liturgical Conference, who looked

---

[2] One of the leaders in Chicago was Reynold Hillenbrand, rector of St. Mary's of the Lake Seminary (Mundelein, IL), who was instrumental in promoting the relationship between the liturgical movement and Catholic Action. See Pecklers, *Unread Vision*, 143–47, 198–99. Program booklets for the following NCRLC meetings mentioned the *Missa recitata*: St. Cloud, 1940; Jefferson City, 1941; Peoria, 1942; Cincinnati, 1944; Green Bay, 1946; Lafayette, 1947; Columbus, 1949. See MUA/ NCRLC, Series 8/1, boxes 3-8, individual convention folders.

forward to future cooperation with the NCRLC through programs that would bring the rural point of view to the Liturgical Conference and vice versa.[3] Luigi Ligutti suggested that "rural cells," a reference to Catholic Action, could serve as places to experiment with present liturgical renewal. Michael Ducey, OSB, of St. Anselm's priory in Washington, DC, had been given the task of studying the history of liturgical practices in relation to rural life. Schlarman and Hellriegel discussed plans for a practical liturgical manual for rural priests. Unfortunately, neither of these last two projects came to fruition. Lastly, in connection to rural culture, plans were drawn up to produce a picture of St. Isidore to accompany a prayer book called "Saints of the Soil," illustrated by artist Lauren Ford. This too never materialized.[4]

As part of the November 1944 meeting in Cincinnati, a "Rural Life Day" was planned for Loveland, Ohio, home to the Grail community.[5] The *Missa recitata* was celebrated and Bishop Schlarman presided. The day included folk dancing and many other rural life activities. A talk given by Fr. George Johnson of Goltry, Oklahoma, "The Liturgy and the Land," was slated for the day.[6] Other recommendations at the meeting called for further development of the liturgical side of rural life in addition to literature and art. Ligutti had given a talk to the Adrian Dominicans of Michigan in the early 1940s. Present at that talk was Sr. Mary Helene, OP, president of the Catholic Art Association. Ligutti saw her again at this 1944 meeting at Grailville and suggested that she paint a picture of St. Isidore. After reading the saint's story, she took as her theme the legend of St. Isidore seen plowing a field assisted by two angels; her rendition was accepted, and the Conference immediately began mass production.[7]

[3] "Minutes," MUA/NCRLC, Series 8/1, box 4, folder "Advisory Board, Executive Committee Meeting, Chicago, IL, January 12, 1944."

[4] Ibid.

[5] See below, 47–54. The Grail will be treated separately due to the amount of material and the important relationship it shared with the NCRLC. The Grail is an international women's movement based in the Christian tradition, but in recent decades has embraced many diverse spiritual traditions as part of its program.

[6] This address and others could not be located.

[7] Witte, *Crusading*, 214. See "Report of the Executive Secretary," MUA/NCRLC, Series 8/1, box 5, folder "Cincinnati Convention Reports and Papers, November 10–13, 1944," 3. The original canvas work hangs in the offices of the NCRLC in Des Moines, IA. See book cover.

The 1949 Columbus, Ohio, gathering proved to be interesting in many respects, for it took some rather innovative approaches to instructing the people about the liturgy and its connection to daily life. A workshop called "Liturgy and the Home" introduced Florence Berger to the Conference for the first time. Her husband Albert also became a regular presenter at annual meetings; the two of them often lectured together on rural family issues. Florence Berger became well known for her book *Cooking for Christ*.[8] The actual blueprint of how she set up her exhibit, which required an entire room, was preserved. She arranged the exhibit in such a way that people would move from one table to the next, represented by a liturgical season or feast day. The people then sampled her recipes designated for that time of the liturgical year. The order was Advent, Christmas, Epiphany, Mardi Gras, Lent, Holy Thursday, Easter, Pentecost, St. John's Day, Assumption, Halloween, and All Saints.[9] Luigi Ligutti wrote in the preface to *Cooking for Christ*: "This book is an extension of the Missal, Breviary and Ritual because the Christian home is an extension of the Mass, Choir and sacramentals."[10] Berger boldly declared in her introduction: "Cook you may call her. I prefer Christian in Action. To some it may seem sacrilegious to connect cookery and Christ but that is exactly what this book means to do." She said that the liturgists have called us back to an earlier vision of Christian worship, which pressed for more lay participation. Berger established a clear connection between

[8] Florence E. Berger, *Cooking for Christ: The Liturgical Year in the Kitchen* (Des Moines: National Catholic Rural Life Conference, 1949). The book is still available from the NCRLC. In 1949 both the *New York Times* and *Time Magazine* gave it favorable reviews. See also Anthony Adams, SJ, "More Everyday Liturgy," *Rural Life Column*, December 6, 1949, MUA/NCRLC, Series 6/1, boxes 9–10.

[9] See actual blueprint, MUA/NCRLC, Series 8/1, box 7, folder "National Convention Columbus, OH, November 4–9, 1949." There was also a list of international leaders who could not make the Columbus meeting, among whom was Msgr. (Dom) Helder Camara. Dom Helder would maintain contact with the NCRLC until the end of his life. He participated in the "Theology of the Land" conference in 1987 held in Collegeville, MN. The conferences were an ongoing reflection on land and religion by the NCRLC and St. John's (The Vigil Michel Ecumenical Chair of Rural Social Ministries). See Bernard Evans and Gregory D. Cusack, eds., *Theology of the Land* (Collegeville, MN: Liturgical Press, 1987).

[10] Luigi Ligutti, in Berger, *Cooking for Christ*, preface.

liturgy and daily life, grounding it on principles advanced by the liturgical movement and fostered a domestic piety.[11]

Also at the Columbus convention, the dramatic performance *The Golden Secret of Green Acres: A Pageant of Rural Life* offered another innovative approach to liturgical catechesis. The pageant was written and produced by Msgr. Joseph Cousins, a priest of the Diocese of Columbus, Ohio, and a faculty member at the Pontifical College Josephinum. Sadly, Cousins died unexpectedly only two weeks before the performance, leaving Fr. Urban Nagle, OP, and others to fill in for him. While pageant might be one word to describe it, paraliturgy would also be accurate. The production was so large that it had to be held in the Coliseum of the Ohio State Fairgrounds. It involved more than 1,200 people including a 180-voice mixed choir, an 80-voice male choir from the Josephinum along with the seminary's 40-piece band.[12] The Coliseum, which held 5,000 persons, was filled to capacity. Cousins explained "The Argument" behind the production:

> Composed to exhibit the nobility and the necessity of Christian rural life, this pageant is set about the Altar of Divine Sacrifice. It shows that all the material elements of Altar and Sacrifice are "from the earth, the good green earth which the Lord has given to us." Man's whole purpose in being is the worship of God. Sacrifice is the perfection of worship. The altar is the place of sacrifice. Thus in the building and furnishing of the altar, man's best activity is symbolized. . . . To the building and fulfilling come those who have labored in earth's green acres: the workers in stone, the goldsmiths, the weavers and spinners, the candlemakers. Last of all—with the altar now prepared—come the farmers bearing the very elements of sacrifice, the wheat and grape, the bread and wine, that will become the Body and Blood of the Divine Victim in the Perfect Sacrifice. Surely, these farmers, these who live the Christian rural life, have, above others, discovered the glorious Golden Secret of the Green Acres.[13]

Following the entry of ecclesiastical and civil dignitaries, flags, officers and delegates of the NCRLC, the invocation of Cardinal Edward

---

[11] Berger, *Cooking for Christ*, introduction.

[12] Joseph A. Cousins, *The Golden Secret of Green Acres: A Pageant of Rural Life* (Somerset, OH: The Rosary Press, 1950), 5. In MUA/NCRLC, Series 8/1, box 7, folder "Annual Convention Columbus, OH, 1949, Golden Secret of Green Acres."

[13] Ibid., 15.

Mooney (Detroit), and the official state welcome by Governor Frank L. Lausche, the pageant began and played out in six movements, here summarized:

1) Prologue—Melchisedech presented as the symbol of all acceptable religious sacrifice.

2) Workers in Stone—who found their work ultimately sanctified by the honor accorded them of building the altar.

3) Goldsmiths—who expressed joy in their art fashioning beauty from crude ore; they lamented the misuse of their precious metal by misguided men; they . . . furnished tabernacle, candlesticks, chalice and paten for His altar.

4) Spinners and Weavers—chanted the need and value of their art to all the race; they claimed the holy privilege of draping the altar of sacrifice and of clothing in sacred vestments the priest who made the offering.

5) Candlemakers—told of the significance of their craft in human history; they, the light makers, offered as a symbol of shining faith and love their tapers of wax for the altar.

> Melchisedech, meanwhile, received all these gifts and reminded them that the most essential gift has yet to be offered—the gift of the tiller of soil and the harvester of its fruits, the gift of the farmer. As the Farm Group entered, Melchisidech finished his speech and retired as his place was taken by "the Priest, ordained in the Eternal Priesthood and for the Perfect Sacrifice of Jesus Christ—the Holy Mass." The choir sang the hymn "Green Acres," which led into the last episode.[14]

6) The Farm Group—entered, led by the priest, and chanted praise to God who had chosen them for the sacred work of renewing and conserving life, of bringing to fertility the good green acres, and so of making all life, all toil, all usefulness and service on the earth; indeed theirs was the gift of providing the material elements of the Perfect Sacrifice itself.

---

[14] The lyrics to *Green Acres* were composed by Cousins: "Green acres fruitful in the sunlight, / Where the kindly earth gives to toil reward. / Place for laughing children there, / Underneath the blessing of the Lord. / Green acres glorious in the moonlight, / Hope of man for all that's best. / Home of quiet peace, when night comes down— / Green acres where our hearts find rest." See Cousins, *The Golden Secret*, 35.

The pageant concluded with priest and members of the cast reciting the opening words of the Mass and the mixed choir singing a hymn of praise.[15]

The pageant made explicit the central role of participation, not only in this paraliturgy but in life as it relates to communal worship. It made clear the close relationship between nature and the fashioning of goods for human use (the guilds). The dignity of work was emphasized, especially that of the farmer. One wonders, however, if singling out one group might have slighted other skilled laborers. In the context of public worship a potential danger exists in stressing the importance of one person (or gift) over another, expressing an inequality within the Body of Christ. The script focused considerably on sacrifice, offering, and priesthood. Liturgical scholars have recovered the ancient notion that the eucharistic liturgy is a multifaceted event comprised of many important parts—introductory rites, Liturgy of the Word, Communion, etc. Overemphasis of any one dimension of the liturgy limits the fuller religious potential of ritual in general. Employing Virgil Michel's language, the pageant expressed both corporality and cooperation in effecting the sacrifice. Overall, it lacked more direct connections to social justice. It did criticize those who used the earth for selfish and materialistic ends. Only near the end does it speak of feeding the hungry and giving drink to the thirsty. Better perhaps would have had the artisans build homes for the homeless, weavers clothe the naked, and, of course, have the farmers feed the hungry, conveying how one's gifts serve the common good.

Finally, at the Columbus meeting, Msgr. Joe Morrison presented a paper entitled "Harmony between Liturgy and Rural Life." In it he treated the usual facets of rural liturgy, such as various sacramentals, Rogation and Ember Days, the Divine Office, blessings from the *Ritual*, particularly agricultural blessings. He linked all such practices to the official public worship of the church, noting how all these "sacramentals" help to bind us more closely to the Mystical Body of Christ.[16]

Bishop Joseph Schlarman of Peoria, Illinois, born and raised on a farm, deserves special mention. As bishop of Peoria (1930–51), he made his first contact with the NCRLC at the 1933 Milwaukee meeting

[15] Cousins, *The Golden Secret*, 6–7.

[16] Joseph Morrison, "Harmony between Liturgy and Rural Life," MUA/NCRLC, Series 8/1, box 7, folder "National Convention Columbus, OH, November 4–9, 1949."

and became one of the organization's outstanding leaders, promoting both the rural and liturgical life. It is uncertain when and where Schlarman took up the liturgical apostolate; however, he made a retreat at St. John's in 1934 and was greatly impressed by the liturgical atmosphere there.[17] After that retreat, he issued a pastoral letter that demonstrated his keen sense of the liturgical movement—the central place of the liturgy, its power to deepen the spirit of the Mystical Body of Christ so as to transform society, active participation by the faithful, and the use of the vernacular, to name a few. What precipitated Schlarman's letter was the poor preaching of his priests and the desire of the people to understand what was happening in the liturgy. For his priests, Schlarman recommended *The Mind of the Missal* by Jesuit C. C. Martindale, a standard reference at the time. Later, as a remedy to the lackluster preaching, he published *Catechetical Sermon-Aids*, a thick tome that followed the liturgical year and carried the slogan "A Sermon or Instruction at Every Sunday Mass." Schlarman also gave a ten-point address to the Provincial Conference of Tertiaries (Franciscan), which had a distinctly liturgical emphasis.[18] The editor of *Orate Fratres* declared that the bishop has "come forth as a champion of the liturgy and its revival."[19]

On October 19, 1934, Schlarman convened what seems to have been the first diocesan-wide Liturgical Day. The editor of *Orate Fratres* remarked that "it was perhaps the most important, and certainly the best-attended Liturgical Day yet celebrated in the United States."[20] In his sermon Schlarman encouraged the faithful to a greater participation in the liturgy. He also offered a critical but faithful assessment of the church's past with regard to her public worship, how it has dampened the Christian spirit, adding: "It is time for us to get out of the rut!" He was clear about the day's purpose:

[17] Colman Barry, *Worship and Work: Saint John's Abbey and University, 1856–1992* (Collegeville, MN: Liturgical Press, 1993) 273.

[18] Editor, "The Apostolate," *OF* 10 (1936): 10–13; and Joseph Schlarman, *Catechetical Sermon-Aids* (St. Louis: Herder, 1942).

[19] Editor, "The Apostolate," *OF* 8 (1933–34): 226. *OF* appended only the first part of Schlarman's letter, noting that the second treats of liturgical music. Father Joseph Kreuter, OSB, took over as editor of *Orate Fratres* from 1930 to 1935 when Michel was sent to the Chippewa reservation. See Marx, *Virgil Michel*, 162, 174–75n91.

[20] Editor, "The Liturgy and the Parish," *OF* 9 (1934): 10. It may have been the first *diocesan* day, but St. John's conducted the first Liturgical Day on July 25, 1929. See Barry, *Worship and Work*, 275.

[It] is to deliberate and discuss how we ourselves can come closer to Christ . . . [to] bring the people closer to Christ and to the altar . . . [to] make them understand their dignity and duty as members of the Mystical Body of Christ; how we can lead them to take an active part in the official services of the Church.[21]

He was also realistic when he added: "This may mean a complete change of heart for some of our priests. What of it? So did the Catholic doctrine of social justice proclaimed by Pope Leo XIII."[22] Even the Episcopalians, Schlarman declared, had become more liturgical-minded than many Catholics.

During the 1940s Schlarman undertook several initiatives connected to both rural and liturgical life. In 1942 he was named president of the NCRLC and hosted the annual convention in Peoria, opening it with a dialogue Mass. It was one of the most successful gatherings of the Conference, and among the attendees were Dorothy Day and the Grail's Dr. Lydwine van Kersbergen.[23] The latter became a regular presenter at the annual NCRLC conventions. The Peoria gathering also included members of the Protestant and Jewish communities, continuing the Conference's ecumenical efforts. Shortly after being named president, Schlarman began translating the agricultural blessings of the Roman Ritual; this became *With the Blessing of the Church*.[24] This prayer book represented one of the best efforts by the NCRLC to integrate the daily life of the farmers with the church's liturgy.

In 1939, the same year the *Manifesto* was published, the NCRLC asked Luigi Ligutti to begin collecting materials for a rural life encycli-

---

[21] Editor, "The Liturgy and the Parish," 10–11.

[22] Ibid., 13. In *Rerum Novarum*, Leo XIII did not use the term "social justice," but Pius XI did in *Quadragesimo Anno*.

[23] Witte, *Crusading*, 126. Day would continue to have lifelong associations with both movements. Naturally, the Catholic Worker farms come to mind as a way of supplying the urban centers with food as well as living out some aspects of the NCRLC's vision. While the Catholic Worker had good intentions with regard to the farms, few succeeded. It was quite the opposite with the Grail women.

[24] *With the Blessing of the Church* has been mentioned several times, and will be considered more thoroughly in chapter 4. It should also be noted that Philip Weller also produced a fully translated English-Latin version of the Ritual. See *The Roman Ritual: The Blessings in Latin and English with Rubrics and Planchant Notation*, translated and edited by Philip T. Weller, 3 vols. (Milwaukee: Bruce Publishing, 1946). See also Philip Weller, "The Liturgy in Rural Parish Life," *National Liturgical Week 1945* (Peotone, IL: The Liturgical Conference, Inc., 1946), 157–62.

cal to present to the newly elected Pius XII. Not until 1946 did Bishop Aloisius Muench (Fargo) have the opportunity to bring the matter before the pontiff, who expressed interest and charged Muench with directing the effort. Many of the Conference's key people wrote sections of the encyclical-to-be, each according to one's expertise. Ligutti continued to bring the matter to the pope's attention until the pontiff's death in 1959, and then to John XXIII; obviously no encyclical was issued.[25] The encyclical draft, much in the spirit of the *Manifesto*, did speak of liturgy this time, and Schlarman was responsible for the text *De Salutari Influxu Liturgiae in Vitam Rusticanam* (The Saving Influence of the Liturgy in Rural Life).[26] The Apostolic Delegate, Archbishop Amleto G. Cicognani, affirmed Schlarman's effort and made a couple of suggestions regarding the Latin text.[27]

Unless Schlarman planned to expand on his rather brief points (and no evidence seems to indicate as much), *De Salutari* did not offer anything noteworthy. The first line below the title stated: "The Liturgy: inspires, satisfies (pleases), sanctifies, honors, blesses, prays, teaches, unites, strengthens, grants."[28] He then proceeded to comment on each of these dimensions of the liturgy. A few examples will suffice to gain a sense of what the document conveyed.

[25] Pius XII did, however, address the delegates at the Convention of the National Confederation of Farm Owner-Operators in 1946. The speech's "author" seems to bear the stamp of Ligutti, and most certainly the NCRLC as the footnotes indicate. See *The Pope Speaks on Rural Life*, Speech delivered by His Holiness, Pope Pius XII, Rome, November 15, 1946, in MUA/NCRLC, Series 5/1, box 2, folder 23. Some vindication came with John XXIII's first encyclical *Mater et Magistra*. The pontiff devoted nearly one-fourth of the entire work to the land and agricultural question, in particular as it pertained to ownership. There was no mention of liturgy of course. See Michael Walsh and Brian Davies, eds., *Proclaiming Justice and Peace: Papal Documents from Rerum Novarum through Centesimus Annus* (Mystic, CT: Twenty-Third Publications, 1994), 103–12, #123–84. Ligutti's influence can also be seen in *Gaudium et Spes*, nos. 71–72. See Bovée, "The Church and the Land," 360–61, and Yzermans, *The People I Love*, 218.

[26] Joseph Schlarman, "*De Salutari Influxu Liturgiae in Vitam Rusticanam*," MUA/NCRLC, Series 1/1, box 3, folder "Encyclical Material." Hereafter, *De Salutari*. I have transcribed the Latin texts exactly as they appear in the document (emphasis is Schlarman's). The Latin *salutari* suggests a broader meaning, and may also imply salutary, wholesome, helping, beneficial, health-giving.

[27] Schlarman to Cicognani, 16 April 1946; Cicognani to Schlarman, 20 April 1946, in MUA/LGL, box H-1, folder "Encyclical Material 1940s."

[28] Schlarman, *De Salutari*. Text: "Liturgia: inspirat, placet, sanctificat, honorat, benedicit, orat, docet, unit, corroborat, donat."

Under the category "honors" he noted: "The liturgy receives from agriculture those things necessary for the celebration of the Most Holy Eucharist, Confirmation, Extreme Unction (Bread, wine, oil); also palms and flowers for the altar." For "prays," specific practices were mentioned: "The liturgy prays in a) in the processions for the Rogation Days for the fruits of the earth, for protection against storms, etc. b) in the litanies for all the holy ones c) in special prayers of the Missal." Lastly, under "teaches," the document expressed the closeness of liturgy and rural life: "The liturgy teaches rural persons to pray in a manner which is suitable to them, truly as in the Psalms, which contain all things connected with rural life."[29]

Schlarman also addressed the 1947 NCRLC convention in Lafayette, Louisiana, the Conference's Silver Jubilee; his talk was entitled "Liturgy and Rural Life." He began by sharing a story of a Jacobite bishop, Mar Ivanios of Trivandrum, India, a convert to the Catholic Church in 1930. During the celebration of the Malankaran Rite the priest kisses the four corners of the altar saying: "Do bind, O Lord, the chain of our feasts to Thine altar with cords." Schlarman added: "I wish every Catholic farmer would kiss the four corners of his land and pray God to bind his acres to the altar, which is Christ."[30] Schlarman recommended that farmers read the Scriptures, especially passages relevant to rural life, as well as knowing the Canon of the Mass so as to participate more fully in the liturgy. The farmer should avail himself of the treasury of blessings and sacramentals. Amid the postwar reconstruction efforts, the U.S. president made a plea to conserve food. Schlarman combined that request with the Holy Father's appeal to give "whatever is over and above our necessity" to the hungry, sick, and naked,

[29] Ibid. Text: "Liturgia accipit ab agricola quae necessaria sunt pro celebratione SS. Eucharistiae, Confirmationis, Extremae Unctionis (Panis, vinium, oleum); etiam palmis et flores pro altaribus."; Text: "Liturgia orat in a) Processionibus in diebus Rogationum pro fructibus terrae, pro protectione a tempestatibus, etc. b) Litaniis omnium Sanctorum c) In specialibus Orationibus Missalis."; Text: "Liturgia docet rusticanos orare in modo qui convenit eis, nempe in Psalmis, qui continent tot res connectas vita rurali." Text: "Liturgia docet rusticanos orare in modo qui convenit eis, nempe in Psalmis, qui continent tot res connectas vita rurali."

[30] NCRLC, "Silver Jubilee Convention of the National Catholic Rural Life Conference," MUA/NCRLC, Series 8/1, box 6, folder "Silver Jubilee Convention Lafayette, LA, November 23–26, 1947." Hellriegel also gave a talk on "Liturgy and Rural Life," as did Fr. A. Wilmes, who presented a paper on "How to Teach Liturgy to School Children."

stressing that the liturgy should inculcate charity as well as justice. To this Schlarman related the communal aspect of fasting, noting the early Christian community's exemplary practice of it. "Liturgy" he concluded, "is God-conscious and land-conscious." The rural family—due to its circumstances—worked, recreated, and prayed together, disposing them for better participation and cooperation in liturgy and life.[31]

It may be argued that Schlarman has not yet received the attention due him as a shepherd of the church, most certainly with regard to his leadership in the liturgical and rural life movements. He had a keen sense for many social justice issues and maintained that the liturgy should serve as the core inspiration of the Christian life. Schlarman became an advocate for a wide range of concerns such as prison reform, international development, ecumenism, ecology, and rural sociology. He also sought to create fraternal bonds between Christians in the United States and Latin America.[32]

Luigi Ligutti's name became synonymous with the NCRLC, being known throughout the world. Ligutti wrote little concerning the liturgy, but he vigorously promoted it. He attended the 1943 Liturgical Week and presented a paper entitled, "The Spirit of Sacrifice in Christian Society." Ligutti noted that farmers in the United States worshiped like other Catholic farmers around the world. The unifying principle that bound them together was the common worship of the Mystical Body of Christ and the sacrifice farmers made in their daily work—here was the bond of true solidarity. This pertained not only to farmers, but to the great diversity of people, jobs, and races in which the doctrine of the Mystical Body acted as a unifying force. Ligutti even extended

---

[31] Schlarman, "Liturgy and Rural Life," MUA/NCRLC, Series 10/1, box 3, folder 36. Schlarman closed on a somewhat pious and patriotic note where he recounted a story of a farmer responding to the question, "Just what is 'our country'—words forever on the lips of people?" The farmer knelt to pray and spoke of turning the soil with spade, the memories, traditions, the beliefs, all "Notre pays!" Then he caught sight of the shotgun on the wall, still kneeling, and said: "I should like to see anyone come and take this land from me! . . . Au nom Pere, et du Fils, et du Saint Esprit. Amen. Notre pays!"

[32] Yzermans, *The People I Love*, 54. He was aided by the social justice oriented priest Fr. Edward O'Rourke who became Executive Director of the NCRLC (1960–70) as well as bishop of Peoria (1971–90). Some of the international trips were taken with Ligutti, during which they introduced their rural philosophy in Latin America. See Witte, *Crusading*, 213ff.

this solidarity to include all creation—rain, sun, and the "millions of God's invisible creatures" that also work in the soil to bring forth the food used on the altar. He also challenged rural pastors to be "convinced that a rural parish is the ideal milieu for a deep, sound, and sensible liturgical movement," since the farmer worked so close to the sacramentals used in worship. Pastors also needed to possess a good sense of architecture and art relevant to rural life that inspired simple but beautiful churches. Saints who were close to the land and soil should adorn rural churches. Education about the liturgy needed to be adapted to the small rural parish. He also emphasized the need for a translation of the *Ritual* into English and sermon outlines for rural pastors.[33]

Father Edward O'Rourke of Peoria, Illinois, related the Conference's social agenda to Catholic Action and the liturgy. For several years he authored a liturgical column for the NCRLC that was often accompanied by a reflection on social justice issues. In the mid-1940s he wrote a very lucid piece entitled "Catholic Action Farmers: Suggestions for the Chaplain." After citing the social teaching of Pius XI and XII, he turned to Catholic Action, noting that it has been solely directed to students, offices, and factory workers. The recently developed "Catholic Action Farmers' Manual," distributed by the NCRLC, was beginning to promote "cells" in the countryside, following the lead of specialized Catholic Action cells. Rural life was most suited to attain the supernatural through the natural, and the liturgy served this purpose in a primary way for Catholic Action. Christians who prayed together were better able to act together. The liturgy also instructed one in the mysteries of faith throughout the year if one was attentive to the major feasts of the church.[34]

[33] Luigi G. Ligutti, "Sacrifice and Society: The Rural Problem," *National Liturgical Week 1943* (Ferdinand, IN: The Liturgical Conference, 1944), 124–25. The archival material has the same talk but it is titled, "The Spirit of Sacrifice in Christian Society," MUA/NCRLC, Series 10/1, box 2, folder 19–24.

[34] Edward O'Rourke, "Catholic Action Farmers: Suggestions for the Chaplain," MUA/NCRLC, Series 10/1, box 3, folder "Edward O'Rourke 1942–45," 4–8. Exact date and context of talk is not known. See MUA/NCRLC, Series 1/2, box 15, folder "Sacramentals and Rural Life," July 18, 1962.

## THE AMERICAN GRAIL MOVEMENT AND THE NCRLC

The Grail, an international women's movement begun in Holland in 1927, was the inspiration of the Dutch Jesuit Jacques van Genneken. Originally, its fundamental aim was to form Christian women as apostles of the Mystical Body of Christ called to transform the world. The Grail's vision has changed in emphasis over the years, but it still has a deep commitment to social justice.[35] One of van Genneken's students, Lydwine van Kersbergen, who became the first president of Grail in Holland, began a correspondence with the Catholic Worker's Dorothy Day in 1936.[36] The Grail leader came to the United States in 1939 to attend the Pax Romana Congress in New York; she stayed and traveled around the country visiting various Catholic organizations. In 1940 van Kersbergen attended the NCRLC meeting in St. Cloud, Minnesota, where she listened to a speech by Luigi Ligutti. Though generally impressed with Ligutti, she stood up and asked him why no one had said anything about the role of women on the land. She pointed out to Ligutti that no renewal of life on the land would be possible without the support of women. Ligutti promptly made her a vice president of the NCRLC.[37] However, van Kersbergen, an urbanite who had to confess to never "having seen a cow," expressed reservations about a life on the land and being settled too far from urban centers. She was also a little uncomfortable with some of Ligutti's tirades against the city.[38]

The Grail entered the United States right on the heels of three other movements that "took off" around 1940: the liturgical movement, the rural life movement, and Catholic Action.[39] The "American" Grail was unique in that it was closely associated to both the liturgical and rural life movements, especially the latter. One found in the Grail a harmonious union of liturgy, culture (rural), and human dignity (especially with regard to women); these coalesced to create a force for social reconstruction. But to "reconstruct" demanded change of mind and

---

[35] See Mary Jo Weaver, "Still Feisty at Fifty: The Grailville Lay Apostolate for Women," *U.S. Catholic Historian* 11 (Fall 1993): 3–12.

[36] Alden Brown, *The Grail Movement and American Catholicism, 1940–1975* (Notre Dame, IN: University of Notre Dame Press, 1989), 23.

[37] Janet Kalven, *Women Breaking Boundaries: A Grail Journey, 1940–1995* (Albany: State University of New York Press, 1999), 65 (hereafter, Kalven, *Women*).

[38] Brown, *The Grail Movement*, 28–29.

[39] Jay P. Dolan, *The American Catholic Experience: A History from Colonial Times to the Present* (New York: Doubleday and Co., 1985), 414.

heart, and as such, Grail initiatives were often met with resistance—principally ecclesiastical. Initially, the Grail settled on Doddridge Farm near Chicago, but after several disputes with Archbishop Stritch regarding the farm, the Grail abandoned hopes of establishing a house there. With this impasse, Luigi Ligutti put van Kersbergen in contact with Archbishop John T. McNicholas of Cincinnati, a strong supporter of the NCRLC, who proved quite amenable to the organization. McNicholas offered the group property near Loveland, Ohio, the Grail's home to this day.[40]

Grailville was a farm in the fullest sense. Its members practiced a self-subsistent lifestyle that immersed the women into nature's full rhythm of planting, harvesting, and animal care. Van Kersbergen had petitioned several bishops to begin an agricultural school for women and supplied them with outlines for it. The courses that were eventually held at Grailville hosted an impressive cast of instructors who moved in both the liturgical and rural life movements and included Martin Hellriegel, Reynold Hillenbrand, Benedict Ehman, Dorothy Day, Gerald Ellard, Godfrey Diekmann, Emerson Hynes, and of course Luigi Ligutti. All of them saw Grailville as fertile ground for liturgical experimentation and church renewal closely associated with rural culture. The NCRLC must have been impressed at how quickly the Grail had established an integrated rural life based on the "family pattern, subsistence economy, and the liturgical life."[41] Obviously, the Grail consisted of women who intentionally came there for this purpose—to be formed as apostles, women with a renewed Christian vision.

As regards this vision, the Grail could be included among the many Catholic Action groups participating in church renewal at that time. However, it was truly unique in that it was completely a lay organization, and *run by women*. Many people simply had great difficulty accepting this, and the organization's work often gave rise to misunderstanding. The Grail, like the NCRLC, put forth a complete vision of life and succeeded at better integrating the liturgy. A 1948 pamphlet described the pillars of Grail this way:[42]

[40] Alden Brown, *The Grail Movement*, 34–35, 43–45. Disputes centered on role of laity, liturgy, property, etc. See also Yzermans, *The People I Love*, 74; Janet Kalven, *Women*, 68; and Pecklers, *Unread Vision*, 118–20; and MUA/LGL, box F-2, folder "Grailville."

[41] Kalven, *Women*, 83.

[42] Ibid., 79–80.

1. A Christian Vision of Life—transforming and unifying all activities of the day, centered on the Mass and living the rhythm of the liturgical year.

2. The Family as the Organic Unit of Society—sharing a common life, organized on a family pattern of mutual giving and receiving.

3. The Nature and Task of Woman—focusing on the woman's spiritual mission and its practical consequences for her role in the social order.

4. Intellectual Formation—directed toward a sure grasp of Christian principles through lectures and discussions led by outstanding Christian thinkers.

5. A Philosophy of Work—both intellectual and manual where "love is made visible."

6. Development of a Christian Culture—understood as the outward expression of our beliefs and values, spirit translated into matter.

The phrase, "love made visible," was used as the title of an article by Grail member Josephine Drabek, which the NCRLC later published as a pamphlet. Kalven added that "agriculture as a way of life" was sometimes excluded from such lists based on the concern that the "novelty of women running a farm tended to obscure our apostolic purpose." Most of the women who came to the Grail understood farm work to be a constituent dimension of the *labora*. Interestingly, Grail founder Jacques van Ginneken was shocked when he discovered that the American Grail was involved in manual labor and rural life. In a letter to van Kersbergen he chided her, saying: "Why did you buy a farm? Revolutions start in the cities and you bury yourself on a farm!"[43] The majority of the women who came to Grail were from the city.

Janet Kalven, a convert to Catholicism, was among the first initiates to the American Grail. In her retrospective on the organization, Kalven said that her attendance at the first National Liturgical Week in Chicago, and especially its fostering of participation in the *Missa recitata*, was the reason for her entry into the Catholic Church. While the Grail was not a monastic community, elements of the cloistered life were in evidence. This was largely seen in its regimen of common work, meals,

---

[43] Ibid., 80–81.

and prayer. Of course, the ultimate bonding factor was the liturgy. There was great harmony between the rhythms of nature and the liturgical cycle. Grace at meals, presided over by one of the members, brought one of the themes from the day's liturgy to the table. The meals were second only to the Mass as a source of unity and a means to nourish mind, body, and spirit. The church's Divine Office structured the day, which allowed the women to stop working and pray in common.[44]

The week's work ceased at noon on Saturday in order to prepare for the worthy celebration of Sunday, the "day of the Lord . . . the eighth day . . . which set the rhythm for the whole week." Sunday meant a larger meal and some frivolity that included folk singing, dancing, plays, and poetry readings. These activities often attracted local residents. Kalven admitted that the pattern was rural and monastic, and this created some difficulties when they tried to establish Grail communities in urban centers. "For us, life on the land gave new meaning to scripture and liturgy." The Grail women experimented with liturgical dancing. The liturgical year provided the structure for their annual activities. The community celebrated Rogation and Ember Days, for these were particularly connected to the spring planting and fall harvesting. These celebrations involved periods of fasting that went beyond their usual observance during Lent, and made the special days of feasting around Assumption and Thanksgiving all the more joyous. Thus, Grailville represented a sound integration of spirituality, work, and culture.[45]

The Grail's simple way of life challenged the unbridled consumerism of the day, and it did so through liturgical prayer and study of the church's social teaching. This challenge was compatible with the vision of the NCRLC, the distributists, and *Quadragesimo Anno*. Recall that in 1938 the NCRLC published its *Manifesto on Rural Life*, which applied current Catholic social teaching to the rural situation. The Grail possessed a lived liturgical spirituality, which was grounded in the study of liturgy, theology, and the social questions of the day. In the first half of the twentieth century, many Catholic organizations worthily focused their energies toward works of charity and education. These organizations, however, lacked a theological and spiritual

[44] Ibid., 14, 83, 87. The meals had a monastic feel to them with silence and reading at table. Kalven's most focused treatment of liturgy can be found on 87–89.
[45] Ibid., 87, 88.

program that was accessible and practical for the laity. Alden Brown rightly critiqued this spiritual lacuna and named Fr. John A. Ryan, the great social reformer and mentor of Edwin O'Hara, as being partly responsible. Ryan's theology "seemed merely an adjunct to social ethics rooted in Catholic natural law theory. Such an approach led not to a renewed spiritual vigor and a sense of the church but to the political arena and close identification with the reform program of Franklin Delano Roosevelt."[46] To Ryan's credit, and others like him, these social justice apostles engaged the modern world in a way that gave new credibility to the church; perhaps his approach had its limitations. The Grail made study and prayer a decisive and integral part of its program.[47] The liturgy celebrated in the rural context was the unifying factor for much of its activity.

The NCRLC promoted the Grail in its periodical *Land and Home* and published some of the members' works as pamphlets. Sometime in 1942, Patrick Quinlan, then vice president of the NCRLC, visited the Grail (Doddridge Farm in Illinois, its first home); he later published a pamphlet entitled *Keep Them Plowing*, which described the Grail's program.[48] The women were fully engaged in farm life—learning "to pray with their hands." Quinlan's visit, during Epiphanytide, revealed an atmosphere permeated with the sense of the liturgical season, with the crib in place, both in the chapel and in the dining room. The Grail women participated fully in the liturgy with processions and singing. After Mass, they invoked the blessing of the Creator upon the whole creation by chanting the canticle of the three youths as found in the

---

[46] Brown, *The Grail Movement*, 19–20. For a lucid discussion of this issue as it pertains to Virgil Michel, see Michael Baxter, "Reintroducing Virgil Michel: Towards a Counter-Tradition of Catholic Social Ethics in the United States," *Communio* 24 (Fall 1997): 499–528, especially 519.

[47] Similar criticism may be leveled at the church with regard to the encyclical tradition. That is to say, while such declarations relied on Scripture and papal teaching, most Catholics did not make use of the encyclicals as a practical program for spiritual formation. Encyclical language required knowledge of natural law and Thomistic philosophy, which, generally speaking, only the clergy possessed. Not only did Grail members read such scholarly works, but they also sought to make such teachings practical for daily living.

[48] Patrick Quinlan, *Keep Them Plowing*, MUA/NCRLC, Series 5/1, box 1 "General Publications 1944–1946." The date of his visit is uncertain. He mentioned the address for Grail as Doddridge Farm in Illinois. The Grail was established in Loveland, OH, on July 17, 1944. See Kalven, *Women*, 306.

book of Daniel. Quinlan quoted from the book of Judith, "Thou hast put salvation in the hands of woman," and painted a very realistic picture of farm life's joys and struggles as these related to the women working there. This realistic picture of farm life was placed in the larger context of reconstructing the social order. The Christian family was the basic unit in society, and a mother who fostered a strong Catholic family life on the farm contributed directly to a more just society.

"Love Made Visible," written by Grail member Josephine Drabek, was a simple and eloquent reflection on the nature and dignity of work.[49] She responded to her city-dwelling friends who doubted her resolve to handle the difficulties of farm life: "It has been my great good fortune to have both the experience and the theory at the Grailville Agricultural School. . . . and I see more and more clearly how work enlarges and enriches human life."[50] Her sound understanding of work was grounded in the creation narratives of Genesis. God, who labored to bring forth creation, endowed humans with physical and intellectual powers to work with him as stewards. The human person was called to employ these bodily and spiritual gifts in a wise and just manner, respectful of the material creation and the human family. Given the time and context in which Drabek wrote, her language with regard to the body was holistic, respectful, yet daring for the time:

> If we learn to use our bodies properly in ordinary tasks—sweeping, digging, hoeing, lifting—we can develop strength and grace of movement. The free and rhythmic gesture of the sower, the magnificent posture of the peasant women accustomed to carrying loads balanced on their heads, are fruits of their daily labor. Intelligence grows too, under the discipline of labor . . . developing initiative and imagination to conceive vision of the finished product. . . . It involves great knowledge of materials, of their properties, and limitations, so that we will use each according to its nature. . . . The work of our hands is

---

[49] Josephine Drabek, *Love Made Visible* (Des Moines, IA: NCRLC, 1946), in MUA/NCRLC, Series 5/1, box 2. The NCRLC also published the pamphlet by Janet Kalven, *The Task of Woman on the World* (Des Moines, IA: National Catholic Rural Life Conference, 1946), in MUA/NCRLC, Series 5/1, box 2.

[50] Drabek, *Love Made Visible*.

our great means of making our love practical and genuine. Work is love made visible.[51]

The body language employed for work was carried over into the liturgy. Work was a gift of self to God and others in the context of community and as such constituted praise of God.

Drabek invoked St. Benedict's maxim *ora et labora* and suggested that a more integral vision of life had been lost—a certain disconnect between body and spirit was evident and needed to be recovered. Christian life was meant to be organic, as the biblical creation narratives expressed, where labor and prayer were meant to be complementary. The notion of work was also reflected in the sacramental principle. Through Christ's incarnation, all creation, all life, and all work were given new significance. Creation pointed to a deeper spiritual reality that human labor innovatively brought to life and gave meaning. It enabled the Christian to see how daily actions were joined to one's life in Christ: "Our daily work is full of meanings and constantly opens new vistas to the mind, if only we know how to read God's sacramental writing in our lives."[52]

In many respects, the Grail, rather quickly put into practice much of what the NCRLC had been trying to engender in its rural adherents for at least a decade. Liturgy was the life and inspiration of all the Grail's activities. It strengthened the dignity and vocation of many women, making them apostles of the Mystical Body of Christ. This integration of liturgy and life was made all the more possible by the rural context in which the Grail lived. Throughout the 1940s the NCRLC continued to incorporate, adapt, and put into practice insights gleaned from the liturgical movement. Bishop Joseph Schlarman and the women of the Grail were particularly noteworthy in their efforts to integrate liturgy and rural life. Martin Hellriegel, the seasoned pastor and leader in the liturgical movement, brought his profound knowledge of worship to bear on the life of rural Catholics. Many of these initiatives laid the groundwork for the further expansion of the NCRLC's activities. The Conference further adapted the faith to the rural context, which strengthened the farmer's vocation, and allowed

[51] Ibid.
[52] Ibid.

him to see the part he played in the church's universal salvific mission.

## SHARING THE BOUNTY: THE LITURGICAL AND RURAL LIFE MOVEMENTS, 1950–1960

In the period leading up to Vatican II, the NCRLC continued to promote rural liturgy and implemented the more monumental reforms of the church at that time—the reform of Holy Week and the restoration of the Easter Vigil. Liturgical practices expanded and exceeded what was witnessed during the 1940s. One observed as well further experimentation that sought to bring the liturgical life into closer union with daily living. Also, several international documents and addresses published by the NCRLC in the early 1950s continued to put forth the liturgy as foundational to rural life. While none of these documents said anything significant or new regarding the liturgy, they illustrated how the Conference attempted to address rural life in a holistic manner. As it did so, it always sought to keep the liturgy, or at least spirituality, as a constitutive dimension to its overall program. In some respects the spiritual dimension was downplayed, perhaps in an effort to cooperate with other religious and secular organizations.

In the early 1950s the NCRLC published two documents, the fruit of two international meetings.[53] One of them, *The Land: God's Gift to Man* (hereafter *The Land*), represented an update of the *Manifesto* (1939); it also drew upon the first international rural life conference held at Castel Gandolfo in June 1951, organized by Ligutti. Both documents manifested a more mature Conference vision; both demonstrated a profound grasp and application of the church's social teaching as this teaching related to rural life. *The Land* was based on natural law, which maintained that humans were created by God, having both a spiritual and physical nature. Human life was directed toward a higher calling and purpose—life with God. God's grace worked through human nature, elevated it, and directed the person toward this higher purpose. The human person was both social and political, endowed with an inviolable dignity and ennobled by work. Work and commerce with

---

[53] NCRLC, *Christianity and the Land* (Des Moines, IA: NCRLC, 1951), in MUA/NCRLC, Series 5/1, box 3, folder 8; NCRLC, *The Land: God's Gift to Man* (Des Moines, IA: NCRLC, 1952), in MUA/NCRLC, Series 5/1, box 3, folder 10. The subtitle is "Statement on World Agriculture and Rural Welfare."

others aided the person in fulfilling one's purpose in life, so as to contribute to a justly ordered society. The human person had a right to liberty and personal property. Access to the material goods of the earth was necessary for one to attain one's purpose. Those who controlled access to these goods had a particular responsibility to assure their rightful distribution for the benefit of all people. The document pointed out that global change and technological advancement did not always benefit everyone, and, in fact, had negative consequences, especially for the poor. The document presented a comprehensive rural agenda, and included liturgy, noting that liturgy "gives wholeness and balance to human life by stressing the proper relationship between spiritual and material things."[54] The section on the liturgy also emphasized the liturgical year, and celebrations "outside" the liturgical life and year proper were to be given a religious accent. Families should "imbue their homes with the spirit of the liturgy making use of the blessings, ceremonies, and Christian customs.[55]

On the national front, at the 1951 Boston convention, the executive committee reported that the circulation of its "Rural Life Page," one of its informational organs, had reached about 1.5 million people. Such large numbers were due in part to its being printed as a monthly column in many diocesan and secular newspapers. The publication covered a wide range of rural life issues and activities. The diocesan directors of rural life noted that the most popular and helpful of the columns were those on liturgy, adding that many of the suggested practices were widespread.[56] Father John Geiser, of Austin, Texas,

---

[54] NCRLC, *The Land: God's Gift to Man*, 29.

[55] Ibid., 29. *The Land* also treated: "Impact of Technology," "Population and Resources," "Technical Assistance," "Land Tenure," "Resource Utilization," "Family on the Land (Family on the Farm, Rural Living for Non-Farm Families)," "Cooperatives," "Rural Credit," "Farm Income," "Farmer's Organizations," "Farm Labor (Wage Workers, Non-Wage Workers, Migrant Labor)," "Rural Education," "Rural Parish Organization," "Liturgy and Ritual in the Rural Parish and Family," and "Recreation in Rural Areas." Also to note, "Commission X," in *Christianity and the Land*, treated the liturgy under the section on religious education. Interestingly, it stressed the "word of God conveyed through the liturgy" as essential to religious education. The liturgy should be celebrated in a dignified manner and explained properly so that the faithful might take an active part, such that they "give expression to it in Christian attitudes in daily life." See NCRLC, *Christianity and the Land*, 28.

[56] "Rural Life Page," MUA/NCRLC, Series 8/1, box 10, folder "National Convention, Boston, MA, October 19–23, 1951." The "Rural Life Page" and its liturgical column will be considered in chapter 6. See Bovée, "Church and Land," 316.

reported on a Mass of Thanksgiving celebrated as part of a harvest festival in which the faithful were asked to bring a portion of their harvest to be given to the poor. In Peoria, Edward O'Rourke led Forty Hours Devotions focused on rural life. In Lafayette, Louisiana, Msgr. Joseph Lerschen observed parish Rogations Days, and celebrated field Masses in conjunction with already established secular festivals such as the Rice, Yambilee (as in yams), and Sugar Cane festivals. In the Diocese of Alexandria, Louisiana, a school for girls modeled after the Grail was established and placed great emphasis on family and liturgy in the home. Much of the Louisiana activity was the work of a young pastor named Joseph Gremillion, who eventually became the executive director of the Pontifical Commission for Peace and Justice established at the Vatican in 1967.[57]

In 1953 the diocesan directors were surveyed to determine which topics they would like to discuss at their meetings. The memorandum listed the following possibilities: discussion groups for rural priests, liturgical practices/retreats, methods for rural schools, the Company of St. Isidore, and publicity for Catholic rural life. While not the number-one priority, many chose liturgical practices.[58] Father Daniel Dunn, the executive secretary, noted that the Conference was considering an update of Florence Berger's *Cooking for Christ*, but no one submitted any liturgical recipes except for those from Luigi Ligutti. Dunn also added: "My request for books in Latin, English, French or Italian of rural liturgical practices brought no reply."[59] The diocesan directors reported that liturgical practices were growing in popularity, mentioning Rogation Days, blessings, the decorating of the altars with fruits and vegetables at the Thanksgiving Day Mass, and devotion to St. Isidore. The director of rural life in the Diocese of Fargo recounted a Thanksgiving Day Mass with one thousand farmers in attendance.

---

[57] "Report on the National Catholic Rural Life Convention, Boston, MA, October 19–23, 1951," MUA/NCRLC, Series 8/1, box 10, folder "National Convention, Boston, MA, October 19–23, 1951," 13–22. On J. Gremillion see *New Catholic Encyclopedia*, 2nd ed., "Gremillion, Joseph Benjamin," 526. See the chapter "Saints of the Soil." As president of the Louisiana chapter of the Future Farmers of America, Gremillion witnessed firsthand the deplorable conditions of black sharecroppers and he was moved to action on their behalf.

[58] "Memorandum, August 5, 1953," MUA/NCRLC, Series 8/1, box 12, folder "National Convention, Kansas City, MO, September 21–24, 1953."

[59] "Reports," MUA/NCRLC, Series 8/1, box 12, folder "Reports, Resolutions, Statements, National Convention, Kansas City, MO, September 21–24, 1953."

This Mass included a long procession in which they brought a small portion of their harvest that was presented along with the bread and wine for Eucharist. In Raleigh, North Carolina (an area where the Catholic Church had few adherents), non-Catholics had begun to express interest in devotion to St. Isidore. Perhaps this spoke to the nature of public ceremony and the manner in which it carried an evangelical purpose, the *lex orandi* expressing the *lex credendi*.

Father Paul Brinker of the Diocese of Covington, Kentucky, recounted how each year he celebrated the "Tobacco Mass" as part of a harvest celebration. Saint Rose of Lima parish, located in rural Mays Lick, Kentucky, comprised about forty-five families, and the majority of them grew tobacco for a living. In the spring, Brinker blessed their soil and seed in the context of the eucharistic liturgy. During the growing season parishioners processed through the fields, blessing what had grown thus far and begging God's protection on the crops. In December the parish celebrated a harvest Mass, decorating the church with sheaves of tobacco. The people processed forward and laid some of their crop in front of the altar. A photo in the *Louisville Courier-Journal* showed Brinker facing the people celebrating a dialogue Mass, while a commentator gave a simultaneous explanation of the liturgy in English. The people also grew the wheat and grapes for the bread and wine used at this Mass.[60]

Father Bill Schimek of Austin, Minnesota, noted that an update to the prayerbook that involved an expansion of *With the Blessing of the Church* was almost complete. (The "update" took three more years to complete!) The Conference wanted to produce a new prayerbook more specifically tailored for rural Catholics, "but not a missal." Alban Dauchauer, SJ, had been responsible for compiling the material, which the NCRLC published in 1956 as *The Rural Life Prayerbook*. This much-expanded prayerbook added more generally practiced devotions that were not particular to rural life. A 1958 letter from Cardinal Alfredo Ottaviani to Luigi Ligutti praised the volume.[61] It contained prayers

[60] "Summary of Reports by Diocesan Directors of Rural Life," MUA/NCRLC, Series 8/1, box 12, folder "Convention Report, National Convention, Davenport, IA, October 8–13, 1954," 2. See Ruth Moore Craig, "Holy Mass of the Harvest," *The Courier-Journal Magazine*, December 27, 1953, 7–9. See Epilogue, 228–33.

[61] "Executive Committee Meeting, October 16, 1952," MUA/NCRLC, Series 8/1, box 10, folder "National Convention, Saginaw, October 17–22, 1952." See *The Rural Life Prayerbook* compiled by Alban J. Dachauer, SJ (Des Moines, IA: National

and litanies to St. Isidore, Rogation Day celebrations, devotions to Our Lady of the Fields, and Thanksgiving Day services.[62]

If the Conference's publications were any indication of how wide-spread these various liturgical and devotional practices were, the executive secretary's 1955 report gave some telling data: 18,122 Rogation Day Manuals, 3,273 Thanksgiving Day leaflets, and 7,328 Our Lady of the Fields devotional pamphlets.[63] These data were usually collected based on the diocesan director's reports that contained a short synopsis of their extensive activities: talks/presentations, retreats, articles/publications, schools/education, distribution of materials from the Conference; parish activities such as days of Christian Rural Living, Rogation Day celebrations, Thanksgiving Day Masses, feast of Assumption with blessing of herbs and flowers, other agricultural blessings, Novena to St. Isidore culminating in a Feast Day Mass, shrines to St. Isidore, cooperatives, and credit unions were also included. A talk entitled "Appreciating Rural Life through Art, Music and Liturgy" addressed the liturgy in the context of art and beauty as it was inspired by rural culture.[64] Father Joseph Hylden (Fargo) spoke of the importance of carrying out the Holy Week liturgy as newly revised. In addition, his parish embraced the dialogue Mass, recited Matins and Lauds in English before funeral Masses, had the baptismal dress made before the child's delivery, and used candles made from the beeswax donated by a parishioner.[65]

---

Catholic Rural Life Conference, 1956); Cardinal Ottaviani to Ligutti, 27 February 1958, MUA/LGL, box E-2, folder "General Correspondence 'O' mid 1930s–60s." It may be noted that much of the Saginaw convention was devoted to the issue of migrant Hispanic workers and the Conference's response to their social and pastoral needs.

[62] "Minutes," 5, MUA/NCRLC, Series 8/1, box 13, folder "Executive Committee Meeting, May 12–13, 1955." It seemed that the purpose for doing so was to have everything in one complete book instead of having to deal with many individual pamphlets the NCRLC published.

[63] "Report of Executive Secretary," MUA/NCRLC, Series 8/1, box 14, folder "Publications, National Convention, Lexington, KY, October 22–26, 1955," 3. See the navy blue bound booklet. For more statistics, "Annual Report" in this same folder, 12.

[64] "Reports of Diocesan Directors," and Sr. M. Magdalen, "Appreciation of Rural Life through Art, Music, Literature," in MUA/NCRLC, Series 8/1, box 15, folder "Diocesan Director Annual Reports, National Convention, Sioux Falls, October 19–23, 1956."

[65] "Specialized Approaches," MUA/NCRLC, Series 8/1, box 15, folder "Speeches, National Convention, Sioux Falls, October 19–23, 1956."

In 1956 the executive committee decided that the Conference would not hold a national meeting the following year; instead, it opted for regional gatherings.[66] While the national gatherings generally drew good numbers, most participants were from the host city, with dioceses or regions being represented by a diocesan director of rural life. The regional directors all agreed that a talk on rural liturgical life should be on every program, and in some cases (Michigan, for example), it would serve as the capstone presentation of the gathering.

At one regional meeting, none other than Godfrey Diekmann, OSB, editor of *Worship*, appeared on the slate to present a talk entitled "The Liturgy and Rural Life." Diekmann, born in rural Roscoe, Minnesota, was neither a pastor nor an assistant pastor in a rural parish. He took as his point of departure an insight from Archbishop Karl Alter of Cincinnati: "Emphasis on living the liturgy should take first place in the program of priests in rural parishes. . . . there is no place where the liturgy can be put into effect more successfully and beneficially than in a rural parish." Diekmann noted all the usual opportunities a rural parish afforded to engage in a rich liturgical and sacramental life, but the substance of his talk dealt with the advantages of fostering the community spirit through the liturgy. The rural context, he claimed, was especially poised for the kind of community that both the liturgical and rural movements wished to engender.

Diekmann took as examples baptism, marriage, and funerals to demonstrate how community spirit was or was not fostered. In each of these, he pressed for the sacrament's communal celebration amid a larger contingent of the faith community. On one hand, he lamented the sad state of affairs at a funeral celebrated by a few family members and friends in a large city parish in which there was no singing and responses to the prayers. On the other hand, he praised a marriage that he had recently witnessed in a small rural parish in which nearly the entire community was present. The assembly knew one another, was happy to share in this important celebration, and actively

[66] "1957 Regional Meetings," MUA/NCRLC, Series 8/1, box 16, folder "Regional Meetings 1957." The regional meetings were held in the following places: St. Cloud, August 4–6; Michigan (four different locations), October 10–11; Wausau, WI, October 20–22; LaSalle, IL, November 3–5; Middlebury, VT, November 21; Malone, NY, November 16; Worchester, MA, November 24. The regional meetings were rather successful as the following attendance data reveal: Michigan—3000, Wisconsin—3500, Illinois—2000, Vermont—275. The Michigan meeting listed in its program book, "The Liturgy and Rural Life—the Heart of a Rural Program."

participated throughout the liturgy. His talk closed with the usual reference to blessings and sacramentals in the rural context. Also, at the St. Cloud meeting, a High Mass was celebrated at Clark Field. This Mass included processions at the offertory by Conference delegates who brought forth "soil, harvest, family, wheat and grapes."[67]

A talk entitled "Liturgy and Rural Life" was given by Alcuin Miller, OSB, at the LaSalle, Illinois, regional meeting. He based his address on a theology of creation, incarnation, and redemption. The divine action of God unfolds in the liturgical-sacramental event, animating the material creation and the human family: "Christ by his coming has sacramentalized and consecrated the world, and Christian man is, therefore destined to live, and grow, and mature into Christian perfection chiefly by means of sacramental action." The liturgy was the principal action in which God divinized the human. Miller captured well the relationship between sacramentality and its central place in the public worship of the church. With this foundation, he addressed the common rural-liturgical themes of blessings and sacramentals as they related to the farm. Nothing stood outside the scope of what the church blessed. Even "the harmful animals" were considered important enough to have a blessing or to have an exorcism directed against them.[68]

Father Michael Dineen, the NCRLC's executive director, gave what may be called a "state of rural life address" at the same LaSalle convention. The farmer, as a member of the Mystical Body of Christ, and due to his unique vocation, was called upon to extend his influence to all parts of the world—to all the people who share in the earth's bounty. The farmer's principal source of grace and inspiration was to be found in the church's liturgy: "The Holy Sacrifice of Mass is the great bridge which reaches from God to man and brings about a unique unification." The farmer was related to the Mass in a special

[67] Godfrey Diekmann, "The Liturgy and Rural Life" MUA/NCRLC, Series 8/1, box 17, folder "NCRLC Regional Convention, St. Cloud, August 4–6, 1957," 1–5; NCRLC, "Program Northwest Catholic Rural Life Convention, St. Cloud, MN, August 4–6, 1957." Other presentations from the St. Cloud meeting included: "Liturgy and the Blessings of Rural Life" by Rev. Joseph Hylden of Edgeley, North Dakota; "The Family, the Mass and the Liturgy" by Fr. William Magee of Immaculate Heart of Mary Seminary in Winona; and Fr. John Gengler of Owatonna, Minnesota, was part of a panel discussion and spoke on specific rural liturgical practices.

[68] Alcuin Miller, OSB, "Liturgy and Rural Life," MUA/NCRLC, Series 8/1, box 18, folder "Regional Meeting, LaSalle, IL, November 3–5, 1957," 1–2.

way through his diligent cultivation of the soil that brought forth the necessary materials for all the liturgical and sacramental celebrations. The liturgy was the "great common denominator," and engendered a worldwide unity with God the Creator. The Mystical Body's union with Christ, forged in the liturgy, manifested "the great social drama in which all men act as social beings in love with God and neighbor." Consistent with what the liturgical movement put forth, Dineen seemed to presage Sacrosanctum Concilium when he asserted: "If to conform personal and public life to the will of God does not begin with Mass, it will never begin."[69] Many of the liturgy talks at these regional meetings covered similar themes. What is important to note is that the NCRLC gave the liturgy a central place in its overall program.

Grail member Josephine Drabek authored a pamphlet entitled *Rogation Days at Maranatha*. Maranatha was the name of a family farm near Loveland, Ohio, and owned by Dan and Mary Cecelia Kane. Mary spent time with the Grail, which had as one of its goals to match good Catholic men and women. Thus, the Kanes were one of the first "couples" who embraced the Grail philosophy and established homesteads near the property. For the rogation liturgy, the priest came to the family's home before Mass. Mimeographed copies of the blessing of fields in English were distributed to facilitate full participation. A short catechesis was provided on the meaning of Rogation Days, and then the prayers and procession began. The intimate experience of church, farm, and home, so closely aligned with the liturgical year, gave "significance and dignity to all our work . . . and has opened new vistas to our understanding and appreciation of the liturgy."[70] Such liturgies in the home established a closer connection between altar and home.

Several other publications may be briefly mentioned that demonstrate how the NCRLC sought to make the liturgy more practical and accessible. The NCRLC published its *Manual of Ceremonies for the Parish Observation of the Rogation Days* in 1953. Rogation Days were often

---

[69] The address is untitled but signed "MPD," which based on other documents stands for Michael P. Dineen. It was often the case that the executive director addressed all such gatherings. See MUA/NCRLC, Series 8/1, box 18, folder "Regional Meeting, LaSalle, IL, November 3–5, 1957."

[70] Josephine Drabek, *Rogation Days at Maranatha* (Des Moines: NCRLC, 1951), MUA/NCRLC, Series 5/1, box 3. See Kalven, *Women*, 76–77.

celebrated as part of an expanded day of Christian rural activities. Rural Catholics also prayed *The Novena in Honor of St. Isidore* at least three times during the year—the days leading up to March 22 (preconciliar feast day of St. Isidore), August 15, and Thanksgiving Day. The novena included reflections for each day that treated various facets of rural life such as family, stewardship of soil, dignity of work, rural works of mercy, prayer, and "Sacrifice of Praise." The Benedictine monks of Collegeville collaborated in the publication of the novena. At home, mother, father, and children were expected to take leading roles in its celebration. The final day had various blessings and prayers for the soil, seeds, animals, and harvests. *Blessing and Prayers for the Feast of the Assumption in Honor of Our Lady of the Fields*, published in 1955, was a fully participative ceremony in English. Other publications treated worship and sacraments but in venues other than those specifically liturgical or devotional. The second part of the NCRLC's *Manual for Rural Retreats and Family Meditation* stressed the importance of the sacramental life in relation to the farmer as well as the rural home, education, soil conservation, and cooperatives.[71]

An address at the October 1956 convention in Sioux Falls, later published as a pamphlet called *A Program for the Family Farm*, declared: "The salvation and sanctification of rural people in and through the circumstances of their own lives is the central aim and objective of the National Catholic Rural Life Conference." No better means existed for accomplishing this objective than that of fostering participation in the liturgy and devotions of the church.[72] Rural life's close proximity to the mysteries of nature gave spontaneous rise "to worship of its Creator." The vital unity of the Mystical Body of Christ, nourished primarily by the liturgy, also depended on sensible pastoral adaptation:

> It is with joy, therefore, that we note the resurgence of interest in and practice of the liturgy as dramatically emphasized in the recent international liturgical congress held at Assisi. The results of this congress, and of the pastoral adaptations of the liturgy which preceded and undoubtedly will follow it, promise even greater strength and vigor in the life of the Church. The welcome action of the Holy See in recogniz-

[71] Many of these publications are rather substantial and will be treated more fully in later chapters.

[72] NCRLC, *A Program for the Family Farm* (Des Moines: NCRLC, ca. 1956), MUA/ NCRLC, Series 5/1, box 3, folder 25.

ing the needs and opportunities of modern times should encourage the rural pastor to use every means to educate and inspire his flock to a fuller realization of the beauty and meaning of the living liturgy.[73]

The reference to Assisi placed the pamphlet's publication sometime immediately after the 1956 Congress held there. It also demonstrated the Conference's consistent eagerness to embrace the liturgical reform of the church, making that reform integral to its wider mission. While the pamphlet said nothing extraordinary regarding the liturgy, the NCRLC did articulate the vital role of worship (and the need to adapt it) as part of a wider program of action that sought to influence many dimensions of Catholic rural life.

Finally, in the period immediately before the Second Vatican Council, Edward O'Rourke, the Conference's executive director, solicited the feedback of Godfrey Diekmann on a sermon he was preparing. Handwritten notes on O'Rourke's sermon appear to have been made by Fr. Michael Marx, OSB. The context of the sermon was to be two field Masses on August 12 and 15, 1962, and O'Rourke petitioned the Benedictine for suggestions to strengthen the sermon and to verify its orthodoxy. (O'Rourke planned to have the sermon published and would need to receive the *imprimatur*.) In his letter to Diekmann, O'Rourke pointed to the central role played by the liturgy and sacramentals in the life of rural Catholics. He expressed concern that the theological basis for these practices had not been clearly spelled out. He hoped that Diekmann and other leaders of the Liturgical Conference might assist in clarifying such theological issues.[74] O'Rourke's critique of the NCRLC regarding the theological underpinnings of sacramentals had some merit. Many of the Conference's publications on the topic were somewhat superficial, contrary to what was seen in the pages of *Orate Fratres*, for example. At the same time, the purpose of such pamphlets was not to give a theological treatise on the subject.

O'Rourke's sermon, "Sacramentals and Rural Life," was later published in pamphlet form under the title *Sacramentals for a More Complete Christian Life*.[75] He elaborated on the theological basis of sacramentals

[73] Ibid., 14–15.

[74] Edward O'Rourke to Godfrey Diekmann, 18 July 1962, MUA/NCRLC, Series 1/2, box 15, folder "Sacramentals and Rural Life."

[75] NCRLC, *Sacramentals for a More Complete Christian Life*, MUA/NCRLC, Series 1/2, box 5, folder 24, 1963.

and their relationship to the liturgy, and he grounded his reflection on the Pauline notion of creation and its role in Christ's redemptive plan (Cf. Rom 8:20-21; Col 2:20). The material creation was affirmed as a good and necessary part of salvation. Interestingly, he made no reference to the incarnation, a theme that often formed an essential part of similar reflections on sacramentality. Of particular value was the manner in which he communicated the salvific sense of "here and now." The redemptive plan set in motion long ago continued to unfold even today when the faithful rightly used the sacramentals:

> This process is begun in baptism and is advanced when we receive a sacrament, say a prayer, accept a hardship or do a good work. The manner of applying the effects of redemption in material things is similar . . . there is a progressive enlisting of creation in His [Christ's] kingdom. Holy Mother Church has instituted many sacramentals. This renders explicit and public the fact that the material world was redeemed by Christ.[76]

The use of sacramentals was explicitly linked to the eucharistic celebration and other sacraments. Yet the Mass was such a profound event it had to be "spelled out for us in the Church's treasury of sacramentals."[77] O'Rourke's assertion with regard to the material creation being redeemed by Christ and possessing an eschatological character was extraordinary only by the fact that he tied it directly to the simple use of sacramentals. This alone justified their frequent employ and more closely joined altar and home.

Throughout the 1940s and 1950s, a variety of liturgical practices were being widely observed in the rural areas. Pastors attempted to make the liturgy even more participative through adaptation to their locales. In this regard, Fr. Paul Brinker's "Tobacco Mass" as well as Fr. Joseph Lerschsen's integration of the Rogation Days and field Masses with already established secular harvest festivals were noteworthy efforts. Overall, the many Conference programs sought to connect home and altar—rural culture and the church's liturgy. In doing so, the vocation and dignity of the farmer was strengthened. Underlying all these specifically liturgical practices was persistent concern for a more just rural social order. The NCRLC and the American litur-

---

[76] Ibid.
[77] Ibid.

gical movement shared a close historical, liturgical, theological, and practical association. In their concern for deepening the true Christian spirit and its allied task of social regeneration, both drew from the primary font of the church's liturgical and sacramental life. This close relationship offered to rural Catholics the opportunity to experience "salvation and sanctification" in and through the circumstances of their own lives. In doing so, both movements cultivated soil and soul, something that Virgil Michel had begun (somewhat more theoretically) in the mid-1930s.

Chapter 3

# A Liturgist Shocks Corn: The Rural Life
# Movement at St. John's University[1]

Virgil Michel and St. John's undertook direct efforts to integrate the
rural and liturgical apostolates. In the Benedictine tradition this was
not too great a stretch, since the *labora* of the order's well-known
maxim presumed wise and effective care of the land to support the
monastery and its works, a tradition that continues today, albeit in
different forms. Recall too that back in the early 1920s Edwin O'Hara
approached Abbot Alcuin Deutsch, one of the "founders" of the
NCRLC, about establishing agricultural courses at St. John's, a proposition to which the abbot was well disposed. Saint John's became a
center for rural life activities, often in collaboration with the NCRLC
and others. At almost every step of the way the liturgy was a central
component to these courses and projects. This practical collaboration
between the two movements provided each with a more solid liturgical, theological, and social foundation upon which to base their programs. Further, Michel and others in the liturgical movement did their
part to recover and make practical a traditional theological precept,
the principle of sacramentality. This would join, in practical fashion,
the material nature of liturgy and agrarian life. All such endeavors
had as their end the renewal of the church and the reconstruction of
the social order.

---

[1] Paul Marx, OSB, *Virgil Michel and the Liturgical Movement* (Collegeville, MN:
Liturgical Press, 1957), 386. A photo shows "the liturgist shocking corn."

## VIRGIL MICHEL'S AGRARIAN ROOTS

Virgil Michel was born and raised in the city of St. Paul, Minnesota, yet significant periods of his life were spent on farms. Between 1900 and 1909 (the year he entered the Benedictine abbey), Michel spent nearly every summer and some Christmas vacations on his grandfather's farm near Jordan, Minnesota, along with his lifelong friend Jack Schmitz. The Schmitz family was quite surprised at how this "city boy" adapted so easily to the difficult farm work. Michel relished the outdoor life and the closeness to nature. He also developed a deeper understanding of the day-to-day hardships and joys of a farming family. Perhaps it was here that his lifelong interest in, and contribution to, the agrarian movement had its beginning, especially his relationship with the NCRLC. If one includes the rural ambience of St. John's Abbey, with its 2,600 acres of forests and farms, which no doubt included *manualia* for some of the monks, then one could posit that Michel spent much of his life on a farm, or at least in close proximity to nature.[2]

Another formative rural experience that may have intensified Michel's commitment to the agrarian and social justice problem was his time on the Chippewa reservation. Upon his return from Europe (1925), Michel threw himself into the liturgical apostolate with abandon. While he was often praised for his incredible capacity for work, it caught up with him just five years into the burgeoning movement. By April 1930, his eyes began to fail him and he was close to having a nervous breakdown.[3] The abbot assigned Michel to a regimen that greatly scaled back his workload, forbade reading, and eventually sent him to the White Earth Chippewa reservation to undertake some light pastoral duties. Michel would take up the agrarian question with renewed energy when he returned to St. John's in 1934.

Michel arrived at the Indian mission in northern Minnesota in September 1930. He easily adjusted to the Indian lifestyle of hunting, recreation, work, and the day-to-day demands of life—a time perhaps

[2] Marx, *Virgil Michel*, 5.

[3] Ibid., 161. It was around the same time that Michel had corresponded with Edwin O'Hara and Bill Busch, and in fact, the latter referred to Michel's poor health in his March 19 letter: "If you are taking a rest—as I hope you are—you may amuse yourself for a little while in reading the enclosed which I wrote to Fr. O'Hara." The enclosed item was Busch's article "Liturgy and Farm Relief." William Busch to Michel, 19 March 1930, SJAA, "Virgil Michel Papers," Z 22.

reminiscent of his boyhood days on the farm. It must have had some curative effect on him. Yet amid this daily interaction, he witnessed the abysmal quality of life the Chippewa experienced and realized the great ministerial need on the reservations. Michel gave himself generously to the work, as one of his fellow monks indicated:

> When he came to White Earth in January, he was a sick man; he inherited a financial mess but straightened it out by August 1; he supervised the 300 acre mission farm having 50 head of cattle, 40 hogs, 500 chickens and big gardens. He took a complete census (200 families), got a confirmation class of 160 together (children and adults), organized a religion class for 30 children in the country, supervised the boarding school for 125 girls, etc.—all this in seven months.[4]

The so-called light pastoral duties seemed an odd remedy to regain health, but in the end they apparently worked. The very simple life he lived among the poor Native Americans further sensitized Michel to social justice concerns. He studied their language and melded with their culture as much as possible. It is unknown whether Michel sought to implement any principles of the liturgical movement, although one might suspect he did.[5]

There can be little doubt that Michel's experience among the Indians, especially their poverty, heightened his awareness of social *injustice*. From 1933 until his death in 1938, the social question occupied considerably more of his thought and energy, always in light of the liturgy's potential to transform the Mystical Body of Christ. A survey of his published works from the same period reveals a prodigious output with an emphasis on the social question.[6] In those works examining

---

[4] Marx, *Virgil Michel*, 164. He also organized some of the largest and most successful Indian Congresses on record. Many Chippewa attended his funeral in 1938.

[5] Interestingly, the same reservation was known for a rather daring architectural project. One of the first American Indian priests, Father Philip P. Gordon, himself a Chippewa, facilitated the building of a new church there in 1922, which incorporated much of the native culture and symbolism. Pecklers, *Unread Vision*, 249–50.

[6] Marx, *Virgil Michel*, 422–34. Virgil Michel told a touching story of his arrival at Cass Lake, and alludes to his deepening sensitivity to justice issues: "Like a conquering hero, depression met me at the door of my new mission among the Chippewa here at Cass Lake Mission. I was in a perverse mood and decided to defy depression. So I bought a young pig believing it would help to support me." Michel had no food for the pig until one day an Indian stops by and gives him some barley to feed it. After the third visit Michel asks, "Where, Simon are you

the rural agricultural question, he provided little in the way of specific practices related to the liturgy. Rather, as with many of his social justice concerns, he expounded on the social nature of participative liturgy and the way it countered those aspects of society that weakened the Mystical Body. Saint John's offered Virgil Michel several venues in which to examine the agrarian question, and the liturgy formed a key part of these explorations.

## THE INSTITUTE FOR SOCIAL STUDY AT ST. JOHN'S

Virgil Michel and Alphonsus Matt led the way in establishing the Institute for Social Study at St. John's in 1934. Because of a misunderstanding with Bishop Joseph Busch of St. Cloud, the first session did not begin until the fall of 1935. The Institute, a collaborative project between the university and the Minnesota Branch of the Central Verein, was geared toward laypeople, but it included a few seminarians. Its central purpose was to train lay leaders in Catholic social principles. While the lectures were theoretical in nature, their ultimate aim was to make that theory practical so as to "reconstruct the social order," ushering in a Christian culture. Integral to the weekend institutes, which covered an array of social topics, was the Saturday evening spiritual conference that treated the Mystical Body of Christ and the liturgy. Active participation in all common prayer for the weekend was strongly encouraged, especially Sunday Mass.[7]

A quick glance at the Institute's topics for the first year reveals a coherent and intentional pattern.[8] Economic and political principles such as capitalism (and its critique), the question of money, reconstruction, and the nature of the state were some of the general themes. In the course of a weekend, these topics were studied by means of five lectures that treated the themes from a historical, cultural, and

---

getting barley?" Simon: "I got a few cents picking berries, Father." Michel: "I could not have you do that Simon. You need things for yourself." Simon: "No Father, I am getting old. I have all I need. I cannot do much for my church. But I can give you a little barley for your pig. Glad to do it, Father. I bring [sic] more when this is used up." Virgil Michel, "Pig to End Depression," *Indian Sentinel* 13 (1932–33): 30. One might note here the wordplay on depression—his and the actual Great Depression—ended by a pig.

[7] Marx, *Virgil Michel*, 368–69.

[8] See Appendix IV where I have provided an outline of the Institute's program for the academic year 1935–36. The materials here are interesting and could warrant further study.

liturgical angle. The liturgy lectures were often titled "The Mystical Body of Christ and . . ." some justice concern such as economic injustice, race, and war. Two other lectures usually amplified the central theme and sometimes looked at specific examples. For instance, when economic cooperatives were discussed, specific enterprises such as the Antigonish Cooperative Movement or the Danish agricultural cooperatives were considered. At the end of the first year (1935–36), certain lectures were selected and bound into a four-volume set having the general title *The Social Problem*.[9] Among the lectures not selected were those on culture by Dunstan Tucker, OSB, a monk of St. John's. In general, the weekend institutes examined the problem of social reconstruction through the lens of liturgy, culture, and justice.[10] Since Tucker's lectures were not included, a brief digression will help situate them within the context of the institutes that had the goal of "restoring all things in Christ."

Dunstan Tucker's thinking on culture exhibits strengths and weaknesses. In essence, his lectures pressed for the establishment of a Christian (Catholic) culture. This was his working definition: "Culture, which is the study of perfection, leads us to conceive a true human perfection as a *harmonious* perfection, developing all sides of our humanity; and as a general perfection developing all parts of our society." The "study of perfection" part of the definition was borrowed from the poet Matthew Arnold, which Tucker then amplified. He noted that the agnostic Arnold "is not an orthodox Christian according to

[9] Specifically, the titles included: *The Social Problem I: Social Concepts and Problems*; *The Social Problem II: Economics and Finance*; *The Social Problem III: Political Theories and Forms*; *The Social Problem IV: The Mystical Body of Christ and Social Justice*.

[10] Fr. Dunstan Tucker, OSB, was born in Tintah, Minnesota, May 10, 1898. He entered Saint John's Abbey as a novice in 1922; professed vows on July 11, 1923; and was ordained to the priesthood on June 2, 1929. He studied at Collegio di Sant' Anselmo in Rome (1925–27). He did graduate work at the University of Minnesota and Chicago, receiving an MA in English literature. He was a dedicated teacher and Dante scholar. He served as chair of the English Department at SJU from 1932 to 1952. He was a chaplain during World War II in the U.S. Navy on a carrier in the Pacific. In 1958 he was appointed academic dean of St. John's University and held that post until 1967. Father Dunstan also was active in athletics; he was the varsity baseball coach for eighteen seasons, winning four intercollegiate championships. In 1978, he wrote the history of sports at St. John's University, entitled *Scoreboard*. He also wrote many articles on Dante's *Divine Comedy* and on liturgy. He died on December 1, 1985. I am grateful to St. John's Abbey archivist David Klingeman, OSB, for this biographical summary of Tucker's life.

our lights."[11] Tucker blamed the Protestant Reformation (Puritan in nature and against the material world) and the Renaissance (seeing the beauty of the created world from a strictly human standpoint) for ushering in the modern notion of culture that is devoid of God. A strength in Tucker's thinking made the distinction between "essential and accidental culture," where "essential" culture is religious and directed toward God (Christian God), while "accidental" culture pertains to all human activities. The accidental qualities of a culture are considered good when they serve the essential.[12] Accidental culture belongs very much to the material world and is necessary for essential culture to flourish; hence the material-spiritual, natural-supernatural dialectic that occupied a key place in Virgil Michel's theology was also evident.

Tucker suggested that essential culture has a universal quality to it:

> It brings men of all races and all accidental cultures into that spiritual unity which is Christianity. The Church does not insist, for instance, that Japanese and Chinese converts accept European art, literature, music, and architecture. She insists only that all men accept fundamental beliefs about God, about human nature and destiny. And herein lies the strength of the Church that all her essential teachings are adaptable to any culture whatsoever. Thereby satisfying the religious needs of all men without separating them from ideas and facts which are traditional and are a part and parcel of their own natures.[13]

The accidental "ideas and facts which are traditional" and "part and parcel of their own natures" affirm the inherent goodness that a culture possesses. This basic insight was affirmed in various ways at Vatican II in the decrees *Sacrosanctum Concilium*, *Gaudium et Spes*, and *Ad Gentes*. Tucker concluded by referring to Christopher Dawson, who said that "a culture finds its roots in the soil and in the simple instinctive life of the shepherd, fisherman, and the husbandman up to its

---

[11] Dunstan Tucker, OSB, "The Nature and Meaning of Culture," 2, lecture at The Institute for Social Study, October 26–27, 1935, in SJAA, Q-9, Social Institute Topics. Tucker and Virgil Michel share some similar understandings of culture.

[12] The accidental-essential distinction of culture comes from Josef Donat, SJ, *Ethica Generalis* (Oeniponte; Innsbruck: F. Rauch, 1928). The Thomistic source of these terms should be obvious. Tucker also relies much upon the work of Christopher Dawson, Cardinal Henry Newman, G. K. Chesterton, and Hilaire Belloc.

[13] Tucker, "The Nature and Meaning of Culture," 5.

flowering in the highest achievement of the artist and the philosopher."
Indeed, all cultures possess the material that can lead them to the
essential, but not everything does in fact do so.

In "Culture and the Liturgy" Tucker reasserted his definition of culture as the "study of perfection," and added that it was best attained
through character training and the church's liturgy. The liturgy relied
upon the "accidental" dimensions of human life and creation so as to
lead the human to the essential culture—supernatural life with God.
He added, "Christian culture derives its strength, solidity and good
sense from Christian dogma, but it is the liturgy which puts dogmas
into action . . . It is the externalization of Christian belief as lived."
This externalization was expressed through the church's use of sacramentals, for example, which facilitated greater union of body and soul.
The externalization evident in the church's solemn public worship
evokes Pius X's motto—*instaurare omnia in Christo*—and relates it to
material understanding of culture: "*All things*, soul and body, and all
that pertains to bodily life. All signifies the whole of life, and this—the
field of culture." The liturgy awakened one to the true meaning of the
Mystical Body of Christ. The church, in her universal nature and
activities, expressed this harmonious union of accidental and essential
culture. The "organic nature of the universe" has but one purpose—
that all things (*omnia*) praise and glorify God, giving the liturgy a
cosmic orientation.[14]

The following month Tucker lectured on "Culture and the Material."
The universe is material, animate and inanimate, and as such culture
"is largely determined by the intelligent use he [man] makes of all
these forms of matter and the mastery he exerts over them in the regulation of life." This intelligent use and mastery is judged according to
the degree to which the human directs the accidentals to the essential
culture (religion and God). "Man gets his ideas from matter, and in
matter he must express them." The extremes, Puritanism (matter as
despised) and idolatry (matter as divine), were counterproductive to
the common good. Tucker stated: "Christian culture arose, and still
arises today, from an entirely different concept of the universe known

---

[14] Dunstan Tucker, OSB, "Culture and the Liturgy," 1–3, lecture at The Institute
for Social Study, February 8–9, 1936, in SJAA, Q-9, Social Institute Topics. I will
take up this notion of the material basis of culture in a later chapter, positing that
culture is constitutive of sacramentality, namely, that one of the unifying threads
joining liturgy, culture, and social justice is the sacramental principle.

as the Sacramental Principle. According to the Sacramental Principle there are two great divisions of reality, spirit and matter." Tucker's wording here can be misleading; he is not advancing any form of dualism. Rather, he simply asserted that the spiritual life of the person is brought to fruition through its material elements (sacraments, sacramentals, etc.). Rightly understood, the sacramental principle regulates and fosters the genuine attitude toward all things material. The incorrect attitude ushers in a host of social problems detrimental to the common good.[15]

Perhaps one Institute weekend can serve as an example to show how these lectures on liturgy, culture, and justice potentially coalesced. In the Institute's second year, during the weekend of November 14–15, 1936, the topic was "Consumer's Cooperatives," and studied various international cooperatives, many of the agricultural type. These lectures were a practical case study of the wider concept of distributism.[16] At its core, distributism promoted as wide a sharing of basic goods as is necessary to provide for human sustenance. It advocated ownership of smaller landholdings that, at a minimum, enabled a family to have a subsistent lifestyle. Distributism stood against both extremes of individualism and collectivism, against too much and too little freedom respectively in the economic order. The distributists maintained that economics was at the service of humanity, not vice versa. This was consistent with Catholic social teaching, which posited the priority of labor over capital and community against individualism. While these particular lectures focused on the economic aspects and benefits of

[15] Dunstan Tucker, OSB, "Culture and the Material," 1–3, lecture at The Institute for Social Study, March 7–8, 1936, in SJAA, Q-9, Social Institute Topics. The "material" in relation to "wealth and property" had been treated in other lectures. It was there that social justice and the common good were often studied.

[16] The previous semester, the Institute focused on economics, in which the basic principles of distributism were covered. While the concept had a wide array of possible applications, Michel gave particular emphasis to the agrarian type. The Institute's participants read works by distributists such as G. K. Chesterton, Hilaire Belloc, and Fr. Vincent McNabb, OP, the latter having taken a special interest in agrarianism. See Vincent Joseph McNabb, *The Church and the Land* (London: Burns, Oates & Washbourne, 1926). In a hypercompetitive market, Virgil Michel upheld distributism's basic principles as a means for the farmer to gain some control and independence from the large farming operations and associated industries. Michel drew some of his basic inspiration from the Scriptures, especially the second chapter of the Acts of the Apostles and from *Quadragesimo Anno*.

cooperatives, the economy of these cultures was one which often retained a "guild" mentality. Such guilds (i.e., woodworkers) prized well-made goods and the human relationships associated with their exchange. The Danish and Belgian cultures of cooperation were especially noted.

It was in the context of this weekend's lectures that Virgil Michel gave the Saturday evening talk entitled, "The Social Nature of Communion." Michel criticized the present-day's individualistic view toward the Eucharist and Communion, noting the overemphasis on Consecration and Real Presence. Eucharistic piety, while well intentioned, focused on what reception of Communion meant for the individual who received it. Devotional prayers conveyed a sense of the communicant's unworthiness and the need to make reparation for one's sins before approaching the altar to receive the sacred Host. Leaders in the liturgical movement made a special effort to correct such imbalances. Michel not only utilized the pages of *Orate Fratres* but venues such as the Institute for Social Study and academic courses to serve as a corrective to this form of piety. During this November weekend in 1936 he told the students:

> This vitalizing union effected by the Eucharist is much more enduring than His mere sacramental presence in us for fifteen minutes or so. This vitalizing union remains and increases with each Holy Communion until we ourselves put a stop to it by becoming dead members of Christ. . . . Christ also comes as our banquet Food. . . . Hence the special sacramental grace of Holy Communion, the specific sacramental effect of the Eucharist, is to strengthen the bond of union between the members of Christ with one another and with Christ Himself.[17]

---

[17] Virgil Michel, "Cooperative Nature of Communion," Institute for Social Study Papers, SJUA 1771, University Topics Rf-T. The article can also be found in Michel, *The Social Problem IV: The Mystical Body and Social Justice* (Collegeville, MN: St. John's Abbey, 1938), 11–16. Another example included a discussion on credit unions along with "The Social Nature of the Offertory." Ibid., 5–10. The archival edition of the article lists it as "The Cooperative Nature of the Offertory." Essentially, he selected parts of the Roman Canon and emphasized those words in the first person plural, "we" and "our." He stressed that the sacrifice is "mine and yours." He continued: "The Sacrificial Offering is essentially a social prayer in which the members of the Church pray officially, as is attested to by the practice of the early Christians, viz. only official members of the Church could attend the Offertory." He spoke too of the ancient practice of bringing gifts of bread and wine

Thus the themes of economics, individualism, and Communion were treated in a weekend series of lectures on cooperatives, combined with common prayer and meals throughout, and concluded with a Sunday liturgy in which all were encouraged to participate. A weekend such as this, and others like it, made for a *potentially* significant formative experience.

## COURSE IN CATHOLIC BACKGROUND AND CURRENT SOCIAL THEORY

In a vein similar to the Institutes of Social Study, Michel conducted a series of seminars between 1937 and 1938 entitled, "Course in Catholic Background and Current Social Theory."[18] The seminars were intended to run for two years and exemplified his desire to integrate the liturgical and social apostolates. Michel directed them, providing introductory comments along with a reading list. The students were required to read some of the books and pamphlets and then write summaries of the authors' position. They also worked collaboratively to answer reflection questions, which, it seems, were generated by Michel. He stated the course's purpose: "It will endeavor to convey a mastery of the best Christian thought of the day, with particular reference to forward looking ideas and programs in regard to every phase of social and cultural reconstruction."[19] The courses and their topics were diverse:

> 1st Semester: Christian Sociologists, Writings of Dawson, Maritain, E. A., The Personalist and Communitarian Movement

> 2nd Semester: The Liturgical Movement, The Corporative Order, The Distributist-Agrarian Movement

> 3rd and 4th Semesters: The Catholic Revival, Theology and Sociology, The New Money Theories, Marxian Theory Today

---

forward, and that cooperation was as necessary for our physical body as it was for the spiritual dimension.

[18] Virgil Michel, ed., *Course in Catholic Background and Current Theory*, SJAA, Virgil Michel Papers, box "Works Published," 1937–1938. See Marx, *Virgil Michel*, 428. The material consists of three stapled collection of typed notes, one for each "course." Each is about 40–50 pages in length.

[19] Ibid., *Course in Catholic Background and Current Theory—First Semester*, 1937, SJAA, Virgil Michel Papers, box "Works Published," 1.

The second semester was Michel's direct attempt to integrate his liturgical and agrarian thinking. The courses were quite theoretical, and the only component that seemed to offer something practical was the session on liturgy.[20] This "2nd Semester" course deserves a closer look.

The course notes did not give an adequate summary statement of what the liturgical movement was, but Michel identified elsewhere its two basic objectives. First, it was to bring the faithful to a better appreciation of what the church's liturgy meant for the life of the Mystical Body of Christ. To arrive at this awareness demanded that one actively and intelligently participate in the church's worship. This formed the Mystical Body of Christ into a corporative and cooperative faith community. Second, the transformation that resulted from this worship was to affect the daily conduct of the Christian. Simply stated, the very nature of the liturgy demanded that Christians become a transformative force in the world. The liturgy was *the* school that engendered such a Christian spirit. The corporate nature and cooperation modeled by the liturgy served as the pattern of conduct in daily life. Michel knew that an individualistic spirit could permeate the liturgy, as it did the world, and if so, that spirit would diminish the Mystical Body's potential to change unjust structures in society.[21]

Michel often stressed the interplay between the individual and the social aspects of humanity when discussing liturgy and social regeneration. In reference to the Mystical Body he noted, "In this holy fellowship we find a harmonious combination of the two complimentary [sic] factors of humankind, that is, organic fellowship coupled with full respect for human personality and individual responsibility."[22] Such thinking expressed, in part, how he understood the liturgy's relationship to the agrarian question. The agrarian-distributism of his time pressed for the freedom of the person's right to own property. Agrarianism, however, was a rather new movement and lacked sound organizational principles, tending to rely on the rugged individualist approach. This, in fact, may have caused its downfall. Michel saw the church, her liturgy and structure, as a privileged place to give due emphasis to both the personal and the social dimensions of life. The

[20] A pamphlet was read that identified specific ways to integrate the liturgy with daily life, and mentioned the use of sacramentals. See Rembert Bularzik, OSB, *Liturgy and Life* (Collegeville, MN: Liturgical Press, 1936).

[21] Michel, "Scope of the Liturgical Movement," *OF* 10 (1936): 485.

[22] Michel, "The Liturgy the Basis of Social Regeneration," *OF* 9 (1935): 541.

liturgy, he believed, could place the agrarian movement on a more stable religious foundation. Michel had at his disposal organizational vehicles to promote his position, including the Minnesota Decentralists and Agrarians, an ecumenical but largely Catholic organization; and of course, he had the NCRLC.

The "corporative order" or the term "corporatism" defied simple description.[23] As its Latin root *corpus* suggested, corporatism was best understood in relation to the body of the individual person and the individual's bodily array of social relationships. Both 'bodies' required at once the need for independence and freedom as well as the awareness that no one person was completely self-sufficient. When the whole organism functioned properly, each body served as a check on the other. Thus Michel employed the term corporatism to counter the hyper-individualism often represented by the liberal economic model and to guard against any collection of individuals who assumed too much local or even national control. The latter could take the form of a large business or an oligarchic political structure, anything that stifled individual freedom and initiative.

According to Michel, though, the distinct spiritual dimension of corporatism was best nourished through the church's liturgy. Through participative celebration, the liturgy bestowed upon the Mystical Body the true Christian spirit, which he labeled as *corporative* and *cooperative*. Michel's philosophical and economic basis of corporatism was grounded in the philosophy of St. Thomas, the personalism of Emmanuel Mounier, and the papal social encyclicals. As Paul Marx noted, Virgil Michel stressed that "every apostolic Christian worthy of the name should support at least one of the following . . . 1) the corporative order, 2) the personalist movement, 3) the cooperative movement, and 4) the distributist-agrarian movement."[24] The corporatism engendered by the church's liturgy and the agrarian-distributist position found in these varied sources a philosophical, theological, and

---

[23] Michel treated corporatism in several places. See Virgil Michel, ed., *The Social Problem III—Political Theories and Forms* (St. Paul, MN: Wanderer Printing Co., 1936), 74–81; idem, *Christian Social Reconstruction: Some Fundamentals of Quadragesimo Anno* (Milwaukee, New York: The Bruce Publishing Co., 1937), 91–107; idem, *Course in Catholic Background and Current Theory*, SJAA, Virgil Michel Papers, box "Works Published," 1937–1938, 7–29; see also Marx, *Virgil Michel*, 307ff.; Hall, *The Full Stature of Christ*, 186–88.

[24] Marx, *Virgil Michel*, 307.

liturgical anchor. The liturgy, however, was primary in its ability to impact more people and unify the other dimensions. Corporate worship served as the school for proper action in the socioeconomic order, originating from a local organic community. The term "organic," was frequently used to describe how the liturgy planted its transformative roots deep into the rural culture. The liturgy nourished both the individual and social *corpus*.

The discussion of the liturgical movement and corporatism laid the groundwork for a consideration of the agrarian-distributist movement. The course bibliography contained about thirty-five works on the topic. Some were specifically about agrarianism, while others addressed the industrial question, often in its harsher capitalistic form. Names such as Herbert Agar, Allen Tate, Ralph Borsodi, Hilaire Belloc, Vincent McNabb, OP, Louis Brandeis, and G. K. Chesterton—all of them of the agrarian-decentralist school—were on the reading list.[25] Several periodicals were recommended, such as *G. K.'s Weekly*, the NCRLC's *Landward*, and *Free America*, the latter identified as the distributist movement's official journal.

In essence, the agrarian-distributist movement was a protest against the unchecked liberal economic model, which often took the form of large industrial complexes. While such business operations were usually located in the cities, they began to extend into the countryside. From its beginning, the NCRLC fought the appropriation of small family farms and placing in their stead large factory-farming operations. Small landowners, associated with the distributist-agrarian movement, tried to band together through cooperatives in order to check this uncontrolled "progress," so designated. This formed part of what was called the "landward" movement. Doing so often drew accusations of being communist. Distributism sought to guard individual rights, access to basic goods, and believed that the state should protect such freedoms (a Jeffersonian ideal). When the state failed to intervene in what the agrarians saw as land/property grabbing, the agrarians believed that the basic liberty affirmed by the Constitution was violated. One keeps in mind that the United States was still in a deep economic depression. Cooperatives were one means among

---

[25] For an introduction to the thought of some of these figures see Allan Carlson, *The New Agrarian Mind: The Movement Toward Decentralist Thought in Twentieth-Century America* (New Brunswick, NJ: Transaction Publishers, 2000).

several that tried to preserve the right balance of individual liberty without devolving into rugged individualism.[26]

Emerson Hynes, of the St. John's faculty and a member of the NCRLC, provided a synopsis of the Conference's philosophy as part of this course. Hynes's presentation on the NCRLC noted that its philosophy coincided very much with that of the general agrarian movement. The "Twelve Southerners" promoted the great dignity of the agricultural vocation, which one pursued with intelligence, attentiveness, and all sensitivity to the culture of the soil. Much of the agrarian South was religious, frequently coming from the Baptist and Presbyterian traditions. These "Southerners" had a strong intellectual, and some argue elitist strain to their agrarian philosophy. Hynes distinguished this form of agrarianism from that promoted by the NCRLC, whose purpose was fundamentally religious in nature. The Conference was concerned with the economic and spiritual well-being of rural Catholics. The rural environment was most hospitable for the family and offered the best opportunity for a balanced lifestyle, attending to all dimensions of human personhood and community. Hynes concluded by saying that the Conference, "is actively going to war against industrialism and advancing a program which will make for a stronger and healthier Church and nation." The NCRLC envisioned a wider purpose in its effort to keep a significant population on the land, not merely to preserve the rural way of life. Rather, he saw its efforts as vital to a stronger national union in the United States of America. In this way, Catholic agrarians viewed their way of life in a countercultural light, which stood against the extremes of individualism and collectivism.[27]

The "Course in Catholic Background" along with the Institute of Social Study afforded Michel the opportunity to explore his agrarian interests in a more theoretical light. Through it all, liturgy gave spiritual and practical vigor to the theory treated in the various lectures and seminars, contrary to the "Ryan" approach to social problems.

---

[26] Michel, *Course in Catholic Background and Current Theory: Second Semester* (Collegeville, MN: St. John's University, 1937), SJAA, Virgil Michel Papers, box "Works Published," 37.

[27] Michel, *Course in Catholic Background and Current Theory: Second Semester*, 37. See also Twelve Southerners, *I'll Take My Stand: The South and the Agrarian Tradition*, with a New Introduction by Susan V. Donaldson, 75th Anniversary Edition (Baton rouge, LA: Louisiana State University Press, 2006).

## THE COOPERATIVE MOVEMENT AND THE
## LITURGICAL MOVEMENT

In 1936, amid the Depression and Dust Bowl, Virgil Michel delivered an address to the attendees at the NCRLC's Fargo convention entitled "The Cooperative Movement and the Liturgical Movement." By the early 1930s, cooperatives had already been established as an integral component of the NCRLC's agenda. In 1934 Fr. Moses Coady of the Antigonish Cooperative Movement spoke at the NCRLC convention in St. Paul.[28] With varying degrees of success rural Catholic parishes set up farming cooperatives and credit unions. Michel declared that the liturgical movement's fundamental aim was to make worship something vital in the lives of the faithful. As for the cooperative movement, it had already been established in many countries and among people of various religious denominations; even nonbelievers embraced it, seeing in cooperatives the potential to improve the economic conditions of its members.[29] But how were the cooperative and liturgical movements related?

Both movements, according to Michel, had a common nemesis—individualism. In the field of economics, individualism thrived in a cut-throat environment and created an unbalanced (and unjust)

[28] The Antigonish Movement began in 1928 as a result of the activities of the Extension Department of St. Francis Xavier University in Antigonish, Nova Scotia. A year later, in response to the great suffering caused by the Depression, the Extension Department presented a series of public speeches and lectures in communities throughout the province regarding self-help and cooperative economic enterprise. It was led by Fathers J. J. Tompkins and Moses M. Coady. Later the movement organized farmers and fishermen co-ops, credit unions, and mutual aid societies. It was, arguably, the most successful cooperative in North America. For a fascinating look at the Dust Bowl see Timothy Egan, *The Worst Hard Time: The Untold Story of Those Who Survived the Great American Dust Bowl* (New York: First Mariner Books, 2006).

[29] Virgil Michel, "The Cooperative Movement and the Liturgical Movement," MUA/NCRLC, Series 8/1, box 2. The talk was given on October 13, 1936, and published in *Catholic Rural Life Objectives: A Series of Discussions on Some Elements of Major Importance in the Philosophy of Agrarianism* (St. Paul, MN: National Catholic Rural Life Conference, 1936). Page numbers will correspond to the reprinted version in *OF* 14 (1939–40): 152–60. See Witte, *Crusading*, 117; Marx, *Virgil Michel*, 381–82. In addition, Michel, like the NCRLC, viewed cooperation in the economic sphere as one way of fostering ecumenism. This was extended to liturgical matters as seen in common celebrations of the Rogation Days.

distribution of the material goods needed for human sustenance and dignity. Such an attitude, he argued, had infected the church. The faithful came to Mass and uttered their own private prayers, generally unrelated to the liturgical celebration. Michel was well aware that people had been "celebrating" the liturgy this way for centuries. This individualistic spirit in the liturgy typified the present state of worship among the faithful, rural Catholics included. This spirit diminished true fellowship in the Mystical Body of Christ as Michel clearly stated: "The two, union with Christ or with God through Christ, and union with all the brethren in Christ, stand or fall together."[30] A person who claimed union with Christ was confronted with the social implications of one's union with the brethren. It was upon this religious foundation that both movements (liturgical and cooperative) coalesced, giving strength to the social regeneration envisioned by Pius XI. The liturgy would both heighten awareness of social injustices, born of individualism, and compel one to take action that would remedy such problems.

Cooperation, more substantively, reflected Michel's basic understanding of social justice, which had as its principal aim the common good. When properly practiced, cooperation acted as a distinct force against individualism. He relied, in part, on his agrarian-distributist position to make his point:

> Instead the movement aims at common cooperative work for all for the sake of a decent livelihood for all; it aims at the maximum distribution of goods among all men. Its attitude toward material goods is the true Christian attitude based on the principle that the goods of this earth are there to serve as instruments for the decent living of men as moral and intellectual personalities, and for decent living of all men without exception.[31]

Combating the common nemesis of individualism, however, was insufficient if a deeper relationship between the two movements was to be forged. This was no small insight on Michel's part. If the two movements were permitted to coexist side by side without intersecting, it would perpetuate the rift between the material and spiritual dimensions of life, resulting in a movement supported by the "natural

[30] Michel, "The Cooperative Movement and the Liturgical Movement," 154.
[31] Ibid., 156.

powers of men" without the assistance of the grace of God.[32] Michel insisted on a religious foundation in order to bring about the full flowering of the cooperative movement. His insight about two parallel movements proved to be accurate down to contemporary times and has in fact occurred more generally. Namely, the liturgical and social justice apostolates have remained two parallel and independent, albeit inestimable, movements in the life of the church. Christians who participated in the cooperative movement, the domain of nature, were to find their inspiration in the grace given by Christ. Michel made it clear for Catholics especially that the cooperative movement *needed* the liturgical movement. This insured that the "social work" found its spiritual source in the common font of grace offered through the liturgy.

## VIRGIL MICHEL THE ANTI-URBANIST?

In light of Virgil Michel's involvement in the rural life movement, was he anti-urbanist? Unfortunately, the most oft-quoted line of Michel's in connection to rural life came from his article entitled "City or Farm?" In it he stated: "I know now that it is indeed very often a misfortune to be born in a larger city; and subsequent experience and contacts have convinced me that it may become an almost irreparable spiritual calamity to be born in some of our largest metropolitan areas." Jeffrey Marlett has argued that such thinking places him among the anti-urbanists of his day. This has some truth to it, but it is very possible that Michel was reacting to what, in truth, were dire times. The cities were not easy places in which to live, contrary to the images in popular magazines. They were crowded and poor for many people, and life was a constant struggle. It was a great comfort only for those with the economic means to share in all its amenities. Recall that Michel was writing in the midst of the Depression and eventual Dust Bowl of the 1930s. It took the Second World War to give the economy a definitive boost. His association with so many people on the front lines of social justice causes—Dorothy Day, Catherine De Hueck Doherty, the agrarians, the NCRLC, and others—provided ample evidence to believe that the ways of "modern progress" (identified as an urban phenomenon) were indeed not beneficial to all.[33]

---

[32] Ibid., 157.

[33] Michel, "Timely Tracts: City or Farm?" *OF* 12 (1937–38): 367. See Marlett, *Saving the Heartland*, 35–36; *idem*, "Harvesting an Overlooked Freedom: The Anti-

The cities, Michel asserted, made the person a "cog in the large machine of city ways," artificial and mechanical. In the city one became divorced from the natural processes and rhythms of life, which he deemed were part and parcel of the liturgy. The family farm (or the family economy) fostered, among children especially, the virtues of cooperation, charity, and justice. "Insofar as a man lives close to the soil he is in all his contacts governed by and cooperating with the functions of life."[34] This loss of contact from the "functions of life" made a deeper engagement in the liturgical and sacramental life of the church more difficult to achieve. The basis of the liturgy is found in the relationship of nature and people—truly organic. Without a doubt, Michel's affinities were for the country, but he was well aware of the work going on in the urban centers. One of the reasons why Dorothy Day wanted to establish Catholic Worker farms was not only to provide food for the urban houses of hospitality but to create a greater connection to nature. Catholic Worker cofounder Peter Maurin was of peasant stock. Certainly, Michel argued for a back-to-the-land movement to counter this negative tendency prevalent in cities. He concluded: "and so the question of city or farm is really a question of restoring the natural basis of Christian living for the greater flourishing of the supernatural Christ-life among men."[35] This affirmation of the natural order formed an essential part of his liturgical and sacramental worldview.

There is no doubt that one can find anti-urban currents in the NCRLC literature and among Catholic agrarians in general. My sense, however, is that Marlett may slightly overstate the case. The anti-urban label he ascribes to Catholic agrarians is given without sufficiently criticizing the urban context. To offer such a critique, one could reasonably begin with Charles Dickens (*David Copperfield* and *Great Expectations*), then move to Leo XIII, Upton Sinclair (*The Jungle*), and Pius XI, among others. They saw that the newly industrialized cities created wealth for a few and enslaved many; urban life was wretched for many people. That such anti-urban thinking constituted a "vision" for Catholic agrarians is doubtful. A vision suggests that programs are

Urban Vision of American Catholic Agrarianism," *U.S. Catholic Historian* 16, no. 4 (1998): 88–108. Luigi Ligutti had published an article entitled "Cities Kill," *Commonweal* 32 (August 2, 1940): 300–301.

[34] Michel, "City or Farm?" 368.

[35] Ibid., 369.

set in motion that become a kind of raison d'être. Based on my extensive reading of NCRLC literature (the face of Catholic agrarianism), such an assertion would be difficult to maintain. If one upholds such a critique of Michel's anti-urbanism, one may have to apply it to Dorothy Day as well. Mark and Louise Zwick note Day's agrarian view:

> Ours was a long-range program, looking for ownership by the workers of the means of production, the abolition of the assembly line, decentralized factories, the restoration of crafts and ownership of property. This meant, of course, an accent on the agrarian and rural aspects of our economy and a changing emphasis from the city to the land.[36]

Day was drawn very much to the Catholic Worker farms and spent as much time there as possible. She especially enjoyed the bucolic retreat-like ambience, but this may have been one reason for their general failure. Peter Maurin, when talking about the social order, always drew the group back to the question of the land.

Michel was not alone in his belief that a nation's stability—economic, social, educational and religious—was very much tied to the countryside. It was also a foundational tenet of the NCRLC. Michel not only criticized the mechanization going on in the cities but on the farm as well. What today are labeled "factory farms" had their beginning in the early twentieth century. Then and now, such operations destroyed family farms and homesteads, and ultimately made the farmers tenants on land they once owned.[37] He knew that an idyllic return to the land was not practical and that agrarian life had to adapt. On one hand, the move back to the land would be countercultural in the face of modernity. On the other hand, this move kept alive a tradition he saw as crucial for the health of a nation. Michel promoted the method of "Biodynamic Farming," which allowed for intensive farming without depleting the soil's vitality.[38] He favored cooperatives as a means to counter the forces of commercialization in addition to preserving

---

[36] Mark and Louise Zwick, *The Catholic Worker Movement: Intellectual and Spiritual Origins* (New York: Paulist Press, 2005), 166–68. Quote is from Dorothy Day, *The Long Loneliness* (New York: Harper, 1952), 220–21.

[37] Land tenure and the small family farm remain on the NCRLC's agenda at home and abroad.

[38] Michel, "Agriculture and Reconstruction," *Commonweal* 29 (January 13, 1939): 318.

some independence for farmers. Thus the "anti-urbanist" label may be too strong in light of the period in which Michel wrote.

Vigil Michel died on November 26, 1938, at the age of forty-eight. Rural life leader Bishop Aloisius Muench offered a memorial testimony on the occasion: "Philosophy gave his thinking unity, social economics gave it modernity, and liturgy gave it life. . . . The cooperative movement was . . . but another manifestation of the workings of the mystical body of Christ among men."[39] Supernatural spiritual fellowship originated in a community that prayed and lived together and thus worked for a true flourishing of the Christian spirit. This formed the thrust of Michel's overall project and served as the antidote to materialistic individualism. Michel had planned to establish a rural life curriculum at St. John's. Perhaps he saw in such an enterprise the most natural means to fully integrate his plan for the reconstruction of the social order, with liturgy as its foundation, believing that agriculture was essential for the welfare of any nation. Just days after his death, the NCRLC's executive committee offered its personal condolences: "Upon motion duly seconded, the executive secretary was instructed to express the sympathy of the National Catholic Rural Life Conference to the Rt. Rev. Abbot of St. John's University, Collegeville, MN on the death of Rev. Dom Virgil Michel, O.S.B."[40]

Michel's death was indeed a great loss for the whole church. By now it should be evident that Michel gave considerable thought and attention to the rural question and consistently kept the liturgical and spiritual aspects at its center. This was particularly true in the years 1935–38. The liturgical movement inspired many rural apostles who pragmatically sought to apply these principles to their situation. In various ways, the NCRLC embraced and put into practice what the liturgical movement retrieved from the tradition. One also notes that Michel gave considerable thought to how the natural life leads to the supernatural life—the way the material and natural world leads the Christian to life with God. This is what is implied by the sacramental principle.

---

[39] Aloisius J. Muench, "A Friend of Rural Life," OF 13 (1938–39): 131.

[40] "Minutes," MUA/NCRLC, Series 8/1, box 3, folder "Executive Committee Meeting St. Paul, MN, November 30, 1938."

## A RURAL SACRAMENTALITY

One of the less discussed aspects of the American liturgical movement was the manner in which it recovered and understood the sacramental principle—a rather traditional precept of the church. Without its being called as such, the principle had been much in evidence among the patristic authors, often alluding to it in the context of the church's liturgical and sacramental life. One contemporary definition of the principle states that "all reality, both animate and inanimate, is potentially the bearer of God's presence and the instrument of God's saving activity on humanity's behalf."[41] The principle was central to Virgil Michel's liturgical theology and ecclesiology. Michel's agrarian interests also show that sacramentality figured into his understanding of socioeconomic reform, grounding such reform in the relationship between the material-spiritual and natural-supernatural. The liturgical movement tried to recover this sense of sacramentality and restore it to its proper place in relation to the church's official, communal worship. The church's natural and practical extension of this principle was its use of sacramentals. Liturgical scholars and practitioners promoted their intelligent use, which included understanding their role apropos of the communal liturgical life of the church. Through the use of sacramentals, the liturgical movement made a deeper connection between the ordinary things of daily life, vis-à-vis agriculture and the liturgical life, between home and altar.

In 1925, a year prior to the official launch of the liturgical movement, Virgil Michel published an article in the *Catholic Educational Review* that demonstrated the liturgy's import with respect to the renewal of society. Michel challenged the assumptions of a modern, industrial, and materialistic society, which he deemed reductionist and negatively influenced educational pedagogy. Education methods stressed the pragmatic and utilitarian approaches that did not educate the whole person, producing a fragmented worldview, not an integrated one.

---

[41] See *The HarperCollins Encyclopedia of Catholicism* (San Francisco: HarperCollins, 1995), 1148. The definition continues: "This principle is rooted in the nature of a sacrament as such, i.e., a visible sign of the invisible presence and activity of God. Together with the principles of mediation (God works through secondary agents to achieve divine ends) and communion (the end of all God's activity is the union of humanity), the principle of sacramentality constitutes one of the central theological characteristics of Catholicism." See also Richard McBrien, *Catholicism* (New York: HarperCollins, 1994), 9–11.

Michel noted that doctrines "must be emphasized in their living aspects, as they should operate in the individual . . . as they find their living expression in all the official acts of the Church."[42] The liturgy offered some insight to a more balanced method that considered the person in a holistic manner. The liturgy could shed a more truthful light on the relationship between the material and spiritual aspects of life:

> It is the essence of the liturgy to give living expression to all the fundamental truths of our religion by means of symbolism that is tangible to the senses. . . . The spirit of the liturgy is well expressed in the sacraments. They always express vitally the most fundamental truths and mysteries of our faith . . . sensible signs of inner truth and grace.[43]

The tangible and spiritual nature of the liturgy provided a balance to the undue emphasis placed upon the material aspect alone, something the modern industrial world had stressed almost exclusively. Michel did not claim the liturgy as a panacea for all of modernity's ills. Rather, the liturgy carried the potential to see the world in a fuller, more spiritual light. When celebrated rightly (as he understood it), the liturgy posed a challenge to the excesses of a materialistic society, be it industrial or personal.

Virgil Michel held the sacramental principle at the very core of his theological worldview and made it constitutive to his understanding of liturgy. It was found throughout his writings. His most succinct description of the sacramental principle stated:

> This general fact, that God has chosen to manifest Himself to men's minds through external visible things, and to act in human souls by means of material things, words and actions, is often called the Sacramental Principle. The word sacramental here refers to external material visible things insofar as they are signs of deeper, hidden, spiritual truths or realities.[44]

---

[42] Virgil Michel, "A Religious Need of the Day," *Catholic Educational Review* 23 (1925): 454.

[43] Ibid., 454–55.

[44] Virgil Michel, *Our Life in Christ* (Collegeville, MN: Liturgical Press, 1939), 76–85, 180–89, esp. 77 and 181. In addition to mention of the sacramental principle above with regard to education, one also finds it in the following works of Michel: *The Liturgy and Catholic Life* (Unpublished Manuscript, 1936), 34–39, 102–5; *The*

Whenever Michel considered the principle he frequently placed it in the context of God's creation, the incarnation, as the supreme expression of it (sacramental principle), and the sacramental life of the church. The Eucharist, communally celebrated by the Mystical Body of Christ, manifested the principle in a special way.[45] The material world was at the service of the spiritual, and the natural world led to, and was essential to the supernatural—here and now. Dualism, in any of its manifestations, found no home in this principle. "Sacramentals" served the vital role of deepening the sacramental life proper, as well as establishing a closer relationship between liturgy and daily life.[46] Finally, he invoked the principle as the basis of a sound world order that kept the common good before its eyes. That is to say, a world order that maintained a proper relationship between the human family and material goods resulted in their just use and distribution. The right relationship toward material goods and their role in the supernatural order were foundational to his agrarian philosophy.

In 1935–36 Michel authored a series of articles on the "natural and supernatural" order, which took as their point of departure the sacramental principle. While they did not treat agrarianism proper, they supported his agrarian views more generally, and placed them on a more firm liturgical-theological foundation.[47] One of the crucial questions for the church in the early twentieth century, articulated by popes and theologians, was concerned with the church's stance

---

*Christian in the World* (Collegeville, MN: Liturgical Press, 1939), 83–111, esp. 101–3; *The Liturgy of the Church According to the Roman Rite* (New York: The Macmillan Company, 1937), 253–73; "Natural and Supernatural Society: I. The Sacramental Principle As Guide," *OF* 10 (1936): 243–47.

[45] In *The Liturgy and Catholic Life* he actually begins his explanation with Anaxagoras then moves on to Plato, Aristotle, and naturally, to St. Thomas.

[46] Virgil Michel, *The Liturgy of the Church According to the Roman Rite* (New York: The Macmillan Company, 1937), 253–73. Of the many examples he could have used, he focused on the agricultural sacramentals and the consecration of virgins.

[47] Virgil Michel, "The Liturgy the Basis of Social Regeneration," *OF* 9 (1935): 536–45; *idem*, "Natural and Supernatural Society: I. The Sacramental Principle As Guide," *OF* 10 (1936): 243–47; *idem*, "Natural and Supernatural Society: II. Spiritual Communion of Goods," *OF* 10 (1936): 293–96; *idem*, "Natural and Supernatural Society: III. Material Goods and the Supernatural Life," *OF* 10 (1936): 338–42; *idem*, "Natural and Supernatural Society: IV. Early Christian Communism," *OF* 10 (1936): 394–98; *idem*, "Natural and Supernatural Society: V. The Christian Possession of Goods," *OF* 10 (1936): 434–38; idem, "Scope of the Liturgical Movement," *OF* 10 (1936): 485–90.

toward two menacing socioeconomic problems, individualism and collectivism, each espousing disordered views toward the material world and inhibited to the full flourishing of the human family. The church wished to identify their limitations and bring them into greater harmony.[48] Michel pointed to this balance that the liturgy inspired: "In this holy fellowship we find a harmonious combination of the two complimentary [sic] factors of humankind, that is, organic fellowship coupled with full respect for human personality and individual responsibility."[49] But this responsibility was inextricably tied to the material creation.

Michel was convinced that if Christians grasped more fully the idea of the church as the Mystical Body of Christ, they would more easily grasp other doctrines. One such teaching was the communion of saints. Prior to the formulation of the fourth-century Creed, Michel argued, one may have interpreted the doctrine as *communio in sanctis*, or the "intercommunication in holy things." The Mystical Body was not just a spiritual communion among the members who worship together, but also "the participation of all members in the supernatural goods and blessings, of the proportionate sharing of all the members in the common treasury of merits of Christ and the saints."[50] Each Christian must personally respond to the grace of Christ, and this was fostered best by a communally celebrated liturgy. Faithful to the sacramental principle, this communion in the supernatural was principally communicated via the natural material goods of the earth and through concrete deeds of human charity and justice. The community that produced the second-century *Didache* gave evidence that the early Christians shared all material goods in common (cf. Acts 2:42-47). This sharing was constitutive of the supernatural character of their community. Thus, for the existence of a truly supernatural Christian order, the right relationship between material goods and their use had to be established. The *just* intercommunion in holy things, here and now, joined the Christian community to the eternal salvific plan. The

---

[48] Michel, "The Liturgy the Basis of Social Regeneration," *OF* 9 (1935): 536, 539. Here is where Michel often made recourse to *Rerum Novarum* and *Quadragesimo Anno*, especially the latter.

[49] Ibid., 541.

[50] Michel, "Natural and Supernatural Society: II. Spiritual Communion of Goods," *OF* 10 (1936): 294.

natural and supernatural orders were one, yet they awaited their full union and manifestation in Christ's final coming.

The modern industrial age had given birth to a "mad race after the goods of this world," which created great disparity between the rich and poor. Throughout the centuries Christianity bounced between extremes regarding the right relationship toward material possessions. Christian royalty often lived alongside the faithful who lived in extreme poverty. Monasteries demonstrated the divine beneficence as they shared their material and spiritual goods with the poor. However, Manichean (and later Jansenistic) tendencies held material goods as sinful, and still other groups maintained that it was not at all Christian to own any material goods. According to Michel, St. Thomas balanced the two extremes: "[The] possession of material goods is necessary as a means, as 'instrumental,' for leading a life of virtue. This relation of material goods to man's spiritual life follows from the nature of man as a material-spiritual organism." Michel promoted a healthy detachment from material goods which, at the same time, showed forth their high dignity in human life, "the positive part they play in the divine dispensation as instruments furthering the life and growth of Christ in his members."[51] In order to fulfill the demands of justice and serve the commonweal, some of the material goods of the earth had to be viewed as a "common treatise," which was given to the whole human race by God. Each human must be granted a minimum free access to such goods. The church tried to articulate a *via media* between private property and that which belonged to the common treasury. In relation to the Mystical Body of Christ, Michel plainly noted: "the supernatural interrelation between body and members must find its counterpart also in man's relation to the goods of the earth, if such relation is to be inspired as it should be by the true Christian spirit."[52]

[51] Michel, "Natural and Supernatural Society: III. Material Goods and the Supernatural Life," *OF* 10 (1936): 338–40. See also Jacques Maritain, *Essays in Order*, trans. J. F. Scanlan (New York: Macmillan, 1931), 21.

[52] Michel, "Natural and Supernatural Society: V. The Christian Possession of Goods," 435. Perhaps it was no mere coincidence that the last article in the series was preceded by a short Mozarabic harvest prayer and followed by this quote from the *Christian Front*, the leading agrarian-distributist periodical of the time: "To restore the Catholic spirit, we must restore the Catholic life. From a vital Catholicity springs a concern for the common good. For the spiritual life of Catholicism is, according to its liturgy, a corporate life, and the social life of Catholicism is modeled

The NCRLC, while not always adopting Michel's specific language, relied on the liturgical leader's thinking to advance a more balanced Catholic position with regard to the agricultural socioeconomic order. Rural Catholics' use of blessings, sacramentals, and Rogation Days, in part, elevated the status of material goods to the supernatural order. The NCRLC also articulated the crucial role played by the material creation (soil especially) in the supernatural life of the Christian.

Other contributors to *Orate Fratres* considered the sacramental principle. James O'Mahoney, OFM, Cap., of Rochstown, Ireland, was one of the founding editors of the journal. He relied on his Franciscan spiritual heritage and its close relationship to creation, authoring several articles that shed further light on the principle's retrieval.[53] Literature, art, Scripture, and theology expressed how nature, in all its materiality, communicated the divine reality. As for stewardship, "Man," he claimed, "is Nature's pontiff; the Christian her true priest." The liturgy was the principal, but not exclusive voice of the church's praise that communicated the truths of its religion. The divine reality was expressed by nature and humanity working in concert. Therefore, to the common understanding of liturgy as "the work of the people," one takes nature in hand, literally, to fashion right praise—*orthodoxy* in the best sense. Religion must appeal to the whole person as a composite of body and spirit.[54] The sensible elements of nature, part and parcel of the church's liturgy, served to uplift the human spirit. "The universe" he remarked, "is a work of art" that both revealed and concealed divine ideas. Art and poetry were also concrete applications of the sacramental principle, since they gave material expression to the ideas imbedded within nature and the human family. Nature itself, O'Mahoney maintained, had been working out a sacramental system

---

after its spiritual life. Out of the ranks of those who live the liturgy will come the Catholic leaders we need. Such leaders will demonstrate the goodness of the Catholic life so well that men of right reason everywhere must recognize the efficacy of Catholicism, and acknowledge its superior contribution to social justice." In *The Christian Front* (1936): 35.

[53] I base this brief assessment on the following articles: James E. O'Mahoney, OFM, Cap., "The Voice of Nature: The Voice of the Church," *OF* 1 (1926–27): 167–71; *idem*, "Nature and the Liturgy: St. Francis," *OF* 1 (1926–27): 301–4; *idem*, "Joy in Praise," *OF* 2 (1927–28): 76–79; "The Sacramental Principle," *OF* 3 (1928–29): 7–9; *idem*, "The Sacramental Principle: Its Source," *OF* 3 (1928–29): 178–80.

[54] O'Mahoney, "The Voice of Nature: The Voice of the Church," *OF* 1 (1926–27): 170–71.

before "the sensible elements of water, of bread and wine, of oil, were selected by our Lord to form the basis of His sacramental system." Just as nature was characteristic of this principle, so also "Man's body itself is a sacrament of his soul."[55] The Christian depended upon the materiality of the liturgical celebration, such that both the material creation and the human person were expressive of the sacramental principle—an extension of the incarnation. "Those who speak of a purely spiritual recourse to God independent of right [sic] and symbol forget that Christ Himself went down into the Jordan to receive Baptism at the hands of John the Baptist."[56]

Bede Sholtz, a Benedictine monk of Conception Abbey, Missouri, became a leader of the liturgical movement and was connected to the rural apostolate. Conception Abbey's association with the liturgical movement began with Patrick Cummins, OSB, who was a founding editor of *Orate Fratres*. The abbot sent Scholtz to St. John's for theological study where he came under the personal tutelage of Virgil Michel. It was at Conception Abbey that the liturgical periodical *Altar and Home* was begun (1934).[57] In 1930–31 Scholtz authored several articles for *Orate Fratres* that highlighted the importance of sacramentals and their relationship to the liturgy, one of which treated the

[55] O'Mahoney, "The Sacramental Principle," *OF* 3 (1928–29): 7–9.

[56] O'Mahoney, "The Sacramental Principle: Its Source," *OF* 3 (1928–29): 180.

[57] *Altar and Home* fulfilled a wish of Michel's that the movement would reach beyond more scholarly circles to the laity, "bridging the gap between the Sunday liturgical assembly and domestic life." Scholtz went on to become Secretary for the Liturgical Conference, and also served as chaplain for the Rural Parish Workers of Christ the King, a secular institute founded in 1942 by LaDonna Herman and Alice Widmer. The "Rural Parish Workers" was one of the first secular institutes founded in the United States. These "city girls," as they called themselves, were inspired by an address of Father Leo Steck, the diocesan director of rural life in St. Louis, who spoke of the great needs of the Catholic faithful in the countryside. They began their apostolate in rural Cottleville, Missouri, about thirty-five miles west of St. Louis, where their remodeled home was blessed by Martin Hellriegel. The thrust of their work was educational and practical with regard to life skills. They traveled throughout the extensive countryside in their 1929 Model T Ford named "Isabelle." Scholtz provided ongoing spiritual guidance for them. See Pecklers, *Unread Vision*, 168–69; and Marx, *Virgil Michel*, 149; Marlett, *Saving the Heartland*, 39–40; and Miss Mary, "A Year with the Rural Parish Workers," *Review for Religious* 12 (September 1953): 242–48.

sacramentals in agricultural life.[58] He took as his point of departure the general blessedness of creation and the manifold ways God placed such things in the hands of the church that then raised them up for use by the faithful. Thus, "The Christian is able to continue, in his ordinary occupations, that divine intercourse which he experiences in a supreme degree in the Mass and in the sacraments. The means hitherto are the sacramentals." Material *things* like holy water, blessed bread, candles, palms, ashes, and sacred *actions* such as the sign of the cross, striking the breast as one prayed the *Confiteor*, and genuflecting, were traditional examples of sacramentals. The experience of God was to be found in the joys and trials that accompanied one's station in life, and sacramentals served to join that experience to the wider redemptive work of the church: "Thus the Christian has opportunities to spiritualize his daily life in the home, in the shop, in the office, at recreation, everywhere and throughout the day."[59] Regarding the agricultural blessings, Scholtz honed in on several from the *Ritual* and pointed to their relevance not only for the farmer but for the entire church. These blessings joined urban and non-urban Christian alike. The blessing of bees and the silkworm, which provide wax for church candles and material for altar cloths and vestments, were especially noted.[60]

Martin Hellriegel enjoined the Christian family to make generous use of the church's sacramentals as it lived the liturgical year. He called the Christian family the "Body of Christ in miniature," and the liturgical year, that "sacred cycle of solemnities by which we commemorate and celebrate annually the Work of Redemption." The sacraments and the Eucharist provided the principal means to enter into these sacred cycles. "The sacramentals," he pointed out, "are the completion, unfolding and radiation of the sacrificial sacrament and the six others, either preparing for the sacraments or accompanying us home as we return from them to our work and duties." Sacramentals

---

[58] There were six such articles on the sacramentals. Bede Scholtz, OSB, "Sacramentals: A General Idea," *OF* 4 (1929–30): 545–49; *idem*, "Family Sacramentals," *OF* 5 (1930–31): 115–18; *idem*, "Sacramentals and the Sick," *OF* 5 (1930–31): 158–62; *idem*, "Sacramentals in Industry," *OF* 5 (1930–31): 268–71; *idem*, "Sacramentals: The Sacramentals and Agriculture," *OF* 5 (1930–31): 323–26; *idem*, "Religious Sacramentals," *OF* 5 (1930–31): 400–405.

[59] Scholtz, "Sacramentals: A General Idea," *OF* 4 (1929–30): 545, 548.

[60] Scholtz, "Sacramentals: Sacramentals and Agriculture," *OF* 5 (1930–31): 323–26.

were created by and for the church, and so he asked, "But who is the Church? Is she not the Body of Christ?" The members of the Body of Christ were the very extension of Christ into the world. Therefore, the sacramentals carried eschatological importance: "In bestowing or bringing about a sacramental does the Church not open another gadget of that one great and precious reservoir which holds the living and transforming waters of the Savior . . . a fountain of water springing up into life everlasting?" Liturgy was the common bond that held together family, sacramentals, and liturgical year. Hellriegel recounted a touching story of his mother's devotion and her concern for the poor. Every Christmas and Easter she prepared fifteen to twenty baskets and delivered them to "Christ's poor." One year, after his father had butchered a "hog of fairly large dimensions," his mother began making baskets for the poor such that when she had finished only "one ham and a few sausages" were left. His father inquired, "Mother, for whom did we butcher?" She replied, "For the poor, I mean, for Christ. . . ." Hellriegel noted that this caused "a few tears to roll down my father's cheek as he smiled back to her." To be noted here is the manner in which Hellriegel tied the use of sacramentals to the church's official liturgy. These blessed baskets of food designated for the poor were sacramentals in a most important way.[61]

More specifically, *Orate Fratres* (and *Worship*) treated the topic of liturgy and rural life with some frequency. In general, one can find in both movements the persistent effort to deepen the relationship between the natural and supernatural dimensions of Christian life as experienced in the liturgy and in social action. One of the first explicit connections made between the liturgical and agrarian life in the pages of *Orate Fratres* was a 1929 article about the Assumption of Our Lady. The church affectionately called Mary, the Mother of God, Flower of the Field, Lily of the Valley, and Mystical Rose. Tradition attested to the blessing of herbs and flowers on this August 15 feast day, a practice that dated back to the ninth century. In part, the practice sought to counter "heathen superstitions."[62] This particular blessing was likely based on a popular tradition that after Mary's assumption into heaven

---

[61] Martin B. Hellriegel, "Family Life, The Liturgical Year and the Sacramentals," *National Liturgical Week, 1946* (Elsberry, MO: The Liturgical Conference, 1947), 95, 96, 103.

[62] Dom Otto Haering, "The Assumption of Our Lady," *OF* 3 (1928–29): 289–91. The article was excerpted from his book *Living with the Church*.

flowers were found in her tomb where her body had been. The blessing, which took place during the late bloom of the growing season, asked God to provide for the "welfare of the body" and for protection against diabolical forces.[63] The thrust of the blessing was health and healing for human and nonhuman alike.

Emerson Hynes, a layman and a sociology professor at St. John's, was actively involved in both the rural and liturgical movements. He offered this lucid insight about rural life and liturgy:

> A true rural society is founded in the soil and receives its tone from it. There is a mutual cause-effect relationship between person and soil; the person cultivates the land, and is in turn influenced and shaped by it. A discussion of liturgy and land will have meaning only if one understands that land is the source of this transcendental quality which makes farming a way of life, and not merely an economic occupation.[64]

Soil, like the liturgy, demanded the work of human hands in order to bear fruit. Hynes supported his thesis about land and the liturgy in three ways. First, land naturally disposed one to the nature of the liturgy. A farmer constantly dealt with "birth, maturity and death" directing intelligently all the farm's organic processes and vitality. Farmers tended to take the "long view" of life, since they fulfilled a vocation versus merely "earning a paycheck." The farmer's close proximity to nature's cycles allowed him to more easily assimilate the church's liturgical year, especially with the help of sacramentals from one's own land.[65] Second, land and liturgy played a central role in advancing the liturgical movement, principally through the family and the parish. Liturgy in the farm-home, contrary to the urban household,

---

[63] NCRLC, *Blessing and Prayers for the Feast of the Assumption* (Des Moines, IA: NCRLC, 1955), NCRLC/MUA, Series 5/1, box 2, folder 3. The blessing will be considered in the next chapter. The NCRLC later amplified this blessing from the *Ritual* in its 1946 publication *With the Blessing of the Church* and again in 1955 when it published an entire booklet for the feast, explaining how to incorporate the blessing into the solemn liturgy. See also Martin Hellriegel, "The Apostolate: Towards a Living Parish," *Worship* 30 (1955–56): 469–70; *idem*, Martin B. Hellriegel, "Family Life, The Liturgical Year and the Sacramentals," *National Liturgical Week 1946* (Elsberry, MO: The Liturgical Conference, Inc., 1947), 102.

[64] Emerson Hynes, "Land and Liturgy I," *OF* 13 (1938–39): 540.

[65] Ibid., 544.

was able to extend and deepen the worship of the parish, since "the symbolism of the liturgy—sun, light, wine, bread, beeswax—is based chiefly on nature, and thus intelligible even to the small rural child."[66] Third, land and liturgy revolved around history; the church has had a long-held predilection for agrarian life. This view originated in the Scriptures with its plethora of agricultural imagery and story. Hynes pointed to the Benedictine tradition, Rogation Days, and blessings from the *Ritual*, of which more than half refer directly to things of rural life. Farming, as a way of life, was "the most fully sacramental of all human occupations, and it is honored in accordance with its dignity. . . . One cannot reflect on the status of agriculture in America without realizing how desperately the land needs the liturgy."[67]

Another renowned liturgical leader, Hans Ansgar Reinhold, frequently contributed to *Orate Fratres* and *Worship*. Perhaps it was his pastorate in rural Sunnyside, Washington, that sensitized him to the daily struggles of the farm family. While the church did indeed have an affinity for the agricultural life, Reinhold noted, her solicitude was not always of a practical nature. The church did not take into consideration the great effort a rural family had to exert to get to Sunday Mass after all the morning chores. After all that effort, the family was treated to a twenty-five-minute religious affair.[68] Such an approach to the liturgy was unlikely to grant one a vibrant faith life, elicit conversion, transform attitudes, and bestow on persons a spirit able to discern the modern world that was advancing into the countryside. On one hand, Reinhold encouraged farmers in their vocation, and on the other, he admonished them as they conceded to the crush of agribusiness and its capitalistic drive. "Secular civilization" had invaded the rural areas, and farmers had bought into a suburban lifestyle guided more by *Redbook*, *Time*, and *Life* magazines. The "contrary civilization"

[66] Hynes, "Land and Liturgy II," *OF* 14 (1939–40): 14. See also Emerson Hynes, "Before All Else," *OF* 17 (1942–43): 204–8.

[67] Hynes, "Land and Liturgy II," 16–17. In a related article, it was reported that the 1940 NCRLC convention in St. Cloud, Minnesota, a field Mass was celebrated with nearly ten thousand people lining the banks of the Mississippi River. Two youths processed forward and presented sheaves of wheat and a platter of grapes collected from the fields of various delegates, making a lucid connection between the liturgy and life, such that "the farmer's daily and intimate contact with nature and the cooperation with the organic forces give farming a purpose beyond that of merely supplying physical needs and making money." Editor, "The Apostolate: With our Readers," *OF* 14 (1940): 561, 562.

[68] Hans Ansgar Reinhold, "Timely Tracks: Rural Liturgy," *OF* 18 (1943–44): 367.

was one rooted in the liturgy with its locus and rhythm close to nature.[69] Reinhold argued for a revolution in the countryside, one that countered these negative forces and allowed the farmer to "regain his soil, organize true cooperation, free himself from pressure groups and make life livable again."[70]

Throughout the 1940s the political and economic state of agriculture was still experiencing some of the previous decade's stagnation. The only agricultural enterprises that flourished were the large factory farms. Reinhold severely critiqued such operations and pointed to the liturgical movement as a remedy, since "it [church] has always had an affinity with traditional values, with the natural order, the soil, the family and 'subsidiary' entities of society," all of which evoked a natural sympathy with rural life.[71] Agribusiness did not merely intrude into the countryside; rather, it was destroying an entire way of life. Reinhold noted that the *Ritual*, wisely used for the agricultural blessings, could counter this trend. He also suggested that the *Ritual* needed to be adapted to developments in society as a whole, making it more relevant and keeping people connected to the land.

Over a decade earlier, Reinhold expressed his fine sacramental sense and pointed to the many animate and inanimate forces that combine to make something as ordinary as bread:

> Bread is something we partake of every day, a thing for every person, a part of our life. It is food, daily food. It makes us grow, be strong and healthy. It comes from farms and has in it the sun, the soil, the rain, the wind and all the good forces of creation. Hard work and human art, a simple and beautiful art, millstone, fire and water helped to prepare it. It is not raw nature, but nature ennobled by our work and intelligence. And then the Holy Ghost has transformed it through divine power. It became the vessel of salvation and spiritual nourishment. That is liturgy: consecration of the true and good things, assumption of created things into the eternal and one sacrifice of creation in its head Jesus Christ.[72]

---

[69] Hans Ansgar Reinhold, "Secular and Religious Civilization," *OF* 14 (1939–40): 560.

[70] Reinhold, "Timely Tracks: Rural Liturgy," 366–67.

[71] Reinhold, "Timely Tracks: Back to What?" *Worship* 26 (1951–52): 255.

[72] Reinhold, "More or Less Liturgical," *OF* 13 (1939): 154. Quoted from Kathleen Hughes, ed., *How Firm a Foundation: Voices of the Early Liturgical Movement* (Chicago, IL: Liturgy Training Publications, 1990), 207.

Rural life, its completeness, afforded a great opportunity to see that something as simple (and taken for granted) as the making and eating of bread was, in fact, a cosmic event. As such, it represented the wider connectedness of people, events, and material creation—all of which rendered praise to God, through Christ in the Spirit. In some respects, he also articulated a sacramentality of eating and nourishment, preeminently shared in the Eucharist.

Father John Sullivan, SJ, also known as "Fr. Co-op," organized several cooperatives in Jamaica in the late 1930s in response to the desperate conditions of the West Indian nation. The Jamaican cooperatives were based, economically, on the Antigonish and Rochdale models.[73] They differed from these other cooperatives in that they were more liturgically based. Under the guidance of Sullivan, fourteen young men formed "Our Lady's Sodality." Sodalities were a common Jesuit work that attempted to foster daily prayer and charitable action as part of one's occupation. However, this sodality matured into something greater.

After the group had been meeting and reflecting for some time, the young Jamaicans posed the question: how should they respond to the economic and spiritual woes of the people? The question implied "what action" should be taken on behalf of the people, and they sought more than simply doing good works. Sullivan expressed the genesis of their discernment this way:

> But action, we felt, radicated [sic] in thought, in study, in prayer. We formed our study club . . . and discussed but one topic: solidarity with one another in Christ stemming out from the revealed doctrine of the Mystical Body of Christ. . . . For at the end of about six months of discussion and prayer these young men, all Jamaicans, all colored, all Catholic, began to become convinced *subjectively* of the *objective* truth of their solidarity with one another in Christ. . . . They decided to form a co-operative, not an economic co-operative precisely but a

---

[73] Yzerman, *The People I Love*, 154. The "Rochdale model" originated in Rochdale, England, a small textile town of about twenty-five thousand people. In the early 1840s the textile industry (mostly flannels) began to dominate the local economy. As mechanization advanced, workers struggled to maintain the standard of living that they had known in the past. Many weavers lived in poverty and worked up to sixteen hours a day and conditions were wretched. The discontent grew into organization, as a class of self-educated workers formed a successful economic cooperative securing better wages and eventually housing.

co-operative devoted to deepening and expressing that social solidarity. Concretely, that meant for them the introduction of the dialogue Mass.[74]

The discussion of the liturgy and its participative celebration were made integral to the sodality. With the eucharistic celebration as their foundation, these young men wanted their social solidarity to extend into the factories, wharfs, markets, and out into the fields of the impoverished nation. The energetic missionary, Fr. Frank Kemple, SJ, founded and orchestrated the rural cooperatives that liberated the small family farmers from the "ruthless middlemen" who often extorted them. Worship and social action must go hand in hand, and the "exclusively sacramental approach is, generally speaking, hopeless on the mission front." The group reasoned that it was unfair to burden the people to pray as a community when they had no bread in their bellies, as the group's slogan indicated: "No Bread! No Prayer!" or *"Co-op worship to Co-op work!"*[75]

Lastly, a Dominican sister criticized the purely consumerist mentality toward the fruits of the earth and the labor of farmers. Soil and its fruits were treated as "commodities" alone or "problems" to be handled by the government specialist. This technical approach, she declared, had caused a loss in the "awareness of the real and symbolic significance of the fruits of the earth." Such thinking created a chasm between creature and Creator, such that even the believers lost sight of their dependence on God. "The Church through her blessings on plantings and harvests, her Rogation Days, and her blessing of herbs and flowers tries to stir us to acknowledgment of the right order between creature and Creator, co-worker and Master."[76] This "acknowledgment of right order," in many respects, goes to the heart of Christian worship and relates to a key liturgical principle—*anamnesis*.[77] At their core,

---

[74] John Sullivan, "Co-op Worship to Co-op Work," *OF* 19 (1944–45): 320–21.

[75] Ibid., 321, 323–24.

[76] Sister Mary Charity, OP, "Thanking for the Harvests," *OF* 23 (1948–49): 538, 540.

[77] *Anamnesis* is "a liturgical term derived from a Greek word for remembering. Following the Jewish tradition, anamnesis is an active form of memory that connects past and present. It functions in two ways: (1) recollection or memorial of a past event and (2) making the past event, present in ritual celebration. Through anamnesis in the Eucharist, the Church both recalls the Paschal mystery, and makes it sacramentally present for the salvation of the world. Anamnesis follows the command of Christ to 'do this in memory of me.' As part of the Eucharistic Prayer, anamnesis follows the consecration of the elements. It occurs as the offering

sacramentals should lead one to a more profound experience of the liturgy and all that it conveys. Liturgy discloses both the order and disorder in the world. Sacramentals, if they are properly directed toward liturgical celebration, potentially augment *anamnesis* in both communal worship and in daily life.

Those authors who contributed to *Orate Fratres* played a pivotal role in retrieving the sacramental principle, showing how the liturgical movement tried to recover sacramentality in general and situate it within the liturgical life of the church. It was shown that this principle also played a role in the church's social mission, delineating a more balanced relationship between the material and spiritual aspects of creation. These authors also advanced the liturgy's relationship to daily rural life through the wise use of sacramentals. While all this was valuable, it was the liturgical year's close affinity to nature's cycles that gave structure and deeper meaning to the celebration of the sacraments and sacramentals, situating them within the universal church's liturgical life.

---

is made and before the intercessions or second epiclesis. This placement suggests that recalling what Christ has accomplished is a prerequisite to petitioning God." See The Federation of Diocesan Liturgical Commissions (FDLC) website < http://www.fdlc.org/>

Chapter 4

# A Year in the Life of a Rural Parish

The natural and civic cycles of time govern the way people live and work. In most religious traditions, days of celebration or days of penance often originated from significant natural or civic events, and these days became integral to the annual cycle of life. One thing remained constant regardless of religious tradition; these significant religious events occurred in the ordinariness of time wherein people lived and worked. Even the most monumental religious events occur (or occurred) within the daily and mundane course of human life. The Christian tradition was no different. On the day of Christ's birth, for instance, all the world's peoples awoke and went about that day in the fashion to which they were accustomed, even in Bethlehem. The church Christianized many cultural and religious practices, which had been based on the annual cycles of time and nature. This was usually done to counter pagan customs.

The liturgical year was yet another facet of the church's life to which the liturgical movement brought a renewed appreciation. Certainly, Pius Parsch comes to mind in this regard.[1] Rural Catholics had a special interest in and a natural affinity for the pulse of the church's year since many of its celebrations coincided with nature's cycles of planting and harvesting. In a manner reminiscent of Parsch, this chapter considers the *lex orandi* proper, structured around the preconciliar liturgical calendar. It highlights those seasons and feasts that were most relevant to rural Catholics and promoted by the NCRLC. Doing so offers a convenient way to demonstrate how the rural Catholics

---

[1] Pius Parsch, *The Church's Year of Grace*, trans. William G. Heidt (Collegeville, MN: Liturgical Press, 1959).

celebrated the mystery of salvation with the universal church. More-over, it shows how they made wise use of the *Missal, Ritual* (blessings), processions, devotions, and uniquely rural practices to manifest how these saving events were part and parcel of their daily agrarian lives. Rarely could a month go by without celebrating a feast or a blessing that had a connection to rural life.

## ADVENT AND CHRISTMAS

Ember Days clearly had agrarian origins and were made a part of the church's tradition. In the church's calendar, the first of the Ember Days was celebrated in Advent after the feast of St. Lucy (December 13). For reasons unknown, however, Ember Days never achieved the popularity (in terms of observance) that the Rogation Days did among rural Catholics, and represent a missed opportunity by the NCRLC and leaders in the liturgical movement. In spite of this and because of their close connection to the agrarian cycles, they deserve a brief digression and reappraisal for the church today.

In the Judeo-Christian tradition, periods of fasting and feasting often coincided with the change of seasons. Etymologically, the word "ember" originated from the ancient use of *Quattuor Tempora* to designate the four seasons. The term was Germanicized into *Quatember* and eventually shortened to the Anglo form *Ember*. Simply stated, the change of seasons impelled people to acknowledge them whether or not it had a specifically religious meaning. Pagan religions observed what were called *feriae messis, feriae vindemiales,* and *feriae sementinae*— harvest time, vintage time, and seed time. In the Jewish calendar, the month of September was of particular importance, celebrating the civil New Year, the Day of Atonement (Yom Kippur), and the feast of Tabernacles. The Jewish prophetic tradition spoke of "the grain, the wine, and the oil," and reference to these periods had profound theological and eschatological meaning. The prophet Zechariah proclaimed that "The fast days of the fourth, the fifth, the seventh, and the tenth months shall become occasions of joy and gladness, cheerful festivals for the house of Judah; only love faithfulness and peace" (Zec 8:19). Jesus' numerous references to fasting, feasting, and the harvest revealed his familiarity with this tradition.[2]

[2] Thomas Talley, *Origins of the Liturgical Year* (Collegeville, MN: The Liturgical Press/Pueblo, 1986), 148–49.

Christians in the first millennium developed these practices. The community of the *Didache* observed Wednesdays and Fridays as days of fasting in preparation for the celebration of their weekly *synaxis* (assembling to celebrate the Lord's Day). The *Liber Pontificalis* credits Calixtus (mid-second century) with the establishment of Ember Days on Saturdays, yielding the eventual practice of Wednesday, Friday, and Saturday. Only during the time of Leo the Great (d. 461) does one find a more developed thinking on the nature of as well as the specified times for the Ember Days. Leo describes four fasting periods throughout the year: the spring fast at Lent, the summer fast of Pentecost, the autumn fast in the seventh month, and the winter fast of the tenth month. The Roman *Ordines*, especially *Ordo Romanus XXXVIIA* (of Frankish origin ca. 800) also confirm the existence of the fast. As the Roman liturgy spread northward to England and the Germanic lands, practices evolved creating some diversity in their celebration. It also created some confusion regarding the actual practice and dates for the Ember Days. Michel Andrieu observes that Amalarius of Metz (ca. 825), in a letter to Hilduin, expressed uncertainty as to when one should observe the Ember Days (*les dates des Quatre-Temps*). At the Roman Synod of 1078, Gregory VII solidified the dates of Ember Days, observed on Wednesday, Friday, and Saturday following the feast of St. Lucy (December 13), the first Sunday of Lent, Pentecost Sunday, and the Exaltation of the Cross (September 14). These days and dates were observed for nearly a millennium, until their reform in the liturgical calendar in 1970.[3]

It would have seemed that the Lenten Ember Days as well as those of September offered excellent opportunities for rural-oriented liturgies. Lent, with its close proximity to spring, would have joined the work of the penitential season to that of preparing the land for planting. The September Ember Days, closely allied with the thanksgiving harvests,

---

[3] See Paul Jounel, "Sunday and the Week," in *The Church at Prayer: The Liturgy and Time*, ed. A. G. Martimort, 26 (Collegeville, MN: Liturgical Press, 1992); Leo the Great, *Sermons*, trans. Jane Patricia Freeland, CSJB and Agnes Josephine Conway, SSJ, in *The Fathers of the Church* (Washington, DC: The Catholic University of America Press, 1996), 95:368–93; Cyrille Vogel, *Medieval Liturgy: An Introduction to the Sources*, trans. William G. Storey and Niels Krogh Rasmussen (Washington, DC: Pastoral Press, 1981), 178; Michel Andrieu, *Les Ordines Romani Du Haut Moyen Age*, Vol. IV (Louvain: Spicilegium Sacrum Lovaniense, 1971), 213, 235; Adolf Adam, *The Liturgical Year: Its History and Meaning After the Reform of the Liturgy* (New York: Pueblo, 1981), 188.

offered yet another opportunity for communities to join prayer and rural life. One author recommended their observance so as to link rural and urban parishes. The NCRLC suggested that urban pastors take advantage of the Sunday preceding the Ember Days to instruct the faithful about Catholic rural life and to highlight the city's dependence on the agriculture. "Such spiritual cooperation will in turn provide the basis for other forms of cooperation between rural and urban peoples: consumer-producer cooperatives, farmer-labor collaboration, etc."[4] In the end, one finds few references to their observance in the NCRLC literature. Their treatment here points to a missed opportunity that invites further study and application for the contemporary church. So what did the NCRLC actually promote and observe during the season of Advent?

For the universal church, Advent principally meant preparation for the birth of Christ, more than the "dual comings" of Christ emphasized after Vatican II. The Advent-Christmas cycle provided only a few opportunities for rural-oriented liturgy. The most frequently mentioned practice was the three-part blessing of wine brought by the faithful on the feast of St. John, Apostle and Evangelist (December 27). It was a special privilege for the farmer who cultivated vineyards to provide wine for the eucharistic celebration. The blessing invoked the incarnation and temporal birth of the Christ so that he could "seek the lost and wayward sheep . . . and cure the man fallen among robbers of his wounds by pouring wine and oil . . . bless + sanctify this wine." Those who drank the wine received strength of body and soul as they made their pilgrimage on earth back to God. The other parts of the blessing had more to do with the legend surrounding St. John, who drank poisoned wine and was unaffected by it. The sacramental image of wine's (and oil's) healing property was taught by the church fathers and representative of their sacramental worldview. A better connection between liturgy and life during the Advent-Christmas cycle was the blessing of stables. This was contained in *With the Blessing of the Church*:

---

[4] Editor, "The Apostolate: With our Readers," *OF* 14 (1939–40): 475–76; Thomas Allen, OSB, "Rural Pastor's Page: Ember Days and the Land," *Land and Home* (September 1943): 76–77; Mariette Wickes, "A Family Celebration of the Ember Days," *Land and Home* (December 1946): 100–102. Neither article from *L&H* was especially insightful with regard to agriculture. However, both made reference to the "fruits of the earth" and one's responsibility toward the poor, a connection which dates back to the time of Leo the Great.

O Lord, Almighty God, who didst decree that Thy only-begotten Son, our Redeemer, should be born in a stable and laid in a manger between an ox and an ass, bless, we beseech Thee, this stable and preserve it from every deceit and snare of the devil that horses and cattle within it may be healthy and secure from all harm.[5]

Winter involved the stabling of animals. In the NCRLC literature surveyed, this blessing was not too prevalent, but this is not to assert that it did not occur.

## THE LENTEN SEASON

Lent, however, set in motion a particularly intense period of rural-liturgical celebrations. This liturgical season also raised the issue of the "piling up" of activities and feasts during a Proper season. So, for example, to observe three special days of fasting (Lenten Ember Days) during the first week of Lent (which had begun the previous Ash Wednesday), seemed redundant. Such was the recommended practice until the 1970 reform of the church's calendar. In the United States, St. Isidore's feast day was celebrated on March 22 and always fell within the Lenten season.[6] Therefore, around this feast day, the NCRLC observed a number of liturgical, paraliturgical, and devotional activities that served to heighten awareness of the farmer's vocation and his place in the larger redemptive plan. Some of these include *The Novena in Honor of St. Isidore* (March 14–22), *Blessing of Seed and Soil on the Feast of St. Isidore*, St. Isidore Feast Day (Mass Proper), and *A Day of Christian Rural Living*. But who was this holy man St. Isidore, saint of the soil and patron saint of farmers?

Saint Isidore the Husbandman (or Farm Laborer) was born in Madrid, Spain, around the year 1070, and was christened Isidore after the famous bishop of Seville. The family was pious and poor; therefore, it could not afford any kind of schooling for the boy. When Isidore was old enough, he began working as a farm-laborer on the estate of

---

[5] NCRLC, *With the Blessing of the Church*, 9.

[6] The rest of the church celebrated the feast on May 15. In 1963 an interesting note appeared in *Catholic Rural Life*. It announced that St. Isidore's feast day would be moved to October 25. The change, anticipating the reform of Vatican II, was made because the "Mass of Lenten week days now takes precedence over most saints' feast days." Obviously, the change remained in effect for only seven years since the final revision of the calendar in 1970 placed the feast on May 15. See "Feast of St Isidore Now October 25," *Catholic Rural Life* (October 1963): 1.

John de Vergas, a wealthy landowner of Madrid. Isidore married a young woman named Maria Torribia; they had one child who died at a young age. After that, the couple decided to "serve God in perfect continence" for the rest of their lives. Like most farmers, he awoke early so as to be in the fields before the day's sun became too hot for work. He differed from many farmers in that he made daily pilgrimages to several churches while en route to the fields. So devout was he that he regularly arrived later than the other workers, who, consequently, became annoyed and reported Isidore to de Vergas. One morning the landowner hid himself near to where Isidore worked in hope of catching this "slacker" in his employ. True to his daily order, Isidore came late to the fields. As the story has been recounted, de Vergas waited a few moments to watch Isidore begin his work, and just when he was about to confront him, de Vergas noticed something strange. He saw a second team of oxen driven by two unknown figures plowing next to the one Isidore was working. Accounts of the legend vary. Another story claimed that the saint was found deep in prayer (not working), but his fields were mysteriously being plowed. These accounts of the story inspired a depiction of the saint by Sr. Mary Helene, OP, in 1945.[7]

Several other miracles revealed his deep faith in God and his concern for those who were much poorer than he and Maria. People came to know that Isidore was indeed a very pious man. He not only attended Mass but frequently served as an acolyte. It was not uncommon to find a train of beggars following Isidore home, hoping to receive something to eat. One day, a story says, after feeding many poor in their home, a beggar arrived late and asked for food. Maria knew that the pot was empty, but Isidore told her to give him what was left. When she opened the pot, she found it full of food. He also demonstrated love for all God's nonhuman creatures. One winter day, on his way to have a sack of grain ground, he noticed some birds sitting on a barren branch, obviously unable to find anything to eat. Isidore spread half the grain onto the ground and the birds happily flocked to it, a good deed that earned Isidore ridicule from his coworker. When the two arrived at the mill, not only was Isidore's sack full of grain, but, when it was ground, his grain produced a double amount of flour.[8]

---

[7] "St. Isidore the Husbandman," *Butler's Lives of the Saints* (Collegeville, MN: Liturgical Press, 1995), 323. See chap. 2, 36.

[8] Leonard J. Doyle in *St. Isidore Patron of the Farmer* (Des Moines, IA: NCRLC, 1947), 11, 13.

These are stories about a saint—poor, devout, and close to the land and to nature. Daily Mass attendance and service at the altar, reception of Communion, and the praying of Sunday Vespers were routine for Isidore. His faithful work in the vineyard moved his master to place him in charge of more land. Isidore died May 15, 1130, and his body remained incorrupt for some time after death. He and his devoted wife Maria became the first husband and wife pair to be canonized by the church, albeit on different dates. He is the patron saint of Madrid. March 12, 1622, marked the day of Isidore's canonization along with a few other notable figures—Ignatius of Loyola, Francis Xavier, Philip Neri, and Theresa of Avila. Maria de la Cabeza was canonized on August 11, 1697. As a simple, faithful, and loving couple, Isidore and Maria served as ideal intercessors for rural parishes and families, models to follow because of their love for the church's liturgy and Christ's poor—human and nonhuman alike.

The hagiography just described gives some background to examine the *Novena in Honor of St. Isidore Patron of Farmers*. The novena extended beyond a mere recitation of prayers; it represented a synthetic vision of Catholic rural life.[9] Published in 1954, about six years after the Mass proper (1947), it exhibited a strong catechetical thrust that emphasized the farmer's vocation and his responsibility to contribute to a more just social order. Faithful to the liturgical movement's agenda, the NCRLC wished to utilize devotions in order to lead the faithful to a deeper engagement in the liturgy of the church. A glance at the novena's acknowledgments revealed the continued cooperation between the rural life and liturgical movements, drawing upon the expertise of "Fr. Abbot and the monks of St. John's Abbey," who were responsible for the redaction and composition. Clifford Bennett, director of the Gregorian Institute, composed the "Hymn to St. Isidore" for the novena.[10]

---

[9] NCRLC, *Novena in Honor of St. Isidore Patron of Farmers* (Des Moines, IA: NCRLC, 1954). On the last page of the booklet used for the *Blessing of Seed and Soil for St. Isidore Feast Day*, the suggestion is made to pray the novena that, "is much more than a series of prayers. It is a manual of spiritual direction for rural people. It offers select passages from scripture which will renew the spirit and bring peace and joy to the rural family, home and farm."

[10] In NCRLC, *Novena in Honor of St. Isidore Patron of the Farmer*, 43. See Appendix I, where I have transcribed a number of the novena prayers in addition to other rural prayers.

The novena was intended for both parish and home use and was fully participative. Father, mother, or children were encouraged to lead the novena if prayed in the home. The novena's order went as follows:

Hymn (changed each day to match the theme)

Antiphon and Psalm

Scripture with response

Prayer (collect for St. Isidore Mass Proper)

Prayer in Honor of St. Isidore

Reflection

Our Father, Hail Mary, and Glory be (three times each)

Other (optional) Prayers

After singing the hymn, the leader read the beginning of the antiphon and psalm "up to the asterisk," at which point the people joined in unison or alternately. The leader then read a Scripture passage, relevant to the day's theme, after which a variety of "call and response" verses were recited.[11] The leader closed with the prayer used for the opening collect of the Mass Proper of St. Isidore, followed by "Amen/ St. Isidore/Pray for us." The "Prayer in Honor of St. Isidore" was recited by all after which a prepared "reflection" was read and concluded with the Our Father, Hail Mary, and Glory be (three times each). Each day the novena closed by praying one of the following optional prayers: Prayer of the Christian Farmer, Prayer of a Rural Family, Prayer for Rain, Prayer against Pests, Prayer against Storms and Floods, Prayer of Thanksgiving, or the Litany of St. Isidore. Benediction was optional.[12]

Each day of the novena had certain set prayers, but otherwise the prayers were tailored to a specific rural Christian theme.[13] As the novena's themes indicate, the NCRLC revealed its comprehensive

---

[11] For example, Day One: Partnership with God used Genesis 1:25 and 2:15 followed by, **R:** Thanks be to God. **V:** You raise grass for the cattle and vegetation for men's use. **R:** Producing bread from the earth, and wine to gladden men's hearts. **V:** The Lord be with you. **R:** And with your spirit.

[12] See Appendix I; in NCRLC, *Novena in Honor of St. Isidore Patron of Farmers*, 6. The *Prayer in Honor of St. Isidore* was composed by Bishop Schlarman in 1936 following the NCRLC's Fargo convention. It was not the one used for the prayer card drawn up in 1947. See Witte, *Crusading*, 141.

[13] See Appendix I.

approach to Catholic rural life. The novena's primary purpose was to "inspire rural people anew with the dignity of their vocation," understanding that dignity as a veritable partnership with God in his creative work. The farmer cooperated with God in bringing about the earth's fruitfulness, ultimately for the well-being of the human family. The earth's fruitfulness was intimately joined to Christian spiritual growth. Family life, love of neighbor, and walking in the presence of God (Days 2, 3, 5) were deemed essential to the unity and vitality of the Mystical Body of Christ.

In the purview of the NCRLC, essential to this vitality of the Mystical Body of Christ was concern for the land; its stewardship was fundamental to a well-lived rural Catholic life. The reflection for Day Six, "Stewardship of Soil," relied upon the thought of Liberty Hyde Bailey, one of America's most famous agrarians and the founder of Cornell University's agricultural college. This was a rather bold move for a Catholic devotional pamphlet in that Bailey was not Catholic but had a Masonic background. Further, at the turn of the century, amid the Catholic church's battle with Modernism, Bailey blended his philosophy and theology with his science, which could have be construed as Deist or pantheist. He saw no conflict between evolution and religion. Nonetheless, he had a keen sense that proper care of the earth was intimately bound up with human welfare: "He [farmer] must handle all his materials, remembering man and remembering God."[14]

"Day Seven: Rural Works of Mercy" honored St. Isidore and St. Maria for the charity they showed to the destitute of their day in spite of their own material poverty. This day's reflection encouraged farmers to care for one's neighbor but went even further. Older farmers were encouraged to mentor younger farmers with less experience and urged young people to remain on the land. The rural faithful were told to take an active role in improving school and health systems in the countryside. Finally, the novena reflection suggested to farmers that they become more aware of those farmers in other countries who were less fortunate and "who comprise three-fourths of the world's population in other lands."

Following on this wider social concern, the last two days of the novena had a decidedly liturgical emphasis. "Day Eight: Trust in

---

[14] NCRLC, *Novena in Honor of St. Isidore*, 24. The quote from Bailey comes from his book *Holy Earth*. See also Alan Carlson, *The New Agrarian Mind*, 7–30. Luigi Ligutti fostered much cooperation between Catholics and Masons.

Prayer" highlighted the importance of daily prayer in the life of the farmer, mentioning St. Isidore's daily church visits as he went to work in the fields. The novena reflection stressed that the farmer's religious life revolved around the parish where one celebrated baptism, confirmation, penance, marriage, and above all, shared in the Eucharist. It also emphasized that the rural pastor's mission field was not just the parish and the diocese but the entire world.

The last day of the novena, entitled "Sacrifice of Praise," concluded on March 22, when the community celebrated the feast of St. Isidore. The novena antiphon read, "Whatever you do in word or in work, do all in the name of the Lord Jesus, giving thanks to God the Father through him." This was followed by the recitation of Psalm 23, a favorite of the early church writers because of its sacramental themes. The Scripture for the day was Hebrews 10:12-14: "Jesus, having offered one sacrifice for the forgiveness of sins. . . . For by one offering he has perfected those who are sanctified." The reflection, naturally, mentioned the farmer's nearness to the materials that gave the church her sacramental life, especially the Eucharist. The emphasis on the consecrated elements was primarily as "spiritual food." The sheaf of wheat and vine of grapes served as the preeminent symbol of the Holy Eucharist, adorning "tabernacle and altar as symbols to give vivid expression to this great and loving mystery of our Catholic faith. These symbols were revealed in art and architecture, and served as the content of many hymns."[15] Thus, even in its official novena, the NCRLC grounded its mission in the spiritual font of the church's worship and social teaching. By 1956 over 100,000 novena pamphlets had been distributed.

*The Blessing of Seed and Soil for the Feast of St. Isidore* is instructive on many fronts and underscores several of the liturgical movement's guiding principles. This rather "simple and noble" blessing ceremony also illustrates how the church's *lex orandi* can potentially and more directly inculcate right belief and action.[16] The ceremony was fully

[15] NCRLC, *Novena in Honor of St. Isidore*, 35. The reflection came from Aloisius Muench's *Partnership with God* (Des Moines, IA: NCRLC, 1941).

[16] The salient parts of this blessing liturgy, which preceded Mass, have been summarized in Appendix V. It should be noted that this blessing liturgy, and others like it, did not always simply transcribe the ceremony from the Roman Ritual. There was some creativity, which in most cases required ecclesiastic approval. It was often granted by those bishops in dioceses where the NCRLC was active. This

participative.[17] It was led by the priest but provided significant roles for the assembly—clearly dialogic in nature, and communal. It may be argued that the liturgy's procession actually began at home as soon as the people gathered themselves and their gifts and directed their attention toward God and the church. They brought something "material" from their homes and farms, which was, in the first place, a gift from God (soil and seed). Yet, it was properly theirs and central to their way of life. The blessing itself—words about God, creation, and people who are creation's stewards—served as a solemn reminder of their dignity as baptized Christians and their unique vocation as farmers. The significance of actually uttering the blessing with one's own voice, in a language that was intelligible and with the gathered community, should not be underestimated. The ceremony involved the key facets of liturgical prayer—blessing, petition, and thanksgiving. The assembly sang two songs, one about the work of the Spirit, yet reflecting orthodox trinitarian belief. The other song beseeched God through Christ, in the Spirit, to make "that work of ours and grace of yours . . . bring the increase that endures."[18] While the blessing could be done in the home, its celebration with the gathered community was preferred.

The blessing oriented those who will use the soil and seed toward God and God's plan of salvation. The farmer and the community, as baptized Christians, have already been made part of the redemptive narrative through baptism. The blessing enabled the farmer's unique life context (narrative) to be more deeply joined to the larger salvific account; this fortified Christian identity. The farmer did not merely partake in a blessing of soil and seed; no, the farmer participated,

---

raises some interesting ecclesiological questions with regard to the local church, liturgical adaptation, and the power of the ordinary (see SC 22.2). In this ceremony, the actual words of the blessing of soil and seed did come directly from the Roman Ritual, while other (non-official) parts were creatively assimilated into the ceremony. See *The Roman Ritual: The Blessings in Latin and English with Rubrics and Planechant Notation*, translated and edited by Philip T. Weller, vol. 3 (Milwaukee: Bruce, 1946), 353, 355. Weller was aided in this translation of the *Ritual* by Godfrey Diekmann, OSB, and Reynold Hillenbrand. Ibid., iii.

[17] It appears that the blessing was said *first* in English (people) and then in Latin (priest and people). The repetition of the blessing was often in English after the official Latin rendition. Weller, in fact, specifically noted this practice. The simple purpose was to aid the people's understanding and participation.

[18] The chant's lyrics can be found in Appendix I.

*hic et nunc*, in the realization of Christ's salvific mission. The blessing liturgy helped to locate the particularities of one's life (culture) within the universal *actio* of the eucharistic celebration and thus the whole redemptive action. As stewards of God's manifold gifts, partners with God, the farmer begs: "Take infertility from the earth, and fill the hungry with Thy gifts, which the fruitful earth will yield in fullness, that the poor and needy may praise the name of Thy glory forever and ever. Amen." Concern for the earth and the poor called the rural Catholic to live out what he or she just celebrated.

In short, the blessing of soil and seed provides one example of how the *lex orandi* is able to straightforwardly express orthodox belief and encourage that social charity be put into practice (*lex orandi, lex credendi, lex vivendi*). Furthermore, the prayers were uttered in a language reflective of a unique culture (rural). They were noble, simple, and intelligible. The work of God (*opus Dei*) mediated through liturgical prayer (*leitourgia*) was drawn into closer union with the daily work (*opus, ergon*) of human hands. Liturgy was expressive of God and life. In some respects, the liturgy began at home with things and people; both passed through the prism of the church's prayer, which is trinitarian, paschal, and communal. The liturgy—prayer, things, and people—concluded at the farm-home where the blessed soil and seed were returned to God's good earth that brought them forth. A crop's growth as well as the Christian's was of the *one* salvific narrative.[19]

On February 22, 1947, St. Isidore was declared the official patron of the NCRLC, even though he had long unofficially been claimed as patron saint of farmers. The Sacred Congregation of Rites granted all dioceses of the United States permission to celebrate the March 22 feast "with the rank of greater-double and with a proper Mass and an Office approved for it." Isidore's feast day was moved to May 15 in the postconciliar reform of the liturgical calendar. In honor of his being

---

[19] Bill Busch's keen insight about what liturgical prayer "does" seems prophetic in light of the above discussion and deserves to be repeated: "Prayer not only implores and honors God, it also educates mankind. This is especially true of liturgical prayer. The liturgy well understood will show us the meaning of the Christian religion in all its scope. The *lex orandi* will help us to know the *lex credendi* and the *lex agendi* [*vivendi*]. We shall be conscious once more of our social solidarity in Christ. We shall see a transformation of social life, agricultural, industrial and political. If this is too much to hope for Christian nations, then the outlook of the modern world is dark indeed." William Busch, "Liturgy and Farm Relief," *Catholic Rural Life* 8 (April 1930): 2.

made patron saint of the NCRLC, Fr. Joseph Urbain published *St. Isidore Patron of the Farmer*. The pamphlet contained the Mass Proper, the Prayer of the Christian Farmer, a Rural Family Prayer, a Christian Farmer's Creed, Suggested Family Practices, along with other suggestions for Participation in Rural Parish Life.[20] Urbain also composed the "Litany of St. Isidore" for the pamphlet, which carried the proviso that it be said only as a private devotion. Later, the litany was added to the list of optional prayers to be said at the end of each day of the novena. The litany's "for private devotion only" caution was somewhat unfortunate since it evoked images from the life of St. Isidore and the rural way of life, virtues extolled by rural Catholics.[21]

For the Mass Proper, there was ample Scripture with agrarian imagery; this made for an easy connection to the life of the farmer. However, because God's word was proclaimed in the context of the Eucharist, it also had the effect of bestowing greater dignity on the farmer's vocation. This liturgy espoused, above all, the virtues of patient faith and humility. The Mass introit was taken from Psalm 92: "The just shall flourish like the palm tree. . . ." The feast's Scripture readings came from the letter of James 5:1-8, 11, 16-18: "Be patient, therefore brethren . . . the farmer waits for the precious fruit of the earth, being patient until it receives the early and late rain." The gospel, John 15:1-7, "I am the true vine, and my Father is the vinedresser . . ." certainly resonated with the farmer. The vinedresser represented the farmer; thus, "In his very trade, the farmer imitates God."[22] The agrarian imagery of the epistle and gospel afforded pastors the opportunity to develop an appropriately tailored sermon for the rural faithful. In fact, the NCRLC received repeated requests from pastors for "rural sermon helps." The epistle from James was also used for the Rogation Day liturgies, reinforcing what was heard during the Mass of the feast day. The day's collect begged St. Isidore's intercession to grant humility to those who work the land.[23] The virtues of

[20] Joseph Urbain, *St. Isidore: Patron of the Farmer* (Des Moines, IA: NCRLC, 1947). See also "Rural Pastor's Page, Litany to St. Isidore," *Land and Home* (September 1945): 77.

[21] See Appendix I.

[22] John Hennig, OFM, "Prayers for Farmers," *OF* 18 (1943–44): 497. Additionally, *Orate Fratres* was known for the artwork that adorned its pages. At the end of Hennig's article, one finds a papal tiara looking very much like a beehive (cross on top and small entrance below) with several bees busily at work.

[23] Urbain, *St. Isidore: Patron of the Farmer*, 4–6.

faith and humility, important for any Christian, did possess greater immediacy for the farmer. Even if the farmer did practice his art wisely, there were still many factors simply out of his control that required his deep trust and patience. Also of note were the references to justice or the just man, which came to the one who walked with humility (from *humus*, earth, soil). No farmer's harvest was genuine, declared Hennig, which overlooked the responsibility to be generous toward the poor.[24] The liturgy made clear connections to the farmer's life situation; combined as it was with the other activities around the feast day made for a potentially formative week.

Urbain's pamphlet also contained a *Christian Farmer's Creed*, which was more vocational than confessional. It spoke of farming as a noble Christian occupation and the farm home as ideal for rearing a family. The earth was God's greatest material gift to humanity. The farmer acted as a conserver of the soil and steward of God's gifts so that the fruits may be justly distributed. The creed ended by stating that "by neighborliness and Christian living we shall draw more to the Faith." The pamphlet also recommended participation in many parish life activities such as rural life communion Sundays, rural retreats, blessings of fields, fruits, animals, rural study clubs, and offering of the firstfruits to the Lord.[25]

The ceremony *A Day of Christian Rural Living* evolved from "Rural Life Sunday," which had been a part of the NCRLC's program since the early 1930s. The celebration of *A Day of Christian Rural Living* involved both official and unofficial liturgical prayer. It was a fully participative prayer service that included prayers recited in unison, processions, and blessings. Father Irvin Will (Diocese of Springfield, Illinois) confirmed that this ceremony was the work of the "priests of Lafayette," Joseph Gremillion, Alfred Sigur, and Joseph Lerschen.[26]

---

[24] Hennig, "Prayer for Farmers," 498.

[25] See Appendix I.

[26] *A Day of Christian Rural Living* (Franklin, IL: Catholic Rural Life Conference of Springfield, IL, ca. 1951) in MUA/NCRLC, Series 5/1, box 2. Hereafter, CRLC (IL), *Day of Christian Rural Living*. N.B. This ceremony is very similar, but distinct from the one I have transcribed for Appendix II (also called *A Day of Christian Rural Living*). I am using here the one published by the Diocese of Springfield. Joseph Gremillion is the author of the ceremony; he replicated and adapted its structure for Thanksgiving Day as well (see Appendix III). See Joseph Gremillion and Alfred Sigur, "Joint Report from the Diocese of Lafayette and Alexandria," MUA/NCRLC, Series 8/1, box 10, folder "National Convention, Saginaw, Oct 17–22, 1953"; and

The ceremony took place sometime during Lent, but it was unclear on which day, and none was suggested. One notable event, yet to be mentioned, was the proximity of the vernal equinox (March 21) to the feast of St. Isidore.[27] There was a possibility that this ceremony could have been held in conjunction with the equinox as part of an entire week of rural devotions and activities. The ceremony began: "IN THE NAME OF OUR LORD JESUS CHRIST—We welcome all of you to this Spring ceremony of the Rebirth of Man and Nature." The brief introduction wove a sound paschal theology with agrarian themes:

> The Season of Spring is the season of renewal. The plants and trees are reborn after the death-like sleep of winter. The farmer prepares for this rebirth by plowing and harrowing the fields, by pruning the trees. Similarly in the liturgical year of Christ's Mystical Body on Earth, Spring is a season of rebirth, climaxed by the Resurrection of Christ from the dead on Easter Sunday. And this too must be preceded by a season of preparation, plowing and harrowing through forty days of Lent, the time of penance and self-sacrifice, the season of inward renewal of the life that really counts. The full meaning of the ceremony is made clear in the words of the ceremony itself.[28]

---

Diocese of Springfield, Illinois Archives, "Catholic Rural Life Bulletins, 1951–66," 22. These bulletins are distinct from the NCRLC's publication of the same name. This bound volume records fifteen years of rural life activity in the diocese—liturgies, study clubs, talks, and conferences. The diocese had one of the most active diocesan rural life conferences in the country.

[27] The connection to the first day of spring did not escape the attention of Joseph Morrison, who pointed (tongue in cheek) to another March 21 coincidence: "My Lord Luigi [Ligutti], was born on the feast of St. Benedict [preconciliar date], hence his love for the liturgy, and the first day of spring, hence his devotion to rural life." See Joseph Morrison, "Using Sacramentals," *OF* 24 (1950–51): 129. One could also add March 19, the feast of St. Joseph, making for a series of celebrations connected to "working folk."

[28] CRLC (IL), *Day of Christian Rural Living*. The basic structure was as follows: I. Why we are here; II. The Wonder of the New Life of Nature ("Men" enter center aisle bearing soil and seeds of wheat, corn beans, hay, fruit and vegetables and place them on a table in the sanctuary); III. The Need for Re-birth within Ourselves; IV. The Joy and Love of Family and Home (Boy and girl enter bearing wedding rings, accompanied by servers with marriage ritual, and holy water); V. Gifts of Redemption (Men enter bearing image of Divine Infant, Crucifix, and Bible); VI. Sermon (optional); VII. Benediction of the Most Blessed Sacrament and Prayer to St. Isidore; VIII. Blessing of Soil and Seed (Blessing/Sprinkling of

The prayer service combined official blessings from the *Ritual*—in participative format—with specially crafted prayers that were recited by the assembly. These prayers were verbose yet quite instructive by their attempt to make direct reference to the lives of farmers. Seed and soil, wedding rings, tractors, farm implements, and animals were also blessed at the close of the ceremony.[29]

The ceremony's sound paschal theology, combined with its participative features and reference to the Mystical Body of Christ, made for good ecclesiology as well: "The persons who bear the Symbolic Gifts up the aisle are the representatives of ALL OF US, of OUR ENTIRE DIOCESE." The presentation of the gifts, an ancient and important liturgical action, had long fallen out of use. The NCRLC clearly played a central role in resurrecting this ancient practice, related as it was to the community's offering of gifts for the eucharistic celebration and to benefit the poor. Overall, the specially crafted prayers put forward an easily understood theology of rural life, expressed in a manner that was at once cosmic and quotidian, universal and folksy. The people approached the altar in a spirit of humility and gratitude as they presented these "tokens and symbols" of God's "daily kindness" to them—soil and seed. God gave the "gift of Physical life," manifested in the sun, rain, soil, seed, fruits, and vegetables that provided food and clothing for human welfare. The people prayed: "All these ordinary things of everyday life are astounding manifestations of your power and wisdom and love."[30]

The ceremony then turned to the need for personal and communal rebirth. It described how in the divine plan the earth has once again made its yearlong journey around the sun and has marked the beginning of spring. Spring marshaled in new life—the good earth is born again, but the people begged: "Lord, we too, need to be renewed." The poetic prayer for rebirth equated the language of one who worked the fields with the discipline of Lent so as to usher in a just and fruitful harvest:

---

envelopes of soil and seed brought by the families); IX. Procession out of the church to bless/sprinkle tractors (vehicle), farm implements, and farm animals.

[29] As Gremillion noted, the ceremony did not have an *imprimatur*; thus, one required special episcopal permission to use it. See Appendix III.

[30] CRLC (IL), *Day of Christian Rural Living*, "The Wonder of the New Life of Nature."

Just as the fields must be plowed and harrowed in order that the seed can bring new life and a good crop . . . so must we plow and harrow our own selves. By prayerful thought we must turn over the great truths of life in our minds. With the pulverizing harrow of fasting we must crush the hardness of our hearts. . . . We must pull out the weeds of passion and we must root up our habits of sin . . . to bring forth the harvest of peace here on Earth and the joy of life everlasting with you in our heavenly home.[31]

At work here was an asceticism that has long been associated with agrarianism. The seasons were a given, but *they* regulated the farmer's life in a manner that did not impact an urban dweller to the same extent. As each season approached, farm life demanded specific tasks that governed the farmer's daily activities. To neglect or grow slack in such daily duties could adversely affect the farmer's livelihood. The farmer knew better than anyone that "for everything there is a season" (Eccl 3:1ff.). Such an awareness of the seasons and their demands is something almost completely lacking in modern society, where everything seems to be available at all times, so that people come to expect it that way. Most important, such asceticism was ultimately joined to the fruit of the physical and spiritual harvest. A bountiful harvest was never for the benefit of a single family, no matter how hard it worked, but for the human family. The NCRLC placed this understanding of harvest at the heart of its program. The asceticism set forth by the Conference was balanced, benefiting the farmer's overall life and health; rarely was asceticism expressed in penitential terms alone. Days of fasting and discipline made those of feasting all the more joyful.

The quality of family life also held a central place among rural Catholics. As rings were blessed, the assembly thanked God for entrusting to mothers and fathers the "seed of life" and allowing them to become "co-creators" with God. True happiness was nurtured in the sanctuary of the home. The family rosary was prayed so as to "relive in thought and prayer Christ's own life on earth." It was also incumbent upon a family not only to share one another's joys and sorrows but to share those in the life of one's neighbors. The prayer for the "Gifts of Redemption" spoke of the incarnation and life of Jesus Christ who shared completely in our human experiences and of "working as

[31] CRLC (IL), *Day of Christian Rural Living*, "The Need for a Rebirth within Ourselves."

a carpenter in the little farming town of Nazareth." The ceremony acknowledged the centrality of the cross and how Christ's death gave a new life of grace to the faithful and established his church. These Christ-events brought the new life that comes to the church through her liturgical and sacramental celebrations.[32]

Finally, the "Blessing of Soil and Seed" was recited by the assembly. Once again, the words conveyed a profound and accessible theology of agrarianism. The blessing began with the solemn reminder of their "dignity and calling as farmers," making them coworkers with God. Soil assumes the nature of a sacrament and the farmer's relationship to the land carries covenantal overtones: "We bring before you this bit of soil from the land through which you gave us life. For this soil we are grateful . . . we know in all truth that this land is yours."[33] The practice of stewardship emerged as well, since the soil and land— these many acres of life-giving ground—were held in "trust." As is the case with all gifts, at the end of time the Lord will call his people to give account of their stewardship of these gifts. The NCRLC made it clear that this was no "privatized" notion of getting into heaven; it ascertained a sense of eschatological justice, reminiscent of Matthew's gospel, chapter 25: "To you one day we must answer for the way we have used this soil which you have loaned to us; and we must answer, too, for the way in which we have used the harvest and the gain of our partnership with you." The value of seed was expressed in paschal terms: "What a great mystery we hold here in our hands. These small seeds apparently lifeless and dead will burst forth from the ground with young vibrant strength." The assembly prayed that God would "cultivate the garden of our souls" so that life everlasting might be their final harvest. Individual envelopes brought by parishioners, holding soil and seed, were then blessed. This was separate from the soil and seed that was carried forth in the opening procession.[34]

---

[32] CRLC (IL), *A Day of Christian Rural Living*, "The Joy and Love of Family and Home" and "Gifts of Redemption."

[33] CRLC (IL), *A Day of Christian Rural Living*, "Blessing of Soil and Seed." This was an oft-repeated insight by the NCRLC, namely, that soil was God's greatest material gift to humanity. The farmer was called to acknowledge God as the giver and to receive it in a manner in keeping with his dignity as a steward of such gifts. It should be noted that these blessings are not from the Roman Ritual. Cf. Weller, *Ritual*, #27, 103.

[34] NCRLC, *A Day of Christian Rural Living*, "Blessing of Soil and Seeds."

*A Day of Christian Rural Living* communicated, by way of a participative liturgical rite, themes such as the vocation of the farmer, soil as
sacrament, stewardship, family life, and justice—liturgy expressed
life. While the prayers and blessings were somewhat verbose, their
language was intelligible. Such ceremonies helped to anchor the
NCRLC's wider spiritual program.

By the early 1950s, for nine days in March (Lenten season), a rural
parish could have done the following: (1) prayed the novena;
(2) blessed soil, seed, and farm instruments; (3) observed *A Day of
Christian Rural Living* (possibly on the first day of spring); and (4) celebrated the Mass Proper of St. Isidore. On one hand, all such rural life
activities gave cause for rejoicing and served as signs of a vibrant rural
parish life. On the other hand (and the council fathers of Vatican II
realized this), all these activities could have been a serious disruption
of the Lenten season. But were they? The novena and the *Day of
Christian Rural Living* provided an opportunity for a deepened prayer
life—one of Lent's three central disciplines of fasting, prayer, and
almsgiving. Not only did the church (along with the NCRLC) encourage fasting, but it did so in a manner that made plain sense to farmers,
for it was connected to the planting and harvesting cycles—periods of
great anxiety for farmers. Might this practice of asceticism have helped
the farmer keep his mind and heart focused? Finally, the prayers and
reflections made clear the responsibility farmers had toward the poor
in being good stewards of the gifts they had been given.

THE EASTER SEASON

The Easter season afforded several opportunities for rural liturgical
practices. While a particular blessing of food (distinct from meals)
could be done anytime, the Easter season was a privileged time to do
so. It was the practice of the early church as the sacramentaries indicate. But the blessings of food grown (or raised) by farmers had a
special significance that was unique to their life and vocation. More
generally, food was connected to the overall health and well-being
(*salus*) of the people who consumed it. The new life associated with
the "Blessing of Eggs" reminded one of Christ's resurrection. The
"Blessing of Bread and Cake" brought to mind the Eucharist and the
way in which "the early Christians brought bread to the altar in the
offertory procession to receive a blessing after the consecration" and
then took it home to be eaten. One has to wonder, though, how the
"health of body and mind" was related to the "Blessing of Bacon or

Lard," an "effective remedy for the human race."[35] Nonetheless, these blessings helped to connect the liturgy at the altar to the liturgy in the home.

Among the rural-liturgical activities during the Easter season, the Rogation Days were by far the most commonly observed. Rogation Days (from *rogare*, to petition or beg) are of ancient origin and developed around two feasts in the Easter season. They were basically days of fasting and prayer. The first, called the *litania maior* because it included a litany (and procession), was the older of the two observances. Its April 25 celebration was on the feast of St. Mark and had a tenuous connection to agriculture. It was likely observed by the church to counter the pagan feast and procession associated with *Robigalia*, which honored the god *Robigo*. Pagan devotees made sacrifice to this god or goddess to protect the harvest against blight or perhaps rust, a wheat fungus that destroyed the crops. The April 25 pagan procession began at the Flaminian Gate and wound its way through Rome to the Milvian Bridge. It concluded by sacrificing a lamb at a sanctuary on the Claudian Way. To counter this pagan procession, Gregory the Great (ca. 590) began the St. Mark procession at the church of St. Lawrence (nearest the Flaminian Gate), stopped to make a "station" at the church of St. Valentine (near the Milvian Bridge), and then veered toward St. Peter's Basilica for the celebration of the Mass and litanies. The Rogation Days that preceded the feast of the Ascension (*litania minor*, since they were established later), were geared toward the protection of harvests. These later-established days originated in the fifth century in Dauphiny (France) and were introduced into Rome by Leo III around 816.[36]

Observance of Rogation Days was an explicit way in which the NCRLC melded liturgy and rural life. Recall that Bill Busch gave them new emphasis in his article on liturgy and farm relief, making them integral to Rural Life Sundays. When *Orate Fratres* offered reflections on the church year, inevitably the Rogation Days were mentioned in connection to agriculture. The days around Ascension were "set apart to supplicate the blessings of God upon us, the first fruits of redemption, as well as upon the fruits of the earth," said Martin Hellriegel.[37]

[35] NCRLC, *With the Blessing of the Church*, 22–27.

[36] Adolf Adam, *The Liturgical Year: Its History and Meaning After the Reform of the Liturgy* (New York: Pueblo, 1981), 191–92.

[37] Hellriegel, "Brief Meditations on the Church Year: Fifth Sunday after Easter," *OF* 18 (1943–44): 292.

In spite of their widespread practice, it would not be until 1953 that the Diocesan Rural Life Conference of Springfield, Illinois, prepared *A Manual of Ceremonies for the Parish Observance of the Rogation Days.*[38]

The introduction to this *Manual* (catechetical in nature) implored God to protect body and soul, and declared that, through the "Sacrifice of the Mass and the Procession on the Rogation Days," we try:

> To move ourselves to penance, arouse confidence and trust in God, acknowledge publicly our dependence on God, ask for plentiful harvest, thank God publicly for the harvest, show publicly our faith, hope and love, and to realize that only through living according to God's will and commandments may they possess a happy, contented, peaceful existence.[39]

The Rogation Day ceremony consisted simply of a procession, during which the Litany of the Saints was recited or sung, followed by the celebration of Mass. The *Manual* provided an English-Latin translation for the litany and an English-only translation for the Mass Proper. The *Missal*, while noting when the days were to be observed, did not provide a rubric to bless anything, let alone fields and animals; rather, the blessing was presumed to be carried out based upon the ancient tradition and practice. In fact, the only noteworthy rubric in the *Manual* pertained to the actual procession: "Procession is according to the custom of the parish. No religious procession may go beyond the limits of the church property without the express permission of the Ordinary." Rural dioceses associated with the NCRLC often received this permission.

Of particular note in the introduction to the *Manual* was the emphasis on the ceremony's public character. Public worship gave witness to faith and, one hoped, a faith reflected in Christians who were living

---

[38] *A Manual of Ceremonies for the Parish Observance of the Rogation Days* (Des Moines, IA: NCRLC, 1953), MUA/NCLRC, Series 5/1, box 3 (hereafter NCRLC, *Manual*). The *Manual* was yet another fruit of the Priest' Rural Life Study Club under the direction of Fr. Irvin Will in the Diocese of Springfield, IL. Among the many articles in *Orate Fratres*, the following were most relevant: A Sister of the Most Precious Blood, "The Apostolate: Ascension Week in the Classroom," *OF* 19 (1944–45): 279; Sister Mary Charity, OP, "Thanking for the Harvests," *OF* 23 (1948–49): 540; Martin Hellriegel, "Brief Meditations on the Church Year: Fifth Sunday After Easter," *OF* 18 (1943–44): 291–308; *idem*, "The Apostolate: Seasonal Suggestions," *OF* 30 (1955–56): 374–77.

[39] NCRLC, *Manual*, Introduction.

justly. The liturgical movement fostered a deeper awareness of the significance of public ritual, understood as essential to the social character of worship. Public worship, as well as worship in the home, called one to a greater accountability for living more authentically the mystery one celebrated. Such thinking supported the liturgical movement's stance against devotions practiced in an excessively private and individualistic manner.

The *Manual's* (and the *Missal's*) only clear reference to the farmer occurred in the litany. The petition was made to protect the people against tempest, earthquake, plague, famine, and to guard the fruits of the earth. It is uncertain whether St. Isidore and St. Maria, who were not included in the general litany, may have been invoked *ad libitum*. The daily Mass of Rogation Days used the reading from James 5:7, "Be patient . . . the farmer waits for the precious fruit of the earth . . ." but otherwise lacked explicit reference to agriculture. These days were celebrated whether or not calamity was imminent. The Roman Missal's rubric stated that the Mass may be said *during* or after the procession. The theme "ask and receive," which began with the gospel for the fifth Sunday of Easter (John 16:23-30), was reinforced during the Rogation Day Masses. The penitential emphasis interrupted the joyful season of Easter, something that even surprised Amalarius of Metz.[40] In spite of these limitations, as early as 1929 the Conference had designated the fifth Sunday of Easter as "Rural Life Sunday." This would have set in motion other rural life activities that augmented the Rogation Days proper.

The May 3 feast of "The Finding of the Holy Cross" (or on the Sunday following) afforded the opportunity to bless crosses that would be placed in fields, vineyards, or gardens. The practice likely originated in Europe in the Middle Ages. The blessing's theme united the suffering endured by Christ on the wood of the cross with the hope of a fruitful harvest.

> Almighty, everlasting God, Father of goodness and consolation . . . in virtue of the bitter suffering of thy Son . . . endured for us sinners on the wood of the Cross, bless + these crosses which thy faithful will erect in their vineyards, fields, and gardens. Protect the land where

---

[40] Amalarius wondered how and why the church could let such a practice evolve, quoting the "Holy Fathers" who forbade fasting in the holy season. See Adolf Adam, *The Liturgical Year*, 190–91.

they are placed from hail, tornado . . . and every assault of the enemy, so that their fruits ripened to the harvest may be gathered to thy honor by those who place their hope in the holy Cross. . . .[41]

Surprisingly, NCRLC literature made scant mention of this practice. The blessing of crosses on this feast held much potential for its proximity to Good Friday—*Ecce lignum crucis*! Wood has played a pivotal role throughout salvation history as the church fathers often noted. The cross that the farmer passed each day in his fields represented a blessing of his work, and reminded him (anamnesis) that his labor too was part of Christ's redemptive work.

## TEMPUS AD ANNUM

For the vigil of the birthday of John the Baptist, he who testified to the light (John 1:7), the *Ritual* suggested the blessing of a bonfire. The feast day was clearly of ancient origin, but the tradition of keeping a night vigil that included a bonfire was less certain. The blessing's overtones were reminiscent of the words that blessed the Easter fire: "O Lord God . . . unfailing Ray and Source of all light, sanctify + this new fire, and grant that after the darkness of this life we may come unsullied to thee Who are Light eternal."[42] As was the case with the vernal equinox, the nearness of the summer solstice (June 21) to the birthday of the Baptist (June 24) suggested another confluence of ecclesial and natural cycles. Depending on the date of Easter, the bonfire blessing had the potential to reinforce the significance of the Easter fire and the fire associated with Pentecost. The blessing of a bonfire was promoted in the Conference's "Catholic Rural Life Page," a publication widely distributed to Catholic and civic newspapers. Additionally, John the Baptist's feast day was also an opportunity to bless baptismal fonts. Again, this afforded an opportunity to deepen the baptismal character associated with Easter and Pentecost as well as with the blessing of nature.[43]

[41] Weller, *Ritual*, #24. See also John Hennig, "Prayers for Farmers," *OF* 18 (1943–44): 501; Joseph Morrison, "Using Sacramentals," *OF* 24 (1950–51): 131.

[42] Weller, *Ritual*, #25.

[43] Fr. Wilfred, OSB, "Liturgical Feature: St. John the Baptist," *Catholic Rural Life Page*, June 15, 1951, MUA/NCRLC, Series 6/1, box 10. On June 23, 2008, the vigil of the feast of John the Baptist's birth, I was at the Benedictine monastery in Montserrat, Spain, for a conference. In the central plaza at around ten in the evening, a bonfire was lit and blessed. About eight runners arrived, having run up the

Throughout the summer months, the *Ritual*'s blessings were employed to beg God's ongoing protection of the crops.[44] On August 15 summer reached a zenith marked by the celebration of the Assumption, a feast that included a blessing of flowers and herbs. This blessing was of ancient origin (ca. tenth century). In 1955 the Conference published its *Blessings and Prayers for the Feast of the Assumption in Honor of Our Lady of the Fields*. The pamphlet's cover page showed the Blessed Mother standing in a wheat field holding a sheaf of the newly harvested crop and provided a fully participative blessing liturgy in English. While the ceremony blessed many of the first fruits, it focused more on the blessing of various herbs and flowers, alluding to the blessing's healing or medicinal purpose. The introduction spoke of the "temporal prosperity" provided by a harvest that prepared one for eternal happiness. Praise and gratitude for the bounteous harvest that God gave to the farmer was coupled with the stark reminder that thousands of people in other countries "go without daily sustenance, have the poorest clothing, and hardly any shelter."

The pamphlet gave the following rubric: "Immediately preceding Mass, the priest stands before the altar and faces the people, who present sheaves of new grain, the finest fruits of the orchards, garden vegetables, flowers, and new herbs. The following prayers are said and the produce blessed."[45] The *Ritual* specified that if the feast of the Assumption fell on Sunday, the blessing was done immediately following the *Asperges*. After placing their produce in front of the altar, Psalm 65 was recited; this psalm was followed by three lengthy prayers that deserve closer examination.

The first of these prayers acknowledged God's goodness as the Creator, who brought forth all kinds of fruitfulness, both as food for creatures and as medicine for the sick: "Bless + these various herbs and fruits, and add to their natural powers the grace of thy new bless-

---

mountain carrying the Catalonian flag. Prayers were recited by presider and people and a couple songs were sung (one was the Catalonian anthem), all in Catalan. After this a traditional dance kept young and old moving for the next hour or so. Firecrackers were set off in abundance. Blessing and prayer aside, the celebration had strong nationalistic overtones, more about the pride of their culture than the dark-dispelling light of Christ and his precursor.

[44] See "The Blessing of Young Crops and Vineyards," in Weller, *Ritual*, #105.

[45] NCRLC, *Blessing and Prayers for the Feast of the Assumption in Honor of Our Lady of the Fields* (Des Moines, IA: NCRLC, 1955), MUA/NCRLC, Series 5/1.

ing. May they ward off disease and adversity from men and beast who use them in thy name." The second prayer invoked the name of Moses, who ordered Israel to carry their sheaves of new grain and present them to the priests and thereby to God:

> Hear thou our supplications and bestow blessings + in abundance upon us and upon these bundles of new grain, herbs . . . Grant that men, cattle, sheep . . . find in them a remedy against sickness, pestilence, sores, injuries, spells. . . . May these blessed objects act as a protection against diabolical mockeries, cunnings and deceptions wherever they are kept. . . . May we laden with sheaves of good works, deserve to be lifted up to heaven.[46]

The final blessing prayer begged Mary to intercede on our behalf before the "fruit of her womb," Christ our Savior: "We pray that we may use these fruits of the soil for our temporal and eternal welfare— the power of thy Son and the patronage of His glorious mother assisting us." Everything brought forth was sanctified by sprinkling and incensing. As with the blessing on St. Isidore's feast day, the NCRLC recommended that the novena of St. Isidore be prayed beginning on August 7 and concluding on August 15.

This blessing on Assumption reinforces several underlying themes of this study. First, it speaks to the holistic nature (*kata holos*) or catholicity of the liturgical and sacramental life of the church. The blessing begged for God's protection and well-being (*salus*) for human and nonhuman creatures alike. The combined events of blessing, novena, and the feast-day liturgy, made clearer the connection between worship, work, and life. Second, the rural community faithfully celebrated the Assumption in union with the universal church, listening to the same readings and praying the same prayers (albeit in Latin and English). But the rural community did so in a manner that highlighted its unique place in culture (as agrarians), yielding an intensified experience of local church. Arguably, rural parishes may have set forth an ideal balance between local church and culture. That is to say, a local faith community celebrated the liturgy that was thoroughly in keeping with its cultural heritage, and yet remained profoundly connected to the universal church. Third, the liturgy honored Mary, but it

---

[46] NCRLC, *Blessing and Prayers for the Feast of the Assumption*.

also honored the work and life of farmers, giving rise to a confluence of worship, work, and life among rural Catholic communities.[47]

Closely associated to the Assumption was the blessing of "seed and seedlings" on September 8, the Birthday of the Blessed Virgin Mary. While some regions of the country or world would have had September plantings, its recommendation for most places in the United States seemed misplaced since most farmers would have been harvesting at this time. The prayer of blessing spoke of the harvest in relation to Moses, who counseled the people to offer their firstfruits upon entering the Promised Land. Otherwise, the blessing begged God to protect the seeds from harm and allow them to germinate and grow. The second part of the blessing said essentially the same thing, calling on God the "Sower and Tiller of the heavenly word, who cultivates the soil of our hearts with heavenly tools . . ." to protect the crop and make it fruitful.[48]

Finally, Thanksgiving Day served as a natural and civic end to the growing season for most farmers in the United States. Writing back in 1925, H. F. Roney had suggested celebrating a Mass on Thanksgiving Day (or on the nearest Sunday) in gratitude for the harvest. He noted how it was fitting to close the year (which began with a blessing of soil and seed back in March) with a Mass of thanksgiving for the harvested

---

[47] Fr. Edward O'Rourke gave a fine homily in 1960 on the occasion of the "Feast of Our Lady of the Fields." In his sermon he concisely integrated the themes of creation, incarnation, and redemption in relation to the eucharistic liturgy and the right use of sacramentals (here, the blessing of herbs and firstfruits). As members of Christ's Mystical Body the blessings (in general) allow the faithful to extend the redemptive act into their daily lives. Doing so "helps to restore order and harmony in our way of life." Thus the eucharistic liturgy, combined as it was with the blessing of the "work of human hands," should lead to a "thoroughly Christian way of life." In rather straightforward terms, O'Rourke gave expression to the adage that forms the basis of this study—*lex orandi, lex credendi, lex vivendi*.

[48] Weller, *Ritual*, #27. At the 1940 Liturgical Week in Chicago, a priest told Hellriegel that on the feast of the Blessed Mother's birthday (September 8) parishioners brought the winter wheat seed to church to have it blessed. Near the Pentecost Ember Days they offered part of the newly harvested wheat, and members of the altar society took it to a nearby mill to have it turned into flour which was used to bake the altar breads for the parish. Hellriegel commented: "God bless a flock that has such a fine Catholic sense!" Martin Hellriegel, "Merely Suggesting I: Sprung from the Seed of Abraham," *OF* 15 (1940–41): 442.

fruits of the land.[49] Once again, the Catholic Rural Life Conference of Springfield, Illinois, took the lead and published the "Ceremony for the Parish Observance Thanksgiving Day" in 1953. It was used in that diocese, and since other diocesan directors of rural life mentioned the ceremony in their reports, it must have been widely disseminated.

The ceremony was observed with a Mass of Thanksgiving in which families were not only encouraged to attend but to receive Communion together. After Mass there was Benediction, which was followed by the recitation of the canticle of the three youths, with priest and assembly alternating the recitation. The day's collect from the Mass of Thanksgiving was prayed by the priest; the Prayer of St. Isidore and the Prayer of the Christian Farmer were recited by the assembly. The ceremony closed with the singing of "Holy God We Praise Thy Name." The pamphlet stated that "the" proper way for any Catholic to celebrate Thanksgiving Day was to participate in the Holy Sacrifice of the Mass and to receive Holy Communion. No suggestion was made to bring any fruits of the harvest to offer at Mass, but parishes adapted the ceremony to do so. This, in essence, rounded out the basic course of the liturgical year and presented what was at least possible for a given rural parish.[50]

## WITH THE BLESSING OF THE CHURCH

In general, blessings attempt to draw into closer relationship ordinary things and events of life and situate them properly in relation to God's salvific plan.[51] Bishop Joseph Schlarman's English translation of the agricultural blessings of the Roman Ritual simply bequeathed to God's faithful of the countryside something that the church long had in her possession. *With the Blessing of the Church* (WBC) made evident

[49] H. F. Roney, "A Thanksgiving Mass," *CRL* 3 (November 1925): 6. As mentioned earlier, this recommendation in 1925 anticipated the Missal of Paul VI, which provided a liturgy for this civil holiday.

[50] *Ceremony for the Parish Observance of Thanksgiving Day* (Sigel, IL: Catholic Rural Life Conference, 1953). See MUA/NCRLC, Series 5/1, box 5, "1951–55." Father Irvin Will, diocesan director of rural life in Springfield, reported 3,273 pamphlets for the ceremony were distributed in 1955. MUA/NCRLC, Series 8/1, box 14, "Annual Report" in navy blue binder. This ceremony was based in part on a paraliturgical celebration created by Msgr. Joseph Gremillion.

[51] Paul Jounel, "Blessings," in *The Church at Prayer: The Sacraments*, ed. A. G. Martimort, trans. Matthew J. O'Connell, one-volume edition, 263ff. (Collegeville, MN: Liturgical Press, 1988).

the closeness rural people enjoyed to God and more important the vital and intimate role they played in God's saving work. Monsignor Joseph Morrison, then the past president of the Liturgical Conference, offered a brief acknowledgment of Schlarman's work, calling him "a scholar of note and an apostle of Christ's Mystical Body" who had done a great service for the church. Morrison highlighted the overall thrust of the book and the relationship between liturgy and life: "Oh thrice blessed be the work of the farmer who uses the sacramentals of the Church while, in close partnership with God, he produces both the essential matter of the Sacrifice and the elements that nourish the body." Thus on one level Schlarman did nothing more than offer, in English, what the church already possessed. Of course, in 1946, to make available to the faithful the church's official rituals in the vernacular was no small matter. This was the same year that Philip Weller produced his English translation of the Roman Ritual.[52]

Perhaps the most valuable feature of *With the Blessing of the Church* was the insightful foreword written by Martin Hellriegel. Hellriegel distinguished the "big" sacraments instituted by the Lord from the "little" sacraments (sacramentals) that were given to the faithful by the church. Sacramentals served as means to receive grace so as to avoid evil and do good; they protected soul and body and remitted venial sin "by virtue of the prayers of the Church and the good disposition of those who use them." By its blessing the church "tears an object out of the claws of the hellish dragon . . . purifies it, and gives it a supernatural dignity" endowed with the power of the Savior.[53]

That the church has blessed "all manner of things" was true from her earliest days—all things (*omnia*) being marked with the sign of the cross. It was here that Hellriegel made the direct connection to the liturgical movement's motto—*instaurare omnia in Christo*—which resonated in a special way with the NCRLC. Hellriegel situated blessings within the larger context of the church's liturgical life. The Eucharist in a certain sense was the preeminent blessing in which all these objects, animate and inanimate, found their true meaning:

[52] NCRLC, *With the Blessing of the Church*, trans. Bishop Joseph Schlarman (Des Moines, IA: NCRLC, 1946), 1 (hereafter NCRLC, *WBC*). See MUA/NCRLC, Series 5, box 3, folder 6. A comparison of the relevant parts translated show that Weller offered a "verbatim" translation, while Schlarman, it appeared, took some liberties. Schlarman also gave brief catechetical notes before many of the blessings.

[53] NCRLC, *WBC*, 2.

By doing so, the Church establishes a divine contact between the Holy Eucharist and these objects, transforming them, making them fit instruments for the daily living, working, toiling and suffering of her children, thereby aiding and sanctifying the redeemed "branches" with the eternal splendor and the sweet fragrance of Christ . . . their Food and Drink.[54]

The blessing of everyday objects and events situates them and the people who use them within the larger salvific plan. The eucharistic celebration was the essential reference point. The source of blessings is to be found in the redemptive act of Christ as the church celebrated this redemption in the liturgy. While such blessings were more often bestowed outside the context of the eucharistic liturgy, they helped the Christian to see that the redemptive act celebrated in the Eucharist continued in one's daily work and life.

According to Hellriegel, the Enlightenment and the secularism it spawned was guilty of the "terrible divorce" that took place between altar and home. The Industrial Revolution deepened this division as more people trudged off to the factories and lost contact with nature and with the organic processes of life. The separation created a "double-track" living: one *with* Christ, done once a week for about thirty minutes; and the other *without* Christ during the rest of the week. In Benedictine terms, the *ora* had been separated from the *labora*. The absence of liturgy in the home deprived the people of that "fecundating hovering-over of the Spirit of the Lord who fills the whole earth." According to this liturgical leader, Pius X initiated the reestablishment of this close relationship between altar and home, something Hellriegel believed the church had lost.[55]

Further, Hellriegel credited the liturgical movement for the healthy growth of such groups as Catholic Action and the National Catholic Rural Life Conference, each finding its inspiration in the church's liturgy or the sacramental apostolate as it was sometimes called.[56] Therefore, *With the Blessing of the Church* sought to reconnect altar and home by taking the natural things of agrarian life and raising them to a supernatural order. It created a "precious mosaic" over which one could write: "RURAL LIFE TO BE INCORPORATED INTO CHRIST!" Finally, of particular note, when no priest was available, Hellriegel

[54] Ibid., 2–3.
[55] Ibid., 3.
[56] Ibid., 4–5.

suggested that the father or another family member recite the blessing. Such was the faithful's right "in virtue of the indelible mark" bestowed on them in baptism and confirmation. As members of the Mystical Body, this was how they shared in the priesthood of Jesus Christ.

Essentially, *WBC* applied this notion of *omnia* quite literally; there were few things on the farm that the church could not bless.[57] The blessings had a central role in the manner by which the farmer joined his particular efforts to the goal of "restoring all things in Christ," advancing his salvation.[58] This approach made for a holistic lifestyle, 'catholic' in the full sense of the word. Some of the blessings (such as the "Blessing of a Water Supply") were quite general and could have been applied anywhere: "grant that, by Thy assistance and blessing and our cooperation, every diabolical attack and confusion may be kept off and that this water supply may always be pure and uncontaminated."[59] The other blessings were proper to rural life and offered some catechesis for their use. Several may be examined here, highlighting their theological and pastoral importance.

Schlarman's catechesis preceding the "Blessing of Horses and other Draft Animals" stressed the role played by these beasts of burden in helping the person along the Christian way: "The animals praise and

---

[57] Of course this notion of *omnia* is expressed in the Roman Canon and could have potentially reinforced those times when rural blessings were done in the context of the Eucharist: "*Per quem haec ómnia, Dómine, semper bona creas, sanctíficas, vivíficas, benedícas, et præstas nobis.*" The translation in the *Novus Ordo*, while adequate, may not do complete justice to the Latin. *Novus Ordo*: "Through him you give us all these gifts, you fill them with life and goodness, you bless them and make them holy."

[58] The blessings are as follows: Blessing of a Farm, Blessing of the Cornerstone of a New Building, Blessing of a New House, Blessing of a Water Supply, Blessing of the Hearth, Blessing of a Stable, Blessing of Horses and other Draft Animals, Blessing of All Domestic Animals, Blessing of Diseased Cattle, Blessing of Diseased Animals, Blessing of Salt and Feed for Animals, Blessing of Bees, Blessing of a Mill, Blessing of a Spring or Well, Blessing for the Sprouting Seed, Blessing of Pasture, Meadows, and Fields, Blessing of Orchards and Vineyard, Prayer Against Harmful Animals, Blessing of the Barn and the Stored Harvest, Blessing of Herbs on the Feast of the Assumption; IN THE MACHINE AGE—Blessing of a Wagon or other Vehicle, Blessing of a Dynamo; BLESSING OF FOOD—Blessing of Eggs, Blessing of Bread and Cake, Blessing of Cheese and Butter, Blessing of Bacon or Lard, Another Blessing of Bread, Blessing of Poultry, Blessing of Grapes, Blessing of Fresh Fruit, Blessing of Wine, Another St. John Blessing of Wine, Blessing of Food in General.

[59] NCRLC, *WBC*, 9.

glorify God inasmuch as they assist man and serve him. In their own way they assist man in attaining his ultimate goal, and for that reason the Church blesses them." Similarly, the "Blessing of Salt and Feed for the Animals" looked to the welfare of the creatures themselves since their health was inextricably joined to that of the farmer's livelihood: "Pour out Thy blessing on this salt (feed, fodder) and fill it with the benefits of Thy invisible power; grant that these animals . . . destined for man's needs may be freed of all disease and protected from the attacks of the evil one when they eat of this salt (feed, fodder)." The "Blessing of Bees" stated: "Thou who hast directed that the ministers of Thy holy Church should light candles made of beeswax when the holy sacrifice is offered . . . send down Thy blessing on these bees, that they may multiply and be fruitful and be preserved from all harm . . . so that the product of their labor may be used to Thy honor."[60] One can hear in this blessing an echo from Genesis 1:28 (be fruitful . . . ) and words that parallel the present-day liturgy (fruits of the earth and work—labor—of human hands). A noticeable lacuna in *WBC* was the "Blessing of the Silkworm." This creature was praised for its dignified role in providing the "matter" for the vestments that adorned altars and ministers alike.[61]

Also of note were those blessings that dealt with diseased animals and various pests. It was often recommended that the priest don a purple stole, alluding to the task at hand as exorcistic, penitential, and reconciliatory. Once again, the blessing tightly wove together the health and welfare of the animals with that of human well-being. The "Blessing of Diseased Animals" begged God to preserve these "dumb" [*sic*] animals without which "man cannot support and nourish himself." It continued by calling down the mercy of God on the animals so that they may be restored to health, and the power of the devil be driven from them: "Be Thou O Lord, the protector of their lives and the healer of their ailments." Finally, the blessing petitioned the Lord

---

[60] Ibid., 10, 12.

[61] It was mentioned in other sources. See Weller, *Ritual*, #90. "O God, Maker and Director of the universe, Who in creating living things didst endow each with the power of propagating its own species, bless + we pray, these silkworms, foster them, and let them multiply. May thy holy altars be adorned with the fruit of their industry. And let thy faithful servants resplendent in robes of silk acknowledge thee with heartfelt praise as the Donor of every Good. Who with thy Sole-Begotten Son and the Holy Spirit livest and reignest for all eternity. Amen."

to turn away from "us" the scourges of God's punishment and drive off this disease that attacks these animals, for God "punishes those who wander from Thy paths, but givest Thy grace when they have amended their lives." At the same time one detected what may be called "wrathful theology." That is to say, any scourge that visited this people was because of its sins.[62]

The "Prayer against Harmful Animals, e.g., mice worms, snails, plant lice, and others" was reserved solely for a "specially authorized priest." Again, it called for the priest to wear a purple stole as he visited the affected fields. Notably, the words were called a "prayer" and not a blessing. This prayer employed stronger language than the blessing for diseased animals just mentioned. Parts of the prayer were reminiscent of ancient exorcism rites connected to Christian initiation. What must be kept in mind was how closely the prayer united the well-being of crops and livestock with that of the farmer—*salus* in the fuller sense of the word. After the antiphon, "Arise, O Lord, help us and redeem us for Thy name's sake," the three-part prayer petitioned:

> Graciously hear our prayers O Lord . . . that we who are justly pun-
> ished for our sins and must bear the punishment of this plague, may
> be freed from it for the glory of Thy name. By Thy power may these
> injurious animals be driven off so that they will do no harm to any one
> and will leave our fields and meadows unharmed, and so that the
> things sprouting and growing in these fields may honor Thy majesty
> and serve our needs.

---

[62] See the opening quote of this study by Msgr. George "Alfalfa" Hildner. While contemporary theology has stood back from such divine wrath scenarios attributed to sinful human beings, there can be little doubt that whatever the cause of such plagues, the impact was most acute for the farmer; consecutive plagues could destroy the farmer's livelihood. Modern society, as it became further removed from natural processes, was spared the effect of such agricultural disasters, save for higher prices in the grocery store. On the one hand, "wrathful theology" is difficult to maintain in principle. On the other hand, one's treatment of the land (soil), not being a good steward of it (greed), carries serious implications for the farmer's livelihood and those who depend on him for food—all of us. For example, the practice of "mono-cropping" saps the soil of vitality and makes crops susceptible to invasive pests. To farm in such a manner jeopardized one's material and spiritual welfare. The NCRLC advanced a more progressive and balanced understanding of agriculture beginning in the 1930s. In short, there is strength to be gained in planting a diversity of crops. The NCRLC gave specific advice to do so.

Almighty, eternal God, Thou the giver of all good things who hast mercy for all sinners, in whose name every knee in heaven, on earth, and under the earth should bend, grant to us sinners by Thy grace that which we ask with confidence in Thy mercy. May we be freed from the plague of these rodents (worms, snails, plant lice, etc.) by Thy strong hand and may we joyously give thanks to Thy majesty.

(Now follows the solemn exorcism of the harmful animals) I conjure you mice (worms, snails, lice, etc.) in the name of God, the Almighty Father, of Jesus Christ, His only Son, and of the Holy Spirit who proceeds from both, that you go out from these fields and pastures and remain no more in them, but depart for places where you can harm no one. In the name of God, the Almighty, of the whole heavenly court, and of God's holy Church, I declare you accursed wherever you go so that you will become fewer day by day. May no part of you be found again, unless it be for man's welfare, May He graciously grant this, who will come to judge the living and the dead and the world by fire.[63]

The ridding of the plague gave glory and thanks to God alone. Interesting to note, excepting the "curse" that the pests decrease in number (which may not necessarily be equated with wishing them death), the prayers asked that they depart for a place where they can do no more harm.

While at times one detected an anti-urban bias among Catholic agrarians, *WBC* saw technological advances as consistent with human progress. Thus, "IN THE MACHINE AGE" offered blessings for a wagon or other vehicles, and for the "Dynamo" (a generator) that aided the electrification of rural areas. Since the church has always accompanied the farmer and blessed his life as he worked in closer communion with nature, so too with the advent of the industrial age: "And the Church did not abandon her children when they went to workshops and factories where a new age sang its chant to the accompaniment of clattering and clanking machines."[64]

*With the Blessing of the Church* proved to be a laudable effort because it offered some of the church's rites of blessing in the vernacular. This not only allowed the people to understand them but enabled the faithful to see how the *little* sacrament of one's farm and home was joined to the larger liturgical life of the church. While Hellriegel's foreword

---

[63] NCRLC, *WBC*, 15–16.
[64] Ibid., 20.

drew upon principles of the liturgical movement, one wonders if the prayer book could not have been better integrated with the liturgical year as the Roman Ritual itself was. It has been noted that *WBC* left out a few significant blessings, such as that of the silkworm, crosses, and bonfires.

One other lacuna deserves mention: the "Apostolic Blessing upon a People and Its Lands."[65] It was one of the few blessings that required an indult—*ex Apostolicus Sedis indulto*. The papal document was explained to the people on the morning it was to be read to the parish. After reading it, the assembly responded, "Thanks be to God." Three days of fasting were begun after a votive Mass for the remission of sins. On the Sunday following the fast, a votive Mass "In Any Necessity" was celebrated, and the blessing was given. The entire rite was rather involved. In essence the blessing spoke of making the land fertile and fruitful so that God "may satisfy the hungry with affluence, so that the poor and needy may praise thy divine majesty." The blessing of the people was given and concluded with the collect from the votive Mass "For Thanksgiving." This blessing is noted here for its solemnity, since blessings of land and people already exist. The additional solemnity of papal approbation had the potential of providing greater esteem and dignity to the farmer's vocation.

In conclusion, the rural parish had ample opportunity to integrate the daily "work of its human hands" with the church's official liturgy, and to some extent, in certain paraliturgical services. The liturgy served to uphold and strengthen the dignity of the farmer's way of life. Through some of these liturgies, with their associated devotions and blessings, direct relationships were established between Christian worship and its role in establishing a more just social order, even as liturgical leaders pointed out that the liturgy alone could not fulfill this goal. Other activities were required for the Christian to make this connection more complete and extend Christ's redemption more deeply into the world. All God's creation groans to be set free and to share in the glorious freedom of the children of God (Rom 8:20-25).

---

[65] Weller, *Ritual*, #37. The *Ritual* has *Ritus Benedicendi Populos et Agros*, which Weller translated "Apostolic Blessing upon a People and Its Lands." However, he also called it "Apostolic Blessing on a Parish and Its Lands." See also John Hennig, "Prayers for Farmers," *OF* 18 (1943–44): 498–99. In my research Hennig was the only one to mention this blessing. Might it have been left out of *WBC* for simplicity's sake and to make the prayer book more participative?

Therefore, the NCRLC promoted extra-liturgical activity (i.e., rural retreats, local conferences and talks, study clubs, rural Catholic Action cells) that sought a more thorough Christian formation of the family and rural leaders. Through it all, the church's liturgical and sacramental life served as the spiritual anchor.

# Chapter 5

# To Restore *All* Things in Christ!

The liturgical reform of the Second Vatican Council affirmed the insights of scholars that the liturgy by itself cannot sustain a complete Christian life. To be certain, the liturgy stands as the source and summit of the Christian life, but other religious practices must also nourish and contribute to the fuller living out of one's baptism. The NCRLC undertook a variety of activities such as summer religious schools, retreats, conferences, study clubs, and Rural Catholic Action. Liturgical-sacramental catechesis was integral to all of them. The same was true for the NCRLC's publications and newspaper columns. Additionally, by considering a potpourri of rural culture—songs, poetry, art, architecture, and pageants—it treats more broadly the notion of sacramentality. All these aspects of rural life, it will be argued, tilled the soil of agrarian religious culture and potentially disposed the faithful for a more active engagement, not only in the liturgy, but in a life marked by works of charity and justice. In all this, insights from the liturgical movement and its leaders imbued rural life with a true Christian spirit. In doing so, the NCRLC sought to realize Pius X's motto: *instaurare omnia in Christo*.

## RELIGIOUS VACATION SCHOOLS

Education held a privileged place in the NCRLC's program as the Religious Vacation Schools indicated. Edwin O'Hara organized his first summer school in 1921 when he was pastor of St. Mary's parish in Eugene, Oregon. (Due to their isolation, families were unable to attend the parochial school during the academic year and often could not even attend Sunday Mass.) A year later, when he was made head of the Rural Life Bureau, he used that office and *St. Isidore's Plow* to promote the summer school program nationally. O'Hara trained lay catechists to help the Sisters of the Holy Names whom he had recruited to conduct the schools. Thanks to Margaret Lynch, Assistant Director for the National Council of Catholic Women, a contingent of lay women also promoted and staffed these schools, calling upon local chapters to staff the schools. The Oregon schools lasted two weeks and offered intensive religious instruction in many facets of the faith—liturgy being one of them.[1] The core curriculum of the Oregon schools included catechism, biblical history, sacred music, Mass prayers, and studies taken from the New Testament. From the mid-1920s to the early 1930s, under the auspices of the summer vacation schools, the Conference tried to inculcate a greater understanding of and participation in the liturgy of the church.[2] The rapid emergence of the Confraternity of Christian Doctrine (CCD), founded by O'Hara, took on much of the work of these vacation schools by the early 1930s.

Luigi Ligutti drew upon the experience of O'Hara's religious vacation schools to establish his own in 1924. At that time Ligutti was pastor of two rural parishes in Woodbine and Magnolia, Iowa. The parishes were poor and the parishioners were spread throughout the surrounding countryside. Religious illiteracy was rampant. According to Ligutti, many children had never seen a crucifix, nor had they said grace before meals, held rosary beads, let alone recited the prayers. Obviously, many had never received the sacraments or attended Mass. In July 1925, "under a spreading elm tree," Ligutti drew up a plan for what he called a "one-horse" religious vacation school, utilizing ideas received from O'Hara and the NCRLC. For three weeks, Ligutti and two Dominican sisters conducted a religious instruction program that began with thirty-five children; but by the program's end, seventy youngsters had taken part in the school.[3]

[1] Dolan, *Some Seed*, 54, 75–76.

[2] Witte, *Crusading*, 181–85. Mention should be made of the efforts of Msgr. Victor Day of Helena, Montana. He is well known for the correspondence courses that he developed for Catholics living in remote areas who were unable to attend Mass regularly. These courses were primarily geared toward sacramental preparation. One lesson was mailed out each week and the child (often with a parent's help) completed the lesson and returned it. Bishop John P. Carroll embraced the idea, and within three months one thousand copies of the First Communion Series were distributed. O'Hara utilized some of Day's courses for his work in Oregon. Victor Day, "Catechism by Mail," *CRL* (November 1925): 6, and Witte, *Crusading*, 187–88.

[3] Luigi Ligutti, "Magnolia Summer Vacation School," MUA/LGL, box J-2, "Religious Vacation Schools, 1925"; and Yzermans, *The People I Love*, 19–20.

It was billed as a summer "vacation" school, but Ligutti ran it like a religious boot camp. It was intense and structured as Ligutti sought to engender in them basic human values of responsibility, commitment, and perseverance; this served to counter the poor and rather haphazard existence of many of them. The day's regimen began with Mass, and this was followed by a series of catechetical lessons led by Ligutti and the religious sisters using the *Baltimore Catechism*.[4] The children learned to sing, especially hymns for Mass and Benediction. Scripture lessons were read aloud by the children and discussed. A class of first communicants was formed so as to receive "our Eucharistic Lord" for the first time at the closing Mass. The Way of the Cross was learned and prayed. The girls were taught to sew altar linens and how to decorate the church. At the conclusion of the school Ligutti received an "alb, altar cloth, twenty-seven purificators, twenty-two finger towels, and two corporals." Eight boys learned to serve, learning all the Latin responses of the Mass to assist Ligutti at the school liturgies. Health and first aid were taught.[5]

In the late 1920s a vacation school was held in the southern Maryland missions. A photo taken from the time showed a mixed group of pupils—whites along with African Americans. In all, two hundred ten children attended and were served by seven Holy Cross sisters, two seminarians, and fifty-three laypeople. While the school taught the Bible, it recommended even more the method of teaching the mysteries of the Lord based on the ecclesiastical (liturgical) year, something the liturgical movement promoted. Daily instruction in sacred singing

---

[4] The *Baltimore Catechism* was the recommended text for the *Manual of Religious Vacation Schools* as well. The *Manual* will be treated below. Eventually, the *Baltimore Catechism* was replaced by the CCD's catechism (1941).

[5] Ligutti, "Magnolia Summer Vacation School." The children's lack of knowledge with regard to first aid was a bit humorous, as Ligutti recorded: "Imaginary accidents took place. The children were told to act as they would if an accident occurred and they were alone. Sad as the accident was, one would have to smile at the first aid rendered. In regard to the severe nose bleed, the boy threw a wet towel across the neck. Water was dripping out of it and running all over the child's clothes. Sister said, 'Dear children, if the boy does not die from a loss of blood he will surely be drowned by that wet towel.' In response to a person's clothes catching fire, the children did not know what to do and delayed in their action, thus the person would have died, and sad to state none of them thought to call for a priest." The children also learned to make "sick call kits" and how to assist the priest when he came to the home.

was given, including the familiar hymns in English as well as those songs that accompanied Benediction. "The meaning of the words of the hymns should be taught phrase by phrase in order that the rendition of the hymn should be not merely a joyful noise but an intelligent expression of religious worship." As with Ligutti's school, this one also sought to impart a comprehensive view of life, thus health, recreation, arts and crafts, etc., were also taught.[6]

According to the 1929 *Official Catholic Directory*, there were ten thousand Catholic churches without a parochial school. Yet in July 1929 O'Hara gave a "state of the religious schools" report that indicated they were flourishing. Some fifty dioceses were conducting almost one thousand religious vacation schools (some were even in cities!). O'Hara spoke of weekday Mass attendance for the children as "devotion" and an opportunity for instruction so as to enhance their participation. The children were furnished with a copy of the prayers for the Ordinary of the Mass, published by Pax Press of O'Fallon, Missouri. This was no doubt the work of Martin Hellriegel and the Precious Blood sisters. O'Hara reported how the children were split into two choirs and recited the prayers and responses along with the priest. This demanded the careful preparation of the presider as well, since such participation was still new for most priests. Generally, it took only a few weeks for the children to ably follow along throughout the liturgy. Once the children became familiar with the structure of the Mass, it was easier to integrate the singing of hymns with the recitation of prayers.[7]

A regular pattern began to emerge for running the summer schools. The schools operated for three to four hours a day, five days a week for four weeks—in all, around sixty hours of instruction. Depending on the number of religious sisters and lay staff, the children were divided into primary, intermediate, junior high, and upper grades. Each day was divided into the following instructional categories: Prayers, Picture Study & Bible Stories, Christian Doctrine, Liturgy and Religious Practices, and Art and Handiwork. Boys were trained to be altar servers, the girls learned to make altar linens and vestments. The schools were open to children of all Christian denominations. O'Hara admitted that "we can well follow the example of the Protestant Daily

---

[6] *NCWC Bulletin*, July 1929. One might suspect that the report was from Father John LaFarge, SJ, who was working in this part of Maryland.

[7] Edwin O'Hara, "Sixty Hours of Religious Instruction," *NCWC Bulletin* 11 (July 1929): 6.

Bible Schools and extend an invitation to all the children of the community without distinction of religious affiliation." O'Hara had attended a Lutheran Bible school as a child before an organized Catholic presence had been established in his native Minnesota. Finally, religious literature, some of it liturgical in nature, was often recommended as a resource for teachers. Sacramental preparation became a regular component of all the schools, with the children often receiving the sacraments (usually First Reconciliation and Communion) at the close of the session.[8]

Because of the schools' widespread success, there was need to develop a more structured general curriculum, yet one that also allowed for local adaptation. This project fell to Father Leon McNeill, Catholic school superintendent from Wichita, Kansas, who authored the *Manual of Religious Vacation Schools* in 1930.[9] The *Manual* stated that the general objective for the primary grades was preparation for "First Holy Communion." The lesson to be communicated was God's love for children. The *Manual* distinguished between "prayers as lesson" and "prayers as an act," where, in the first part they learn *how* to speak to God, and in the second part they *actually* speak to God. Mass was not to be mandatory for the primary grades, "nor should the children be bribed" to attend. They should be instructed about the Mass and how to pray it: "With this new understanding, they will want to attend of their own accord. Teaching them by practice is preferable to the recitation of the Rosary during Mass." This put into practice the liturgical movement's goal of intelligent and active participation in the liturgy. In the section "How to Receive Holy Communion," much of the eucharistic piety typical of that time was in evidence. Interestingly, the words "real presence" were not given much emphasis. Rather, the *Manual* noted: "We must know that what looks like bread is not real bread, but is really the live body and blood and soul of Christ, and Christ not only as man, but as God. . . . Holy Communion is going to our Lord's table to receive Him."[10] Recommended teacher resources were *Our First Communion* by Msgr. Kelly, *The Visible Church* by John F. Sullivan, and *Mass Prayer Cards*.[11]

[8] Edwin O'Hara, "Religious Vacation Schools," *CRL* 8 (March 1930): 2, 4.

[9] Rural Life Bureau/NCWC, *Manual for Religious Vacation Schools* (Washington, DC: Rural Life Bureau, 1930), 5–6. In ACUA, NCWC/USCC, box 53, folder 31 "Printed Material."

[10] Ibid., 11.

[11] Ibid., 10–12.

For the intermediate grades, the children used the *Baltimore Catechism* for general religious instruction and the same liturgical materials as the primary grades. The "Christian Doctrine" component of the day often treated the sacraments. The "Liturgy" section was practical, that is, geared toward active participation. Also under the liturgy section, basic devotions were taught, making the distinction between private prayer and the public prayer of the church—another aim of the liturgical movement. Lessons included instruction on vestments and items used at Mass. Even the topics of religious life and vocations were treated under liturgy.[12]

With the junior high grades, naturally, the schools began to expect more from the students with regard to worship. Teachers stressed the "duty of public social worship, the eminent dignity of the Mass." The students were taught about the liturgical year and told what a privilege it was to live the "liturgical life of the church in spirit and practice." The students constructed a miniature altar complete with candlesticks, crucifix, and altar linens. In general, it seemed that most instruction took a hands-on approach complete with props (sacramentals); this was especially true with sacramental teaching (ambry, water, sacred vessels, and vestments). The Real Presence was taught along with devotion to the Blessed Sacrament (Forty Hours); more important, frequent Communion was encouraged.[13]

Depending on the level of instruction high school students had received, the *Manual* suggested using the junior-high template for instruction and adapting it as needed. For the high school group "we suggest that major attention be given to the liturgy, with special emphasis on the Holy Sacrifice of the Mass." Each student was told to obtain a copy of *The Mass* by Moorman and a missal (Lasance was recommended). The teacher, equipped with a copy of Sullivan's *The Visible Church*, "should introduce into the course instruction other phases of the liturgy, e.g., services, devotions, religious practices, and the sacramentals."[14] Hymn singing was practiced with emphasis placed on Gregorian chant, especially for use at Benediction and during

[12] Ibid., 19–22. The *Manual* used the term "liturgy." Some of the "devotions" taught were: to one's Guardian Angel, for Poor Souls in Purgatory, the Stations of the Cross, Forty Hours, the Blessed Sacrament, and the saints.

[13] Ibid., 25–29.

[14] Ibid., 30. See John Francis Sullivan, *The Visible Church, Her Government, Ceremonies, Sacramentals, Festivals and Devotions: A Compendium of the Externals of the Catholic Church*, 4th ed. (New York: P. Kennedy Pub., 1922).

one of the Gregorian Masses. In the resource list, Virgil Michel's pamphlet "My Sacrifice and Yours" was one of the recommendations for high school students.[15] The students were also taught to answer "objections" from non-Catholics. Much attention was given to health concerns—a perennial problem in remote rural areas where flush toilets, running water, and electricity for food storage were often lacking.

Overall, the schools attempted to foster active and intelligent participation in the liturgy. While they clearly had a religious focus, they also fostered a wider appreciation of life in general. This was especially true of health education and the promotion of responsible citizenship. The schools afforded an opportunity to learn music, handcrafts, and various forms of recreation. They sought to foster a well-balanced Catholic life for the children living in rural areas. This tended to have good effects on their parents and the parish community as well.

FARMERS' RETREATS

The lay retreat movement began in the mid-nineteenth century in Europe, but only gained wider popularity here in the United States in the 1930s and 1940s. It was a response to the growing need to provide the laity with a sound spirituality that animated other activities such as Catholic Action. Combined with study and liturgy, retreats helped to round out one's basic Christian formation.[16] The retreats often required laypeople to go to a retreat house for a weekend (or week), and they were mostly conducted by members of religious communities. This arrangement was simply not practical for a farmer. So the NCRLC decided to take the retreat to the farmer. For the Conference, this accomplished two immediate goals. First, it afforded the chance to have the entire family participate (or at least the mother and father). Second, the retreats were often parish-based events, serving to strengthen the parish community as a whole. Parish and family were the pillars of a rural community. Obviously, a parish-based venue

---

[15] Ibid., 40–42. See also Edgar Schmiedeler, OSB, *Catholic Rural Activities* (NCWC, 1933), CUAA/SAD, Box 61, folder 24, "Catholic Rural Activities."

[16] Joseph P. Chinnici, *Living Stones: The History and Structure of Catholic Spiritual Life in the United States* (New York and London: Macmillan Publishers, 1989), 157–71; Joseph P. Chinnici, and Angelyn Dries, eds., *Prayer and Practice in the American Catholic Community* (Maryknoll, NY: Orbis Books, 2000), xxvii–xxvii; and Pecklers, *Unread Vision*, 94–96.

provided the opportunity to tailor the retreats specifically to the farmer's life and needs.[17]

Requests poured in from many dioceses, moving the Conference to publish its *Manual for Rural Retreats and Family Meditation* in 1947.[18] The foreword also distinguished how these retreats differ from traditional ones: "The Rural Retreats . . . do not reason from eternal truths to their application here and now [traditional retreat]. Instead, they start with the daily life of the farmer and move from there to the purpose of his life and the will of God. The farmer is a man who deals with *things*."[19] The retreats lasted either one day (five conferences) or a day and a half (nine conferences); the talks were interspersed with quiet reflection, spiritual reading, and round-table discussions. Mass, with an offertory procession, was celebrated, and the day concluded with Holy Hour and Benediction.

The retreat was divided into two parts. The first, "Christian Rural Principles," largely focused on the dignity and vocation of the farmer. Much emphasis was given to the materiality of creation and the role it plays in aiding the farmer on the path to holiness. Raising good crops with the right intention gave glory to God. "Work on the land . . . is the working out of our salvation . . . a continuation of God's glory effecting the salvation of souls." The manual employed many rural images taken from Scripture, encouraging farmers to read the Bible daily. "Family Duties" highlighted the cooperative nature of the family unit, praying together in the home. Participation in the liturgical and devotional life of the church was emphasized, especially receiving Communion as a family.

---

[17] Witte, *Crusading*, 203–5; Bovée, "Church and Land," 328. Witte's reference to Fr. "Joseph" McShane, SJ, is incorrect. James McShane was a Missouri Province Jesuit ordained in 1943 and spent time at the Jesuit parish in Mankato, MN, this according to the *Catalogus Provinciae Missourianae* of 1943. The first such retreat was held at Queen of Angels parish on January 3, 1945, in Austin, Minnesota, given by Fr. James McShane, SJ, who received his rural training at the Jesuit seminary in St. Mary's, Kansas. At the Green Bay convention in 1946, the NCRLC made the retreats an official part of their rural program.

[18] NCRLC, *Manual for Rural Retreats and Family Meditation* (Des Moines, IA: NCRLC, 1947), in MUA/NCRLC, Series 5/1, box 8, folder 4. There seems to have been an earlier version of the retreat manual. The archival material is incomplete, but it appears that the 1947 *Manual for Rural Retreats* was based on this earlier format. The earlier version offered a little more substance with regard to content. It too suggested that the leader adapt the material to local circumstances.

[19] Ibid., foreword (emphasis original).

"Stewardship of the Land" occupied a significant portion of the retreat. Land, the manual noted, was a gift for all time to humanity and therefore demanded proper care: "Spiritual rewards follow good stewardship." Scripture was used to demonstrate that God had intended harmony between humans and the land from the beginning. Biblical institutions such as the jubilee, seventh-year remission of debts, and relief from tilling were the practical manifestations of the mandates: "Subdue does not mean abuse. Rule presumes wisdom and respect." Good practices such as crop diversification and natural fertilization were recommended; bad practices (mono-cropping) were condemned. The care of animals, machinery, barns, house, and yard contributed to the overall "art" of farming and expressed the beauty and order reflected in creation. The retreats also stressed the farmer's duty to humanity and situated this responsibility in the papal "call to arms" via Catholic Action. This was one way the church countered secularism, by forming Catholics to live spiritually vital lives in the midst of their rural daily circumstances. The parish served as the primary locus of Christian formation since "it is a place for social worship of the community." It was recommended that farmers join any organization that upheld social principles consistent with church teaching (i.e., Christian-inspired cooperatives).[20]

The second part of the retreat, "The Sacraments and the Farmer," tried to make explicit the relationship that existed between the two; in essence, this consisted of liturgical and sacramental catechesis. A line from the sacramental rite and an explanation of the ceremony was sometimes provided. For baptism, it stated:

> Receive this white garment. . . . Most important day in your life next to death. Baptism makes us members of the Christ's Mystical Body. The spring rains which bring freshness and new growth to the earth, so in like manner do the blessed waters of Baptism poured over a child bring new freshness and growth of grace to the soul; the spring rains which wash away the dirt and dust, so also, the waters of Baptism wash away the dirt of sin.[21]

[20] Ibid., 13–18. Finally, the farmer must engage in the political process, principally by voting: "There is not a two-fold morality, public and private."

[21] Ibid., 25–26. The method of catechesis based on the liturgical rites was something Virgil Michel brought back in the 1930s and used it in his Christ-Life series. Of course, this was the preferred method of the early church as seen, for example, in the works of Cyril of Jerusalem, Ambrose, and Theodore of Mopsuestia.

The manual recommended that one observe baptismal day rather than one's birthday. The virtue of purity—in thought, word, and action—was emphasized for baptism. The "actions of animals," it cautioned, "can be a source of impure thoughts . . . give children facts of life according to age; use examples from life on the farm."

The other sacraments were treated in a similar manner. The words "I sign thee . . . and I confirm thee with the chrism of salvation" was the beginning of a talk on confirmation. The seven gifts of the Holy Spirit that one received had to be strengthened through prayer and frequent reception of the sacraments, "just as fertilizer is added to the soil to increase and strengthen the crops." For penance, "just as the farmer must constantly fight with weeds on his land, so he realizes the necessity of constantly pulling the weeds of sin from his soul" in this sacrament. The Christian farmer fills his bins and barns in preparation for the long winter, so must he prepare for his death through prayer and the reception of extreme unction. With regard to prayer, the manual suggested converting "the ordinary actions of planting, sowing, choring [sic], sewing, and washing into prayers through the morning offering." As for matrimony, "just as the farmer chooses well, and only after careful study, the breeding stock for his farm, so he realizes the necessity to prepare well and choose his or her life partner in the contract of marriage."[22]

The Eucharist was explained as sacrifice and sacrament. "Sacrifice," since there was an offering of a "sensible object by a priest to God alone, and destruction of an object to show man's dependence on God."[23] The sacrifices offered by Cain and Abel and the Jewish people were products of the farm. The sacrifice of the Mass has the same priest and

---

[22] Ibid., 31, 33.

[23] The concept of Eucharist as sacrifice has a long and theologically complicated history. This is especially true as it relates to the role of the priest as the one who "offers" *in the person of Christ* and in the name of the church. The NCRLC maintained the traditional (if somewhat problematic) understanding of Christian sacrifice—something being offered to God for something in return. Robert Daly, SJ, has dedicated the last thirty years to studying the notion of Christian sacrifice, rooting the concept in trinitarian and liturgical theology. He identifies a threefold movement of the Father offering the Son (incarnation), the Son freely offering himself on the cross, and then, and only then do the people of God offer themselves (joined to this pattern of offering of Father and Son) in the Holy Spirit. See R. Daly, "Sacrifice Unveiled or Sacrifice Revisited: Trinitarian and Liturgical Perspectives," *Theological Studies* 64, no. 1 (2003): 24–42.

victim, Christ. The importance of the farmer in this action was stressed this way: "Great artists may design a magnificent cathedral, masons can build beautiful altars, goldsmiths make the chalices . . . and popes, cardinals and priests may be present, but if the farmer has not provided the wheat and the grape, there can be no Mass." As "sacrament" there is an exchange of gifts, and at the offertory the farmer gives meaning to these gifts "by placing his heart into the chalice." At Communion, "God offers to share our gift to Him by receiving Holy Communion." The body needs food daily to live and the crops need moisture to grow; "so our souls need Communion daily to grow to full vigor."[24]

The retreat material examined here, based solely on the *Manual*, made a modest attempt to integrate the Catholic faith with the farmer's daily life, especially regarding the sacraments. A closer study of actual retreat notes from one of the leaders may yield other creative approaches. The strength of the retreats may not have been the creative approach to liturgical-sacramental catechesis, but the manner in which the farmer's vocation was situated in a thoroughly religious context. This served to join the life of the farmer to God's saving work as members of Christ's Mystical Body.[25]

THE FORMATION OF RURAL LEADERS

Edwin O'Hara knew from the start that if his rural program was to succeed, he would have to prepare strong leaders, principally the priest-pastor. So it was natural for him to approach seminaries and present his program in the hope that he could inspire some of the young men to take a greater interest in the rural apostolate. It would not be until the late 1930s that the Conference made direct efforts to form rural leaders. Initially, this training focused on priests, religious (mostly women), and seminarians. In the 1940s this training was extended to the laity as well. Once again, the liturgical and sacramental life of the church occupied a central place in the various curricula,

---

[24] Ibid., 29–30.

[25] Some of the suggested points for reflection were blatantly anti-urban. For example, several comparisons were made between one who works with dirt, animals, and machines versus a man in a suit (city bred) "working with mortal sin on his soul." The Prodigal Son lost his soul in a city, only to return to the family farm. Humanity began and flourished in a garden (farm). The point that Christ worked in the "country" was a bit overstated.

which provided the spiritual grounding for rural missions. Seminary formation was important, as were various programs for priests who, as diocesan directors of rural life, were considered the primary rural leaders. In both cases such formation took the form of rural life study clubs and institutes.[26]

In 1936 the NCRLC's executive secretary Father James Byrnes, of St. Paul, Minnesota, proposed that the Conference sponsor a course in rural sociology during the summer specifically geared toward women religious. Schools in Wichita and St. Paul were formed but little else emerged from the idea.[27] In 1938 Luigi Ligutti wrote to Virgil Michel on behalf of the NCRLC and asked if St. John's would be interested in offering a course for rural priests or diocesan directors of rural life. Abbot Deutsch, Michel, and his fellow monks were quite sympathetic to the idea, and Michel suggested a six-week program with the following topics:

1) Lectures on *Quadragesimo Anno*

2) Society and Economy (Fundamental principles)

3) The Liturgy and Social Life

4) Rural living or rural problems or the general program in prospectus of the National Catholic Rural Life Conference.

Michel preferred to stress theory and principles, but he was also disposed toward a practical component. Ligutti too believed in stressing the academic dimension if the NCRLC was to develop able leaders.[28]

---

[26] The first diocesan director's institute was held in 1936 at the NCRLC's Fargo convention. Before that they were conducted under the auspices of the Rural Life Bureau. See MUA/NCRLC, Series 15/1, box 1, "Diocesan Rural Life Directors Institute, 1936." In 1926 the Conference outlined a few "immediate steps" to be taken for its overall agenda and included here was the training of clergy and seminarians. See Bovée, "Church and Land," 157–58; and Editor, "Immediate Steps in Catholic Rural Life," *CRL* 5 (December 1926): 1–2.

[27] Witte, *Crusading*, 199.

[28] Ligutti to Michel, 24 February 1938; Michel to Ligutti, 26 February 1938; Ligutti to Michel, 3 March 1938, in SJUA 1771, University Topics Rf-T, "Rural Life Schools Correspondence 1938–42." Aloisius Muench, bishop of Fargo, also wrote to Michel encouraging him to promote the course. Muench apparently submitted a draft outline. He pointed out that the diocesan rural life directors had not been adequately prepared for their work. Michel's response indicated something of the substance of Muench's program: "I can see the point of your suggestions very well,

Michel also consulted Pauline Reynolds of the State Agricultural College in Fargo, who was the Assistant State Leader of 4-H Clubs for North Dakota. Reynolds had become associated with the NCRLC at the 1936 Fargo convention. Michel listed several "theoretical" courses he had in mind, but Reynolds may have convinced him that a purely theoretical tract may not be the most effective way to impart a rural philosophy, as her following practical suggestions indicated:

1) Art and architecture in rural life.

2) Chant, community singing, and choral projects.

3) Home crafts.

4) Social and community recreations in the country.

5) Youth projects and movements in the country.[29]

This list, combined with the more academic courses listed above, better reflected the NCRLC's desire to provide comprehensive training for its leaders.

Because planning had begun too late in 1939, the first school was not held until July 15–27, 1940. This particular school treated numerous topics including soil conservation, home care, recreation, cooperatives, credit unions, parish life, foreign trade in relation to agriculture, cate-chetics, and two seminars on liturgy and the rural parish.[30] Roger Schoenbechler, OSB, addressed the school's participants on the subject of catechetics. He and Reinhart Kroll, OSB, were the first men that Abbot Deutsch had sent to Sant'Anselmo (Rome) for liturgical studies. Upon their return to St. John's Abbey, they collaborated on several

---

although my first reaction was that the courses as outlined by you would be too much the kind of thing that can be given at a secular university. Of course, that was not what you meant." One might gather that Muench's proposals may not have given due emphasis to the "supernatural" Michel would want in a rural life program. See Michel to Muench, 17 March 1938; Muench to Michel, 12 March 1938; SJUA 1771, University Topics Rf-T, "Rural Life Schools Correspondence 1938–42." Muench's draft outline could not be located.

[29] Michel to Pauline Reynolds, 12 March 1938, SJUA 1771, University Topics Rf-T, "Rural Life Schools Correspondence 1938–42." For Reynold's association with the NCRLC see Witte, *Crusading*, 117.

[30] "Rural Life Summer School," July 15–27, 1940, SJUA 1771, University Topics Rf-T, "Rural Life Schools Correspondence 1940–41," 1–5; See also "Rural Life Summer School," CRLB 3, no. 2 (May 1940): 3.

liturgical projects.[31] At the St. John's summer school, Schoenbechler asserted that all religious instruction must have a firm basis in the liturgy: "For nineteen hundred years the Church has had the task of educating the masses; this was done through word of mouth and the liturgy, which was the first teaching means of the Church." Children need to be shown how to live the liturgy, and this called for an experiential, narrative approach to catechesis. One source he recommended was the *Christ-Life Series* by Virgil Michel.

Abbot Alcuin Deutsch's remarks on the last day of the summer school asserted that the "liturgy is the chief means of improving the conditions of and doing away with the general dissatisfaction now prevalent among rural peoples." The *Missa recitata* and congregational singing were the first steps.[32] After Michel's death in November 1938, the responsibility of the summer schools passed to Martin Schirber, OSB. Michel had left on his desk several unfinished projects, among them a four-year college curriculum for rural living as well as an article on agriculture for *Commonweal*. Without a doubt, St. John's set the pattern for schools around the country, and those at St. John's endured into the 1950s.[33] John Sullivan, SJ (who had worked in Jamaica), visited St. John's and commented on the school's effort to meld theory and praxis, placing participative worship at the center: "It stands for the whole man, the whole farmer. It is a nice fusion of co-ops, rural life, and social worship."[34] Few facets of rural life were left untreated by this summer school.

---

[31] Barry, *Worship and Work*, 262, 268, 289, 303. Yet another interesting confluence of persons in both movements is represented here. Bishop Schlarman (Peoria) asked Abbott Deutsch to send two men to serve at the University of Illinois Newman Center. A team of four Benedictines were sent, Schoenbechler among them. He developed an innovative religious education program based on the liturgy. Newman Hall was occupied by the U.S. military in 1943 and the Benedictines were pulled out by the abbot. Father Edward O'Rourke (Peoria), connected to the NCRLC, succeeded them and continued using the Benedictine's approach to catechesis.

[32] "Rural Life Summer School, St. John's University," MUA/NCRLC, Series 15/1, box 1, "Rural Life Summer Schools, 1940–43," 20, 37.

[33] Marx, *Virgil Michel*, 391.

[34] John P. Sullivan, *Forward on the Land: Benedictines Set Pace in Complete Rural Life* (Kingston, Jamaica: The Social Action Department, St. George's College Extension School, ca. 1944). Sullivan was mentioned in chapter 2 for his article "Co-op Worship to Co-op Work" *OF* 19 (1944–45): 320–24. See also Eva J. Ross, "School for

Nationwide, by the summer of 1945, the NCRLC had conducted 55 such schools or institutes ranging from 1 to 5 days and enrolled 1,700 priests, 9,600 sisters, 9,900 laypeople, and 775 seminarians. James Byrnes was correct when he remarked to Ligutti in 1938: "It looks very much as if this were the beginning of the most important developments in Conference history . . . inasmuch as it represents the first orderly attempt to offer training opportunities for Rural Life Directors."[35] It was indeed a critical juncture for the NCRLC, for up until that time, save for the religious vacation schools, the annual conventions largely gave rural leaders ideas to implement in their dioceses and parishes. The 1940s witnessed a tremendous expansion in its programs and publications, interestingly enough in conjunction with similar stirrings of the Liturgical Conference.[36]

Other efforts were begun to train leaders. In 1943 Father Edward O'Rourke of Peoria, closely associated with Bishop Schlarman's rural activities, noted that the efforts of Catholic Action (CA) had largely been directed toward the cities and factories. Thus O'Rourke felt it necessary to put together some "suggestions" for the chaplains to Catholic Action Farmers (CAF), which he shaped into a manual for the group the previous year. "The supernatural," he asserted, had to be "approached through the natural." Attention to all the natural dimensions of farm life and how they lead one to the supernatural state will move the CAF to right action, seeking to remedy that which is not reflective of a just social order. The "best means for incorporating the supernatural objective and motivation" is to help leaders better understand and participate in the liturgy. Baptism, confirmation, and Eucharist incorporated one fully into the Mystical Body of Christ, and according to O'Rourke, this ecclesial incorporation leads to action:

---

Living," *Columbia* (September 1941): 7, 24; *idem*, "Rural Priest Leads the Way," *Columbia* (October 1942): 9, 18–19. Dr. Eva Ross was a sociology professor at Trinity College in Washington, DC, who had interests in rural life. See her *Belgian Rural Cooperation: A Study in Social Adjustment* (Milwaukee: Bruce Publishing, 1940).

[35] Witte, *Crusading*, 199–201; Bovée, "Church and Land," 319–20; Barry, *Worship and Work*, 288.

[36] A further manifestation and application of the holistic view of life that the Conference took was its pamphlet entitled *Rural Life in a Peaceful World* (1944), issued at the height of World War II. It asserted that amidst the total destruction wrought by the war, a plan for total peace must follow. To reconstruct the social order (literally), the agrarian question would have to remain at the forefront of all such programs. See NCRLC, *Rural Life in a Peaceful World* (Des Moines, IA: NCRLC, 1944), MUA/NCRLC, Series 5/1, box 2, folder 16.

In the Sacrifice of the Mass, we participate in the corporate act of worship of the Mystical Body. Having learned to pray together as an organic unit we are better able to act together. . . . [We] are associated very intimately with Christ in His offering Himself to his heavenly Father for our redemption and the redemption of all men.[37]

Such active participation was indispensable to the Catholic Actionist. The liturgy taught the Christian the truths of the faith by way of the annual feasts (Pius XI). This was far better than knowing "solemn expositions" and was accessible to all no matter what one's state in life. The mysteries would not be known in a "cold and academic" fashion, O'Rourke concluded, "one would live them."

At a 1947 institute for diocesan directors of rural life in Des Moines, Martin Hellriegel conducted a full-day program on liturgy and rural life in which he made clear: "Rubrics are not the essence of liturgy. They are the shell which surrounds the Mass, sacraments, sacramentals, divine office and liturgical year."[38] He discussed the nature of sacrifice, the Mystical Body of Christ, and various arrangements of the dialogue Mass. In some cases, he added, a reader may be assigned to read the collect, epistle, gospel and postcommunion, and the assembly may recite some of the offertory prayers. Congregational singing should be fostered with preference for Gregorian chant. For baptisms, he also recommended that a white garment and candle be made for the child; a prayer card (from Pio Decimo Press) should be sent to the mother after the birth. A study of that prayer, Hellriegel insisted, makes clear that this is not a "purification ceremony" but rather a blessing and petition. First communicants may be led into the church by the deacon carrying the paschal candle, with each child in tow carrying a smaller taper as a reminder of their baptism. It was only after establishing this more substantial liturgical foundation that he began to discuss the usual rural blessings and sacramentals.[39]

A Study Week for Priests was held at Notre Dame in 1947. Theodore Hesburgh, CSC, reaffirmed that Catholic Action (CA) was an external action of the laity in conjunction with the hierarchy. However, he

---

[37] Edward O'Rourke, "Catholic Action Farmers: Suggestions for the Chaplain," MUA/NCRLC, Series 10/1, box 3, "Edward O'Rourke File." I have not been able to locate the CAF manual.

[38] "Diocesan Rural Life Director's Institute," Des Moines, IA, July 15–25, 1947, MUA/NCRLC, Series 15/1, box 1, "Diocesan Rural Life Director's Institute," 4.

[39] Ibid., 4–6.

asserted that there was a deeper "ontological reality" that was essential to a sound theology and spirituality of CA, one that shared in the priesthood of Christ: "Here is a beautiful pattern . . . collaboration with Christ in work and prayer . . . a work of participation in the two great priestly actions of Christ's Mystical Body, the *Ora* and the *Labora*, the public prayer and the universal apostolate."[40] The call of the laity to share in Christ's work was grounded in baptism and confirmation. At this same study week, Raban Hathorn, OSB, from St. Meinrad Seminary, made explicit the connection between the liturgy and CA. Communal liturgy must animate all Christian action in the world so as to restore the social order: "social collapse follows upon the loss of social worship." The ten- to fifteen-minute allotment for liturgy discussion at CA meetings was important but it was better to actually *do* the liturgy. The "dialogue Mass, Prime and Compline, and the sacramentals of the various seasons, especially those connected to work and home," animated the Christian life. Gerald Ellard, SJ, led a discussion following Hathorn's talk, while Luigi Ligutti represented the NCRLC in promoting the "rural cells," noting that the small-cell technique— think, judge, act—was especially suited for rural people.[41]

*The Family, Church and Environment* was a study-discussion outline for seminarians, sisters, priests, and lay leaders. The one-hundred-page booklet had as its subtitle the liturgical movement's motto "*Instaurare Omnia in Christo.*" The booklet was the joint effort of the NCRLC and the Institute for Social Study at St. Louis University. It was divided into six main divisions, eighteen units, with four topics for each unit—

[40] Theodore Hesburgh, CSC, "Theology of Catholic Action," 4, in *The Lay Apostolate and the Priest: Talks Given at the Fifth Annual Week of Catholic Action Study For Priests, University of Notre Dame, August 4 to 8, 1947* (South Bend, IN: Fides Press, 1947). Hesburgh's doctoral dissertation was entitled "The Relationship of the Sacramental Character of Baptism and Confirmation to the Lay Apostolate." See Pecklers, *Unread Vision*, 32n24.

[41] Raban Hathorn, OSB, "Liturgy and Catholic Action," 33–39; Luigi Ligutti, "The Rural Movement," 11–12, in *The Lay Apostolate and the Priest*. A decade later in 1956, Notre Dame hosted one of the NCRLC's rural life workshop for priests, sisters, and lay leaders. Monsignor Joseph Morrison led an entire day devoted to liturgy. His talk, "Secularism Meets Its Challenge in the Liturgy," was followed by workshops and discussions entitled: The Liturgy and Blessings at Work on the Farm, Liturgical Ceremonies for the Country Parish, Liturgical Practices in the Home, A Day of Christian Rural Living, and The Young Christian Farmer Apostolate. See "Rural Life Workshop, Notre Dame University, August 15–18, 1956," MUA/ NCRLC, Series 15/1, box 1, "Institutes for Priests."

seventy-two lessons in all. It was sweeping in scope, examining nearly every facet of rural life and providing an extensive bibliography. Ligutti and Jesuit Anthony Adams wrote the foreword. They emphasized that the manual's disciplined approach was needed for today's rural leaders so as to counter any sort of utopian idealism: "The social order will never be restored in Christ by either daydreams or a plethora of activities which are not preceded by serious thought and planning . . . leaders who lack an integrated concept of the interdependence of the natural and supernatural orders."[42]

Unit Nine of the manual, "Toward a Spiritual Renaissance," proposed a study of the CCD, A Living Liturgy, Rural Street Preaching (i.e., Catholic Evidence Guild), and Retreats. The purpose of the liturgy component was to gain a greater appreciation of the close bond between rural living and the church's official worship. Topics such as the Mass, special collects, Rogation Days, and blessings in the *Ritual* were suggested. Under "Remarks" it recommended a study of the St. Andrew Daily Missal to show the close relationship between liturgy and rural life. The *Proceedings* of the 1946 Liturgical Week, with a special focus on "The Family in Christ" were recommended for study. In addition to the *Proceedings*, the short liturgical bibliography recommended *Grailville: A Program of Action*, and Emmanuel Mounier's *Personalist Manifesto*. The general bibliography suggested "Ember Days" and "Holy Spring-Lenten Sundays," both published by the Grail, *Orate Fratres*, and Martin Hellriegel's *Holy Sacrifice of the Mass*. Virgil Michel's *Christian Education for Rural Living* and *Christian Social Reconstruction* were also included. Saint John's was listed as the liturgical resource for further consultation, and the manual's authors even went so far as to give the contact information of the following persons who could offer further insights: H. A. Reinhold, Benedict Ehman, OSB, George Hildner, and Martin Hellriegel.[43]

Direct efforts were also made to inculcate seminarians with the NCRLC's program for rural life.[44] Some of these endeavors were

---

[42] NCRLC, *The Family, Church and Environment* (Des Moines, IA: NCRLC, 1947), 3.

[43] Ibid., 51, 106, 112. The 1946 *Proceedings* carried Hellriegel's "The Family Life, The Liturgical Year and the Sacramentals," which was treated in chapter 3, 93–94.

[44] Even though it took some time to organize a concrete program, a beginning was made at the 1928 convention in Atchison, Kansas, where the NCRLC established a seminary committee and made Fr. Philip Kiley the chairman. See MUA/NCRLC, Series 8/1, box 1, black binder. Also, the Jesuit theologate of St. Mary's (Kansas)

wholly centered on rural life; others gave a place to the rural apostolate in the wider context of Catholic Action. Institutes and study clubs for seminarians were held all around the country as the diocesan director reports indicate. The institutes frequently cooperated with a state university that had a strong agricultural extension program—Kentucky, Illinois, Vermont, and Wisconsin—to name a few. The University of Wisconsin at Madison was especially noteworthy as it hosted summer institutes for over a decade. Several institutes and study clubs for seminarians can be highlighted to gain some sense of the formation the men received.

As early as 1931, St. Mary's College (Kansas), the Jesuit theologate for the Missouri Province, began to address rural life issues as part of a sodality project. The seminarians studied issues centered mostly on farm ownership, not surprisingly, since the Depression had precipitated the foreclosure of thousands of farms. This study group was the initiative of Fr. Robert Demeyer, SJ, and a handful of seminarians. They published a number of pamphlets dealing with private ownership, cooperatives, credit unions, village planning, and 4-H clubs. At the time, these pamphlets were considered groundbreaking, in part because they were the only publications in this field, and they directly applied Catholic social teaching. The group disbanded in the mid-1930s, only to be resurrected by Anthony Adams in 1938, who became a long-time leader in the Conference. Adams had the seminarians take a survey of American Jesuits to determine their interest in rural life. The response was less than enthusiastic. One Jesuit responded by questioning whether a relationship existed between rural life and the salvation of souls. "This irked the members and moved them to write *Is Rural Life the Answer?*"[45]

Adams taught courses in rural sociology and pastoral action. An elective was offered for both priests and lay leaders who are "seeking methods of applying rural life principles to parish and community life." The course placed the spiritual dimension at the forefront: "Monday: Initial Motivation—Farmer's Retreats, Days of Recollection,

---

had begun work in the early 1930s (see below), as did St. Francis Seminary in Milwaukee, Wisconsin, under the leadership of Aloisius Muench.

[45] Witte, *Crusading*, 207–8. Anthony Adams was the principal author, and it was published in *The Queen's Work* in 1941. Adams also penned a liturgical column that was widely disseminated to diocesan and civic newspapers. This will be considered below in the section titled *Disseminating the Rural Life Message*.

Rural Life Sundays, sermons, and liturgy." Once again, the course was meant to be comprehensive and included such topics as street preaching, radio broadcasts, ethics of land use, home culture (blessings, native art, etc.), cooperatives, and credit unions.[46] The Jesuits of St. Mary's literally put theory into practice; they operated a large garden that employed "biodynamic" farming techniques and were able to feed over two hundred seminarians and faculty on campus. A labor shortage caused by World War II moved the Jesuit seminarians to give over three thousand hours of manpower harvesting crops on local farms.

Saint Mary's also embraced the Catholic Action movement that was being established at many seminaries around the country. One study group utilized an outline entitled "Catholic Action and the Rural Problem." The seminarians reflected on the problems facing rural communities—inferiority complex, isolation, life on land stripped of its value, and deterioration of family life. They offered solutions as well—independent farming, cooperation, reform of rural education, dissemination of the best technical methods in agricultural, and revival of rural home life. "Services" described the methods employed by the group to respond to the problems. They were meant to put into practice the Christian spirit and included rural liturgy, retreats, and days of recollection. James T. Meehan, SJ, was inspired by such programs and wrote his 1941 licentiate thesis on "Cooperatives: A Phase of Pastoral Theology." His thesis demonstrated the broad reach that the Conference advanced with regard to seminary formation, further trying to meld theology and praxis, altar, and home.[47]

[46] Anthony Adams, SJ, "Rural Life in Action," Midwest Jesuit Archives, St. Louis, MO, "Rural Life Committee St. Mary's, KS, 1946."

[47] James T. Meehan, SJ, "Cooperatives: A Phase of Pastoral Theology," (Licentiate Thesis, St. Mary's College, KS, 1941), in MUA/NCRLC, Series 12/1, box 2, "Reports and Theses." There was another thesis on rural life from St. Mary's. See J. H. Millet, SJ, "Catholic Action and the Rural Problem," MUA/SCA, Series 2, box 1, "St. Mary's College, 1943–46." Mention should also be made of the "Semana Rural" held at Montezuma Seminary in New Mexico, August 1–6, 1943. This seminary was established for Mexican clergy during the period of persecution. Bishop Schlarman, Luigi Ligutti, and John Rawe, SJ, were the main presenters. The agenda included: a study of soils, Biodynamic Farming, land use, homesteads, cooperatives, and a full day devoted to liturgy (led by Schlarman). A Pontifical High Mass was celebrated in a field and a sermon was preached. There was a blessing of fields followed by songs and a picnic. In MUA/NCRLC, Series 15/1, box 1, "Semana Rural." See also

An extension of St. Mary's work was undertaken by one of the Conference's outstanding leaders, Fr. John Rawe, SJ, who with Luigi Ligutti authored *Rural Roads to Security* in 1940. Rawe, who was raised on a farm in Carrollton, Missouri, made his first contact with the NCRLC in 1936 at the Fargo Convention, the same conference Virgil Michel attended. In 1942 Rawe established the Creighton University Rural Life Institute on the grounds of the Omar Research Farm near Omaha. The program was geared toward laymen and showed great promise; however, half the class was conscripted for military duty and it came to an abrupt end. This short-lived institute taught progressive stewardship of the land, one that employed the best scientific and technical knowledge of soil and animals: "The students will learn how to deal intelligently with the 'wholeness' and the 'completeness' of nature on each small farm; how to keep a state of balance on the land, i.e., varied crops, animals, and organic matter for renewal." The twelve-month course went beyond the science of farming and included topics such as rural culture, philosophy, religion, social reconstruction, home life, recreation, economics, and food storage/ processing. Unfortunately, Rawe became sick while working in Maryland and died at the age of forty-six.[48]

The seminarians at the Sulpician-run Theological College in Washington, DC, conducted an active CA program. Tom Reese, from the Diocese of Wilmington, Delaware, served as the college's CA leader.[49] In 1944–45, the college began several CA study groups. Topics included The Popes and CA, Jocist Movement, Cell Technique, CA and the

---

Anne M. Martínez, "From the Halls of Montezuma: Seminary in Exile or Pan-American Project," *U.S. Catholic Historian*, 20 (Fall 2002): 35–51.

[48] *Forward on the Land: Creighton University Rural Life Institute*, Midwest Jesuit Archives, St. Louis, MO, "Biographical: John Rawe, SJ," ca. 1942. See also "Fr. John Rawe Leaves Classroom to Become Real Dirt Farmer," *Eastern Kansan Register*, February 13, 1942; and Obituary for John Rawe, Midwest Jesuit Archives, St. Louis, MO. Rawe began similar projects at St. Stephen's Indian Mission in Wyoming, as well as in southern Maryland among whites and blacks at the Cardinal Gibbon's Institute.

[49] Reese's name litters the Seminarian Catholic Action files at Marquette. He coordinated national gatherings such as the one discussed below at Notre Dame. One has to wonder if and when he managed to study any theology. Perhaps this says something about the nature of seminary life at that time. Then again, in its most rudimentary form, a theology of CA had as it core curriculum liturgy and ecclesiology, both inseparable from the moral life and social justice, as it was noted in Theodore Hesburgh's work above.

Liturgy, The Rural Challenge, CA and the Home.[50] "The liturgy is the primary means of glorifying God and the indispensable means whereby she saves and sanctifies mankind . . . the liturgy comprises the Mass, Sacraments, sacramentals, Office and liturgical year . . . [it is how] divine life must be communicated to mankind from Christ." It was left to the CA apostle to bridge the divide between modern life and the liturgy; one must act as a "mediator" who has feet in both spheres of life. In "The Rural Challenge" the seminarians highlighted the difficulties faced in the countryside—isolation, the farmer's independence and aversion to organizing (contrary to Europe), "factories in the fields," lack of pastor-leaders, and few opportunities for youth. The ultimate success would be found in developing rural leaders, a task for CA. Among the group's recommended solutions, rural liturgical practices did not make the list. This is of course not to say it was not discussed elsewhere.[51]

The University of Notre Dame was a hub for liturgical as well as Catholic Action programs. On that campus, Moreau Seminary served as a house of studies for the Holy Cross men in formation. In 1944–45, the seminarians adopted a Catholic Action study plan developed by the group at Montezuma Seminary the previous year. Study groups were organized around such topics as: liturgy, foreign missions, education, labor, rural life, "the Negro, and the Jews."[52] The group's primary liturgical source was Dom Wesseling's *Liturgy and Life: The Common Act of the Mystical Body*. The study group moved beyond principles to consider the liturgy's role in forming one's moral life. Does the liturgy affect the whole Christian, imparting a worldview? Is it the *sacramentum unitatis et pacis*? How does corporate worship counter excessive sentimentalism and individualistic piety? What is its particular relationship to labor and race issues, education, politics, missions, and the parish? The Rural CA group studied the dignity and

[50] "Catholic Action Seminar: A Resume of Papers Given at Group II," MUA/SCA, Series 2, box 1, "Seminaries, Theological College, 1944–48." There was no specific date for the seminar but it correlates with the following item in the same file, "Plan for Catholic Action Study Group I and II: 1944–45."

[51] "Catholic Action and the Liturgy," 22–23, and "The Rural Challenge," 24–25, in the same "Catholic Action Seminar" booklet just noted above.

[52] "Moreau Seminary Catholic Action Plan, 1945–46," MUA/SCA, Series 2, box 1, "Moreau Seminary, ca. 1946," 1–8.

vocation of the farmer, family life, rural liturgy, cooperation, steward-ship, and the role of the layperson.[53]

Saint John's seminary in Kansas City, Missouri, hosted the first rural life institute for seminarians, July 1–9, 1948. At this gathering several leaders reported on the activities at their respective seminaries. Eugene Robl recounted the establishment of a study club at Kenrick Seminary in St. Louis in 1943. By 1948 the club had evolved into a cycle course taught over four years in this order: philosophy of the *Manifesto*, cooperatives, rural Catholic Action/Farm Organizations, and liturgy. The seminary had even planned a course on folk dancing for the fol-lowing year in addition to establishing a credit union. On July 8, at the same institute, Martin Hellriegel addressed the men on "Liturgical Rural Living." He stressed the close relationship between the NCRLC and the Liturgical Apostolate, calling rural life and Catholic Action two branches on the tree trunk of liturgy—the indispensable source of the true Christian spirit. The liturgy is not just rubrics and ceremonies but is the vital expression of the Mystical Body of Christ: "The liturgy is to the Mystical Body what speech and thought are to the human person. Christian people then are people who live the liturgy." At nearly every institute conducted between the years 1949 and 1955, each one allotted a place for the liturgy to be discussed as the primary spiritual foundation for rural living and a just social order.[54]

In 1955 the Conference created the "Seminarians Manual for the Study of the Rural Family, Church, and Community," which was

[53] Ibid., 4, 8. Also to be noted, the "Cross and Plow Conference," held at St. Francis Seminary in Milwaukee, spearheaded an effort to encourage seminarians to take up rural ministry. Bishop Aloisius Muench served as rector there in the 1930s and had been instrumental in fostering interest in rural life. The "confer-ence" functioned more like a study club, running through 1948 with almost seventy men taking part. It was not mandated for all of the seminarians. Liturgy, as well as rural social problems, rounded out the comprehensive curriculum. The seminarians relied on the "Family, Church, and Environment" outline (examined below) and modified it as needed. "Cross and Plow Conference," MUA/NCRLC, Series 8/1, box 6, folder "Cross and Plow Conference, ca. 1947, 1947."

[54] Eugene Robl, "Session Briefs," St. John's Seminary Rural Life Institute, Kansas City, MO, 2 July 1948; "Msgr. Hellriegel Explains Liturgical Rural Living," 8 July 1948, in MUA/NCRLC, Series 15/1, box 1, "Institute for Seminarians, 1948–55." Even the thought of making a "folk dancing" course part of a Roman Catholic seminary's curriculum in the 1940s, let alone actually conducting it, was astounding. As far as I could determine no archival material about the course or its rural life program was preserved.

intended to be a three-year-cycle course that treated the religious, social, and economic aspects of rural life. It was a condensed format of *Family, Church and Environment.* Six topics were suggested for each semester, and it provided (unlike the previous manual) questions for discussion and a bibliography for each topic.[55] The liturgy's import for rural life was studied and the "Questions for Discussion" not only probed the general nature of the liturgy but its meaning for rural culture and its social implications:

> What is the definition of the liturgy? What are the rural implications and associations with the Holy Sacrifice of the Mass? List some of the liturgical blessings especially suited to rural living. How can the liturgy be a source of unity within the family and a common bond of unity in the community? What influence has the reception of the sacraments on the way of life rural people [live] socially as well as religiously? How successful has the new Easter Vigil been in rural parishes?[56]

The manual's bibliography relied upon literature from the liturgical movement and the Conference's liturgical publications, combining theory and praxis. Once again, it demonstrated the NCRLC's "catholic" approach, which utilized many sources—secular and religious—that would advance its program to restore all things in

---

[55] NCRLC, "Seminarians Manual," MUA/NCRLC, Series 5/1, box 6, folder 18. *Religious Aspect*: The popes and rural life, rural pastor, parish organizations and study clubs, liturgy, catholic rural leadership, diocesan rural life director, dignity of the farmer, family prayer, rural retreats, CCD, home missions (Glenmary), institutes for seminarians. *Social Aspect*: history of agriculture, population trends, rural environment, rural-urban relations, international sphere (migration and immigration), rural settlement, education, youth activities, vocations, homemaking, and health. *Economic Aspect*: family type farm, ownership vs. tenancy, father-son partnership, soil conservation, extension service, scientific farming, farm mechanization, distribution, far organizations, producer and consumer co-ops, and credit unions.

[56] NCRLC, "Seminarians Manual." All of the bibliographical sources had either a strong liturgical-sacramental emphasis, or at least a reference to the liturgy, and included: *The Land: God's Gift to Man, Sacramental Protection of the Family, Seven Keys to a Christian Home, A Day of Christian Rural Living, Rural Sociology, With the Blessing of the Church, Twenty-Five Years of Crusading, Rogation Day Manual, Novena in Honor of St. Isidore, Thanksgiving Day Manual,* "The Cooperative Movement and the Liturgical Movement" (V. Michel), and "Living the Liturgy" (a column from the Catholic Rural Life Page).

Christ. By 1956 there were twenty-three rural life study clubs in major and minor seminaries.[57]

The NCRLC made a consistent effort to imbue its rural leaders with a wide breadth of knowledge, one that was not purely academic in nature. Each facet of its program imparted knowledge of the rural socioeconomic order, soil conservation, recreation, and art/crafts. All these were balanced by a spiritual agenda that gave primacy to the church's liturgy. In doing so, the NCRLC relied on the leaders of the liturgical movement and its various publications. Clearly, active participation in the church's worship was fundamental. More generally, the Conference nourished deeper engagement in the life of the church, a fuller living out of one's baptism in the Mystical Body of Christ.

DISSEMINATING THE RURAL LIFE MESSAGE

With regard to the periodicals and the rural life columns (distributed to diocesan and local newspapers), the NCRLC understood its mission as a kind of rural *propaganda fide*. In many respects, the periodicals were a constant challenge for the NCRLC, requiring considerable time, effort, and money to produce and distribute. The various editors gave emphasis to issues they thought were more important. The Conference's main informational organ changed names, and to some degree its focus, eight times in thirty-five years.[58] Another problem was the language of the periodicals, namely, it was technical and beyond the reach of the average farmer (their complaint). Ligutti sought to change this when he took over as executive secretary in the early 1940s, giving it a folksy feel. More substantial material continued to appear, but the simpler format enabled the farmer to see more clearly the relationship between his daily toil, the liturgy, and a more just social order.

Among the broad spectrum of topics treated, one finds much material dealing with rural culture, justice, and liturgy. Selections will be guided by these three areas, noting how the NCRLC informed rural

[57] Executive Committee Meeting, October 19, 1956, Sioux Falls, SD, MUA/NCRLC, Series 8/1, box 15.

[58] All Conference periodicals and columns can be found in MUA/NCRLC, Series 6/1. *St. Isidore's Plow* (1923–25), *Catholic Rural Life* (1925–30), no journal 1930–33, *Landward* (1933–37), *Catholic Rural Life Bulletin* (1938–41), *Land and Home* (1942–47), *The Christian Farmer* (1948–51), *Feet in the Furrow* (1952–55), *Rural Life Conference* (1957–58), *Catholic Rural Life* (1958–present). See Bovée, "Church and Land," 312–17.

Catholics (and the general population) about these topics through the various publications. By now, it has been made clear how the NCRLC understood and celebrated the church's liturgy in relation to rural life; but how did the Conference understand the terms culture and justice, which it frequently employed? The NCRLC set forth its understanding of culture and justice in its core vision statement, the *Manifesto on Rural Life*. The Conference employed these terms in a manner that was not so specific as to limit their application.[59]

The NCRLC wanted to free the term "culture" from the common association with intellectual and artistic superiority based on wealth and leisure. One could possess culture without knowledge of Shakespeare and Mozart. At the same time the *Manifesto* honestly acknowledged the paucity of culture in the countryside due to isolation and poverty. It often referred to the etymology of the word culture, which is related to the cultivation of the soil, yet admitted that the term was difficult to define. At its core, "It designates the harmonious development of man's moral, intellectual, and esthetic faculties . . . a synthesis of the gentleman, artist, scholar, and saint." The *Manifesto* further clarified:

> Culture cannot be superimposed on a group. It must grow out of the life of the rural community. It will be deeply rooted in their modes of thinking and in their philosophy of living. Culture implies the right appraisal of values and an appreciation of both material and spiritual good. Culture is best expressed in its creative aspect. Rural Catholic culture will find expression in refined manners, artistic homes, neat farmsteads, modern conveniences, music, art, and literature; in folk drama; in the liturgy and church chant; church architecture; and above all in virtuous living.[60]

This "harmonious development," the Conference believed, occurred in the context of community such that a flourishing culture would be reflected in closer social and economic bonds as well. "When farmers work together [co-ops], perhaps they will play together."[61] Religion

---

[59] The overall goal here with regard to the periodicals will be modest since the volume of material is extensive. Therefore, I will treat the magazines and columns chronologically, providing a general sense of their scope and content as it relates to the themes of liturgy, culture, and justice.

[60] NCRLC, "Catholic Culture in Rural Society," in *Manifesto*, 110–11.

[61] Ibid., 116–17. See Edwin O'Hara, *The Church and the Country Community* (New York, Macmillan, 1927). John LaFarge made a similar argument, namely, religion,

provided the unifying thread that ran through the whole of rural culture, permeating all spheres of life.

The *Manifesto* made a distinction between "social charity" and "social justice," but not always in a clear manner. "Charity cannot be exercised without consideration of justice," said Pius XI. Justice aims to correct those structures within a culture that inhibit the true flourishing of the human person, his or her "harmonious development." Lack of access to fair wages, basic resources, education, and recreation were problems whose basic cause was rooted in poverty and unjust social structures. "Justice is fundamental in the social order because it defines and defends the individual at points where he is in danger from others or social conditions against which he is helpless." Charity served to counter the "selfish impulses" of society that could institutionalize individualism, leading to a law of the jungle. While the *Manifesto* provided no extensive treatment (or definition) of social justice per se, discussion of justice emerged in the chapters on farmers' cooperatives, land ownership and tenancy, rural health, farm labor, and credit unions. Soil erosion, the *Manifesto* claimed, was intimately bound up with human erosion. These concerns were (and still are today) at the heart of social structures that prevented rural people from having a more just share in America's bounty.[62]

With the inauguration of the *Catholic Rural Life Bulletin* in 1938, the Conference began to address in a more comprehensive manner the issues important to Catholic agrarians. Contributors were often experts from governmental and other civic groups. They were also leaders in the liturgical movement and the arts. Virgil Michel voiced his hope and approval of the new endeavor this way:

> I have just read the first issue of the Catholic Rural Life Bulletin. . . . We Catholics need to learn anew the true philosophy of Catholic living. Catholic life must be a life close to nature, for the supernatural dispensation of God builds on the natural. Instead of commercial exploitation of the soil, which is but a pagan counterpart of the

---

and especially Catholicism (principles, not a wholesale imposition of the church's teaching), could serve as the basis of a just American society. John LaFarge, "Religion, the Groundwork of True American Culture," *Landward* 5, no. 1 (Spring 1937): 1, 8–10.

[62] NCRLC, "Rural Social Charity," in *Manifesto*, 145–46, 192. See also Benedict XVI, *Caritas in Veritate: On Integral Human Development in Charity and Truth* (Rome: Libreria Editrice Vaticana, June 29, 2009).

unchristian mechanization of our big city life, we must get back to cooperation with the forces of nature for more wholesome Christian living. We must learn again, how to build up the soil itself even while getting a fuller cultural life itself. A vast field of discussion and re-learning opens up before us here, and we need to probe it to the very bottom . . . to the bottom foundations of sound natural living and sound Christian principles.[63]

In the same issue Michel also set the tone for what could be expected from a program for Christian rural living. Concerned about the "citify-ing" of rural curricula, he stressed that a course of study should not merely duplicate what agricultural schools are doing in their focus on the science of farming. Rather, his three-point program began with the supernatural aspect imparted to a member of the Mystical Body of Christ who actively and intelligently participated in the official worship of the church. Second, natural knowledge should be grounded in the philosophy of personalism, inclusive of the ideas of corporatism and cooperation. Finally, there was the need to be steeped in the agricultural aspect of rural living—to stand against commercial farming, embrace organizations that will advance the betterment of the family farm and rural life in general. In short, Michel recommended a "living" school versus the vocational-technical programs that were popular; no mere traditional classroom instruction would suffice. He named the Danish folk schools as being exemplary, in which one was suffused completely with the local culture.[64]

"Rural Life Sundays" were a celebration of rural Catholic culture. Their observance "becomes an occasion for earnest Christians to gain an increase in Grace . . . it gives emphasis to the honor and dignity of the agricultural occupation, to the economic, social, and spiritual securities . . . blessedness of life on the land." Sociologically, their observance revealed the approach the church took to involve itself in the daily life of the farmer. The Rural Life Sundays drew large numbers

---

[63] Virgil Michel, no title, *CRLB* 1 (August 1938): 3. A quick perusal of the articles will give some sense of the breadth of topics treated: "The Land and Human Values," "The Middle Way in Belgium," "Ruralizing Rural Education," "Wheat" (poem), "Christian Education for Rural Living" (Virgil Michel), "Rural Life Sundays," "Rural Orchestras," "Agriculture in the Industrial Encyclicals," "Missionary Work of Canadian Nuns."

[64] Virgil Michel, "Christian Education for Rural Living," *CRLB* 1 (August 1938): 19–21. As mentioned earlier, a rural curriculum was one of the projects he left unfinished on his desk when he died.

of faithful for a day filled with Mass, blessings (seed, soil, crops, farm machinery, etc.), and talks; it was a celebration of rural life and culture. Such days served as a countervailing force to the strong individualistic spirit spawned by "liberalistic economies. . . . They form the individual heads and hearts of farmers in the demands of God's laws of justice and charity."[65] In a similar vein, one reader wrote to the editor asking how rural Catholics were to foster a communal rural spirituality:

> If we are to develop an indigenous rural culture based on Catholic principles, we must develop an indigenous spirituality with which the people of that culture can bind themselves to God. And we can't do it with the forms of 16th century Europe. . . . I think if we go back to the psalms and breviary hymns and [the church fathers] . . . we would find a society and spirituality much more to the point. I was beginning to discuss this with Fr. Virgil Michel, but now he is gone. . . . I usually get little but uncomprehending looks when I mention any of this.[66]

The reader expressed some frustration with "business as usual" religion, a mere repetition of what cities were doing as well as the devotions and practices of a time and place that were not relevant to his or her situation.

---

[65] "Rural Life Sundays," *CRLB* 1 (August 1938): 20.

[66] "Found in the Editor's Mail," *CRLB* 2 (February 1939): 12. Several other people deserve mention as regards promoting culture. Pauline Reynolds wrote about her association with "The Little Country Theater," a program at North Dakota State College. She called the theater a "real social center," complete with plays, lectures, library, and people skilled in crafts. Pauline Reynolds, "Live Nobly and Well," *CRLB* 2 (February 1939): 8–10; *idem*, "Rural Dramatics in North Dakota," *CRLB* 2 (August 1939): 12–13, 16–17. Willis Nutting was a sociology professor at the University of Notre Dame once noted: "It has been the case before that when people became Christian their peculiar characteristics [cultural] . . . were not eradicated but consecrated. Why could not our religion take these distinctive elements in our traditional rural culture and make them strong, beautiful and holy?" Nutting put forth in seed form what is understood today as inculturation and points to the inherent good in all cultures (*Gaudium et Spes*, no. 53). Willis Nutting, "Pattern for a Native Rural Culture," *CLRB* 3 (May 1940): 9–11, 28–29; *idem*, "Foundations of a Rural Christian Culture," *CRLB* 2 (February 1939): 1, 26–28. See also pieces by the well-known architect Ralph Adams Cram, "Strength from the Good Earth," *CRLB* 3 (May 1940): 1–3; *idem*, "The Status of Church Art and Architecture," *CRLB* 1 (May 1938): 7–9. Cram presented a paper at the Conference's 1937 Richmond meeting.

In terms of social justice, economic (labor) issues predominated in the late 1930s, often focusing on credit unions and cooperatives. The dignity of the human person, created in the image and likeness of God, was also put forth by the NCRLC—a tenet that has been more thoroughly advanced in contemporary church teaching. The priority of labor (the person) over capital was a deeply held conviction of Emmanuel Mounier in his *Personalist Manifesto*. Saint John's University, under the influence of Virgil Michel, applied personalist philosophy to both the liturgical and rural life movements. Emerson Hynes, a sociology professor at St. John's, relied on Mounier's work and further integrated it with the Catholic agrarian viewpoint. The Catholic agrarian, Hynes argued, was one who honored individual freedom and dignity nourished by the corporative-cooperative order. The joy and dignity of work comes, in part, from ownership and holding creative power over one's farm and production, being able to provide food for family and world—a dignity that factory farms wrested from the family farmer.[67]

Human rights regarding migrant labor were also a regular feature in the *CRLB*. (The Conference had placed this issue on its agenda in the late 1920s.) Patrick Quinlan depicted well the issue prior to the coloring of the American imagination in John Steinbeck's *The Grapes of Wrath*. While the present-day image of South and Central Americans easily comes to mind, Quinlan included as well the Italians, Swedes, Poles, Portuguese, Southern mountaineers, and blacks. He urged cooperation between churches, civic entities, and employers to better their precarious lot. Quinlan sounded prophetic:

> So vast a homeless, neglected group of human beings threatens the life of a nation. Migrant labor camps can become the slums of rural life. All the elements which are the germs of crime could easily find nourishment in the labor camp about which nobody cares.[68]

[67] For two outstanding examples of cooperative projects see Donald Hayne, "Westphalia: Pattern and Promise," *CRLB* 2 (August 1939): 18–19, 28; and Editor, "Coops Again," *CRLB* 3 (February 1940): 9. The latter article tells of Fr. Wilfrid Soucy, who reversed a deplorable socioeconomic situation in rural Maine. The monks of St. John's Abbey translated Emmanuel Mounier's *Personalist Manifesto* with Virgil Michel writing the foreword. See also Emerson Hynes, "Consider the Person," *CRLB* 2 (May 1939): 9–11, 28–29; idem, "The Joy and Dignity of Work," *CRLB* 1 (November 1938): 16–18, 24–25.

[68] Patrick Quinlan, "Rural Migrants on the March" *CRLB* 2 (May 1939): 12–13, 25–26. Steinbeck published *The Grapes of Wrath* in 1939.

The Conference defended the cause of migrant labor when it supported such initiatives as the Bracero Program begun in 1942. Later, the NCRLC also lent its support to Cesar Chavez and the United Farm Workers, not without controversy, however.

Another group with agrarian connections that upheld the dignity of the human person was the Catholic Worker. William Gauchat argued how the CW farm communes offered freedom and security that was both corporative and cooperative. This was how the Mystical Body expressed itself best. Peter Maurin repeatedly claimed that the key to social reconstruction would be the "cultivation of lands and crafts—*cult, culture, and cultivation.*" Skilled labor on the farms was one escape route from the poverty that dogged so many people in the 1930s. Gauchat's vision of the CW farms (Catholic agrarianism) was much aligned with the NCRLC's and placed the Mass at the center of such a Christian community.[69]

The NCRLC's publication changed names and tenor with the first edition of *Land and Home* (1942–47). This journal represented one of the better efforts of the Conference to impart its rural philosophy to the average farmer. *Land and Home*'s purpose seemed geared toward persuading rural people to remain on the land; thus, it vigorously promoted rural culture. Contributors included housewives and professors, and topics ran the gamut from farming's relation to classical Greek poets and philosophers to the housewife's contribution to the home economy while her husband held a job in the city. The "Rural Pastor's Page" (a column in *Land and Home*) offered practical suggestions to strengthen parish life and served as an idea bank. Every issue contained reviews of current literature dealing with agricultural economics, liturgy, and politics. While "substantial" articles continued to appear in its pages, the overall tenor seemed more down-to-earth.[70]

Almost every issue of *Land and Home* contained articles on liturgical and sacramental topics, providing sound catechesis consistent with the liturgical movement's agenda. The use of sacramentals was encour-

[69] William Gauchat, "Cult, Culture, and Cultivation," *CRLB* 4 (August 1941): 64–66. See also Marlett, *Saving the Heartland*, 76ff.

[70] In my estimation, *Land and Home* (especially) and all of the Conference's periodicals warrant an independent study. They are quite rich in terms of the people solicited to write for them and the topics they covered. *Land and Home* would make an interesting study of rural culture in 1940s America. Below, I will draw on this journal for some of the poetry that was frequently published in its pages.

aged as a means to deepen one's connection to the land, and so a blessing (in English) from the Roman Ritual appeared in many issues. It was suggested that families recite the blessing in their homes, one way in which the NCRLC promoted liturgy in the home (and on the farm). The prayers used in the agricultural blessings, according to Martin Hellriegel, should be prayed in the family home in the absence of a priest. Bede Scholtz, OSB, of Conception Abbey, spearheaded that monastery's use of blessings on its farm. The revival of these sacramentals gave impetus to greater engagement in the seasonal ceremonies joined to the church's liturgy. *Land and Home* relied on *Altar and Home* for such insights, most certainly for translations of the blessings (this prior to Schlarman's *With the Blessing of the Church* in 1946). The journal *Liturgical Arts* was also promoted in this NCRLC periodical.[71]

*Land and Home* continued to advocate the Conference's social justice concerns. More interesting, in some respects, was how their cooperation with different civic and religious groups may have contributed to greater ecumenical, interreligious, and interracial accord. In 1944, no less, with the Second World War still raging, Samson Liph of the Jewish Agricultural Society gave an overview of his organization's work. If Liph had not identified himself as Jewish, anyone reading the

---

[71] *Altar and Home* was also the recommended journal for high school students as part of the Aledo-Peoria Plan, a creative project for religious education in rural areas. The following is just a sample of articles on liturgy and sacraments: Thomas Allen, OSB, "The Land and Sacramentals," *L&H* 5 (September 1942): 2–3. Allen also reported on the 1942 Liturgical Week held at St. Meinrad in the pages of this journal. He was especially moved by the thousands who actively participated in the liturgies and the impact it had on them. "Go home and be apostles of the liturgy seemed to be the slogan on the minds of all at the end of the inspiring and instructive week." Thomas Allen, OSB, "The Liturgical Week," *L&H* 5 (December 1942): 20. Other liturgically oriented materials include no less than the following: "Rural Pastor's Page," *L&H* 6 (March 1943): 16; Lee Bowen, "Symbolic Plowing," *L&H* 5 (December 1942): 5; "The Rural Pastor's Page" *L&H* 6 (June 1943): 46; Thomas Allen, OSB, "Ember Days and the Land," *L&H* 6 (September 1943): 76–77; Sr. M. Joanna, "The Aledo-Peoria Way," *L&H* 6 (December 1943): 111–12; Luigi Ligutti, "Communism Goes to Mass," *L&H* 7 (June 1944): 32–33; Ignatius Esser, OSB, "Farm Home—Kingdom and Sanctuary," *L&H* 7, no. 2 (June 1944): 34–36; Edward O'Rourke, "Sermon Outline: A Valiant Woman," *L&H* 8 (June 1945): 47–48; Benedict Ehmann, OSB, "Gather Ye into My Barns" *L&H* 9 (September 1946): 66–68; Mariette Wickes, "A Family Celebration of the Ember Days," *L&H* 9 (December 1946): 100–102; "Notes and Comments, *L&H* 9 (December 1946): 105, has a picture by Edmonde J. Massicote that shows a father with hands extended giving a new year blessing to his family, who are kneeling in a simple wood cabin.

article would have thought it written by a Catholic farmer urging the same lifestyle on the land. One year later, a group of Catholics, Protestants, and Jews signed the "Land Policy" that set forth a program for just stewardship and distribution of land.[72]

Present-day racial problems are almost exclusively framed in relation to African Americans. In the 1940s, the word "racial" may have conjured up images of "American Indians, Orientals, and Mexicans." It was John LaFarge who in 1924 brought the issue of African Americans in the countryside to the NCRLC's attention. He devoted much of his life to this issue and founded the Catholic Interracial Council. He also pressed for relocating more blacks on farms as a means of strengthening community and "building up the morale of a depressed racial group." Responses to this issue took the form of agricultural schools and cooperatives for blacks in Virginia, North Carolina, Alabama, Mississippi, and Louisiana. Father Arthur Terminiello, a Massachusetts priest, founded St. Theresa's Village in Bolling, Alabama, in 1937. Terminiello was known to be an avid preacher, often showing up in small Alabama towns in the countryside to expound upon the faith. He established the village along with a cooperative farm operation; it resembled a medieval village, complete with a church in the center. The sign at the village's entrance read: "Founded and Operated on the Principles of Catholic Social Justice."[73] The above-noted ecu-

[72] Samson Liph, "Jewish Farm Settlements," *L&H* 7 (September 1944): 62–63. John LaFarge, "Returning Veterans to the Land," *L&H* 8 (March 1945): 16–17; See also Patrick Quinlan "Rural Solidarity," and "The Amish People," in *Rural Life Column*, March 6, 1946, MUA/NCRLC, Series 6/1, box 11, folder "Rural Life Columns, 1946." The United States had been instrumental in the postwar rebuilding of Europe, and agriculture was center stage in feeding millions of displaced persons. *Land and Home* regularly advertised for two postwar international relief agencies—CROP and the Heifer Project. The NCRLC joined arms with the Church of the Brethren's "Heifer Project" in 1944, and then teamed up with the Church World Service and Lutheran World Relief in establishing the "Christian Rural Overseas Program" (CROP) in 1947. These groups delivered aid to numerous countries regardless of creed. The programs were more than mere handouts; they empowered people to become self-sufficient. In April 1950 the NCRLC received an award from the National Conference of Christians and Jews for its promotion of understanding between Catholic, Protestant, and Jewish farmers. See Yzermans, *The People I Love*, 70–71.

[73] John LaFarge, "Rural Racial Problems," *L&H* 7 (September 1944): 66–67; On Terminiello, see Marlett, *Saving the Heartland*, 67–68, where he notes that one Catholic magazine published a photograph of the sign outside St. Theresa's Village with "KKK" printed across it.

menical cooperation, along with involvement in racial issues, it may be argued, broadened the church's self-understanding as the Mystical Body of Christ. In the name of justice and charity, denominational differences were set aside to serve God's reign.

Lastly, *Land and Home* regularly featured articles on soil conservation. Biodynamic farming continued to be promoted. Care for the soil remained a crucial social justice concern since, if a farmer "mined" instead of planted his land, the soil would be left poor for the next person; erosion and pesticide use poisoned a neighbor's field. Edward O'Rourke drew upon Romans 6:23 to state in no uncertain terms the implications of poor stewardship: "The wages of sin is death; the wages of soil depletion is poverty and degradation of peoples."[74]

Information published by the NCRLC also took the form of weekly and monthly columns that were disseminated to diocesan and small-town papers. From 1945 to 1950 the one-page *Rural Life Column (RLC)* was distributed weekly and treated the usual broad spectrum of concerns. One article dealt with rural solidarity and criticized the tendency of agrarians to assert too much independence. The Amish were named as an example of such cooperation that stressed both independence and solidarity. Even the American Federation of Labor (AFL) took an interest in organizing farmers but with little success. The *RLC* regularly discussed agricultural policy, which it understood as being crucial to national health. Advocacy on behalf of war veterans pressed for a just land resettlement policy.[75]

Good nutrition was discussed in connection to human dignity and well-being. The mistreatment of soil (a violation of the eleventh commandment) prevented the growth of diversified crops, causing health problems for those who consumed the produce of the land. In 1947

[74] John Rawe, "Biodynamics," *L&H* 6 (September 1943): 67; Editor, "Land Policy" *L&H* 8 (September 1945): 61–62; Edward O'Rourke, "Soil Saving—A Plan," *L&H* 9 (March 1947): 22–23; Paul Sacco, "Soil Reconstruction," *L&H* 9 (December 1947): 91–93; Editor, "Gleanings" *L&H* 9 (December 1947): 111–12.

[75] Other columns with a social justice orientation include: Anthony Adams, SJ, "Coops and the Survival of Small Communities," *RLC*, September 4, 1946; *idem*, "Upholding Radicalism," *RLC* (four parts), August 31 and September 7, 1949; A twelve-part series on communism begun December 28, 1949, addressed materialism and secularism as it applied to economics and farming, offering biblical and religious remedies. Adams spoke of the impersonal nature of materialism vs. the personal nature of sacramentality. Added to this was the harmful effect of strip mining on farm land and the environment in general. See MUA/NCRLC, Series 6/1, boxes 9–10.

Anthony Adams produced a masterful seven-part series on the seventh commandment (stealing), which situated this sin in a broader social context. It was written in a style that placed the reader in an eighth-grade religion class with "sister." The first part of the series dealt with the notion of waste and the impact it had on the poor. It promoted stewardship since "Everybody has a right to life and health." The rest of the series (now with a visiting priest in sister's classroom) was titled "Soil and the Seventh Commandment," in essence making the connection between poor stewardship and stealing. Soil, God's greatest material gift, was the common inheritance of all humanity—for all people, for all time. Adams asked the children what they would do if some enemy of our country came and took all the land in the "corn belt." The youngsters valiantly responded, "We'd fight to get it back." Thinking they would be battling some external force (like communists), Adams led them right back to themselves, forcing them to consider that they may be accomplices to a great social injustice by the way their families cared for the soil. "Soil and soul" the priest said with great seriousness, "both need saving."[76]

The *RLC* also related liturgy directly to agrarian culture. The "heartfelt public thanks" expressed in the civic celebration of Thanksgiving was directly linked to the eucharistic celebration. It also provided an opportunity to connect rural and urban people in their common need for food. But the farmer was especially close to this harvest feast in all the obvious ways: "Every festive table represents the patience and toil of the man of the soil, working not only to produce for himself, but likewise for his fellowmen in the Mystical Body of Christ." From the eucharistic table, where *the* great act of thanksgiving was made, one was led to the family table at home, where one ate the goods harvested from the land, enjoyed homespun music, singing, and games. Music was also to be an integral feature of the parish liturgy by singing appropriate hymns. "The meaning of the feast is best taught to the little ones through attractive songs," and this applied to adults as well. Ember Days consecrated the seasons to God with prayerful petition, fasting, and thanksgiving. Sunday's worship must be carried into the workplace: "Participation in the Mass is man's greatest and most important act of worship. . . . Full-blossomed liturgical worship of God

[76] Anthony Adams, SJ, "Soil and the Seventh Commandment," *RLC*, May 28, June 4, 11, 25, July 2, 16, 23, 1947.

is the antidote for secularism." Gerald Ellard's *Men at Worship and at Work* was noted as being most helpful in making this connection.[77]

There is an ancient monastic adage that went something like this: "You can tell the state of a monk's soul by the way he sweeps the floor." The NCRLC fostered the practice of rural home beautification, holding contests in order to motivate rural Catholics to take pride in the farmstead. It was not simply an exercise to fight against boredom in the countryside. To the contrary, homemaking and beautification efforts reflected a "loving, cooperative, and alert soul" attuned to rural culture. Care of the home was part and parcel of rural living, strengthening the dignity of the person; it was also seen as a way of keeping young people on the farm. Not only was the body a temple of the Holy Spirit but so was the home. "Environment plays an important role in either expanding the holiness or the shrinking degradation of a soul. Disorder, decay, rubbish have no resemblance of godlikeness."[78]

Begun in 1951, the *Catholic Rural Life Page* (*CRLP*) further shaped rural Christian identity. Each month the Conference mailed a packet (10–20 pages) to diocesan and local newspapers, which could use the material as each saw fit. The mailing combined an editorial (often oriented to rural justice issues), feature stories on rural life/persons, homemaking topics, a liturgical column, book review, and a question box answered by "Uncle Phil." The column "Living the Liturgy" had various authors: Joseph Urbain (Archdiocese of Cincinnati and Grail connections), Anthony Adams, "Father" Wilfred, OSB, "The St. John's Seminarians" (of the Liturgical Academy at Collegeville), and

---

[77] Joseph Urbain, "A Farmer's Thanksgiving," *RLC*, November 28, 1945; *idem*, "Music in the American Countryside," *RLC*, August 14, 1946, *idem*, "Ember Days in the Country," *RLC*, September 3, 1947; Anthony Adams, SJ, "Everyday Liturgy," *RLC*, November 2 and 16, 1949 (parts 1 and 3 are missing); *idem*, "More Everyday Liturgy," *RLC*, December 6, 1949; *idem*, Everyday Liturgy Again," *RLC*, December 14, 1949; Gerald Ellard, *Men at Work at Worship: America Joins the Liturgical Movement* (New York: Longmans, Green, 1940).

[78] Anthony Adams, SJ, "Your Yard Pictures Your Soul," *RLC*, April 6, 1949. It would be judgmental to liken a messy home to the state of the family's (or homemaker's) soul. Nevertheless, the role of environment does impact the moral life and dignity of the person. In our own times, one can witness this in any locale mired in poverty—in developed and underdeveloped nations. The earth's environment is sacramental, presenting both an opportunity for grace and sin. The NCRLC reiterated time and again that the home was the ecclesiola, and just like an adorned cathedral, it too should manifest the glory of God. Home care shared in the wholeness of rural life in general.

"Father" Francesco. It is unclear from where Fathers "Wilfred" and "Francesco" wrote their columns. Subjects for the monthly liturgical columns were guided by the church year and particular feasts. In 1951, according to David Bovée, the *Catholic Rural Life Page* was received by 60 of the 96 dioceses in the United States with a circulation of approximately 1.5 million, exceeding by far the numbers attained with the regular periodicals.[79] Some issues of the *CRLP* were translated into Spanish.

As a whole, the subjects treated in the *CRLP* were extensive, many of them already mentioned above, and need not be repeated. "Uncle Phil's" question box handled very practical queries: How many acres of a particular crop should be planted? How far apart does one space these crops? Should one use pesticides? What does one do about certain invasive pests? "Uncle Phil" relied on his own knowledge to respond, as well as that of experts in entomology, economics, and geology. One could get information on crops, livestock summaries, price outlooks, safety material, and reviews of new farm machinery. Edward O'Rourke's "Crossroads Comment" brought rural justice issues to readers' attention.[80]

The homemaker's column by Sr. Anne Dolores, SND, should not be so easily dismissed as quaint reflections for women in the home. To be sure, advice was practical and included recipes, interior decoration suggestions, home safety, hospitality, child-care tips (this from a female religious), spinning/sewing, gardening/canning, and even what vaccinations pets should receive. "Thrift" should be a conspicuous virtue of the homemaker. On a spiritual level, here was a woman who seemed to be acquainted with psychology; thus advice was given on family, relationships, personality development, and dating. One finds here a veritable theology (philosophy) of homemaking. The homemaker is a woman "who softens the hard edges of materialism," giving true spiritual significance to the daily tasks. In essence, Sr. Ann

---

[79] Bovée, "Church and Land," 312–17, esp. 316.

[80] Here is a sample of the *CRLP*'s "Crossroads Comment" topics by O'Rourke: "Rural Life in Our Cities," August 14, 1953; "Better Farm Housing," August 20, 1954; "Bread, Rural Life and Our Schools," September 17, 1954; "Justice on the Farm," March 18, 1955; "Revolution in Soil Use," June 17, 1955; "Migratory Agricultural Workers Suffer—A Nation Sins," September 14, 1956; "Work," October 16, 1956; "Humane Slaughter," June 13, 1958.

Dolores put forth a homespun aesthetics, a "beauty of the common-place," for which woman was the chief artisan.[81]

The *CRLP*'s liturgical column, aptly titled "Living the Liturgy," sought to accomplish at least two things: provide liturgical catechesis and relate liturgy to the life of the farmer. Topics were guided by the liturgical seasons and feasts; thus a May mailing of the *CRLP* had a column that focused on a June feast (i.e., Corpus Christi). Overall, the catechesis was sound and relied on insights from the liturgical movement, fostering active, intelligent participation, often expressed as "assisting at Mass." Lent was explained in its relationship to baptism and the meaning of Easter. Pentecost deepened one's commitment made in confirmation and was sustained by the Eucharist. Authors described the church's worship as the true source of "being Church," the Mystical Body of Christ. Liturgy served as the common bond of Catholics around the world, both rural and urban. Plainsong (Gregorian chant) had the simple goal of glorifying God as it unified the community. English in the liturgy, which the NCRLC had promoted since the 1930s, continued to be set forth as a desirable goal. The common praying of the psalms using "The Finest Prayer Book" (Breviary) was promoted. Devotions were considered in their relation to the official worship of the church, making the distinction between private and liturgical prayer.[82]

"Living the Liturgy" treated feast days in their rural bearing as well. Corpus Christi was described as the "farmer's feast" because of his close association to wheat—planting, cutting, threshing—all such work being at the service of producing the altar breads. Processions, long a tradition with this feast, should pass through local fields; children could present baskets of wheat for the eucharistic bread and for the breakfast breads served to continue the feast day at home. Liturgy was understood as a way to counter secularism and bring religion to bear on civic holidays. For example, bonfires marked many occasions—college and high school homecomings, the end of bond

---

[81] Sr. Anne Dolores, SND, "Homemaker's Column," *CRLP*, December 1955, 8–10.
[82] All the following are from the *CRLP*: "Last Weeks of Lent," March 13, 1953; "Rosary," September 8, 1953; "Christmas for All," December 18, 1953; "Plainsong for all Men," January 15, 1954; "Vine and Branches," March 19, 1954; "Rogation Days," April 19, 1954; "Pentecost and Confirmation," May 14, 1954; "Pope St. Pius X," June 18, 1954; "English in the Liturgy," September 17, 1954; "Know Your Church," June 17, 1955; "The Finest Prayer Book," September 16, 1956.

drives, and annual clean-ups. The "sacramental bonfire" on John the Baptist's feast day (June 24) acted as a "symbol of the darkness-dispersing light of Christ," and thus gave some religious meaning to its secular practice. Similar efforts were made in regard to Independence Day and Thanksgiving. The discipline of Lent, which prepared one for Easter, was joined to the routine of readying the soil for spring planting; joyful hope in the resurrection and a great harvest were the fruits of that toil. Lent fostered an asceticism to which the farmer easily related. Rogation Days continued to be put forth but in relation to justice for the farmer and for world peace.[83]

Exemplary leaders of rural life, ancient and new, were presented to readers. Saint Bertrand was a sixth-century bishop and cultivator of soil known for his wise use of the land and generosity toward the poor. Parallels were drawn between St. Bertrand and the monk Gregor Mendel (1822–84), the father of modern genetics. City-born Father Paul Brinker from Kentucky integrated the daily life of his tobacco-farming parishioners with the liturgical life of the church. The feast of Assumption, with its blessing of the firstfruits, communicated to the faithful "how even things were freed from the curse of Adam."[84]

The *Rural Life Column* and the *Catholic Rural Life Page* seemed to be especially effective in disseminating the liturgical movement's agenda

---

[83] All the following are from the *CRLP*: "Corpus Christi in the Home," May 1951; "St. John the Baptist and Lighting Fires as Sacramentals," June 1951; "Independence Day," June 1956; "Three Times Thankful," November 1956 (This column linked eucharistic gratitude for family, church, and nation to Thanksgiving Day.); "Days of Rogation—For Prosperity and Peace," *RLC* April 13, 1956. Rogation Days were connected to justice largely through specific petitions (intentions). Thus, after a brief liturgical explanation of these days of petition, "Fr. Francesco" suggested: "This year we might not only pray for an abundant harvest but also for a sound agricultural economy. In many localities farm income has fallen so low that it jeopardizes the very existence of family farms. Farm legislation is becoming so involved in politics. . . . Let us ask God to enlighten the minds and instill a spirit of justice and charity into the hearts of individual farmers, the rural leaders, and the congressmen who are involved in this problem." He further suggested that the faithful pray for peace among the nations because of the possibility of an "atomic war."

[84] All the following are from the *CRLP*: "Steward of the Land," June 19, 1953; "Assumption," August 14, 1953; "Ashes and Crosses," February 19, 1954; "Work and Worship," April 15, 1955; "Daily Mass and Communion," February 17, 1956; "Blessings and Dedication," August 15, 1956; "The Farmer Views the Sacraments," August 17, 1956; "Ember Days," September 14, 1956.

among rural Catholics. These two are especially noted because their readership was not only Catholic. These columns may have served the additional purpose of informing non-Catholics about the church's liturgy and social teaching, correcting common misconceptions about Catholicism and revealing points of common belief and practice. In all the periodicals, the NCRLC consistently treated the issues of rural social justice, liturgy (spirituality), and culture as central to a complete rural life. It supports the argument that a deepened sense of one's particular culture, concomitant with the official worship of the church, brought to light and fortified the dignity of the farmer's vocation. Not only was this way of life worth preserving in itself; more significantly, such a vocation contributed to the basic human need of feeding the world. "Food security" is crucial to a just social order.[85]

## ARS RURALIS

Bishop Vincent Wehrle's 1923 insight that rural life had a sacramental quality about it begins to take on fuller significance. He seemed to envision a culture that engendered wholeness of life, a culture especially pervaded by religion. In what follows, the case is made that "culture" participates in the broader notion of sacramentality. If "all reality" (*omnia*) is potentially the bearer of God's presence, then it may be asserted that culture is constitutive (a bearer) of a sacramental worldview.[86] This interpretive key must remain at the forefront as the various artistic genres are examined. That is to say, a particular culture's language and symbol grows organically and carries the "potential" of both bearing God's presence and tilling the soil of the Christian community's spiritual life, disposing it for a more fruitful reception of the Gospel and grace. Thus a brief survey of rural-oriented art—songs, poetry, pageants, and architecture—generated by Conference leaders and other agrarians advances the above argument regarding sacramentality. There is another interpretive key that must be kept in mind. Since these various genres (poetry, songs, etc.) accentuated the

---

[85] This phrase, "food security," has only recently become familiar to the general public but was used over sixty years ago by the NCRLC. It means that food can be readily grown or supplied that provides at a minimum basic sustenance and health. It is presently estimated that eight hundred million people worldwide are food *insecure*.

[86] The notion of culture being constitutive of sacramentality is a subject that I will take up in the next chapter.

feet, healed the blind (the spittle-clay mixture of Mark 8:23 and John 9:14), and was given life by the blood that flowed from Christ's side. The latter image was a favorite of the church fathers, later depicted in art that showed flowers growing beneath the crucified Christ. The poem conveyed soil's sacramental quality.

Harvests, especially of wheat, were popular subject matter for poems. Consistent themes ran through many of the poems about this crop: the simple glory and awe when standing amid wheat fields; themes of human labor, thanksgiving, Eucharist, and justice were often connected to the feeding of humanity:

### Harvest Thanksgiving

Thrust in your sickle
Reap the shining morn;
Bind up the crimson
Poppies with the corn.
Stack the golden harvest
And then let it lie
In the tawny heat-haze
Under the sky.
See the rich harvest
Gleaming in the sun.

Te Deum laudamus,
Every theme's outrun,
Te confitemur,
As our harvest days
Fill the air with gladness
And the land with praise.
Pray Him at dawning
For the hungry lands.

Raise above our altars
Bread in priestly hands:
Bright Sun of justice,
Conqueror of the dead,
Let no man be wanting
This miracle of bread![92]

---

[92] John Roberts, "Harvest Thanksgiving," *L&H* 7 (December 1944): 98.

### En Route

O Wheat fields, restless in the wind,
The crowds that care less and pass and glance,
Will one day bend in awe, when you
Have donned Omnipotence.

O waving fields of golden grain
Envisaged thro' my tears,
And priestly hands uplifting high
White Hosts of future years.[93]

### Wheat

Patiently I churned the loam,
And waited for the warmth that surges through the earth
O mother-round my seed
And nourish forth the living blade.
I prayed for rain and sun,
And for deliverance
From wasting blight.
(A thousand times I dreamed
That hail had prematurely scythed me down.)
But now a regiment of ripened grain
Stands stoutly as some old barbaric horde,
Tossing rusty golden tufts upon the wind. . . .
A proud work, this, of God's and mine,
That needed elemental earth and air and sun and rain,
That needed Life Itself,
And something, too, of human hope and pain.[94]

In these poems about wheat, one detects a sense of awe amid nature's beauty—as it exists naturally and that which has been brought forth through human labor (harvest). Creation in general has always been a primary bearer of God's presence. "*Te Deum laudamus . . . Te confitemur*" invoked words from the ancient hymn praising God's glory. More obvious and prominent is the role played by humans who work so closely with creation to manufacture spiritual and material

---

[93] Sr. M. Raphael, BVM, "En Route," *L&H* 7 (June 1944): 39.
[94] John J. Walsh, SJ, "Wheat," *CRLB* 1 (August 1938): 8.

good for a hungry world ("A proud work, this, of God's and mine
. . ."). Themes of Eucharist and justice were explicit (holy things for
holy people), the work of liturgy joined to the work of justice. There
was also an inherent ambiguity in the sacramental principle. That is to
say, the very same creation that ushers in the farmer's praise of God
could also leave the farmer questioning his faith. This can be seen in
the fact that farmers will inevitably face "a daunting horde of pests"
or thousands of acres in need of plowing. The sweat and tears,
"human hope and pain," was sometimes couched in terms of an
apocalyptic showdown between man and nature.[95]

Nature's elements constantly occupied the farmer's life and conversation—and rightly so. Weather conditions confronted the farmer with
the precariousness of his livelihood; humility, his dependence on God,
was kept before him on a daily basis. Sister M. Madeleva Wolff, CSC,
who served as president of Saint Mary's College (Indiana) from 1934
to 1961, was a frequent poet-contributor. For several years she
submitted poems that often took up rural-nature themes, which
captured well the human lack of control over nature, and highlighted
human dependence on God:

*Limitations*

Words I can pattern
Row after row.
How to plan a snowflake
I do not know
I can fashion raiment
For me, for you.
But to cloth a pansy
What can I do?

I can plant a garden,
Set its paths with care.
Who will tell a dawn wind
To wander there?

---

[95] For an interesting treatment of the connection between ambiguity and sacramentality see Susan A. Ross, *Extravagant Affections: A Feminist Sacramental Theology*
(New York: Continuum, 1998), 38–40. Ambiguity, according to Ross, has less to do
with confusion than it does with mystery.

I can fly forever
Where my love may be
And no bird, no thought can
Follow me![96]


Farm life regularly brought unforeseen predicaments, no matter how meticulously one planned. This poem by Sr. Madeleva further elaborated on the relationship between ambiguity and sacramentality. It must be admitted that while the church's liturgy is a primary bearer of God's presence, it is also limited and cannot convey the fullness of what is implied by the sacramental principle. By using nature imagery and metaphor, these poems expressed the human's dependence on God exercised in faith and humility.

For over two decades, Florence Hynes Willette was by far the most published poet in the Conference's periodicals. She authored many poems for the annual Christmas card sent out by the NCRLC, which were later collected into a small volume called *A Handful of Straw*. These poems unfolded the mysteries surrounding the incarnation in a language that any farmer who grew hay and owned a barn would easily recognize.

### all nature labored

Some man in his few acres scattered seed
And scythed and flailed it as of ancient law;
And unaware how hallowed was the deed
Bedded his stable with the broken straw.
No lodgings at the inn . . . but here were rest
And humble shelter; here were kine and sheep
To warm the chill about the strawy nest
Whereon the new-born Child lay hushed in sleep.

All nature labored fully for this night:
Earth took the grain and warm rain did its part;
Sun drew the slender spears into the light
And burnished them for delicate sure art;
And some good man, unknowing and unknown,
Forked up the golden straw to make a throne.


[96] Sister M. Madeleva, CSC, "Limitations," and "The Pepper Tree," *L&H* 3, no. 2 (May 1940): 10, 26. Sister Madeleva's legacy continues in the Madeleva Lectures, held annually since 1988 at St. Mary's.

*the astral laws*

For that one night the astral laws gave place
To change unprecedented. Zodiac
And all its glittering galaxy drew back
As formed and sank a wondrous star through space.

Its pointing finger touched a hillside town
And earth, too, altered, never more the same;
The Promised kindled into certain flame
And all the walls of Adam tumbled down.

Transformed were ancient ritual and law
And alchemized by Love all human ways . . .
O there was change when shepherds in amaze
Knelt down with angels by a throne of straw . . .
Even in the pit where hate is might
The prince of darkness changed his plans that night![97]

In both these poems, Willette conveyed a sense of how the entire cosmos, its sacramentality, labors to prepare a place for the birth of the Savior (Cf. Col 1:12-20). There was here too an inherent eschatology at once transcendent and imminent. From the "glittering galaxy" to "some good man, unknowing and unknown" forking up straw one finds a thoroughly incarnational theology expressed therein.

Willette also found a way to connect church architecture and sacramentality that would have resonated with any rural community that had built its own church. Yet she concludes that the church that endures is the one made of believers:

### New Church

Designed by man and raised beneath his hand;
Formed of the things of the earth, cleft stone and wood,
A church new built is beauty on the land;
Men praise its purpose, bless, and call it good.
Through golden summers and the winters' white,
Dawn, dusk, and Sabbath, men steadfastly fare
To holy walls that house the soul's Delight . . .
Great lives and little lives are leveled there.

---

[97] Florence Hynes Willette, *A Handful of Straw* (Des Moines, IA: NCRLC, 1958), 22, 26. In MUA/NCRLC, Series 5/1, box 1, folder 6.

Something there is most precious and inspiring
In walls of beauty reared on sacred sod;
Something holy sprung from hearts desiring
A fitting place wherein to worship God;
A thing outlasting rugged wood and stone
No church was ever built of these alone.[98]

Church architecture has long been a manifestation of the principle of sacramentality in which the building of a church relied upon the material elements and human ingenuity of a particular locale. Willette had her ecclesiology right as she notes: "A fitting place wherein to worship God; / A thing outlasting rugged wood and stone / No church was ever built of these alone." The Mystical Body of Christ is not "made" by a church building (although it contributes); it is made through the celebration of the Eucharist for which the church exists.

Little evidence of any bold architectural projects emerges in the NCRLC literature. One example, the "King's House," a retreat center built in the Diocese of Bellville, Illinois, used a converted stable for its chapel. The people creatively and generously funded the center's construction through the donation of produce from their land, animals, and bees. One farmer donated grain sales from two acres of his land ("God's Acres" he called them) for a five-year period. Another pledged milk and cream sales for one year from one of his cows (a $250 value). Lastly, a St. Louis woman offered revenue from the sale of honey and wax from one of her bee hives. One farmer remarked: "The first 'King's House' was really the stable at Bethlehem and I feel even today the farm animals could lend their services to honor and shelter the king of men as animals did at the stable in Bethlehem." These contributions represent a good example of how the notion of "offering" was broadly understood and applied in the rural communities.[99]

[98] Florence Hynes Willette, "New Church," *CRLB* 3 (February 1940): 21.

[99] "New Retreat Center Draws Unique Support," *CRLP*, August 17, 1951. Such forms of giving should not be underestimated. On June 16, 2006, I attended the "Future of Farming and Rural Life Forum" sponsored by the Wisconsin Academy of Arts and Sciences. There I spoke with a Wisconsin dairy farmer who owned a cow named "Shirley," if I recall correctly. In the twenty years of that cow's life, she has produced 400,000 pounds of milk—and she's still going strong. The point being made is that the food we eat has a history connected to people, places, labor, and environments. I have found author and agrarian Wendell Berry to be most eloquent about these relationships. Nowhere is this more true than in the church's Eucharist—word (the salvific narrative) and sacrificial meal are inseparable. It was

Music too was a vital part of rural culture. Rural songs were sung at annual conferences as part of the liturgy and during rural life days and retreats. The NCRLC drew upon the expertise of musicians—religious and secular—to generate songs that reflected, upheld, and preserved rural culture. At times, words of rural songs were arranged to go with more familiar melodies. After a 1939 trip to Europe, Luigi Ligutti brought back six rural religious folk songs and translated them for the Conference under the title *Catholic Rural Life Songs.* Ligutti's concern about urban culture's encroachment on rural life noted: "The Conference feels that real rural culture voicing everyday rural living, has to be restored."[100] Lyrics of two such songs will suffice to gain some sense of their style.

### For God, Our Home and Our Fields

In Holy Mother Church Working let us spend our days,
And this shall be our motto We gladly work always:

Refrain:
We pray, we love, labor happily, for God,
for our homes, and fields (2x)

Companions of the soil Farmers guard your treasures all,
God calls us to that labor We gladly heed his call. Refrain.

Now let us join our work with the goodness of his hand,
And serve out bread with happiness to all within the land. Refrain.

What matter if the hail ruin our harvest when it comes,
Still faithful is our Father to bless and save our homes. Refrain.

---

just such a web of relationships with people and the natural processes of life that Virgil Michel believed was threatened. I would also contend that such a disconnect forms part of the present-day misunderstandings of the Eucharist.

[100] Witte, *Crusading,* 174–75. "Catholic Rural Life Songs," MUA/NCRLC, Series 5/1, box 2, folder 17. The songs were: *For God, Our Home and Our Fields*; *Mary, Queen of Rural Youth*; *The Chapel in the Fields*; *Painter of the Fruits and Flowers*; *Our Lady of the Fields*; *March of Rural Youth.* The songs were sung at the 1944 Rural Life Leadership School at St. John's. See SJUA, box 1771, University Topics Rf-T, "Rural Life Schools Misc."

*March of Rural Youth*

Refrain:
Come, come, come, the breezes blowing
Tell us now is time for sowing.
We are children of the soil,
On the land we gaily toil
Till the fields of golden grain are growing.

We are of that favored band
Who are living on the land
Close to nature's heart we rest
Knowing we are truly blest.
Purple fruit and grain of field
In the most abundant yield
Make secure the happy hours
In this rural life of ours. Refrain.

Land we'll till and fields we'll sow
As the seasons come and go,
Through the sunshine and the show'rs
Partners in the mighty pow'rs.
Proud and happy then are we,
Rugged though our paths may be,
Ever sterling, staunch of soul,
Lives of manliness our goal. Refrain.

The songs were arranged by the relatively well-known composer and musician Walter Goodell, who collaborated on a number of sing-along books.[101] In 1945 Ligutti asked Sr. M. Vincent, RSM, of Mt. Mercy Academy (Grand Rapids), if she could create some new rural life songs. What she did was put the NCRLC's four principles to music.[102]

---

[101] Ruth Heller, and Walter Goodell, eds., *Singing Time Music Book* (Chicago: Hall and McCreary, 1952); N. H. Aitch, ed., *The Golden Book of Favorite Songs* (Chicago: Hall and McCreary, 1920). Goodell may have also collaborated in the musical arrangement for two 1920 films *The Blue Moon* and *The Gamesters*.

[102] Ligutti to Sr. M. Vincent, RSM, 23 August 1945, MUA/NCRLC, Series 12, box 2, "Music 1942, 45, 54." Lyrics: "To the cause of the National Catholic Rural Life, we pledge our fellowship, we'll work with all our might to further your aims and preserve our rural right to live on the land in God's countryside. To care for the underprivileged Catholics living on the land, to keep on the land those Catholics

Sister Agnes Marita, a Sister of Charity, responded to a similar request by Ligutti and suggested putting rural lyrics to popular tunes by Stephen Foster or to melodies from songs such as *Jingle Bells, Comin' Through the Rye, Frere Jacques, Yankee Doodle, My Bonnie Lies Over the Ocean, Pop Goes the Weasel,* and *La Cucaracha.*[103]

The Conference also enlisted the talents of Clifford Bennett, director of the Gregorian Institute, to put rural lyrics to chant modes. Ligutti's handwriting across the top of one score noted, "First Day—Partnership With God," suggesting that he used the chant at a farmers' retreat or rural life day. The untitled song's lyrics went this way:

> Maker of man, who from thy throne
> Does order all things, God alone;
> By whose decree the teeming earth
> To reptile and to beast gave birth.
>
> The mighty forms that fill the land
> Instinct with life at thy command
> Are giv'n subdued to humankind
> For service in their rank assigned.
>
> Glory to Thee O Father, Lord,
> And to Thy sole-begotten Word,
> Both with Holy Spirit one,
> While everlasting ages run.[104]

---

who are now on the land, to settle more Catholics on the land, to convert the non-Catholics on the land. Happy the man whose wish [and . . .] a few paternal acres bound, content to breath his native air—on his own ground."

[103] Sister Agnes Marita to Ligutti, 16 August 1945, Ligutti to Sr. Agnes Marita, 23 August 1945, MUA/NCRLC, Series 12, box 2, "Music 1942, 45, 54."

[104] Clifford Bennett, July 14, 1954, Gregorian Institute, MUA/NCRLC, Series 12, box 2, "Music 1942, 45, 54." See also Pecklers, *Unread Vision,* 274–76. One finds further ecumenical cooperation with regard to music. Mrs. Albert Magnuson, whose son Ray headed the Methodist Rural Fellowship, translated several Swedish folk songs; it's uncertain if or how the NCRLC actually used them. One of them, "The Happy Plowman," sung of how a loving husband and wife cooperated even when one worked the field and the other in the kitchen: "Near a home in a wood, with horse very good, a poor young farmer smiled as he stood; / looking down at his plow, in his heart was a glow, then he sang as he plowed the row: / *Refrain.* / Heigh-ho, my little buttercup! We'll dance until the sun comes up! Thus he/she sang as he plowed/she stirred and he/she smiled as he/she sang, While the woods and the wel-kin rang. In the house near the wood, where the farmer stood,

Rural-themed music of a religious nature expanded the sacramental worldview of Catholics, and singing it reinforced the inherent goodness of rural culture.

A three-part series entitled "Catholic Rural Artists" appeared in the NCRLC's journal *Land and Home* in 1947; the author signed each one "An Agrari-Ann." The author worked out of Studio Angelico at the Dominican-run Siena Heights College in Adrian, Michigan. The articles were directed toward young women and encouraged them to remain on the land; more generally they addressed rural life. Anthony Adams, SJ, commented on the "Agrari-Anns" in his *Rural Life Column* and identified another underlying purpose—getting Agrari-Anns and Agrari-Andys together for married life on the land. (He referred to the "Andys" who resided at the University of Notre Dame and St. John's in Collegeville.)[105]

In the first part of her series, the author promoted rural artists and craftsmen; she chided Catholics on the land for not supporting talented local persons. She highlighted Collegeville, calling it a "Mecca for rural life leaders, for those interested in the liturgy, for scholars, and for Catholic action advocates." Also at St. John's were a collection of artisans, one who carved in wood and stone, "lending significance to cradle and tombstone." One artist served as an apprentice under the well-known liturgical artist Ade Bethune.[106] Metal smiths, she added, could produce a nice chalice for a rural seminarian or a ring for the rural groom. These artists produced all manner of furnishings for rural churches.[107]

The Agrari-Ann called attention to a number of artisans and their studios. Saint Leo's Shop in Upton, Massachusetts, distributed the works of Ade Bethune. Mary Paulson, protégé of Bethune, fashioned stained-glass windows and wood carvings. Printing houses, like Sower Press, put out rural literature. The Catholic Worker's Maryfarm in Easton, Pennsylvania, was a temporary home to many artists, thanks in part to Tamar Hennessy (Dorothy Day's daughter), who recruited artists to come and work there. The Agrari-Ann noted: "Busy as

---

there lived his helpmate lovely and good; / As she cooked and she stirred, she was glad she heard, and she echoed every word. *Refrain*."

[105] An Agrari-Ann, "Catholic Rural Artists," *L&H* 10 (March 1947): 3–4; and Anthony Adams, *RLC*, April 30, 1947.

[106] Ade Bethune's art and writing, often carrying a social justice theme, graced the pages of *The Catholic Worker* and *Orate Fratres*.

[107] An Agrari-Ann, "Catholic Rural Artists," *L&H* 10 (March 1947): 4.

Dorothy is, she finds time when at the farm with her daughter to spin wool from Tamar's sheep and angora goat." The Grail was identified as a center for rural artisans as well. Monsignor Fridolin Frommherz of St. Mary's parish in Assumption, Ohio, hosted local "spinning institutes." The Toledo diocese dubbed its own Father Sassong the "spinning priest." Fathers John and Walter Harbrecht, blood brothers, were master weavers; Walter's "damask and his yardage for clerical suiting is cherished for those fortunate enough to secure his produce." The Agrari-Ann also prudently slipped in some social commentary, noting that a rural artist achieves a certain "rightness of his own efforts" that an assembly-line worker will never experience.[108] Indeed, the arts and hand crafts manifest the sacramental principle in a most obvious way.

Luigi Ligutti studied classics at The Catholic University of America. Although an immigrant, he possessed great facility with the English language and became known for his "Ligutti-isms," snippets of wisdom that revealed his agrarian philosophy. On the surface they seemed innocent and were often humorous. On a deeper level they pierced social reality in a way that critiqued it. Rural culture is known for such homespun wisdom and humor, at times born from necessity caused by isolation, a lack of books, and other media. Rural cultures are among the last authentic preservers of "oral" culture. Oral traditions shape worldviews and give people a language that helps them make sense of life—words matter.[109] No doubt, this tradition could be narrow, exclusive, and even anti-urban as was sometimes evident in the NCRLC's literature. Regardless, the oral culture affected how one came to the liturgy and other religiously oriented activities. It potentially disposed the rural Christian to be more receptive to a sermon that tried to deepen the Christian roots of rural living. Ligutti was steeped in this kind of wisdom, and coupled with his intellectual training, made him a very persuasive charismatic figure.

---

[108] An Agrari-Ann, "Catholic Rural Artists," *L&H* 10 (June 1947): 42–43; idem, "Catholic Rural Artists," *L&H* 10 (September 1947): 70–71. Frommherz was another outstanding rural leader who embraced the liturgical movement and initiated several cooperative ventures. The most well known was St. Mary's Cooperative Meat Locker (basically, a common refrigerator) in Ottoville, Ohio. In the 1930s, it was a brilliant move considering the lack of rural electrification programs.

[109] The deliberate play (words matter) suggests that words themselves have a sacramental quality about them. They convey narrative which affects people and potentially changes them. Words shape worldviews—negatively and positively. I would note again the value of Susan Ross's use of ambiguity.

Ligutti convinced a group of women religious to repeat the following:

> A garden and a cow
> A smokehouse and a sow
> Twenty-four hens and a rooster
> And you'll have more than you usta'.

To an audience of farmers in North Dakota, he quipped: "*Ora et labora* —and use a lot of fertilizer!" His wisdom demonstrated knowledge of history and the social influences incumbent on a given epoch:

> *1880*
>
> Farmer is at the plow,
> Wife milking the cow;
> Boys threshing in the barn,
> Daughters spinning yarn—
> All happy to a charm.

> *1920*
>
> Farmer's gone to see a show,
> Daughter is at the piano;
> Wife is dressed in satin,
> All the boys learning Latin;
> And a mortgage on the farm.

A youngster from his parish in Granger, Iowa, picked up on Ligutti's social commentary about the disintegration of family farms and added his own thread to the history:

> *1940*
>
> Farmer's tinkering with tractor,
> Daughter made beautiful by Max Factor;
> Mother is busy cooking from a can,
> Sonny at tavern discussing Sally Rand.
> No wonder father is renting land—
> Soon he'll be a hired hand.

Finally, in an audience with Pius XII discussing international problems, Ligutti said: "When a poor family becomes the owner of a cow, then communism goes out the back door."[110] Such charisma endeared Ligutti to many audiences. He used his good will and wit to get people's attention and then he led them to the more serious issues confronting agrarians.

This brief survey of the various art forms found in rural culture served to highlight and broaden the notion of the sacramental principle. A culture that generates beautiful artwork, poetry, and music accentuates the inherent good it possesses, giving it material expression. In the case of rural culture, this carries the added purpose of bestowing dignity on rural life in general and on the vocation of the farmer in particular. In some cases, rural art contributed directly to liturgical life of the church.

Overall, this chapter demonstrated the NCRLC's thoroughly *catholic* approach to its many endeavors as it ministered to the Catholics living on the land. It did so through rural life schools, retreats, institutes, and study clubs, revealing how the Conference wished to extend its philosophy into nearly every facet of life. Liturgy, culture, and justice anchored and gave direction to much of this activity. It relied on the church's liturgical and sacramental life as *the* spiritual source to animate its social agenda; in the words of *Sacrosanctum Concilium*—the liturgy served as "source and summit" of the Christian life. The Conference also took seriously Pius XI's call to reconstruct the social order; that "order" was, in the first place, the rural culture in which Catholics lived. But it was seen that the Conference's understanding of the Mystical Body of Christ extended beyond strict identification with the Roman Catholic Church.

---

[110] Bovée, "Church and Land," 309–11; Yzerman, *The People I Love*, 50, 58, 59. Two regular features of *Land and Home* were "Cracked Corn" and "On and Off the Track," which offered such tidbits, quotes, and facts that were expressive of this genre, some of it pithy, some more substantial.

# Chapter 6

# Weaving Together Liturgy, Culture, and Justice

Good liturgy and sound agrarianism share a common bond. Both are paschal practices to which these two insights allude:

> By not conserving it [soil], the farmer has sinned against it. By conservation man is expiating his sin and making restitution. This makes soil conservation a pious act.[1]

> [It] is not to suggest that we can live harmlessly or strictly at our own expense; we depend upon other creatures and survive by their deaths. To live, we must daily break the body and shed the blood of creation. The point is, when we do this knowingly, lovingly, skillfully, reverently, it is a sacrament; when we do it ignorantly, greedily, clumsily, destructively, it is a desecration . . . in such desecration, we condemn ourselves to spiritual and moral loneliness, and others to want.[2]

---

[1] "Alfalfa George: A Rural Pastor Talks about God, the Land, and His People," *Jubilee* (August 1960): 19. Hildner called the soil "sacred" and its conservation "a holy cause."

[2] Wendell Berry, "The Gift of Good Land," in *The Art of the Commonplace: The Agrarian Essays of Wendell Berry*, ed. Norman Wirzba, 304 (Washington, DC: Counterpoint, 2002). Hereafter *The Art of the Commonplace*. A brief word about Berry's background is in order. Born in Henry County, Kentucky, in 1934, Berry grew up on a family farm. He attended a military institute for high school and then went on to earn a BA and MA in English from the University of Kentucky. In 1957 he married Tanya Amyx. They have two children and several grandchildren who live nearby and also farm. Berry received several postgraduate fellowships that took him to Stanford and Italy. He taught English at New York University's University College in the Bronx, showing much promise as a writer, having published his first novel, *Nathan Coulter*, in 1961. However, in spite of all the opportunities for a writer living in New York, in 1965 Berry left all of that (much to the

Liturgy and rural life should in no uncertain terms be treated as some bucolic liturgical romanticism. Liturgy, especially the Eucharist, is the celebration of the paschal mystery, our salvation in Christ. The very health (*salus*) of our God-given planet along with its myriad cultures—the diversity of land and people—born from the soil are threatened. Even though a number of twentieth-century prophets warned us, we are now beginning to see that the ways we have chosen to be in the world, scandalously wasting our God-given resources for our sustenance and development, have come at great cost. One among the many prophets who have pointed out our dilemma, especially in the United States, is the noted author and agrarian Wendell Berry. As one of the "New Agrarians" he offers an integral vision of *how* to be in the world, justly and harmoniously. His thoroughly sacramental world-view is, it will be argued, consonant with the work of the NCRLC.

Culture, according to Wendell Berry, includes the entire scope of human activity that occurs in a unique place with the distinct inclusiveness of nature (creation), the whole ecological framework in which humans enact their lives. Berry states: "People are joined to the land by work. Land, work, people, and community are comprehensible in the idea of culture."[3] Culture encompasses all of life, arising from the

---

chagrin of his department chair who thought him crazy) and returned to Kentucky where he purchased land and began to farm again in addition to teaching at the University of Kentucky (1965–77). Berry's output since moving back to Kentucky has been prolific—close to fifty books in the form of essays, poetry, short stories, and novels. While Berry attends a Baptist church in Port Royal, KY, he has challenged organized religion for its complacency, its lack of involvement in the world. His writing and other awards are numerous. See Jason Peters, ed., *Wendell Berry: Life and Work* (Lexington: University of Kentucky Press, 2007); Kimberly K. Smith, *Wendell Berry and the Agrarian Tradition: A Common Grace* (Lawrence: University of Kansas Press, 2003).

[3] Wendell Berry, "People, Land and Community," in *The Art of the Commonplace*, 189. This purview of culture is partially consonant with the contemporary cultural studies, as per Clifford Geertz: "A system of inherited concepts expressed in symbolic forms [language, gesture, music, dance, etc.] by means of which men communicate, perpetuate, and develop their knowledge about and attitudes toward life." See Clifford Geertz, *The Interpretation of Cultures* (New York: Basic Books, 1973), 89. According to Geertz, meaning, drawn from religious symbols, motivates one's actions. However, Vincent Miller, relying on the critique of Talal Asad challenges this position, namely that the direct connection between religious symbols (rites included) do not necessarily inform the religious practices of believers. Further, Geertz is criticized by Kathryn Tanner for "projecting onto culture the anthropologist's need for coherent order." See Vincent J. Miller, *Consuming Religion:*

soil (*cultus*) organically, and becomes a key pillar of the New Agrarian philosophy. Yet soil needs to be cultivated (*colere*), tended, and tilled, and thus *worked* by and for humans. From *cultus* one derives *cultum divinum*, liturgy, which also requires work done by and on behalf of the people. The NCRLC understood that a close relationship between the rural culture and liturgy was integral to achieving a lasting, vital justice. Examining the work of the New Agrarians, especially Wendell Berry, attempts to carry the good work begun by the NCRLC into our contemporary context. A key link between the two movements can be found in a theme that has permeated this book—the sacramental principle, writ large in nature and culture.[4]

Therefore, what does it mean to posit that culture is constitutive of a sacramental world? That is, wherever a more profound confluence of liturgy and culture occur, the potential for a fuller flourishing of justice as it relates to people, land, and community, indeed the whole cosmos, will be in evidence—salvation made more manifest—*hodie*.

## THE BROKEN WORLD

In the first two decades of the twentieth century, agriculture in the United States experienced somewhat of a boom. However, that began to shift in the early 1920s.[5] At this time Fr. Edwin O'Hara witnessed firsthand the disintegration that was occurring in the American countryside, especially but not exclusively among Catholics. This compelled him to found the NCRLC in 1923, setting forth an ambitious program for those living from the land. As a priest he not only cared

---

*Christian Faith and Practice in a Consumer Culture* (New York: Continuum, 2004), 20–21, 23.

[4] The term "rural" here will refer to those specific communities whose culture is rooted in concrete agrarian practices (farming), with some extension to rural life in general. However, the term has evolved and there is at present no wide consensus on its precise meaning. The rural designation is more often used for demographic purposes (census, funding, infrastructure, etc.), which Berry would call a cultural reductionism. See John Cromartie and Shawn Bucholtz, "Defining the 'Rural' in Rural America," *Amber Waves* 6, no. 3 (June 2008).

[5] For a good concise history of rural America, see David B. Danbom, *Born in the Country: A History of Rural America*, 2nd ed. (Baltimore, MD: John's Hopkins Press, 2006), chap. 8; For an agricultural history in the U.S. see R. Douglas Hurt, *American Agriculture: A Brief History*, rev. ed. (West Lafayette, IN: Purdue University Press, 2002); Bruce L. Gardener, *American Agriculture in the Twentieth Century: How It Flourished and What It Cost* (Cambridge, MA: Harvard University Press, 2002), 1.

for the faithful's religious life but their socioeconomic (agricultural), educational, and *cultural* life. The ensuing 1929 Stock Market Crash and consequent Depression and Dust Bowl only compounded the despair. It is interesting to note, however, that during these difficult years small, independent farmers faired pretty well because they could produce their own food. During the 1940s longtime rural leader Luigi Ligutti traveled throughout the world and witnessed the great extent of rural problems—injustice and starvation, civil strife, and world wars, moving him to remark: "The problems of the world today are the problems of the land and the people on the land."[6] Its profundity should not be missed, since from time immemorial land has played a pivotal role in the birth, life, and death *of nations*.

Indeed, Walter Brueggemann calls land "the central theme" of biblical faith, a faith in pursuit of historical belonging. Ellen Davis's recent work gives an agrarian reading of the Hebrew Bible, noting how the contemporary agrarian vision has roots in the culture and agriculture of ancient Israel, yielding an ethics of land use. For the last half century, Wendell Berry has put forth a stinging critique of contemporary American life as one that is profoundly unconnected to land and community—this, our fundamental brokenness. No longer do we belong anywhere historically. There exists no *affection* for *a* place, Berry often writes, no deep intimate knowledge and love for land and people and their profound interconnectedness. A healthy farming community was understood as crucial to the well-being not only of a local community but of the whole inhabited world—prophets, popes, presidents, economists, farmers, ecologists, and homemakers have said so.[7]

As with land, liturgy too plays a central role in the birth, life, and death *of Christians*. God's salvific plan unfolds in and through the blessing of and exchange of earthly gifts, making and forming Christians and, it is hoped, imparting to them a sacramental way of viewing the world. Not only does liturgy depend on the land for its

---

[6] This quote may have been an adaptation of a line from Fr. Vincent McNabb, the English Dominican philosopher and agrarian.

[7] Walter Brueggemann, *The Land: Place as Gift, Promise, and Challenge in Biblical Faith*, 2nd ed. (Minneapolis, MN: Fortress Press, 2002), 3; Ellen Davis, *Scripture, Culture, and Agriculture: An Agrarian Reading of the Bible* (New York: Cambridge University Press, 2009); Wendell Berry, *The Unsettling of America: Culture & Agriculture* (San Francisco: Sierra Club Book, 1996), 3–16.

sacramental materials but the whole sacramental economy has unfolded through creation, took on a new intensity in the Word made flesh, and was consummated in Christ's paschal mystery, "for us and our salvation." The NCRLC frequently called soil God's greatest material gift. Berry sees soil as the most Christ-like of materials "in its passivity and beneficence, and in the penetrating energy that issues out its peaceableness."[8] Thus the liturgy not only fashions 'right praise' (orthodoxy) using the fruits of the earth and work of human hands, but its celebration makes demands of 'right action' (orthopraxis) in the world. Christians use the same created matter as a sacramental extension of salvation into a beautiful but fragmented land, people, and community. The sacramental economy must be at the service of healing our broken world. More often than not, Wendell Berry directs his incisive critique toward what he perceives to be the source of a very fragmented world, a *culture* ignorant of the ways that foster true and just human flourishing. His worldview, to which we will shortly turn, is sacramental in the fullest sense even though he tends to steer clear of organized religion in his essays.

In an era of heightened ecological awareness, perhaps it may be timely to expand upon the well-known corporal works of mercy found in chapter 25 of Matthew's gospel: "When you saw the body of my good earth wounded and neglected and did not care for it or heal it, you did it to me." In 1990 Pope John Paul II called the ecological crisis a moral problem with wide-ranging social effects wherein "the indiscriminate application of advances in science and technology" have led us to see that "we cannot interfere in one area of the ecosystem without paying due attention both to the consequences of such interference in other areas and to the well-being of future generations."[9] In 1999 the Society of Jesus (Jesuits) published its first authoritative statement on the environment, *We Live in a Broken World: Reflections on Ecology*, stating in the introduction:

---

[8] Wendell Berry, "A Native Hill," in *The Long-Legged House* (Washington, DC: Shoemaker & Ward, 1969, 2004), 204.

[9] "The Ecological Crisis: A Common Responsibility," Message of His Holiness John Paul II for the Celebration of the World Day of Peace, January 1, 1990, Vatican City, in *And God Saw That It Was Good: Catholic Theology and the Environment*, ed. Drew Christiansen and Walter Grazer (Washington, DC: United States Catholic Conference, 1996), 217.

Unscrupulous exploitation of natural resources and the environment degrades the quality of life; it destroys cultures and sinks the poor in misery. Such serious injustices may be understood in terms of human rights: Respect for the dignity of the human person created in the image of God underlies the growing international consciousness of the full range of human rights, including rights such as development, peace and a healthy environment.[10]

There is an intimate connection between care for the earth and the flourishing of human cultures that combines for an integral justice so needed in our world. Catholic tradition has consistently maintained (although not always in practice) that we humans inhabit a sacramental world. But therein lay a certain ambiguity and challenge. Namely, the one sacramental world both manifests the glory of God and is abused by humans who participate in a rapaciousness that is simply not sustainable—for the land and people—*omnia*. There is the common-place tendency to assert that we have "environmental problems," as if nature *in se* is to blame. Wendell Berry identifies such thinking as *abstraction*. But if John Paul II is accurate in calling it a "moral problem," then the issue is people (moral actors), not the rest of creation. *We* are the stewards and tenants in God's world. The pontiff and the Jesuits are right to assert that this is not just a matter of preserving the beauty of creation for human enjoyment but a human right that sustains all life on the earth. It is paramount to name ecological sin, call people to conversion, and inspire a new corporal work of mercy.

While the brokenness of our world is becoming more obvious, it has yet to yield a sustained call to moral responsibility; we continue to destroy creation and cultures.[11] Eric T. Freyfogel has identified some

[10] The Society of Jesus, "We Live in a Broken World: Reflections on Ecology," *Promotio Iustitiae* 70 (1999).

[11] In 2003 alone, over seventeen thousand farmers in India committed suicide. The sources of this problem are many but are principally tied to the rapid embrace by India to be a major player in the global agri-markets. This move thrust millions of small-scale farmers to embrace farming methods that were driven by technology and the agricorporations (Monsanto's Terminator Seeds). Such ways of farming were quite at odds with centuries-old indigenous cultural practices that were more sustainable. This has not only resulted in a destruction of land but cultures and communities. The basic cause is tied to enormous debt that farmers cannot repay. Among the groups in the United States who have the highest suicide rates, farmers are near the top of the list. In a personal conversation with one of my Jesuit confreres in 2005, Fr. Xavier Bosco, working in central India, shared with me that

specifics of our present crisis: the degradation of nature through water pollution, soil loss, resource consumption, the radical disruption of plant and wildlife populations; worries over our food system—its security, nutritional value, safety, freshness, and taste. This leads to a declining sense of community, blighted landscapes, the separation of work and leisure, the shoddiness of mass-produced goods, a heightened sense of rootlessness and anxiety, decline of the household economy, fragmentation of families, neighborhoods, and communities. "Permeating these overlapping concerns is a gnawing dissatisfaction with core aspects of modern culture, particularly the hedonistic, self-centered values and perspectives that now wield such power." As Berry often says, to destroy nature is to destroy culture: "To live at the expense of nature is not just bad farming, it's suicidal." Berry also understands these problems as vulnerabilities to our national security.[12]

## THE NEW AGRARIANISM OF WENDELL BERRY

The New Agrarianism is a movement that includes rural, suburban, and urban dweller alike; and it is experiencing somewhat of a surge. Part of the reason stems from the growing ecological consciousness among peoples the world over, highlighted by international gatherings of governments and concerned groups. Perhaps, and even more so, it originates from a postmodern exhaustion with contemporary life, which, in spite of our technologically "connected" world, only seems to breed deeper fragmentation and despair among people, land, and community. That agrarianism deals principally with those living on the

---

125 Dalit farmers with whom he works committed suicide in one summer alone. See Somini Sengupta, "On India's Farms, a Plague of Suicide," *New York Times*, September 19, 2006. Accessed December 15, 2008. <http://www.nytimes.com/2006/09/19/world/asia/19india.html?pagewanted=1>

[12] Eric T. Freyfogel, "Introduction: A Durable Scale," in *The New Agrarianism: Land, Culture, and the Community Life*, ed. Eric T. Freyfogel, xvi (Washington, DC: Island Press, 2001); One need only look to the present financial crisis in the United States to see its corollary side effects. See also Wendell Berry, "The Agricultural Crisis as a Crisis of Culture," in *The Unsettling of America: Culture and Agriculture* (San Francisco, CA: Sierra Club Books, 1996), 47; Wendell Berry, "Property, Patriotism, and Nation Defense," in *Home Economics* (San Francisco: North Point Press, 1987), 98–111; In 2004, upon his resignation as secretary for housing and urban development, Tommy Thompson quipped: "For the life of me, I cannot understand why terrorists have not attacked our food supply, because it is easy to do." In Bill McKibben, *Deep Economy: The Wealth of Communities and the Durable Future* (New York, NY: Times Books, 2007), 61.

land, especially farmers, is obvious. Yet to think that the work of the farmer does not concern the urbanite would be foolish in the extreme. Many of the issues raised by the NCRLC in the 1920s and 1930s about the demise of the family farm and all the associated challenges to rural life and culture have, in greater part, come to pass. The Conference tried to stem that tide, and its efforts should in no way be an admittance of failure. In the post–World War II era, their efforts were simply overrun by a policy-driven economics that shifted to "big" industrial-scale farming. The Conference understood these problems and attempted to foster a sacramental worldview and praxis that would counter the march of "progress," so called. The New Agrarians approach life (read culture) in a way that is integral and just, and whose core concerns remain "the land, natural fertility, healthy families, and the maintenance of durable links between people and place."[13] For over forty-five years Wendell Berry has been a voice of one crying out in the wilderness, calling us back to covenanted communities rooted in the land and people.

In the *Timbered Choir*, Berry's collection of Sabbath poems, he writes:

> Be thankful and repay
> Growth with good work and care.
> Work done in gratitude
> Kindly, and well, is prayer.[14]

Norman Wirzba notes that "Berry makes plain the goal of human life . . . to attain the peace and rest that marked the climax of creation," ushering in a "dance of joy and delight that mirrors the creator's pleasure in the goodness of creation." For the authentic celebration of Sabbath, all that we long for, all that we know, and all the work that we do (*culture*) must not be done out of simple religious obligation or to "pull back" from the week's toil. No, as Abraham Heschel has written in his slim but profound work *The Sabbath*: "What we are depends on what the Sabbath means to us" and that it is no mere "interlude," but the "climax of living." Wirzba adds that a vision of

---

[13] Freyfogel, *The New Agrarianism*, xvii.

[14] Copyright © 1999 by Wendell Berry from *A Timbered Choir: The Sabbath Poems 1979–1997*. Reprinted by permission of Counterpoint.

the Sabbath becomes a "transformation of all work in light of the goodness and interdependence of creation . . . a vision founded on [its] wholeness and health."[15] Agrarianism is, above all, a practice. Gratitude, work, care, and prayer, as Berry puts it, places him alongside St. Benedict (d. 547), whose motto *ora et labora* still shapes a rule (way) of life. Gratitude and work captures as well what Christian tradition has long held to be the substance of *leitourgia*, for just like agrarianism, it too is a practice, a work of gratitude. Modern industrial-technological culture has alienated humans from many of nature's simplest and most joyful processes as well as from the attention and care that go into making quality goods. A consumerist, throw-away culture fosters ingratitude, unkindliness.

Berry posits that one of the results of industrialism "is the separation of people and places and products from their histories . . . we do not know the histories of our families or of our habitats or of our meals."[16] Virgil Michel raised a similar concern in the late 1930s, referring to the manner in which the industrial revolution contributed to a fragmentation of person, land, and community, of well-made goods. In the industrial economy, *all things* became cheap and easily discarded, lacking in the basic relationships that produced, exchanged, and used such goods. Berry calls this the industrial "one-night stand." Interestingly, both Wendell Berry and Virgil Michel believe the "industrial way" contributes to the destruction of culture, pulling people away from 'home' and the wider network of human-nature relationships that gives a person roots. Large-scale industrial farming drove people off the land, breaking up the traditional household economy. This was followed by the wider disintegration of rural communities and a loss of shared memory.[17]

---

[15] Norman Wirzba, "The Challenge of Berry's Agrarian Vision," in *The Art of the Commonplace*, xvii; Abraham Heschel, *The Sabbath* (New York, NY: Harper Torchbooks, 1966).

[16] Wendell Berry, "The Whole Horse," in *The Art of the Commonplace*, 236.

[17] Berry's novels often highlight the recovery of shared memory and community. See especially *Andy Catlett*, *Remembering*, and *Jayber Crow* to name a few. Numerous contemporary studies highlight the breakdown of community life in the United States. See Robert Bellah, Richard Madsen, William M. Sullivan, et. al. *Habits of the Heart: Individualism and Commitment in American Life* (Berkeley: University of California Press, 1985); Robert Putnam, *Bowling Alone: Americas Declining Social Capital* (Thousand Oaks, CA: Sage Publications, 2001); James Howard Kuntzler, *The Geography of Nowhere: The Rise and Decline of America's Man-Made Landscape* (New

Berry and the New Agrarians see nature as the final judge of how humans use the earth. "We should not work until we have looked and seen where we are . . . consult the Genius of the Place." The industrial mind (often an outsider, absentee) sees in a place only materials to be extracted and human life as expendable, having no regard for the long-term health of the community. Agrarianism is a way of thought based on the land; *nature and culture* must cohere in a manner that not only brings forth the fruit of the land but also works and conserves the land in a way that is sustainable for future generations. This allows the local culture to truly flourish. "An agrarian economy rises up from the fields, woods, and streams—from the complex of soils, slopes, weathers, connections, influences, and exchanges . . . local community." This economy requires an agrarian mind that is *placed*, intimately and affectionately, knowing that particular place's limits and possibilities. The industrial mind is indiscriminate and prefers to deal with figures and abstract quantities. The agrarian mind is "threatened and sickened when it hears people and creatures and places spoken of as labor, management, capital, and raw materials." The industrial mind is incapable of honoring truly good work, skillful—mindful of the whole—people and creation. The agrarian *works* thoughtfully, asking: how should *this* field be plowed? Should *this* tree be cut and where should the skid road pass through the woodland? What are the best types of animals for *this* pasture? "Agrarianism can never become abstract" says Berry, "because it has to be practiced in order to exist." Human ingenuity as practiced by the agrarian toils for the harmonious union of nature and culture, which are in fact one, making agriculture a true art form. Attention and devotion to the "lowly" and "menial" arts of farm and forest are the "foundation of human life and culture."[18]

It should be no surprise then that Wendell Berry calls the crisis of agriculture a "crisis of culture," precipitated in large part by industrial-technical development. Agrarian life, as a culture, attends to the whole of life. Culture is a single yet diverse organic body. All the attendant

---

York: Touchstone, 1993); Charles Pinches, *A Gathering of Memories; Family, Nation, and Church in a Forgetful World* (Grand Rapids, MI: Brazos Press, 2006).

[18] Wendell Berry, "The Whole Horse," 239–41, 244. See also Ellen Davis, *Scripture, Culture, and Agriculture*, 139–54; See also Wendell Berry, "Going to Work," in *The Essential Agrarian Reader: The Future of Culture, Community and the Land*, ed. Norman Wirzba, 259–66 (Washington, DC: Shoemaker and Hoard, 2004).

disciplines (work) undertaken to enact and sustain it must simultaneously preserve the community and animate-inanimate creation, *omnia*. Berry argues that certain *cultural* influences have contributed to the fragmentation of the home culture, agrarian in this case, but it may be applied much broader. For example, the onset of technology on the farm may have relieved farmers of some of the "drudgery" of their work, but in point of fact such "progress" forcibly displaced millions of people, since there was no longer any "use" for them on the farm.[19] Can a person honestly claim that one is "set free" from a type of work one enjoys only now to take up other work that he or she finds less satisfying? Our nation was too busy consuming to take notice of this crisis. Officials from the U.S. Department of Agriculture—experts, technological specialists—often expressed this *policy* as "get big or get out," meaning, increase the size of the farm, embrace technology, and watch productivity rise. As a social or economic goal, Berry posits, "getting big" amounts to totalitarianism since the official system will then employ the necessary means to make the policy's vision (so called) a reality. Decisions made in this manner, abstracted as they are from the real life of farmers, have caused this fragmentation of land and people, culture. From a cultural point of view it "involve[d] a radical simplification of mind and character" that is born of the industrial mindset—the rote tasks of the assembly line. In relation to knowledge, Berry calls this simplification *ignorance*.[20] Such a policy did not simply result in an exodus of jobs from the countryside but further marginalized an entire way of life. There is a close relationship between vocation and justice. Since work is so fundamental to culture, the vocation of the authentic agrarian demands that his or her work attends to the "rightness" of all relationships, encompassing the land, workers, and

[19] Wendell Berry, "The Agricultural Crisis as a Crisis of Culture," 41. In 2007, in each of the states of Washington, Oregon, and Idaho, one thousand independent family farms were either shut down or bought up by "bigger" farmers.

[20] See the opening chapters of Wendell Berry's novel *Remembering*, where Andy Catlett, working as a farm journalist, is invited to speak at a conference on farming, "big" farming that is, abstract and unconnected as it often is to land and people. Andy departs from his prepared text and delivers a stinging critique of farming as such. The moving story tells of the power of remembrance and knowing intimately a place, its land and people. Berry also calls it "ignorant arrogance" in the title essay to *The Way of Ignorance and Other Essays by Wendell Berry* (Berkeley, CA: Counterpoint Press, 2005), 53.

all creation. Yet such "job losses" are treated as a statistic, not a loss of vocation. This is a real crisis.[21]

Food as well is a cultural product that demands a complex and synthetic knowledge. A one-day visit to a farm that practices either organic or other sustainable methods—kind to land, animals, and people—will prove this.[22] Such praxis is not reducible to a technological innovation. The discipline (art) of agriculture has become so compartmentalized (and simplified) based on technology that "the practicalities of production and the network of meanings and values necessary to define, nurture and preserve" such a culture are lost. Their uniqueness and wholeness have been sacrificed to automation, efficiency, and inferior products. "Farming, the *best* farming, is a task that calls for this sort for complexity, both in the character of the farmer and in his culture. To simplify either one is to destroy it." Resilient cultures have "strong communal memories" and "traditions of care."[23] This loss of memory has occurred in our eating habits, con-

---

[21] Norman Wirzba situates human dignity and vocation in the context of the wider creation: "That we willingly destroy and disregard the natural habitat and social contexts that make our lives possible, and on which we daily depend, indicates a profound confusion over what constitutes a proper human identity and vocation." More specifically, the human vocation "consists in the hospitable gesture of welcoming and enabling the whole of creation to share in the peace and joy of the divine life. It is a vocation that demands that we be attentive to those forces which distort or disfigure life and so doom some elements of creation to a life of loneliness and suffering." Norman Wirzba, *The Paradise of God: Renewing Religion in An Ecological Age* (New York: Oxford University Press, 2003), 2, 21. Recall too that in the face of the industrialization of agriculture and rural disintegration of the twentieth century, the NCRLC frequently nourished and supported the vocation of the farmer; this was in fact one of its central aims.

[22] Examples abound of living practitioners, farmers acquainted with this very complexity, to which Berry both refers and practices. Mention should be made of farmer Joel Salatin of Polyface Farms in Virginia, who, it may be said, farms in "nature's image." Interestingly, Salatin is not a "certified" organic farmer but his methods clearly are. See Michael Pollan, *The Omnivore's Dilemma: A Natural History of Four Meals* (New York: Penguin Press, 2006), 123–33. Visit Polyface Farms at <http://www.polyfacefarms.com/>; Judith D. Soule, and Jon K. Piper, *Farming in Nature's Image: An Ecological Approach to Agriculture* (Washington, DC / Covelo, CA: Island Press, 1992). One farmer who has blazed this path is Wes Jackson of the Land Institute in Salina, Kansas: <http://www.landinstitute.org/>.

[23] Wendell Berry, "The Agricultural Crisis As a Crisis of Culture," 41–45. The sources of this rupture are many according to Berry, but he names the universities, Land Grant Colleges included, which have ushered in this compartmentalized,

suming fast food, eating it on the run, or in front of our television(s), with no sense of its history. Ask elementary school children where their food comes from and the response will be the neighborhood grocery store. True enough, and if pressed they might wind their way back to the farm and beyond. Food has become an industrial commodity like any other to be consumed, often with little reflection on or regard for its origin or meaning. As Berry says, "I begin with the proposition that eating is an agricultural act. Eating ends the annual drama of the food economy that begins with planting and birth."[24] *Narrative* has come unhinged from *meal*, and this, not only the fundamental structure of the eucharistic liturgy but essential to the building of culture. Eating is a sacramental act as well, or it is?

The industrial way has given birth to humans as consumptive machines.[25] This *way* is rooted in a superficial economy based on money, which has "infiltrated and subverted the economies of nature, energy, and the human spirit." It is interesting that the words economy, ecology, and ecumenical share the same Greek root, *oikos*, or household. But this is not merely the physical house one lives in but the wider network of familial relationships, management of the household. In the ancient world and even in twentieth-century agrarian cultures such maintenance of subsistence farm-homes involved the very complexity to which Berry refers. Fundamentally *oikos* denotes relationship. "The people and their work and their country are members of each other and of the culture."[26] In Christian terms, one understands "members" as the wider Mystical Body of Christ, inclusive of creation (Cf. Rom 8:22; Col 1:15-20). It would be suicidal for one to pillage the land (*oikos* as in ecology) that feeds and sustains a family unit, a region, or nation. *Oikoumenos* is also relational, standing for the whole inhabited world. At present though there is perhaps no other word more abused in our contemporary language than economy (*oikonomia*), a word that has become so unhinged from its fuller relational reality.

---

specialized approach to learning and most of all praxis. He would add that they are under the considerable sway of big corporations.

[24] Wendell Berry, "The Pleasures of Eating," in *What Are People For?* (New York: Northpoint Press, 1990), 145.

[25] For a clever, entertaining, and well researched glimpse of our extractive, industrial, consumer culture, see *The Story of Stuff* by Annie Leonard: <http://www.storyofstuff.com/>

[26] Wendell Berry, "The Agricultural Crisis As a Crisis of Culture," 46.

If one were to be so bold as to try to capture the substance of Berry's critique of American (Western) culture, one might call it the *perversion of oikos*. The economies of industrialism are first a "way of thought based on monetary capital and technology," yielding a priority of capital over labor.[27] Agrarianism is based on land, and furthermore it is a *culture* at the same time it is an economy. Industrialism is an economy before it is a culture, compared to agrarianism's economy that rises up from field and forest—*cultus* in the best sense. One who degrades the land degrades oneself and others who rely on it, ruining culture and committing a grave injustice. In the end, Berry says:

> Between the two programs—the industrial and the agrarian, the global and the local—the most critical difference is that of knowledge. The global economy institutionalizes a global ignorance, in which producers and consumers cannot know or care about one another, and in which their histories of all products will be lost. In such a circumstance, the degradation of products and places, producers and consumers is inevitable.[28]

One need not look any further than the present "global" financial crisis. According to Berry's logic, such a crisis marks the epitome of such global ignorance and hubris, a degradation of people, land, and vocation. Which "way," one may ask, will more clearly manifest the *economy* of salvation?[29]

To counter this abstract way of thinking and choosing, Berry often speaks of *affection* for *a* place and people, an intimate knowledge of local plants, animals, soils, histories, biographies—in short, culture. It is, namely, all that goes into forming a people, enabling them to flourish in the *hic et nunc* of their life situation. It is, in the words of Jesuit John Kavanaugh, to choose the "Personal Form," that is, deep covenantal relationships, over the surface-level, abstract way of the

[27] Wendell Berry, "The Whole Horse," 239.

[28] Ibid., 244.

[29] In Berry's essay "Thoughts in the Presence of Fear," he states: "I. The time will soon come when we will not be able to remember the horrors of September 11 without also remembering the unquestioning technological and economic optimism that ended on that day. II. This optimism rested on the proposition that we were living in a "new world order" and a "new economy" that would "grow" on and on, bringing a prosperity of which every new increment would be unprecedented." See Wendell Berry, *Citizenship Papers* (Washington, DC: Shoemaker & Hoard, 2003), 17.

"Commodity Form."[30] This affection was present, with limitations, in the romantic poets Thoreau and Wordsworth. But a more knowledgeable expression is found in twentieth-century agrarian-scientists such as Liberty Hide Bailey, Sir Albert Howard, Aldo Leopold, and Wes Jackson, the latter of the Land Institute of Salina, Kansas. In essence, the above-mentioned persons cultivated the practice of farming in nature's image. "Let the forest judge" and "take note of the Genius of the Place," Berry writes. True and good use of the land, and therefore the true flourishing of culture, can only come about through the "stability, coherence, and longevity" of human occupation and great attentiveness. That is, one takes up residence in the oikos in the fullest measure possible—to know it, care for it, and love it, becoming one with a local culture, place, and land. In the words of Norman Wirzba, such a labor of love and conviviality ushers in an "economy of gratitude," giving hope in the face of great resistance.[31]

In his essay, "The Body and the Earth," Berry contends that the "modern urban-industrial society is based on a series of radical disconnections between body and soul, husband and wife, marriage and community, community and the earth." This contributed to the physical and spiritual disintegration, dis-ease, and dismemberment of cultures, the creation, and community. "Our economy is based upon this disease."[32] How do we begin to reconcile these radical disconnections? Interestingly, Berry begins his essay recounting a letter he received from someone who wrote about a person who committed suicide. The letter had asked and answered the question: "How does a human pass through youth to maturity without breaking down? [It does so] with help from tradition through ceremonies and rituals, rites of passage through the most difficult stages." The writer continues, and Berry concurs, that "the theme of suicide belongs in a book on

---

[30] John Kavanaugh, *Following Christ in a Consumer Society: The Spirituality of Cultural Resistance* (Maryknoll, NY: Orbis Books, 2006), 38, 75, 124–25.

[31] "The Whole Horse" in *The Art of the Commonplace*, 240–41, 244; Norman Wirzba, "An Economy of Gratitude," in *Wendell Berry: Life and Work*, ed. Jason Peters, 142–55, esp. 145 (Lexington, KY: University of Kentucky Press, 2007).

[32] Berry, "The Body and the Earth," in *The Art of the Commonplace*, 132. This essay is one of Berry's most synthetic and provocative. The subsections of this lengthy essay are indicative of the breadth with which he approaches our "disease," suggesting also its treatment: "Health, The Isolation of the Body, Competition, Connections, Sexual Division, The Dismemberment of the Household, Fidelity, Home Land and Household, The Necessity of Wildness, Freedom from Fertility, Fertility and Waste, Health and Work."

agriculture." The fragmented approach of the technicians is misguided and contrary to the holistic, agrarian one. Do we not often hear various leaders in the United States declare that "America is healthy," by which they mean the "economy" is "humming" along, growing, and people are consuming. This notion of health is an abstraction, and nothing could be further from the truth. There is a basic misunderstanding of the word *health*:

> To be healthy is to be whole, a word related to *heal, whole, wholesome, hale, hallow, holy*. . . . If the body is healthy it is whole. . . . It is therefore absurd to approach the subject of health piecemeal with a departmentalized band of specialists. A medical doctor uninterested in nutrition, in agriculture, in the wholesomeness of mind and spirit is as absurd as a farmer uninterested in health. Our fragmentation of this subject cannot be our cure because it is our disease. The body cannot be whole alone. Persons cannot be whole alone.[33]

In Christian theology health (*salus*) relates to salvation. Thus when a person is saved (healed) it is not just the sick part that is redeemed, made whole, but the entire person. One is saved in the waters of baptism and grafted onto the body of all believers. Becoming whole is a communal action. But our place in this world also joins us to the body of all humanity and the body of God's good creation. This expresses well the notion of the communion of saints.

Wendell Berry suggests that the path toward deep "healing," while complex, includes seeing "health and work" through a wider lens. At a rudimentary level, restoration and reconciliation of the disconnections can come through seeing the relationship between "living and eating, eating and working, working and loving." He names gardening, for example, as a way to work with the body in an act that produces something to feed the body, making it healthy. He adds, "the work, if knowledgeable, makes for excellent food . . . nourishing and joyful, not consumptive, and keeps the eater from getting fat and weak." The work of growing and preparing one's food is not "drudgery," which is what agribusiness makes it through the monotony of mono-cropping and the use of big machinery to *simplify* work. The work of growing, preparing, and eating food is at once a practical act and a sacramental one, "by which we enact and understand our one-

---

[33] Ibid., 98–99.

ness with the Creation, the conviviality of one body with all bodies," this, *oikoumenos*. Not only with food, but all good work, according to Berry, becomes the *enactment* of these necessary connections for a lasting health (*salus*), work that originates in the soil, penetrating every dimension of creation—land and people, indeed, *omnia*.[34]

By way of transition let us be explicit about this relationship between health and work, that is, salvation and *leitourgia*. Christian liturgy, especially the Eucharist, is the celebration of our salvation in Christ. The place of its enactment is the culture where one lives and works. Salvation is *worked* there, here and now. If Berry's purview of culture, rooted in the *wholeness* of creation, is accurate, then the New Agrarian's comprehensive vision of life may just offer contemporary liturgical theology a valuable insight into the potential confluence of liturgy, culture, and justice. It is to see the celebration of liturgy as cultivating an "economy of gratitude," *oikonomia* in the fullest sense, reflective of the economy of salvation set in motion from the beginning of creation. Saint Paul's "household of God," (*oikiou tou Theou*, Eph 2:19) encompasses no less than the whole blessed cosmos.

Wendell Berry offers us a complex but praxis-oriented sacramental worldview. It will be argued that sacramentality can serve as the common thread weaving together liturgy, culture, and justice, advancing the thesis that *culture is constitutive of sacramentality*.

Perhaps two analogies may help to focus the above aim of this book: In order for the two rivers of liturgy and justice to form one life-giving, socially transformative stream, it seems they must meet, flow, and draw their energy from the riverbed of culture. Or, to phrase it another way: the tree trunk of liturgical prayer (orthodoxy) must sink its roots into—draw its nutrients from, be nourished by—the culture in which it is celebrated and lived, so that just living (orthopraxis) may flower and flourish.

## SACRAMENTALITY AND THE
## CHRISTIAN THEOLOGICAL TRADITION

Kevin Irwin argues that the principle of sacramentality carries the potential to ground all liturgical and sacramental theology. This entails recovering a broader patristic understanding of a sacramental

---

[34] Ibid., 132–33.

world, grounding the study of liturgy and sacraments in a theology of creation. This would shift their study toward a more fundamental sacramental (and traditionally Catholic) worldview rather than beginning with more dogmatically oriented treatises. Doing so would offer a more "contemporary paradigm for sacramental theology."[35]

It is primarily in the celebration of the liturgy and sacraments that the sacramental economy unfolds for, and is communicated to, the faithful in an *explicit* manner. The communal nature of the liturgy points to the interdependence of all creatures inherent in the liturgical action.[36] God uses creation within the liturgy (and outside of it) to unfold the salvific plan. Irwin states:

> We humans have been saved through the things of this earth, including human culture. . . . Liturgical and sacramental rites by their nature are *inculturated* in the sense that they respect and derive from the human cultures which celebrate them. Liturgical rites make sense in that they derive from culture and reflect the ways human cultures communicate and operate. They are not meant to be mysterious in terms of unknowability. Rather they are taken from what and how humans communicate so that the irrevocable union of God and humanity in Christ becomes the paradigm and the medium through which salvation is accomplished.[37]

For example, the ordinary human meal takes on greater significance in light of the fact that Christ also ate similar meals, but more so based on what happened at the Last Supper. Those two deeds became paradigmatic for the church. Irwin rightly cautions against any naïve romanticism that only exalts God's creation and redemption. For the reality is that heaven and earth are *not* always full of God's glory (injustice). The liturgy does not simply "right" these wrongs. Rather, it awakens the consciences of those who profess to be members of Christ's Body and who, with God's grace, work to further unfold the sacramental economy.

[35] Kevin Irwin, "Sacramentality and the Theology of Creation: A Recovered Paradigm for Sacramental Theology," *Louvain Studies* 23 (1998): 159–60, 166.

[36] Ibid., 167. Irwin notes here the creation motif in the *Catechism*, nos. 280, 288, 294, 300, 302, and 340–43.

[37] Ibid., 169–70. This is a key insight with regard to liturgy and culture and will be taken up again when the NCRLC's program is examined in light of sacramentality.

Practically speaking, Irwin suggests that one way to accomplish this is to consider the meaning of liturgical blessing. Since Vatican II there has been an effort to correct the notion that it is things that are blessed. While true in part, a blessing is given to persons. In the blessing liturgy (a communal action as in *De Benedictionibus*) an object is blessed by speaking words that join that object's use *by people* to the salvific deed done *by God*. This is why the church requires the word of God to be read when imparting a blessing, since doing so recounts, in part, salvation history. For example, in the blessing of water the prayers speak of how God has used water to demonstrate his goodness, recalling (*anamnesis*) God's saving action throughout history in the presence of people today. This means that "the prayer is thus effective by drawing us into the paradigmatic events of salvation history while at the same time through this blessed water it makes present an act of recreation and redemption here and now through creation's gift of water."[38] Blessing liturgies were clearly one of the principal ways in which the Conference made a direct connection between worship and life, weaving their daily agrarian lives into "the paradigmatic events of salvation history." The *one* sacramental world was at the basis of the NCRLC's liturgical, cultural, and social program—the ground of these being the principle of sacramentality.

Prosper of Aquitaine's axiom and its retrieval by contemporary theologians was an attempt to reestablish the vital connection not only between liturgy and theology but between liturgy and life. This endeavor ultimately concerned the renewal of the church.[39] The NCRLC, without explicitly invoking the axiom, had its spirit in mind and intuitively applied it to the rural context. The church's official liturgy (*orandi*), primarily in the form of the *Missal* and *Ritual*, served as an authentic theological source that engendered orthodox belief (*credendi*). This rural-oriented prayer and belief helped rural Catholics to live in accord with Gospel-centered values (*vivendi*). As valuable as this more direct application use of the axiom is, one must be careful not to apply it in too strict a manner. There is room for reading the axiom

---

[38] Ibid., 175–76.

[39] On Prosper of Aquitaine, see above, p. xix. With regard to the magisterium, Irwin points out that the most recent *General Instruction of the Roman Missal* and many contemporary popes make reference to Prosper's insight. See Irwin, *Models of the Eucharist*, 25–26.

differently, in a reciprocal or dialectical manner, bearing new fruit for the liturgy-life question.[40]

When one says or reads the words *lex orandi, lex credendi*, the natural inclination is to understand them in that order. The *lex orandi* can and should be a primary and normative source of theology. At the same time, the *lex orandi* can be a primary source without its being first in the order of Christian experience. For instance, someone may come to experience the richness of the *orandi* proper only after he or she has received a new insight to faith through simple catechesis (*credendi*) outside the liturgical celebration. The same is true with regard to the *lex vivendi*. Some rural Catholics discovered the value of farmers' cooperatives (a form of social action) in light of the church's social teaching. This moved them to join one. Yet it was only after a pastor introduced a more fully participative liturgy in the parish that one potentially saw the intrinsic relationship between economic cooperation and communal worship. Dorothy Day had already been hard at work establishing Catholic Worker houses (*vivendi*) before her encounter with Virgil Michel and the liturgical movement. She then discovered the power of participative liturgy and made it integral to her work. This deepened the transformation already underway. This demonstrates how the axiom's dialectical nature may be at work in Christian life. Indeed, Christian experience indicates that they operate in a dialectical manner.[41]

---

[40] See chapter 4, 110–14, where I examined *The Blessing of Seed and Soil for the Feast of St. Isidore*. Blessings seemed to have more potential to form those who liturgically participated in them. *SC* 21 states: "The Christian people, as far as is possible, should be able to understand them [liturgical rites] with ease and take part in them fully, actively, and as a community." This issue becomes all the more pertinent in light of the debates surrounding the present translation of the Roman Missal. Edward Kilmartin, SJ, pressed for balance (dialectic) and cautioned against overemphasizing either term of the equation. To do so would "threaten to obscure the unique value of two different kinds of expression of faith. . . . Consequently, it seems legitimate to state the axiom in this way: *the law of prayer is the law of belief, and vice versa.*" See Edward Kilmartin, *Christian Liturgy: Theology and Practice* (Kansas City, MO: Sheed and Ward, 1988), 97.

[41] See Irwin, *Context and Text*, 54–56. Applying his thought: "we understand there to be an *ongoing dialectical relationship* between *text* and *context* where the ecclesial and cultural settings in which liturgy takes place—*context*—influence the way we experience and interpret liturgy—*text*. But just as *context* influences how the *text* of liturgy is interpreted, the other side of the equation concerns how that data we call *text* necessarily influences the Church's theology, spirituality, and life—*context.*"

## CULTURE AS CONSTITUTIVE OF SACRAMENTALITY

To propose that *culture is constitutive of sacramentality* suggests an alternate reading of Prosper's axiom that retains its basic form and applies it differently. This involves viewing the *vivendi* in a broader way, considering it as indicative of a comprehensive sacramental worldview—*omnia*—and hence, all of life.[42] The "law of right living" derives from this more fundamental understanding of sacramentality.

The created world communicates something to humans about God. In the incarnation, that communication became emphatic. *Sacrum commercium* is the phrase that the church employs to express both the exchange of gifts at Eucharist and the saving mystery of Christ taking flesh.[43] The incarnation and the exchange of gifts are foundational to liturgy being sacramental *and* relational. The church itself is constituted by the diversity of cultures that make up the Body of Christ. If culture is constitutive of sacramentality, then a culture's words, symbols, gestures, and its materiality comprise its basic language and are able to communicate the presence of God. The unique elements of culture are how that culture understands itself and, in the end, how it comes to know God. If that basic language is utilized in a local church's prayer, making it intelligible (and orthodox), it will better serve the relationship between liturgy and life. This implies that the *vivendi* is synonymous with culture. It refers to everything (*omnia*) that makes up a people's way of life, inclusive of the local material creation, as Wendell Berry would contend. Liturgy, even as "source and summit," is a means to an end. God will use *that* culture as a means to achieve the end that God desires—salvation!

This broader understanding of the *vivendi* makes it *a* possible source of liturgical-sacramental theology. To be certain, the *lex vivendi* implies the "law of right living." Yet a more literal translation is simply "the law/rule of living" and encompasses something more than the moral life. Humans experience first the demands of existing. God addresses humans there, in their unique context. A Christian belongs to a culture first, and it is there that he or she is evangelized. Then one comes to the liturgy and, therefore, to the church. It is safe to presume that more

---

[42] It is helpful to recall that the root of the word *vivendi* is *vivus*, which can mean a human person, living being, life, and alive.

[43] *Sacrum commercium* conveys a "holy exchange" or interchange. For the relationship between sacramentality and liturgy see Irwin, *Models of the Eucharist*, 42–49, and on the *commercium*, 58–59.

Christians understand their own life situation far better than the church's liturgy and most assuredly better than any of its dogmatic pronouncements. Yet the church's liturgy and doctrine offer a necessary structure for living the Christian life.

What, then, can be drawn from the thesis that culture is constitutive of sacramentality? One begins with the basic human desire to experience a full and abundant life. The total flourishing of a given people and its culture (*vivendi*) is something that the church ardently desires. In the Christian context, such a desire directs one's actions *instaurare omnia in Christo*. God redeems people and things; the two are inseparable. The eucharistic liturgy is the privileged *sacrum commercium*, the salvific meeting point of God, people, and creation. The NCRLC's blessing liturgies joined what was constitutive of a given culture more closely to the church's official prayer. If the sacramental principle is maintained, then all life (culture) becomes the material God uses to redeem people. Culture *is* a sacramental reality. God redeems these particular things, peoples, and events, fashioning a people after God's own heart in ways they understand. How could it be otherwise? Thus culture is constitutive of sacramentality, and this, the means toward salvation.

Culture and sacramentality formed part of Virgil Michel's thought as well. According to Michel, "man" was at the center of culture.[44] The human being was to direct those God-given human capacities to know the world surrounding him or her in its totality. This fostered an integral human development, drawing out the best that was in him or her. The human person will endeavor to know "his entire environment insofar as this is intimately connected with human life. The whole field of human culture in its widest sense embraces all activities and abilities of man, all the aspiration and inspirations of his nature, the entire field of human existence."[45] This comprehensive knowledge of one's place and circumstance, and having *affection* for it, is central to Berry's understanding of culture and greatly impacts his understanding of justice.

---

[44] Marx, *Virgil Michel*, 255ff., esp. 257–58. See pp. 70–73 above the material on the Institute for Social Study at St. John's. There, Dunstan Tucker delivered a series of lectures on culture, relating it to social change.

[45] Virgil Michel, "Christian Culture," *OF* 13 (May 1939): 296–97. He continues elsewhere in the article: "Being truly catholic, the Church is opposed to no particular traits of culture such as are peculiar to an individual nation or an individual period of history. She has room for all . . ." (300).

There was a conspicuous convergence in Michel's notion of how liturgy and culture were joined. That nexus was the sacramental principle, and it is writ large throughout the entire chapter that Paul Marx devoted to the liturgical leader's thought on liturgy and culture.[46] Michel seemed to intuit something fundamental in this relationship since he understood both terms as being rooted in the sacramental principle and as playing key roles in a more just social order. At the basis of Michel's thinking was his notion of the natural-supernatural, material-spiritual dialectic:

> Any culture has to do greatly with the material things of creation, and a wholesome Christian culture will depend very much on the proper position of the material in the entire Christian scheme of life. According to the latter, the whole material world was created to be an instrument and as it were an extension of man. . . . Proper use of the material in human life needs knowledge of the dispensation of God. . . . In all of this the liturgy is again the model as well as the source of true inspiration. . . . The primacy of the spiritual will be assured in human life and culture under the inspiration of the liturgy, but in conjunction with the full employment and rightful enjoyment of all the material goods God has placed at the disposal of man.[47]

This insight succinctly captures how Michel understood that there was a material and natural, and thus, sacramental basis to the liturgy, culture, and a renewed social order. The *one* sacramental world can serve as a source of *both* justice *and* injustice. The church must employ the very materials that are constitutive of that culture to transform what is unjust within it. This is thoroughly incarnational and spiritual. It also expresses the inherent ambiguity of sacramentality. The relationship between liturgy and culture has as its ultimate aim the true flourishing of the Christian spirit among the members of the Body of

---

[46] With regard to the sacramental principle and its rather pervasive role in connection to culture, see Marx, *Virgil Michel*, 260–61, 263, 264 (on culture and Catholic Action), 265, 274–75, 281, 283, 285. In fact, Michel also based his conception of art, architecture, and most especially a more just social order on this central Catholic principle. His agrarian-distributist position was also grounded in the natural-supernatural dialectic, which I treated in chapter 3.

[47] Michel, "Christian Culture," 301–2. He continues: "The average living out of this spirit in daily life will thus result in a Christian culture, according to which all material progress will be put into greater service of man . . . and will enter also through man into the service which the Christian renders to God in his daily life" (302).

Christ. The nature of the liturgy demanded that those who celebrated the mysteries were then called to transform those negative aspects of the very culture in which they lived. That social order is, in the first place, one's home culture. As Virgil Michel stated in various ways, God transforms people through the liturgy, and people transform culture.

Several ecclesial documents also support the thesis. The 1939 *Manifesto on Rural Life* devoted one chapter to the discussion of rural Catholic culture. Its understanding was wholly consistent with NCRLC's insight that "the salvation of the farmer occurs in and through the circumstances of his life [read culture]." The authors of the *Manifesto* state that culture "designates the harmonious development of man's moral, intellectual, and esthetic faculties . . . a synthesis of the gentleman, artist, scholar, and saint." Culture is not to be imposed on any group; rather, it is far better that culture grow out of the life of a rural community—organically. It is something deeply rooted in the agrarian person's mode of thinking and philosophy of living. Rural culture implies "an appreciation of both material and spiritual good." In the end, rural Catholic culture will manifest itself "in refined manners, artistic homes, neat farmsteads, modern conveniences, music, art, and literature; in folk drama; in the liturgy and church chant; church architecture; and above all in virtuous living."[48] This "harmonious development" arises from one's home culture and is finally judged by the manner in which one lives "rightly."

Twenty-five years later *Gaudium et Spes*, no. 53, offered a strikingly similar insight about culture as that found in the *Manifesto*:

> It is one of the properties of the human person that he can achieve true and full humanity by means of culture, that is through the cultivation of the goods and values of nature. Whenever, therefore, there is a question of human life, nature and culture are intimately linked together. The word "culture" in the general sense refers to all those things which go into refining and developing of man's diverse mental and physical endowments.[49]

---

[48] See NCRLC, "Catholic Culture in Rural Society," in *Manifesto Annotations*, 110–11.

[49] Austin Flannery, ed., *Vatican Council II: The Conciliar and Post-Conciliar Documents* (Northport, NY: Costello Publishing Co., 1992); see also *GS* 42, 44, 56, 58 (mentions the liturgy).

The insight that "nature and culture" form the basis of the "good" among humans is a theme that pervades Wendell Berry's work and was consistent with the thinking of the NCRLC and Virgil Michel.[50] When "man" maximizes his natural faculties (knowledge and physical labor) in harnessing the earth's resources, "he humanizes social life both in the family and in the whole civic community through the improvement of customs and institutions." The council fathers understood this human effort as being of a spiritual quality and eminently at the service of human progress and the common good (the overall thrust of GS). The authors of Gaudium et Spes rightly acknowledged that the human person "can achieve true and full humanity only by means of culture." God redeems "this" particular people, bringing them to "full humanity." Indeed, how else is it to occur?

In Ad Gentes, no. 22, the conciliar document on the church's missionary activity, agrarian imagery was used to declare that the local church bears much fruit when it grows out of the soil of the culture in which the Gospel was planted: "The seed which is the word of God grows out of good soil watered by the divine dew, it absorbs moisture, transforms it, and makes it part of itself, so that eventually it bears much fruit." Because of the "economy of the incarnation," Christ, who was born in time and yet transcends it, makes it possible for the created good that already exists in a culture to reach its "full humanity." Thus, the "young churches" are encouraged to make use of all that is in their culture so as to render fitting praise to God, and this, most of all, by the "right ordering of Christian life."[51]

Sacrosanctum Concilium, nos. 37–40, offered four brief statements that served to guide the church's cultural adaptation of the liturgy. These statements have been interpreted broadly, generating much discussion and debate. The key insights from Gaudium et Spes and Ad Gentes noted above lend further support for the adaptation the liturgy set forth by the decree, as noted in SC 37: "Even in the liturgy the Church does not wish to impose any rigid uniformity in matters which do not involve the faith or the good of the whole community."

[50] See especially, Berry's The Unsettling of America, 17–48.

[51] Of course AG 10 is the seminal reference with regard to the incarnation and inculturation: "If the Church is to be in a position to offer all men the mystery of salvation and the life brought by God, then it must implant itself among all these groups in the same way that Christ by his incarnation committed himself to the particular social and cultural circumstances of the men among who he lived."

The conciliar decree asserted that the church wished to honor anything good in a culture so long as it is not bound up with superstition or anything erroneous, even admitting certain customs into the liturgy itself. To impose a "rigid uniformity" as such partakes in what Berry calls "simplification" and becomes a grievous act against people and land. *SC* 40 spoke of how in certain places and circumstances "radical adaptation" of the liturgy may be necessary. *GS* 58 highlighted the history of such adaptation and how God spoke according to the culture proper to each age:

> Similarly the Church has existed through the centuries in varying circumstances and has utilized the resources of different cultures in its preaching to spread and explain the message of Christ, to examine and understand it more deeply, and to express it more perfectly in the liturgy and in various aspects of the life of the faithful. . . . In this way the Church carries out its mission and in that very act it stimulates and advances human and civil culture, as well as contributing by its activity, including liturgical activity, to man's interior freedom.[52]

These select conciliar insights along with those of the NCRLC and Vigil Michel point to the crucial relationship that exists between the liturgy, culture, and a more just social order. The evidence presses for a more "radical adaptation" of the liturgy grounded in the soil of a community's culture—with attention, knowledge, and *affection* of the local *oikos*. However, in no way should "more radical" be equated with some great departure from the church's *credendi*.

Virgil Michel, along with the authors of the *Manifesto* and the conciliar decrees, confirmed that the flourishing of Christian life originated in one's cultural milieu, using what is constitutive of it. The ways of a culture become the "material" through which God saves this particular people—to praise the glory of the Creator. The authors also stressed that "right living," true human progress, was inseparable from one's culture. That is, the human person who accepts the Gospel will express its values in a manner consistent with the culture where he or she resides. It may be helpful at this point to recall the "nature" analogies above, suggesting an intrinsic relationship between liturgy, culture, and justice. The thesis that culture is constitutive of sacramen-

---

[52] *GS* 58.

tality means that the unique sacramental makeup of a culture is the very material that God redeems, and that redemption is reflected by deeds that are "right and just," *hodie*. Why should this material not become part of its liturgical-sacramental celebrations proper?

Inculturation can never be limited to the liturgy. Thus the many programs that the NCRLC offered to rural Catholics also supported this relationship between culture and sacramentality. Such activities led the faithful to both a deeper engagement in the liturgy and in rural life, often integrating both. The discussion on rural arts also supported the relationship. Arts and crafts, music, poetry, snippets of rural wisdom, literature, and architecture all contributed to the flourishing of rural life. When the church extended a blessing upon people and things, they were brought into closer union with the redemption wrought by Christ. Study clubs and retreats led rural Catholics to reflect more deeply about their culture. In doing so, they found confirmation of their vocation as farmers through the church's doctrine and social teaching. The liturgy also confirmed their vocation in a unitive and doxological way. Farmers gathered together to praise and thank God, offering back to God the fruits of their land—God's gifts to them, stewards of a sacramental universe.

Assuredly, the Conference tried to integrate liturgy and life. Here *vivendi* was broadly interpreted to include the entire sacramental world, that is, *oikos* and *omnia*. This grounds the thesis that culture is constitutive of sacramentality. Once again, the lucid insight of Bill Busch in 1929 is noted and serves as a cogent conclusion to the foregoing discussion. The liturgical leader rightly intuited the direct relationship between how "the liturgy speaks in a familiar way" to the agrarian people who celebrated it and the implications it carried for right living. Wendell Berry too offers us a sacramental view of the world, one that is grounded in concrete paschal practices and not mere theological speculation, as he so eloquently states:

> Culture is not a collection of relics and ornaments but a practical necessity, and its corruption invokes calamity. A healthy culture is a communal order of memory, insight, value, work, conviviality, reverence, and aspiration. It reveals human necessities and human limits. It clarifies our inescapable bonds to the earth and to each other. It assures that necessary restraints are observed, that the necessary work is done, and that it is done well. A healthy farm culture can be based only upon familiarity and can grow only among a people soundly established

upon the land; it nourishes and safeguards a human intelligence of the earth that no amount of technology can satisfactorily replace.[53]

Berry's thought on culture, while not strictly liturgical, provides keen insight into the demands for a true flourishing of communities. For the Christian community, in all its diversity, a more profound, organic approach is needed that will make the liturgy truly inculturated, honoring all that is good in it, and allowing it to become an integral source of justice. *Ad Gentes*, no. 19, noted how the faith should be imparted by means of a well-adapted catechesis and celebrated in a liturgy that is "in harmony with the genius of the people." This shapes communities of faith and love, leading the faithful to strive for a "public order based on justice and love." Our mission orders have been given. Dare we receive them with grace!

---

[53] Wendell Berry, "The Agricultural Crisis As a Crisis of Culture," 43.

# Saints of the Soil:
# An Eschatological Epilogue[1]

LOOKING FORWARD WHILE REACHING BACK

In his 1975 response upon receiving the North American Academy of Liturgy's first Berakah Award, the Benedictine liturgical scholar Aidan Kavanagh spoke of his work as being "unfinished and unbegun."[2] This study has attended to some unfinished liturgical business, namely, an unexplored piece of twentieth-century U.S. Catholic history has been brought to light. These explorations unearthed the many historical, liturgical-theological, and practical relationships shared between members of the American liturgical movement and the National Catholic Rural Life Conference. For over forty years, the NCRLC consistently sought to engender an integral approach to Catholic life and made the liturgy key to that effort. At the same time, chapter 6 suggested that there was also some work, not so much "unbegun" but perhaps work that invited redirecting liturgical and theological discourse toward the notion of sacramentality.

Central to the work of the liturgical movement was the historical recovery (or rediscovery) of those dimensions of the church's worship that had fallen out of practice or became so encumbered within the liturgy that certain actions lost their original meaning. The thrust of these scholarly and pragmatic efforts was to restore to the assembly a more participative role in the church's public prayer. Further, roles in the liturgical assembly that once belonged to the laity had been usurped by the priest and/or acolyte. Leaders of the movement wanted to make the liturgy once again a vibrant source of Christian piety, the ultimate purpose being the renewal of the church. The NCRLC

---

[1] "Saints of the Soil" was the suggested title of a proposed rural life prayer book in the 1940s.

[2] Aidan Kavanagh, "Liturgical Business Unfinished and Unbegun," *Worship* 50 (1976): 355.

adopted and implemented many of these rediscovered aspects of the liturgy among which the following can be mentioned:

1. Centrality of the liturgy, especially the Eucharist, as the basis of Christian life

2. Active and intelligent participation in the liturgy; this principally accomplished by way of the dialogue Mass or *Missa recitata* and blessing liturgies

3. Such participation was understood as formative of the Mystical Body of Christ and indispensable for a broader ecclesiology

4. Use of the vernacular in the liturgy

5. Frequent Communion

6. Catechesis on the liturgical year was made practical in the celebration of feasts that had rural orientations

7. It gave new and significant meaning to processions, in particular, with regard to the "offertory" or presentation of the gifts. This was directly related to the farmer who produced the wheat and grapes as well as its relationship to social charity

8. It encouraged communal celebrations of the sacraments

9. Congregational singing in Latin and the vernacular

10. A broader understanding of sacramentality with respect to the liturgy was advanced; it took seriously the motto *instaurare omnia in Christo*; *omnia* being directly related to the notion of sacramentality

11. Deepened the understanding of sacramentals and their role in relationship to the church's public worship

12. Rural devotions rightly understood in relation to, and sometimes integrated with, the liturgy

13. Attempted to make a direct link between liturgy and life; liturgy was fostered in the home and on the farm

14. It made a connection between baptism and vocation; a way of life (farming) was affirmed via the liturgy, another conjunction of liturgy and life

15. The Conference made liturgical formation and catechesis integral to all its other activity (retreats, study clubs, etc.)

Leaders in both movements catechized rural Catholics in one or several of these dimensions of the liturgy. At times it seemed that the whole of the liturgical movement's agenda could be reduced to intelligent and active participation in the church's communal prayer. Many thought that this would automatically instill a more socially conscious piety among other things. In spite of many good efforts, the integration of liturgy and social concern was not embraced by a significant number of the faithful. This is noted as a possible limitation of the liturgical movement. That is to say, the tendency can be to place too great a burden on what the liturgy alone (Sunday Eucharist especially) can accomplish in deepening the spiritual life of Christians. Perhaps this suggests directing more attention to other sacraments or to the more frequent use of something like the *Book of Blessings*.

The NCRLC offered to rural Catholics an integral faith formation. Liturgical and sacramental catechesis was constitutive of nearly every facet of its overall program. The NCRLC's central aim was to impact the whole of rural life—its religion, culture, economy, education, health, and environment. It can be argued that the NCRLC practiced a nascent form of what is today called "Total Community Catechesis" (TCC).[3] TCC is a holistic faith formation program that fosters a broader understanding of what faith in the triune God means in practice—praying, learning, and serving. Sunday Eucharist is at the center of this enterprise, but TCC tries to cultivate a regimen of prayer (private and communal), catechesis, and Christian action reflective of the paschal pattern established by (and in) Christ. It is Catholic in the best sense of the word. In part, such an approach was necessitated by the isolated rural environment.

---

[3] The NCRLC's comprehensive approach to catechesis (faith formation) also invites further study. "Catechesis" is one dimension of the larger field of "faith formation" and is distinct from "religious education." Catechesis is often reduced to didactic religious instruction (information input) and thus, can be found to be spiritually lacking. "Total Community Catechesis" is preferred over "Whole Community Catechesis" but both imply the same basic idea. Thomas Groome has offered some clarity to the subject: "catechetical education is to inform, form, and transform Christian persons and communities as apprentices to Jesus for God's reign in the world." See Thomas H. Groome, "Total Catechesis/Religious Education: A Vision for Now and Always," in *Horizons and Hopes: The Future of Religious Education*, ed. Thomas H. Groome and Harold D. Horell, 6–12 (New York: Paulist, 2003). Groome draws principally from the scriptures and the *General Directory for Catechesis* to articulate what he means by catechetical education. Central to being an "apprentice of Jesus" entails "right belief (*orthodoxia*), right action (*orthopraxia*), and right worship (*ortholeitourgia*)." *Idem*, 10.

One reason that some rural faith communities were successful in integrating liturgy and life was their ethnic and vocational homogeneity. This enabled a rural parish to be united in its common endeavors—liturgical, educational, and economic. Rural communities celebrated local liturgies that strengthened the local church and did so in union with the universal church. Could attempts to so localize a liturgy (in any cultural context) obscure the more universal sense of church? This did not seem to occur with rural parishes but could be raised as a more general concern regarding liturgical inculturation. In today's globalized society, with the greater movement of peoples and other cultural factors, such a homogenized community is less likely to exist. The NCRLC's attempt to integrate agrarianism and Catholicism invites a more thorough examination in light of contemporary research on liturgical inculturation.[4]

Two of the chief nemeses of the liturgical and rural life movements were individualism and capitalistic materialism. In spite of the efforts to thwart the determined march of these two socioeconomic forces, both movements eventually succumbed to them. In the United States, the family farm has almost completely disappeared, being replaced by large corporate (factory) farms.[5] This raises deeper questions about both liturgical inculturation and the liturgy's countercultural role in society. Inculturation implies that a local church adopts local customs for worship and catechesis. Yet inculturated practices that indiscriminately adopt certain local customs without asking whether or not they perpetuate injustices in that culture need to be more critically examined. An uncritical acceptance of a culture's symbols and traditions might undermine the potentially countercultural impact of the liturgy and other evangelizing efforts. In North American culture an unbridled consumerism persists that poses very serious challenges to a truly *catholic* sacramental worldview—engagement with symbol, ritual, and

[4] Some of the NCRLC's anti-urban tendencies were noted. Could such a narrow purview have been the result of so ardently trying to preserve the rural (local) way of life to the detriment of the universal communion? The work of Anscar Chupungco, OSB, and Robert Schreiter would be two (among many) authors to consider on the topic of inculturation and the local church.

[5] I would add, however, that this is not necessarily the case in places such as Africa, where the church is experiencing rapid growth where agrarian cultures are still predominant. Eighty percent of the farms in Nigeria are family run and depend on cooperatives. Possibilities still exist for carrying forward some of the NCRLC's agenda, adapting it to the unique "ecclesial and cultural setting."

justice. Virgil Michel believed that the ever-present dominance of an industrial, commodity-driven world removed people from the many natural processes that govern daily life (i.e., food production and the corporate relationality it fostered). This, more than anything, shapes Wendell Berry's tough but realistic criticism of American culture. Vincent Miller has recently put forth a persuasive argument concerning the commodification of culture and how this potentially distorts the inherited tradition of symbols and belief. The problem is manifested in "consumption," which is substituted for religious practices and the "distribution" of select elements of a religious tradition as a commodity. The consumer culture *is* a formation system that engenders alienation (Marxian to a certain degree) not only from "production" but also from the traditional symbols of religious faith. A rupture has occurred; belief and practice become more tenuously joined since they are grounded in beliefs that are *personally* chosen—a consequence of the consumer culture. Miller identifies theology, liturgy, and church communications infrastructures as "tactical resources" that can potentially counter some of the deleterious effects of consumerism.[6]

The church's official prayer can and must serve as a source of doctrine and theological reflection. This is so because the *lex orandi* (along with the Bible and Lectionary) serves as a common text for the manner in which the faith is expressed for all who participate in the church's liturgical and sacramental life. Such was the case for Christians in the first millennium. Through the celebration of the liturgy and the sacraments they were able to perceive a world that was thoroughly sacramental, a world "charged with the grandeur of God," as Gerard Manley Hopkins wrote. The National Catholic Rural Life Conference tried to recover such a Christian sacramental view of the world—in its own time and place, not by returning to an "alleged" glorious past. All things—*omnia*—potentially gave glory to God. The heavenly blessing of God and church accompanied the agrarian's daily and earthly tasks, which fulfilled in part the petition in the Lord's Prayer, "thy kingdom come . . . on earth as in heaven," and in the words of the *Sanctus,* "heaven and earth are full of your glory. . . ." In these simple rural blessings, which are extensions of the preeminent *berekah* of the

---

[6] Vincent J. Miller, *Consuming Religion: Christian Faith and Practice in a Consumer Culture* (New York: Continuum, 2004), 32–43, 154, 188–209. Miller's work is a thorough and dense examination of the past century of consumerism and its impact on religion, especially Catholicism.

eucharistic celebration, the people of God are fashioned into instruments that manifest the kingdom of God—eschatology is realized *hic et nunc*.

Both Edwin O'Hara and Virgil Michel knew that if their respective movements were to take hold and flourish, they would need leaders, both lay and ordained, who did not merely impart information; rather, they had to be people imbued with the true Christian Spirit. Within the rural life movement there were numerous outstanding leaders who captured the vision and spirit of the NCRLC, promoted it, and implemented it. The defining traits of these leaders were many and varied, but all of them saw that a vibrant liturgical life coupled to a penchant to reconstruct the rural social order was central to each of them. A number of charismatic leaders have been chosen who, it may be articulated colloquially "simply got it." They put forth and lived an integral Catholic life and inspired the same in the faithful whom they served.

## MONSIGNOR GEORGE "ALFALFA" HILDNER

George Hildner was tagged with the nickname "Alfalfa" after he had returned from an NCRLC meeting in Kansas City in 1943. His parishioner-farmers had been hit by a drought that withered the alfalfa crop used as animal feed. While en route to Kansas City he spotted from his train window large stacks of good alfalfa. He disembarked at the next stop, went back to the place where he had seen the crop, and bargained for five hundred tons. With the help of some parishioners he formed the "Alfalfa Association" that gave him the economic leverage to purchase the crop, helping the farmers survive the drought. This incident was vintage Hildner, who always saw to the material and spiritual well-being of his parishioners. He worked just as persistently in the sanctuary as in the fields that he himself farmed.[7] Hildner attended the inaugural NCRLC meeting in St. Louis (1923) and served as its secretary for many years.

Born in 1881 in Carlyle, Illinois, but raised in St. Louis, Hildner was one of the NCRLC's most colorful figures. As a young man, he was tempted by offers to play professional baseball, which he refused in

---

[7] "Alfalfa George: A Rural Pastor Talks about God, the Land, and His People," *Jubilee* (August 1960): 15. Sadly, the personal papers of Msgr. Hildner have not been preserved as far as I was able to ascertain. They were not in the St. Louis Archdiocesan collection, nor that of Kenrick Seminary, nor the parish of St. John's.

order to enter the seminary. A cartoon entitled "All Things to All Men" depicted the life story of the ballplayer turned priest.[8] He earned a master's degree in fine arts before seminary studies; his affinity for colorful arrangements was expressed in his dress as well as in the churches where he served. He was known to have worn plaid jackets, tan hats, and wine-colored scarves with his clerics. He shocked some of his parishioners when he decorated the church with liturgical symbols of green, red, and blue, and even once propped up the choir loft with abandoned railroad ties. Hildner labored in a city parish for ten years before "scandalizing older pastors with innovative youth work." In 1915 the bishop assigned him to a rural parish on the Mississippi River. He knew nothing about farming but took seriously the apostolic mandate of St. Paul to be "all things to all men." Within the year he was raising prize-winning chickens at county fairs; sale of his "hatching eggs" helped to fund church repairs. He relied on the local extension agents at agricultural schools to learn the most current methods of farming, a move that made his parishioners suspicious. Once they saw the awards he was winning, they quickly changed their minds. The parish was rather run-down, but the first building he constructed was a chicken coop next to the rectory. The following year he organized a farmer's cooperative. Hildner's philosophy was simple: "A pastor is supposed to live for his flock, not off of it."[9]

One witnessed the kind of service he rendered to his parish during Holy Week in 1922. Rain inundated the area and the Mississippi River began to rise. The devoted pastor found himself piling sandbags on the levee and patrolling it with a shotgun, protecting it from poachers downstream. Easter Sunday morning before Mass, he saw a boat coming down the river that threatened to break the levee. He prevented it from hitting the wall by firing some shots over the bow. "Thank God," he told his parishioners that morning, "we didn't have to kill anybody before Easter Sunday Mass." That night the levee broke, flooding homes and farms throughout the region. Hildner rowed through his parish, rescuing parishioners from rooftops as well as livestock. The incident motivated Hildner to raise a half-million dollars in bonds (through parish chicken dinners, held to this day), which the federal government matched to build new levees. It was fundamentally a soil

[8] See "All Things to All Men," *The Young Catholic Messenger*, September 24, 1943.
[9] Witte, Crusading, 38.

conservation issue. Land that was constantly threatened by floods had low value, and this project stabilized property values and eventually allowed parishioners to build more permanent homes. This earned him yet another nickname, the "Levee Priest."

In 1935 he was moved to the parish of St. John (Gildehaus), in Villa Ridge, Missouri, about forty miles southwest of St. Louis. Hildner's pastoral and civic responsibilities increased. He ran a thirty-three-acre demonstration farm where he continued to experiment with various crops as well as make a closer study of soil conservation methods. Farmers, Catholic and non-Catholic, came from around the state seeking his advice. In the mid-1940s he received the state of Missouri's first "Master Conservationist" award, and by 1960 held over twenty-five church and state leadership roles and titles. He served on numerous conservation and agricultural committees throughout the state. When the local electric company was reluctant to run power lines to his area, he threatened to form a cooperative, forcing the company to concede. New schools, road construction projects, dairy and meat cooperatives—all formed part of Hildner's plan to improve the temporal well-being of his parishioners. It is no exaggeration to assert that Hildner was instrumental in transforming a regional economy. He possessed a broad understanding of the Mystical Body of Christ that was not limited to the Catholic Church alone. This self-taught expert on soil conservation and economics advanced the NCRLC's balanced vision of the material and spiritual dimensions of life: "It's no use trying to teach farmers conservation unless you know it from the grass roots up. You can't do it with a pious prayer, sanctimonious look, and a Roman collar."[10] His willingness to defend his parishioners on many fronts earned him yet another oft-used nickname, "The Fighting Priest."

Liturgical life at St. John's was vibrant. Hildner embraced the reforms recommended by Pius X and the liturgical movement. A parish report submitted in 1935 noted changes in the church that removed steps to the Communion rail, accommodating older parishioners. Banners and vestments were made by the Precious Blood sisters of O'Fallon, Missouri. He regularly preached for forty-five minutes and used the opportunity to speak about stewardship of the land. The school opened

[10] No author, "Alfalfa George: A Rural Pastor Talks about God, the Land, and His People," 16–17.

every day with the children fully participating in the *Missa recitata*. Sunday Holy Communions, he reported, "increased over a thousand in 1935 and mass attendance is nearly 100%." Full use was made of the *Ritual*, with Hildner singing the blessings and then translating them into English for the faithful.[11] On Corpus Christi, the congregation walked "in a night procession to five altars in the fields," the way lit by flares with flowers strewn over the paths. He attended to marriage preparation personally. After the morning ceremony in which almost the entire community participated, he invited the couple to his house for breakfast where he further discussed and counseled them on married life. He reported very few divorces or separations in the parish during his pastorate. Funerals, similarly, were community celebrations. Hildner "eulogized" the dead person but included parents and family. He led the procession to the cemetery past other family tombstones to a grave dug by neighbors; Hildner planted the flowers and shrubs himself.[12] In the late 1940s he boasted to Luigi Ligutti about the new altar and shrine to St. Isidore recently built at the parish.

Religious vacation schools, retreats, and rural life days were regular parish activities at St. John's. In 1956 he reported that the Rural Parish Worker's of Christ the King were active in his region.[13] Hildner was called upon to give talks to seminarian and priest study clubs and, of course, at the annual NCRLC meetings, which he continued to attend and at which he served as an officer. Here was a true pastor who spoke with authority that came from close contact with his flock on a daily basis, attending as much to their spiritual needs as to their material ones. Hildner's approach was holistic and organic, with its origins in the soil and souls of the faithful, as he eloquently declared:

> Conservation is such a holy cause that pastors of all churches in rural
> communities should help their people advance in their economy by
> this means, working for soil conservation as well as soul conservation.
> The soil is sacred. It has taken thousands of years for the creation of

[11] George Hildner, "Parish Report of St. John's Church, Gildehaus, MO, for 1935" Archdiocese of St. Louis Archives, folder "St. John's Gildehaus."

[12] No author, "Alfalfa George: A Rural Pastor Talks about God, the Land, and His People," 16.

[13] Hildner, "Diocesan Director Report," MUA/NCRLC, Series 8/1, box 15, folder "Jan 11, 1956–Oct 23, 1956."

six to seven inches of topsoil sufficient, with sunshine and rain, seeding and work, to support generations of man. Mankind, though, has sinned against the soil by depleting it and destroying its fertility. Man has been given the stewardship down through the ages. By not conserving it, he has sinned against it. By conservation man is expiating his sin and making restitution. This makes soil conservation a pious act.[14]

Community (public) worship and devotions along with public works unified the Mystical Body of Christ who prayed and worked in Villa Ridge, Missouri. Monsignor George "Alfalfa" Hildner brought to fruition the NCRLC's vision for a vital Catholic life that enabled farmers to remain on the land. He nourished a lived piety formed by the liturgy and the land.

### FATHER PAUL BRINKER—THE TOBACCO PRIEST

In Fr. Paul Brinker one discovers yet another city-born priest who became an outstanding rural leader. Born in 1910 in Covington, Kentucky, he entered the seminary in 1928 and was ordained on June 7, 1936.[15] Bishop William Mulloy called him one of the more gifted men of the diocese, intellectually and pastorally. After a number of assistant pastor assignments and chaplaincies, he was made the diocesan director of rural life in 1945, a position he held until 1957. From 1951 to 1957 he was pastor of St. Rose of Lima parish in rural Mays Lick, Kentucky. The small parish community was comprised mostly of tobacco farmers even though the town's welcome sign said: "Mays Lick, the Asparagus Bed of Mason County." Brinker, like Hildner, knew little about farming. One thing he readily noticed, however, was that his flock's well-being was closely tied to tobacco farming. Thus he began his "worship-work program," and it was at St. Rose that he became known for celebrating the annual "tobacco Mass."[16]

---

[14] "Alfalfa George: A Rural Pastor Talks about God, the Land, and His People," 19.

[15] It was often the case that when I inquired at various diocesan archival collections about certain persons, I presumed many of them had since gone onto happier, heavenly pastures. Brinker was one of them who recently passed away in December 2008, at ninety-eight years of age.

[16] Ruth Craig Moore, "Holy Mass of the Harvest," *The Louisville Courier-Journal*, December 27, 1953, 9.

Brinker immersed himself in the life of his parishioners, visiting their homes and farms. He often asserted that there must be a direct connection between a "man's life and his liturgy, his cult and his culture." One's religion must be a part of one's daily life. Brinker quickly familiarized himself with the daily and annual rhythm of the local farmers. When he saw the first spring burning of the tobacco beds (a procedure that prepares the ground for planting), he set in motion for the following Sunday a blessing of soil and tobacco seed that occurred during Mass. In the middle of the growing season he celebrated a blessing of the crops for their protection, susceptible as they were to severe droughts. The people processed to an altar set up in or near someone's tobacco patch where a blessing was given and the litany recited. Brinker's very brief report at the NCRLC meeting in Saginaw declared: "Living the Liturgy on the Land seems to have been the theme of the Rural Life program for the past year in Covington. Blessing of seed, the tobacco fields, and the Thanksgiving ceremonies along with the dialogue Mass in the vernacular, were carried out with dignity and benefit to all participating."[17]

It was the annual Mass held to give thanks to God for the tobacco harvest that demonstrated how Brinker joined liturgy and life. On one Sunday in December after the crop had been harvested, farmers brought to church a "stick" of the finest "hands" of tobacco from their crop. Depending on the size of the hands, one could place about eight to twelve hands on a single stick.[18] The farmer removed one or several hands for family members to carry forward during the Mass as part of the "offertory," and was laid on a table in front of the altar. The rest of the crop was collected in the basement and then taken to the market. Sales of the crop went toward the purchase of coal to heat the church or to insurance. The choir sang the following Brinker-composed hymn while the congregation processed forward with tobacco in hand:

[17] Paul Brinker in "Summary of Diocesan Director's Reports, Saginaw Convention," MUA/NCRLC, Series 8/1, box 10, folder "National Convention Saginaw, Oct 17–22, 1952."

[18] The entire plant is cut, or likely uprooted by "hand," hence the term. The stalk is split or speared and left to wilt on "sticks" in the field for a day or two before it is hung in a curing barn. Wilting the leaves helps dry them out, preparing them for curing. A "stick" is approximately 53–55 inches long (4½ feet).

Lady of tobacco fields,
Golden leaves we offer thee;
God has blessed our field of labor,
In tobacco crops of gold.

Brinker composed other songs that he put to familiar church hymns. They were appropriate to certain feasts and facilitated congregational singing. Even the church was decorated with bouquets of beautiful golden tobacco that flared from tall vases.

This Mass as well as other feast days involved further liturgical innovation for which Brinker always asked Bishop Mulloy's permission. He faced the people to say Mass while a lector narrated the Mass in English. Brinker believed that one can never be entirely happy in one's religion until he or she achieves a sense of participation and possession in this worship. In his petition to Mulloy to celebrate Mass facing the people, he argued: "I hope in this way to increase their active and intelligent participation in the holy liturgy. May I also occasionally use the offertory procession?"[19] Mulloy responded in the affirmative to both requests, but he cautioned that the liturgy should be preceded by a thorough explanation and the offertory procession should be reserved for the greater feast days. In September or October, St. Rose also celebrated the "Wheat Mass." The wheat was grown by the parishioners, who also cleaned and ground it before taking it to the local convent where the sisters baked the altar breads. A small portion of wheat was brought forward during the offertory procession and the surplus wheat was used for the poor.

Brinker made incremental requests for the use of musical instruments during the liturgy, beginning with the Midnight Mass of Christmas. He started with the violin and then added the flute and eventually a flute-violin ensemble for the feast of the Assumption later that year (1954); he did the same for the Midnight Christmas Mass. Saint Rose had parishioners who were "quite skilled" at playing these instruments and it "could greatly edify the people, especially the non-Catholics." Mulloy gave him permission for this use of instruments, saying, "it will be an inspiration to the people. I know of no other instrument that I love more than the violin."[20] In 1954 Brinker broadcast the

[19] Brinker to Mulloy, 23 June 1953, Diocese of Covington, Kentucky Archives, folder "St. Rose of Lima, Mays Lick" (hereafter, DCA).
[20] For the correspondence on music see the following: violin, Brinker to Mulloy, 3 December 1952, Mulloy to Brinker, 6 December 1952; flute, Brinker to Mulloy,

Midnight Mass on a local radio station, with his brother Maurice, also a priest of the diocese, serving as narrator.

Brinker reached out to all people in the area. Even though the Catholics of St. Rose were a denominational minority, he often stretched out a hand of good will to other Christians. So trusted was he by them that Brinker alerted Mulloy that he would be receiving an invitation to preach at a small Christian church that had been without a pastor for some time. He added, "They are good people, fervent in faith." Mulloy did not grant his request to preach, fearing that "it would give scandal to the faithful." He did give permission to explain Catholic doctrine to them in their church hall.[21] Ecumenical cooperation often extended to social, educational, and economic programs.

Beyond the sanctuary the devoted pastor engaged in a wide array of activities on behalf of rural people. He collaborated with a broad spectrum of people, anyone willing to promote rural welfare. A glance at his diocesan director report for 1953–54 was indicative of his zeal and the fervor he inspired in other rural pastors:

> Worked to establish a new Catholic hospital [nearer to rural areas]; one credit union; Southern States Cooperative in two counties; Rural CYO organized; three new rural grade schools; Rogation Days observed (litany in English, paraliturgical); Feast of St. Isidore observed; St. Isidore Shrines in every home of St. Rose; Tobacco Masses—blessing of seed, blessing of crops with procession, harvest Mass facing people; four study groups for clergy; gave first broadcast in Soil Conservation Week, July 25–31, statewide 30-station hook-up; Aug 23–28, gave 30 minute broadcasts over station WFTM, World's Finest Tobacco Market, disseminating the Catholic rural philosophy; distributed 5000 pieces of literature at R.E.A. Fair, July 28–29; Weekly article in diocesan newspaper; Dialogue Mass established in several places; collaborating with rural Life Committee of Diocesan Council of Catholic Women in promoting family shrines; Wheat Mass, every year at harvest time. Wheat used for altar breads; surplus for the poor.[22]

---

3 September 1953, Mulloy to Brinker, 21 November 1953; ensemble for Assumption, Brinker to Mulloy, 1 August 1954, Mulloy to Brinker, 6 August 1954; ensemble for Christmas Midnight Mass, Brinker to Mulloy, 10 December 1954, Mulloy to Brinker, 13 December 1954. In DCA, folder "St. Rose of Lima, Mays Lick."

[21] Brinker to Mulloy, 13 November 1951, Mulloy to Brinker, 23 November 1953, DCA, folder "St. Rose of Lima, Mays Lick."

[22] Brinker, "Diocesan Rural Life Activities, 1953–54," MUA/NCRLC, Series 8/1, box 13, folder "Diocesan Director Reports, Davenport, IA, Oct 8, 1954." REA stands for the Rural Electrification Association.

Brinker worked closely with the University of Kentucky, collaborating on a number of projects. Some of them were religious in nature such as the seminarian institutes that were conducted at this and other universities. He worked with Professor Howard Beers of the University of Kentucky Sociology Department on how to more effectively organize rural communities. Brinker helped to organize the "Rural Leadership Institute" in 1948 at the university.[23]

Health issues were a perennial challenge in rural communities. Brinker requested permission from Bishop Mulloy to work with legislators on a rural health bill, wanting to identify with them and add strength to the cause. More interesting, he pointedly asked Mulloy: "How far shall I go in recommending that this bill be extended to rural coloreds?"[24] A year later he worked with sewage authorities to use a byproduct (of human waste) for fertilizer; this to help farmers improve their farms the "organic way."[25] The project was considered quite progressive for its time in terms of conservation and sustainability.

In August 1950 Brinker formed part of the rural think tank that gathered at Blue Ridge Summit, Pennsylvania; the fruit of that meeting was *The Land: God's Gift to Man* (1952). Brinker commented to Mulloy on the collection of brain power in attendance, but the bishop expressed his esteem for Brinker by telling him that he topped the list.[26] He also attended the Mid-century Whitehouse Conference on Youth in Washington, DC, where he made an appeal for rural facilities and rural youth development. He teamed with Lydwine van Kersbergen to give several talks at Grailville and sent some girls from the diocese to Loveland so as to further develop and invigorate the lay apostolate back home.

Indeed, to modern sensibilities the concept of a "tobacco Mass" could not be more politically incorrect. In any case, Dolores Donovan, who was a parishioner at St. Rose during Brinker's pastorate, said of

[23] Mulloy to Brinker, February 24, 1947; Brinker to Mulloy July 18, 1947, DCA, folder "NCRLC 1945–47." Brinker had asked Msgr. George Hildner to give one of the talks on soil conservation.

[24] Brinker to Mulloy, February 24, 1947, DCA, folder "NCRLC 1945–47."

[25] Brinker to Mulloy, December 30, 1947 and January 2, 1948, DCA, folder "NCRLC, 1948–50." Such a project, the use of human waste as fertilizer, has gained support in recent years and research is under way. The capture of human waste to convert into energy is also being explored. All such research has the goal of greater sustainability in mind.

[26] Brinker to Mulloy, 8 September 1950, DCA, folder "NCRLC, 1948–50."

the beloved priest: "He could bring a dead ant back to life. He was simply the most personable man and knew everyone; he made you feel essential to the parish—all in order to keep the engine oiled." She added, "he'd also stare you down in church and 'call you out' if he saw you weren't singing." During Advent and Lent, the seven o'clock morning daily Mass was in dialogue form and had congregational singing accompanied by organ. His homilies made an explicit connection between religion and rural life. Fifty years later one could hear in Mrs. Donovan's voice the joy that Father Paul Brinker imparted to his flock. More significantly, after all this time, one sensed the great impact left on her by the intelligent and active participation in the liturgy that Brinker fostered. Of all the activities in this small but bustling faith community, liturgy made the greatest impact, and it was explicitly joined to the daily lives of the faithful at St. Rose of Lima parish.[27]

## DIOCESE OF SPRINGFIELD, ILLINOIS— SPREADING THE RURAL FAITH

The Springfield diocese was a veritable hub of rural life activity and played a significant role in disseminating rural literature, especially liturgical services. Fathers George Nell and Irvin Will deserve special mention. Each one coordinated rural life activities and served as diocesan directors covering a span of forty years.

Nell was a founding member of the NCRLC and spent most of his life as pastor of St. Joseph's Church in rural Island Grove, Illinois, which Nell often quipped, was "neither an island nor a grove." Nell was yet another pastor who was ignorant of farming, and he humbly admitted that "the people gave me an education." Upon Nell's arrival at St. Joseph's he was confronted with many socioeconomic challenges. He instinctively knew that if they were not remedied in some way, the people would leave the land, and consequently the parish. He tackled first the social problem and this through various forms of entertainment—plays and movies using a "stereopticon." When the people gathered, he used the occasion to talk to them about more substantial issues. A 1923 parish bulletin reported how the social program invited interest in educational initiatives that eventually led to addressing economic concerns. He was instrumental in starting a parish library, the Young People's Social Action Committee, and a Farm Bureau

[27] Personal telephone conversation with Dolores Donovan, October 2006.

Baseball League. All this activity had the purpose of instilling in the people a certain pride in the rural-agricultural life. In 1920 Nell established the "Co-op Parish Activities Service," an educational service to rural people that distributed catechetical materials as well as movies and plays.[28] At every step of the way Nell always invited the non-Catholics to participate.

The land in Jasper and Effingham counties was not especially fertile and certainly not suited to "row crops." Nell slowly convinced farmers, suspicious of change and any "progressive farming" ideas, to consider dairy farming, which they did. With the help of the county extension programs, dairying began and farmers eventually formed a cooperative. A regional milk strike tested the resolve of the farmers, but "Nell traveled throughout the milkshed to encourage farmers to stay united and after two years they secured a fair contract."[29] Saint Joseph's and its avant-garde use of films were also employed for farming courses held in the parish hall. In conjunction with the University of Illinois Extension Service, Nell conducted short courses for rural pastors (Catholic and Protestant), which were comprehensive in breadth and expressive of the NCRLC's total vision for rural life. Serge F. Hummon, a colleague of Nell's from a congregational church, said of the beloved pastor: "the test of greatness in a clergyman is a stature so large that all denominations claim him. This we could say of Fr. Nell. He belonged to the community."[30]

Father Irvin Will began his rural life activities in the late 1940s and soon became one of the great animators of the Catholic Rural Life Conference of the Springfield diocese. In many respects the Springfield chapter fully implemented the Conference's vision. Father Will held several national roles within the NCRLC, mostly organizing seminarian institutes and study clubs. In 1951 he surveyed the diocese

---

[28] Susan Karina Dickey, OP, "Father George Nell, the Farmer's Friend in Jasper County," paper delivered at the Conference on Illinois History, October 9, 2003, 3, 6, 8. I have especially relied on this paper for the information on Nell. Also, Miss Edith Feldhake was indispensable to Nell in establishing the cooperative service. It marked a rather bold step with regard to clerical and lay cooperation, especially with women. A long-time parishioner, Angela Jensen, noted "Fr. Nell would have been lost without her [Feldhake]." She was more than an able administrator, but also offered constructive feedback to Nell on the catechetical materials he authored. The "Co-op Services" achieved worldwide distribution.

[29] Ibid., 10.

[30] Ibid., 12–13.

and discovered that 15 percent of the Catholics actually farmed, while over 30 percent lived in rural areas. The survey also revealed that rural pastors needed much help, and this gave birth to the priest study clubs. The first one met on December 13, 1951, and quickly became a model to follow. They were voluntary and typically drew about twenty-five priests to each meeting (three times each in the fall and spring). Topics covered the full array of NCRLC issues and provided the pastors with practical information about governmental and university programs. The study club published its own "Catholic Rural Life Bulletin" (hereafter Bulletin).

Rural liturgical activity as a whole was quite vigorous in the diocese. Clearly, one of the fruits of the study club was the liturgical and paraliturgical materials it produced and distributed in the 1950s. One such publication was *A Manual for the Parish Observance of the Rogation Days* published in 1953; over 11,000 copies were sold ahead of the May observance with over forty parishes participating. A "Day of Christian Rural Living," was held in Newton, Illinois, in which over 1,000 priests and laity participated.[31] A similar "Day" was held on March 22, 1953, in the neighboring Diocese of Bellville at St. Boniface Church (Germantown, Illinois), with Bishop Arthur Zuroweste presiding; over 1,200 people participated. Will's 1953 annual report to the NCRLC made specific mention of the "six-part ceremony of the rebirth of man and nature." This ceremony was the work of the "priests of Lafayette, LA" who composed the prayers. The priest was Father Joseph Gremillion, whose work will be taken up shortly. The study club was especially responsible for publishing three such ceremonies under the auspices of the NCRLC: the *Rogation Day Manual* and *A Day of Christian Rural Living*, just mentioned, and a *Thanksgiving Day Ceremony*. The Bulletin of the study club enjoyed posting the numbers of the various ceremonies and rural life days that were observed. By 1957 over 20,000 *Rogation Day Manuals* had been distributed, and by 1960 over 60,000 Thanksgiving Day leaflets found their way into the hands of the faithful. No doubt with some pride, one leader remarked in 1955: "Thousands of rural people will process and bless crops using the litany and recite the Mass . . . they will remember that the priests of the diocese of Springfield produced the manual. . . . [They will]

---

[31] "Diocesan Director Reports," MUA/NCRLC, Series 8/1, box 12. See Appendices II and III for examples of these ceremonies, which were discussed in chapter 4.

create in the mind and soul of the rural dweller the kinship of the church and farm."[32] It was true, they did.

The Bulletin also provided "Sermon Notes" for the Thanksgiving Day service. The homily or sermon was another facet of the liturgy that the liturgical movement tried to restore. The sermon notes for the service spoke first of gratitude—thanks for the soil and the harvest should rule the day. It then suggested that such gratitude must usher in "corporal works of mercy" for the thousands of poor and dispossessed. It tied grace before meals to the intelligent use of the *Missal*, noting how often "we lift our hearts in gratitude during the sacrifice of the Mass." The sermon notes included points that could be used throughout the harvest season. The feast of All Saints reminded the farmer of "the immense harvest of souls who have already arrived in Heaven. The saints whom we honor on November First are not only the canonized saints . . . but ordinary people like you and me who struggle against weaknesses and temptations."[33]

There were many other activities that rounded out the program in Springfield. The study club organized field trips to study the best farming and conservation methods being employed. On one such trip to Dixon Springs Experimental Station, fifty-one people (lay and ordained) from the Springfield and Belleville dioceses listened to a forest service representative lecture on conservation. "The real highlight," one pastor noted, "was the exchange between priests and laity." As part of a "Farm and Home Week" in February 1953, a short course for farmers offered much interaction with non-Catholics and allowed them to share their visions for rural life. During this ecumenical exchange the NCRLC was noted many times for its good work that fostered better understanding between the various denominations. Father Irvin Will accompanied nine seminarians to the summer institute in Madison, Wisconsin, and he conducted four workshops for women religious in 1953. At a 1956 workshop, the Sisters of St. Mary

---

[32] "Catholic Rural Life Bulletin, 1951–66," Diocese of Springfield, Illinois, Archives, 65, 96, 135, 171 (hereafter, DSA). This bound volume is a collection of all the reports from the study clubs. It was compiled by Fr. Hugh Cassidy, diocesan director in the mid-1960s. It provides a rather detailed glimpse into how one diocese concretely implemented the NCRLC's agenda. The pages are consecutively numbered.

[33] "Sermon Notes for Thanksgiving Day, November 22, 1956," Catholic Rural Life Bulletin, 122, DSA.

Immaculate (Joliet, Illinois) demonstrated "how the Catholic rural school can be a powerful influence on the rural community when it adjusts and adapts its teaching methods of the curriculum to the pupils' way of life." Finally, the club suggested that a rural health award be given to a nurse, doctor, or institution that makes an outstanding contribution to rural health. Retreats, talks, and vacation schools were all utilized to better the material and spiritual well-being of the rural people in the Diocese of Springfield.[34]

## MONSIGNOR JOSEPH GREMILLION— A SOUTHERN PASTOR

If there was one phrase that characterized all the work Msgr. Joseph Gremillion undertook, it would be "The Church *Katholikos*," expressing this "Southern Pastor's" approach to everything.[35] Gremillion was a Renaissance man and a true pastor who appropriated the best of the liturgical movement and made it integral to his numerous social justice concerns. As a seminarian at The Catholic University of America and then as a young priest, he was involved in both the Liturgical Conference and the NCRLC.[36] Gremillion was ordained in 1943 for the Diocese of Alexandria, Louisiana, and was first assigned to the cathedral in Alexandria, the parent diocese of Lafayette from 1943 to 1947. It was when he was made pastor of St. Joseph's in Shreveport (1950–57) that Gremillion conducted most of his rural activity. Gremillion came from a farming background, and it is likely that they had sharecroppers working for them. Imagine for just a moment Gremillion, a recently ordained priest traipsing across the Louisiana countryside in the 1940s, organizing black sharecroppers—there, this Southern pastor would say, is the Church *Katholikos*.[37]

[34] No author, "Sermon Notes for Thanksgiving Day, November 22, 1956," Catholic Rural Life Bulletin, 40, 46, 54, 64, 123, DSA.

[35] The phrase is found throughout his writings from, at least, the mid-1940s to 1950s, the period especially connected to his rural life work. See Joseph Gremillion, *The Journal of a Southern Pastor* (Chicago: Fides Publishers Association, 1957). A full-length biography of Gremillion's life has yet to be written.

[36] Yzermans, *The People I Love*, 228–29. This would have made him a contemporary of the many Catholic Action seminarians active at Theological College.

[37] Gremillion attended the Gregorian University in Rome (1958–60) and upon his return worked at Catholic Relief Services in New York (1960–67). From 1967 to 1974 he worked in Rome at the Pontifical Council for Justice and Peace. He taught and served as co-chairman to the University of Notre Dame Committee on Social

What did he mean by this phrase the Church *Katholikos*? Gremillion's most succinct statement of the phrase came during a 1955 address to the annual teachers' institute for the Diocese of Lafayette. Opening with the Prologue of John's gospel, he challenged these Catholic educators to be "Bearers of the Power, Bearers of the Light" so as to "beget, upbuild, and nurture our Lord's Mystical Body. You are the voice of the God-man speaking forth His Way and His Truth *hic et nunc*, in the *hic* of the Diocese, in the *nunc* of 1955." The breadth of the term was expressed this way:

> Katholikos, the word Catholic, means: universal, all-embracing, geographic wholeness, it embraces all the human family, it looks to the whole man, envisions the totality of society—family, economy, the body politic, education, the arts; in the words of Pius XI, all things must be restored to the dominion of Christ Our King. Katholikos stretches through the whole of time: the year 33 to the year 1955 to the consummation of the world.[38]

After depicting a picture of the world and all its struggles, he delivered the blow that many came to expect from him. As bearers of light and truth, these teachers (and all Catholics) must strive for the "total integration of the negro." Those who don't, he charged, were guilty of the heresy called racism. "How can we," he added, "refuse association with him in whom God dwells, because his body is brown, his hair kinky and because *his* grandfather was bought and sold like furniture by *my* grandfather? . . . Racial discrimination forms a blood clot, an occlusion in the flow of grace and love within Christ's Mystical Body." He warned that this road to integration will indeed be difficult to travel.[39]

---

Development and Peace 1974–78. He went back to the Diocese of Alexandria to serve as its Director of Social and Ecumenical Ministry. He returned once again to Notre Dame in 1983 were he stayed until his retirement in 1989 and his death in 1994. I am grateful to Christine Rivers, chancellor of the Diocese of Shreveport, for this biographical background on Gremillion.

[38] Joseph Gremillion, "Bearers of the Power, Bearers of the Light," in opening address to annual teachers' institute, Diocese of Lafayette, 30 September 1955, 2–3. In University of Notre Dame Archives, Joseph Gremillion Manuscripts, box 2, manila folder (hereafter, UNDA/CGRM).

[39] Ibid., 9, 11–12.

He experienced such difficulty firsthand at St. Joseph's parish the day he invited some African American parishioners into the rectory for dinner. This scandalized his white parishioners and some left.[40] He worked with Betty Delaney of Maria Laach Farm in Burnley, Virginia, to establish Friendship House, a work that was much in the spirit of Madonna House Apostolate foundress Catherine de Hueck Doherty. These houses had as their basic apostolate hospitality, no matter who you were. The house in Lafayette endured constant pressure to close because of the "mixed crowd" who met there, and they frequently received threats from people in the neighborhood.[41]

As diocesan director of rural life, Gremillion was involved in numerous social justice initiatives. The young priest noted that the postwar resettlement of Displaced Persons presented a splendid means of planting the seeds of faith in an area where Catholics made up only 2 percent of the population. Displaced Persons were a great concern of Pius XII, and many diocesan rural life conferences responded in charity and justice toward the veterans. Secondarily, reaching out to the veterans was seen as a means of keeping people on the land.[42] This applied to African Americans as well, and Gremillion organized a "Farm and Home Day for Negroes" that proved quite successful. Prizes were awarded by Bishop Charles Greco for canned goods, handwork, and produce. Oratorical contests were held on the subject "Why I want to own my own farm." Gremillion said: "It proved a magnificent weapon for the Apostolate. This county has 20 Catholic Negroes among a colored population of over 10,000. It gave the Josephite pastor of this mission a chance to meet hundreds of persons under the most favorable conditions." This led to speaking engagements for Gremillion in public schools and countywide assemblies addressing issues such as stewardship of the land, farmers as coworkers with God, and

[40] Joseph Gremillion, *The Journal of a Southern Pastor* (Chicago: Fides Publishers Association, 1957), 44–53.

[41] UNDA/CGRM, box 1, folder 1 "Friendship House." Also in the folder was a pamphlet signed by Catherine Doherty from Madonna House in Combermere, Ontario.

[42] Ligutti and Gremillion were two of six American priests appointed by the War Relief Services of the NCWC to study postwar conditions in Europe. They went to Frankfurt, Germany, on June 16, 1948, where they studied the situation and pondered possible solutions. The resettlement of displaced persons was one such program. See Yzermans, *The People I Love*, 96–97. Gremillion also worked closely with Ligutti as *Gaudium et Spes* was being crafted in August of 1965. Ibid., 225.

gratitude for the commonplace gifts of soil, sun, and rain. Trailer chapels, run by the Josephite fathers, were moving throughout the diocese conducting weeklong street-preaching workshops.[43]

At the 1950 NCRLC convention in Bellville, Illinois, Gremillion spoke to a group of priests and asked them to recall the day they awaited their first assignment: "the primary fear which gripped you. . . . The horror of being sent to Muddville, the threat of being 'stuck out in the sticks' even for a few years haunted you as an impending doom." A decade of work by the Conference with its study clubs and seminary institutes have paid off and allowed men to see how magnificent the rural apostolate is. He listed the usual litany of rural issues that must be the concern of the rural priest—he must move deftly between the sanctuary and the field. The priest cannot do this alone; he will need coworkers.[44]

In the spirit of Catholic Action and central to the Church *Katholikos*, Gremillion believed in a well-formed laity. Gremillion had close contact with the Grail and relied on the group for liturgical insights as well as methods to train lay leaders. He sent several young women to Loveland, the first in 1948, and noted that "Her influence upon returning will be invaluable." He conducted a weekend school for girls based on the Grail pattern, which emphasized family and liturgy in the home. He held a leadership school for college and high school students (four high schools and ten colleges), which treated both urban and rural social problems. He formed three study groups of laymen (ages 25–35), which examined such problems in light of Christian social teaching. One such group, rurally based, was composed of "1 lawyer, 2 farmers, 1 county worker, 2 rural physicians, the president of a rural bank, 2 merchants, and a stock feed manufacturer." Plans

[43] Joseph Gremillion, "Report of the Director of the Diocese of Alexandria, October 15, 1948," MUA/NCRLC, Series 1/1, box 2, folder "Diocesan Director's Reports, 1944–48." Also mentioned was CROP, 4-H Club and Future Farmers of America (FFA), Knights of Columbus, National Conference of Catholic Men (NCCM), and the "Washington Institute," which alerted rural leaders to the agricultural issues from the side of Washington, DC. The institute was directed by Fr. William Gibbons, SJ. Gremillion commented to the other directors that many secular groups "were hungry for contact with the NCRLC. . . . Don't rest until you've been through the Washington mill."

[44] Joseph Gremillion, "The American Priest and Rural Life," address delivered at the 28th National Convention, NCRLC, October 17, 1950, UNDA/CGRM, box 3, folder 5 "Articles and Talks."

were underway to form eight other such groups around the state. At an "Arch-diocesan Moderator's Meeting," he led discussions on the development of Lay Leadership with special emphasis on the rural areas and called for a "Lay Department of the NCWC." The goal was clear; he wanted intelligently formed lay leaders who knew the church's social teaching and who would actively implement it wherever they worked and lived. Later the same year, he stated: "Are we priests afraid of an intelligent, militant laity? Don't we feel much more at home with the pious 'old reliable' who will never contradict our position, to whom explanations are unnecessary?"[45]

In 1953 Gremillion noted the immediate fruits of such work by and with the laity:

> The growth and development of the [lay] men has been truly heartening. They are acquiring a Christian conscience because throughout the harsh realities of day-to-day economic and political crises are squared off against the challenge of Christ and the teaching of our Holy Fathers. . . . An over-all result of inestimable value is the progress made under this impetus for the solution of the very serious racial problem in our rural areas. These leaders have aided their Negro brothers in Christ in the fields of education, economic security, registration and voting, etc., and principally by becoming their friends.[46]

The group's impact was felt in parishes, agricultural schools, public schools, medical societies, bar associations, and labor groups. Gremillion also cooperated with numerous state and local authorities in government and education. The Southwest Louisiana Institute (now University of Louisiana at Lafayette) became a center of Catholic rural life. The secular school's enrollment was around 2,000 and 80 percent were Catholic, including many of the faculty. Several Louisiana

---

[45] Joseph Gremillion, "Report on Activities of 1950–51," MUA/NCRLC, Series 8/1, box 10, folder "Diocesan Director's Reports, Boston, Oct 19, 1951;" Idem, "Problem of Men's Organizations in the Province of New Orleans," November 8, 1950, address to Moderator's Workshop, in UNDA/CGRM, box 1, folder 2.

[46] Joseph Gremillion, "Report of the Diocese of Alexandria, Louisiana," MUA/NCRCL, Series 8/1, box 12, folder "Director's Meeting, Kansas City, MO, Sep 21–24, 1953." He was also much informed about the migrant labor issue and encouraged more cross-border cooperation between the U.S. and Mexico. In one report he mentioned the fine work of H. A. Reinhold among the migrants of Washington state. See MUA/NCRLC, series 8/1, box 11, folder "National Convention, Saginaw, Oct 1952."

priests and some missionaries earned agricultural degrees from the school. (The university hosted the NCRLC's silver anniversary convention in 1947.) Farmers' unions, Catholic Action of the South, the Catholic Committee of the South, 4-H, Future Farmers of America, to name but a few, were organizations with which Gremillion associated. All of this activity contributed to a well-formed laity.

One should not be surprised by what Joseph Gremillion considered *the* most vital and animating force of all this social action—the liturgy. He had embraced the liturgical movement in the early 1940s just when it was gaining both popular and episcopal support. Gremillion's diocesan director reports regularly accounted for the usual fare of rural blessings and Rogation Days. Gremillion went further though and made adaptations, integrating the church's official liturgy with numerous secular harvest festivals that had begun in the 1930s and 1940s.

Days set aside to celebrate rural life had been observed by the Conference beginning in the early 1930s. "A Day of Christian Rural Living" (hereafter, DCRL) was a paraliturgical service authored by Gremillion circa 1950. It combined both official prayers and blessings from the Roman Ritual as well as other prayers written by Gremillion. The DCRL service was catechetical in nature, and it was eventually published by the Catholic Rural Life Conference of Springfield, Illinois. Gremillion noted in his director's report for 1952:

> In addition to the development of the dialogue or community Mass, the introduction of the liturgy in the home a la Grailville and other increasingly accepted rebirths of our liturgical tradition, we have with the approval of our Bishops begun the development of a para-liturgy. These too are experiments subject always to review and revision. Two such examples are attached as Appendices II and III.[47]

---

[47] Joseph Gremillion and Alfred Sigur, "Joint Report from the Diocese of Lafayette and Alexandria," MUA/NCRLC, Series 8/1, box 2, folder "National Convention, Saginaw, Oct 17–22, 1953." The extensive combined report (over fifteen pages) accounted for most of the activity in both dioceses. Here is a partial summary: fifteen priests focusing on the "total apostolate," rural/urban issues, the lay apostolate—think groups, leadership institutes, house of apostolic formation for men, a rural newsletter, Summer School of Catholic Action, farm workers and organization, liturgy, collaboration with secular agencies and the "public farm festivals—rice, yams, sugar cane, and dairy." Appendix I of his report gave the schedule for a weekend "Leadership School for Catholic Men," which carried the theme: "What Christ Expects of the Practical Catholic, 1952." Highlights included

The appendices were adaptations to the DCRL, which was a ceremony more associated with springtime. Gremillion used this service as the basic template and adapted it for other times of the year. Through such adaptation he attempted to bring out the *hic et nunc* of the Church *Katholikos*.[48]

Gremillion further adapted the above ceremony for Thanksgiving Day, November 22, 1951, in his parish of St. Joseph's (Shreveport, Lousiana). His primary motivation for doing so was based on a national feast that had lost its religious moorings. The entire ceremony was held before the Mass for that day and carried the proviso that "it should not be held without the approval of diocesan authorities . . . and naturally, it should be adapted to the locality, according to the products of the earth, the crops and minerals produced in the region and other factors."[49] Reading these prayers (*lex orandi*) would have provided a glimpse into this people's way of life in Louisiana in the 1950s, revealing the variety of human labor and activity of the members of the parish—farming, textiles, and petroleum industries. The basic structure had a procession and presentation of gifts.

Interestingly, the longest of the prayers was that for the "Products from the Earth," since it was quite likely that many of the faithful worked in the oil industry. This particular prayer not only expressed God's omnipotent powers, but the human's gifts of intelligence used to harness the earth's minerals for the common good. It spoke of the diversity of ores and minerals, the physical and chemical laws that govern matter, plants, and animals with "ordered biological principles," and scientists and researchers with the intellects and wills to

---

the social situation, the Mystical Body of Christ's response (clergy and laity), "Restoring all Things in Christ—restoring the economy, the body politic, education, the professions, race relations, the human family, and the family. Part III of the weekend addressed the "Total Vision and Total Apostolate" in which it noted: "The very Complexity of the Social Crisis demands an INTEGRAL approach." This led to a discussion of the liturgy.

[48] See Appendices II and III, p. 251ff.

[49] Joseph Gremillion and Alfred Sigur, "Joint Report from the Diocese of Lafayette and Alexandria," MUA/NCRLC, Series 8/1, box 12, folder "National Convention, Saginaw, Oct 17–22, 1953," Appendix II. The basic outline of the ceremony went this way: I. Our Offering of Thanks (general); II. Fruits of the Field; III. Products from the Earth; IV. The Beauty of Creation; V. Blessing of Human Rights and Duties in America; VI. The Joy and Love of Family and Home; VII. The Gifts of Redemption; The Sacrifice of the Mass.

discover a "glimmer of God's glory." "Compressed within the atom" was a force beyond imagining, a "mirrored inkling of God's almighty power." The prayer then mentioned the *hic* of Louisiana:

> Your natural laws drew order out of the chaos . . . and in *our region* was compounded a marvelous storehouse of hydrocarbon, petroleum, and natural gas . . . to release from its mile-deep reservoir the energy and brilliance of the sun . . . to serve now as fuel and fiber to provide us your children with goods far beyond our needs and meriting.[50]

This part of the service was followed by "The Beauty of Creation," in which "men" presented plants and flowers to decorate the altar, sheet music, and a hymnal that were to be used in the liturgy, and concluded by singing *America the Beautiful*.

Of special note was the "Blessing of Human Right and Duties." Led by the American flag, Boy Scouts and scoutmaster entered bearing large "scrolls" with the Constitution and the Declaration of Independence. Gremillion's prayer spoke of being endowed with "certain inalienable rights" written "deep within our nature." It mentioned as well that such rights belong to all: "For letting us all realize that we are brothers because we of all this world are members of your one human family despite our variety of race, color and appearance." The veterans who defended these rights and freedoms also received mention. Post–World War II Catholics were experiencing greater assimilation into the American mainstream, but not completely; this part of the ceremony validated being Catholic *and* American. Photos of this service have been preserved and show a table in front of the altar completely covered with the gifts symbolically offered—a can of "Esso" brand oil right alongside the sugar cane, corn, Constitution, crèche, and crucifix.[51] *Omnia*, restored in Christ!

Finally, perhaps in the spirit of Fr. Brinker's "tobacco Mass," Gremillion and other Louisianan priests wanted to recognize some of

[50] Appendix IV (emphasis mine).
[51] "A Thanksgiving Liturgy," *Jubilee* (November 1955): 64; See also UNDA/CGRM, box 7, photos. A similar service was done for Candlemas which involved processions with the blessed candles as well as a blessing of mothers and presentation of their children. The prayers are especially eloquent with regard to manner in which "that little bee . . . transforms the fluid of flowers to the perfection of wax and honey." See "The Sowing," UNDA/CGRM, box 2, manila folder. "The Sowing," begun by Gremillion, is still the name of the parish bulletin.

the many secular harvest festivals in their state (still celebrated to this day). Many of these harvest festivals began in the 1930s and 1940s, and Gremillion mentioned several in his report:

> Plans are practically complete for opening the Sugar Cane Festival with its customary High Mass; the Dairy Festival with High Mass and sermon; the Yambilee with same. Correspondence with the Rice Festival authorities and the pastor is not completed, but the same arrangements are projected there.[52]

The properly religious dimension of the festivals seemed to include a procession and presentation of the particular crop (rice, yam, etc.) followed by a blessing and then Mass. The harvest Mass is still a tradition at many of these festivals.[53] It should be recalled that most of the Catholics who lived in Louisiana were eighteenth-century exiles from Nova Scotia and other Atlantic coastal colonies. Estimates suggest that over half the Catholics in the South resided in these areas of Louisiana. Thus to hold such Catholic religious ceremonies in areas where Catholics were a minority was a bold initiative in itself.

The festivals were true celebrations of a unique culture, complete with indigenous music, dress, arts, crafts, games, parades, and food— prizes being awarded for champion recipes. Of course there was the much-anticipated crowning of the cotton, rice, and yam "queens," as well as "King Sucrose and Queen Sugar." The crowning has been a part of the festivals from the start. Today's queens are often college students involved in sororities and advocates of a charity of their choice. Of course, the young women are also quite beautiful. In 2006, Sarah Owens, a twenty-one-year-old student from Nichols State University bore the title "Queen Sugar." Following her coronation ball on Saturday evening, a Sunday morning harvest Mass was celebrated. Sarah is in store for a very busy year as she will travel throughout Louisiana promoting sugar cane and its associated industries.[54]

---

[52] Joseph Gremillion, "Rural Life Report, 1952–53," MUA/NCRLC, Series 1/1, box 2, folder "Diocesan Director Reports, 1953."

[53] The respective schedules for the current rice, yam, and sugar cane festivals all mention the celebration of at least a Mass; some also have a crop blessing, at times separate from Mass and more inclusive regardless of denomination.

[54] Staff Report, "St. Charles Does It Again . . . Owens Crowned Sugar Queen," *St. Charles Herald*, September 28, 2006. As one can only imagine, web sites for many

The importance of situating the liturgy in the context of such festivals cannot be underestimated. Simply stated, it had as its purpose preventing the celebrations from devolving into something merely secular. This was much in the spirit of Catholic Action, which sought to "return the exiled Christ" to the present culture. In the spirit too of the conciliar document *Ad Gentes*, the liturgy acknowledged what was genuinely good in a given culture and wove this local patch of history into the one large tapestry of salvation history—*hic et nunc*. On one level such integration and accommodation seemed genuinely sound and good, something the church has done for centuries. On another level it raises the question of how the liturgy may challenge what is *not* genuine in the social order of a given culture. Sharecroppers, upon whom the sugar industry relied in the past, rarely received just wages. Today they have been replaced by migrant labor from Central America with even fewer rights. Does the "queen," if her reign is to be one of justice and charity, concern herself with such issues? One wonders, did she make this issue a part of her "platform" in order to be "chosen"? If so, would she have fared as well? Did (does) the homily at the harvest Mass draw attention to the fact that many harvests come at the great expense of human dignity? Finally, it would be interesting to know if a young woman from Gremillion's parish was ever crowned queen, and if so, were any of them formed at Grailville?

These crucial issues and their relationship to religion and the liturgy were not missed by the above-mentioned apostles of rural life—saints of the soil. All of them shared a profound understanding of sacramentality closely joined to liturgical worship that was corporal, cooperative, and communal. This understanding placed the materiality of the created order into "right relationship" with the spiritual, making them one. It helped to reconcile the tragic divorce of the material and spiritual dimensions of life, the fruit of many dualisms eradicated by the incarnation. The sacramental principle, concretely applied, enabled the people to see more clearly how daily work and living were part and parcel of God's redemptive plan. This served to affirm a way of life (vocation) such that the basic human dignity of a marginalized group was strengthened. The very nature of rural ministry and leader-

---

of the festivals abound. The Rice Queen dons a long beautiful handmade train with a bundle of the crop embroidered in the center.

ship could not be relegated to the pastor alone; thus, laypeople played significant roles in parish life. Nor could the Catholic Church accomplish the reform of the social order alone; the common good was just that—it involved everybody and everything. Therefore, in part out of necessity, rural Catholics joined efforts with Protestants and Jews to bring about a more just and vital rural life. The NCRLC's slogan, "Christ to the Country, the Country to Christ" never implied an overt proselytism. This, it has been argued, significantly broadened the ecclesial self-understanding of the Mystical Body of Christ and the manner in which the church engaged the world.

By the mid-1950s all the activity described above manifested a unified vision of life, "catholic" in the fullest sense. It can safely be asserted that the marvelous vision of the Second Vatican Council, the *hic et nunc* of the true Christian spirit, was indeed operative at least a decade before the formal decrees were issued. One can hear the voices of *Sacrosanctum Concilium, Lumen Gentium, Gaudium et Spes, Ad Gentes, Unitatis Redintegratio, Optatam Totius,* and *Apostolicam Actuositatem* in the declarations and actions of the National Catholic Rural Life Conference and the American liturgical movement. Monsignor Joseph Gremillion must have been quite pleased with the newly crafted postconciliar preface for Thanksgiving Day.[55]

[55] The Roman Missal, Preface 84, p. 541.

# Appendices

## Appendix I. Rural Prayers and Devotions

*Novena to St. Isidore*

Themes:
Day 1: Partnership with God; Day 2: Family Life in Christ; Day 3: Love of Neighbor; Day 4: Dignity of Work; Day 5: Walking in the Presence of God; Day 6: Stewardship of Soil; Day 7: Rural Works of Mercy; Day 8: Trust in Prayer; Day 9: Sacrifice of Praise.

The Daily Format:
> Hymn [changed each day to match the theme]
> Antiphon and Psalm
> Scripture with response
> Prayer [collect of St. Isidore Mass Proper]
> Prayer in Honor of St. Isidore
> Reflection
> Our Father, Hail Mary, and Glory be (three times each)
> Other (optional) Prayers [see below]

Other (optional) Prayers: The Litany, Prayer of the Christian Farmer, A Christian Farmer's Creed, Rural Family Prayer. Not included here are the following: Prayer for Rain, Prayer against Pests, Prayer against Storms and Floods, Prayer of Thanksgiving.

*St. Isidore Litany*

The substance of the litany may be summarized as follows:

St. Isidore . . . patron of farmers, illustrious tiller of the soul, model of laborers, devoted to duty, loaded down with the labors of the field, model of filial piety, support of family life, confessor of the faith, example of mortification, assisted by angels, possessor of the gift of miracles, burning with lively faith, zealous in prayer, ardent lover of the Blessed Sacrament, lover of God's earth, lover of poverty, lover of fellowmen, most patient, most humble, most pure, most just, most obedient, most faithful, most grateful . . . *pray for us*.

Jesus, Our Lord: we beseech You, hear us. That You would vouchsafe to protect all tillers of the soil: we beseech You, hear us. That You would vouchsafe to bring to all a true knowledge of the stewardship of the land . . . That You would vouchsafe to preserve and increase our fields and flocks . . . to give and preserve the fruits of the earth . . . to bless our fields . . . to preserve all rural pastors . . . to grant peace and harmony in our homes . . . to lift up our hearts to You. Be merciful, graciously hear us, O Lord . . . *From* . . . lightning and tempest, pestilence and floods . . . winds and drought . . . hail and storm . . . the scourge of insects . . . the spirit of selfishness . . . deliver us, O Lord.

### Prayer in Honor of St. Isidore

O God, who taught Adam the simple art of tilling the soil, and who through Jesus Christ, the true vine, revealed yourself the husbandman of our souls, deign, we pray, through the merits of Blessed Isidore, to instill into our hearts a horror of sin and a love of prayer, so that working the soil in the sweat of our brow, we may enjoy eternal happiness in heaven.

### Prayer of the Christian Farmer

O God, Source and Giver of all things, who manifests your infinite majesty, power and goodness in the earth about us, we give you honor and glory. For the sun and the rain, for the manifold fruits of our fields, for the increase of our herds and flocks, we thank you. For the enrichment of our souls with divine grace, we are grateful. Supreme Lord of the harvest, graciously accept us and the fruits of our toil, in union with Christ, your Son, as atonement for our sins, for the growth of your Church, for peace and charity in our homes, for salvation to all. Amen.

### A Christian Farmer's Creed

We believe that: Farming is a noble Christian occupation. The farm home is the most suitable place for the rearing of a Christian family. The good earth is the greatest material gift of God to mankind.

A farmer must be a conserver of soil, a steward of God's gifts,
a producer of the essential elements of life for his family and society,
a good neighbor, faithful parishioner, a good citizen. By good example,
participation and sharing within the family we shall encourage the
children to follow the vocation of farming. By assistance and organization within the parish and diocese we can increase the number of
Catholic families living on the land. By neighborliness and Christian
living we shall draw more to the faith.

*Hymn to St. Isidore* [First Day of novena: Partnership with God]

O Lord, as you have made the earth / to man and beast have given
birth / have given sun and rain that thence / the soil might give them
sustenance.

We beg you make us willing to / perform the law we get from you /
that work of ours and grace of yours / may bring the increase that
endures.

*Refrain*: Through Jesus Christ let this be done / who lives and reigns
our Lord your Son / whom with the Spirit we adore / one God with
you for evermore.

Hymn [Fourth Day of novena: Dignity of Work]

O Lord, our God, whose mighty hand / carved out the seas and built
the land; Who, by the labors of our Lord / the honor Adam lost,
restored.

Let us be joined to Christ, your son / that in His work we may be one;
So shall we in our work partake / of God, Whom we by sloth forsake.
*Refrain*

Hymn [Sixth Day of novena: Stewardship of the Soil]

O Lord, as you by your command / for all men's use have made the
land; Yet have allowed man's wise decree / rule it be cared for
privately.

Let us know that what we control / is made for mankind as a whole;
And we must an accounting give / of what God lends us while we live.
*Refrain*

*Rural Family Prayer*—by Mrs. Florence Hynes Willette

Wise and compassionate God, accept this our prayer;
Sheltered from storm and darkness, under this roof,
This family kneels to adore Thee.
For the day just past,
For keeping us safely, body and soul,
Now we most humbly thank Thee.
For hilltops and verdure,
For sunlight and wind and boundless space,
For rain and the sky's rich color,
For boughs and blossoms and cold clean snow,
We are eternally grateful.
For birds, and beasts,
For the good black earth and the seeds producing
The plenteous harvest; for times without number
When we have eaten of that same harvest,
We thank Thee and bless Thee forever.
Deliver us safely, if such be Thy will.
From deluge and drought,
From famine and war and disaster.
Give us tomorrow as yesterday and today,
All things most needed for rightful living;
And move our hearts that we may have sorrow
For sinning against Thee.
God of the hearth and the harvest,
Thy children here kneeling, adore Thee.
Bless now our rest,
And cherish us safe till the morrow.

## Appendix II. A Day of Christian Rural Living

A Day of Christian Rural Living
The First Sunday of Lent
March 2, 1952

Parish of St. Paul the Apostle
Mansura, Louisiana
Diocese of Alexandria

Pastor: Msgr. M. P. Nothfer; Ass't Pastor: Fr. Roland Bordelon
Conducted by Fr. J. B. Gremillion, Diocesan Rural Life Director

In the name of our Lord Jesus Christ—we welcome all of you to this spring ceremony of the Rebirth of Man and Nature.

The Season of Spring is the season of renewal. The plants and trees are reborn after the death-like sleep of winter. The farmer prepares for this rebirth by plowing and harrowing the fields, by pruning the trees. Similarly in the liturgical year of Christ's Mystical Body on Earth, Spring is a season of rebirth, climaxed by the Resurrection of Christ from the dead on Easter Sunday. And this too must be preceded by a season of preparation, plowing and harrowing—the 40 days of Lent, the time of penance and self-sacrifice, the season of inward renewal of the life that really counts.

The full meaning of the ceremony is made clear in the words of the ceremony itself.

The persons who bear the Symbolic Gifts up the aisle and to the altar are the representatives of all of us, of our whole parish and community. We should join together our minds and hearts and wills as a family of families in presenting those offerings to God our Father and Christ our King and Brother.

All will please speak slowly and aloud the thoughts which follow, in unison with the Priest at the Altar.

* * * * *

I. Why We Are Here

Almighty God, Our Creator and yet our Father, we your sons and daughters of St. Paul parish humbly kneel at your feet this day. We have gathered as your children to express our love to you our God and Father. We have come together as a family of families here before your earthly throne in our Father's house where you dwell in our midst night and day. We jointly recognize and proclaim as a family group of friends and brothers your great fatherly goodness to us. As an open demonstration of our affection we place before you here present on the altar tokens and symbols of your power and greatness, tokens and symbols of your daily kindness to us.

II. The Wonder of the New Life of Nature
(Men [sic] representing all of us enter up the center aisle bearing soil
and sod, cotton, corn, clover and soybeans, vegetables and fruits, hay
and grain. Place on the table before the altar.)

Great God, our Creator and yet our Father, we thank you for the gift
of physical life. We thank you for the gift of food and clothing which
in your providence you give us for the continuance of healthful living.
Realizing the infinite greatness of your power we adore you and
honor you. We thank you for the sun and rain, for the soil and seeds
and animals which bring forth in due season the cotton and corn, the
vegetables and fruits, the clover and the hay, the milk and butter, the
eggs and meat, which in your wonderful design keep us breathing
your clean air and walking your good green bountiful earth. All these
ordinary things of everyday life are astounding manifestations of your
power and wisdom and love. For all this we adore you.

III. The Need for Rebirth within Us

Almighty maker of the universe, once more your planet Earth has
reached that point in its yearly voyage around the sun which marks
the spring season of the year according to the wondrous nature you
have given them. Soon your trees will be sprouting their leaves, soon
your grass will be a radiant carpet of waving green, soon we will plant
your seeds in the fields and they will push up their tiny stems marking
the rows with beautiful green lines of growing cotton and corn and
beans.

Every year by your great omnipotence, through the magnificent
powers which you have given to soil and seeds, rain and sun, your
good earth is born again, renewed and reborn in the outburst of spring.

Lord we, too, need to be renewed, we too need the inward rebirth of
your life within us. Help us to better know you and to love you and
each other.

Today is the first Sunday of Lent, the season of penance and self-
sacrifice. Just as the fields must be plowed and harrowed in order that
the seed can bring new life and a good crop in the fall, so Lord, during
this Lenten season must we plow and harrow our own selves. By
prayerful thought we must turn over the great truths of life in our
minds. With the pulverizing harrow of fasting we must crush the
hardness of our hearts to prepare them to love you and each other.

We must pull out the weeds of passion and we must root up our habits of sin so that the seed of eternal life will fall on good ground and will bring forth fruit a hundredfold, the harvest of peace here on Earth and the joy of life everlasting with you in our heavenly home.

Lord we offer you this penance and prayer, the willing sacrifice of and fast and abstinence of this Lenten season. With all your good earth we yearn to burst forth anew with the life of true and lasting love for you our Father and for each other.

IV. The Joy and Love of Family and Home
(Boy and girl enter bearing wedding rings and server with Marriage Ritual and holy water)

Lord our Father, please strengthen and renew the bond of love which unites family and home. We thank you, Good Father, for the Sacrament of Matrimony by which man and wife become one in Christ. For the vows we took before you in marriage giving each other to each other which vows we will renew this afternoon. We are amazed at the awesome power you the author of all life share with mother and father by entrusting to us the seed of life and allowing us to become co-creators with you, the creator of all.

We thank you Good Father for embracing our children, the fruit of our love. For the joy of beholding our little ones grow and develop from helpless infanthood in the full perfection of mind and body, soul and character, qualities with which you have endowed them.

We thank you for allowing us to share one another's happiness and sorrow, laughter and tears in the sanctuary of our well-blessed homes. For letting us join together in the family Rosary, to relive in thought and prayer your own life on earth, for being present in our homes when we gather in your name. For giving us friends, far and near with whom we share one another's burdens. For the unity of brotherliness which pervades our community and neighborhood.

For all these gifts, Father of humanity, we thank you.

V. Gifts of Redemption
(Men enter bearing image of Divine Infant, Crucifix, Missal, Bible; men servers carrying hosts for the sacrifice, wine and water; boy servers carrying candles for the altar; Father Bordelon carrying chalice and ciborium.)

Kneeling before you, O Christ Our King, Redeemer and Savior, we adore you and thank you. For coming down to our earth as a baby, joining your divine nature to a human nature like our own, in your One Person as Jesus Christ the God-Man.

For living with us, for sharing our human experiences, for eating like us bread and meat, sharing our joys and tears, for working as a carpenter in the little farming town of Nazareth. There you knew sweat and fatigue like the rest of us humans. We adore you and thank you for showing us the Way, the Truth, and the Life.

For carrying our Cross, for dying on the cross so that we might live.

For establishing your Church, for preserving us from error and your own words in Holy Scripture. For the gift of sanctifying grace, for the forgiveness of our sins in the sacraments of Baptism and Penance.

For giving us your own living Self, Body and Blood, Humanity and Divinity as food for our souls in the Holy Eucharist. For becoming our Offering and Victim in the Sacrifice of the Altar.

For remaining here in the tabernacle as our Friend and our Consoler in this Home which we have with your help built for you in our community.

For the promise of everlasting happiness and for the grace and strength you give us daily to take up our cross and follow in your footsteps. For all these Lord we adore and thank you.

Now we present this bread and wine, made from wheat and grapes and grown by farmers like ourselves through the wonder of God-given nature.

And now we offer the Sacrifice of your Body and Blood as a living memorial of your great Sacrifice on the Cross which you offered on Good Friday, a memorial Offering of Praise and Thanksgiving, of sorrow and petition to you our God and Father.

(A chorus of voices will now offer the community Mass, speaking certain prayers in unison. You are all invited to join in aloud.)

The Sacrifice of the Mass: The Ordinary of the Sacrifice begins on page 35 and today we shall use the prayers for the Proper on page 136.

## Appendix III. Suggested Ceremony for Thanksgiving Day

Suggested ceremony for Thanksgiving Day—before the Sacrifice of the Mass

The following ceremony was held November 22, 1951, in St. Joseph's Parish, 216 Patton St., Shreveport, Louisiana, with the approbation of the Most Reverend Charles P. Greco, D.D, Bishop of Alexandria. This is not a liturgical ceremony. It has been called para-liturgical. To my mind it should not be held without the approval of diocesan authorities. And naturally it must be adapted to the locality, according to the products of the earth, the crops and minerals produced in the region and other factors. We had one rehearsal on the eve of Thanksgiving. The congregation was led and paced by a chorus of ten speaking voices, all men, who had also practiced as a group. They were kneeling together in the center of the congregation. As they entered the Church all the people were given a mimeographed copy of the whole program as presented below.

Father Sigur had a similar ceremony in his Parish, adapted to the crops of his locality.

Father J. S. Gremillion, Pastor

Thanksgiving Day

IN THE NAME OF OUR LORD JESUS CHRIST—we welcome you all to this Thanksgiving Ceremony.

The full meaning of the Ceremony of the Offering of these Gifts of Gratitude is made clear in the words themselves of the ceremony. The men who bear the Gifts two by two up the aisle and to the Altar are the representatives of ALL OF YOU, of our whole Parish and Community. You should join together your minds and heart and will as a FAMILY OF FAMILIES in presenting those Offerings to God Our Father and Christ Our King and Brother. All will please speak slowly and aloud the thoughts which follow, in unison with the Priest at the Altar.

## I. OUR OFFERING OF THANKS
(All together, pause at dashes)

Almighty God, our Creator and still Our Father, we your sons and daughters of St. Joseph Parish humbly kneel at your feet this day, we have gathered as your children to say thank you to our Good Father.

We have come together as a family of families here before your earthly throne in our Father's house where you dwell in our midst night and day.

We jointly proclaim as a family group of friends and brothers your great fatherly goodness to us. As an open demonstration of our gratitude we place before you here present on the altar tokens and symbols of your daily kindness to us.

## II. FRUITS OF THE FIELD
(Six men representing all of us enter up center aisle two by two bearing Fruits of the Field, cotton and corn, vegetables and fruits, hay and grain. Place on table before the Altar.)

Great God, our Creator and yet our Father, we thank you for the gift of physical life. We thank you for the gift of food and clothing which in your providence you give us for the continuance of healthful living. Realizing the infinite greatness of your power we adore you and honor you. We thank you for the sun and rain, for the soil and seeds and animals which bring forth in due season the cotton and corn, the vegetables and fruits, the alfalfa and the hay, the milk and butter, the eggs and meat, which in your wonderful design keep us breathing your clean air and walking your good green bountiful earth.

## III. PRODUCTS FROM THE EARTH
(Six men representing all of us enter up center aisle two by two bearing petroleum products, oil cores, well-logs and synthetic compounds. Place on table before the Altar.)

Good God Our Father, we thank you for storing in the depths of the earth an amazing variety of ores and minerals and compounds.

You have so constituted all matter that it follows a wondrous pattern of physical and chemical laws. In giving life to plants and animals you have endowed them with ordered biological principles. You have given our scientists and researchers the intellect and will to discover and grasp a glimmer of the glory of your blueprint of creation.

You have compressed within the infinitesimal space of the atom a force beyond imagining a mirrored inkling of your own almighty power, you have joined together the atoms into molecules and the molecules into elements and the elements into compounds. Such is the overwhelming over-ascending ladder of your creation.

257

In untold ages past your natural laws drew order out of the primeval chaos and in the workings of your providence in our region was compounded a marvelous storehouse of hydrocarbon, petroleum and natural gas. In these products you have preserved for centuries unnumbered the energy and heat and light of the sun captured by the green chlorophyll and the minute creatures of land and sea, during the infant days of our mother earth and stored in her bosom in the microscopic might of the millioned molecules of a droplet of oil and a jet of gas.

In the soul of man you have rooted firm the light to know the true and the drive to will the Good. Embryo-like this unfolding human genius of engineering and geological skill faintly flickering glimmer of your own intelligence plumbs the dark reaches of the earth to release from its mile-deep reservoir the energy and brilliance and warmth of the sun for centuries held captive to serve now as fuel and fiber to provide us your children with goods and comforts far beyond our needs and meriting.

Aghast at the wonder of it all awe unutterable we lisp childlike murmurs of praise for what we so dimly behold of your eternal glory echoed in the space and time of the plan of your creation. For all this goodness and greatness Father, we thank You.

IV. THE BEAUTY OF CREATION
(Four men enter bearing plants and flowers in vases for the Altar, hymnal and sheets of music.)

Good Father we thank you for all the beauty you have showered upon our earth.

We thank you for the blue of the sea and the green of the grass, for the due [dew] and harmony of your flowers and plants for the azure blue bowing—to the blushing bloom of simmering sunset on the careening canvas of the sky the masterpiece of a Painter profusely prodigal to please His little ones with colors catching the eye and calling the heart to rejoice.

We thank you for endowing us with sight sensitive to loveliness of line and symmetry of shape with hearing attuned to the symphony—of sound and measured music awakening our inmost being with a glow of peace and treasured tranquility grooming the spirit, grant O Lord, the grace for the vision of beauty itself, the soul-searing sight of you face to face when we walk through the dark door of death into the Light of True Life. For earth's frail foreshadow of beauty unbounded Father, we thank you.

"AMERICA THE BEAUTIFUL"
(All rise and sing together.)
O beautiful for spacious skies, For amber waves of grain,
For purple mountain majesties above the fruited plain,
America! America! God shed His grace on thee,
And crown thy good with brotherhood, from sea to shining sea.

## V. BLESSING OF HUMAN RIGHTS AND DUTIES IN AMERICA
(Boy Scouts and Scoutmaster enter bearing large scrolls inscribed with the Declaration of Independence and the Constitution and Flag)

We thank You God Our Father—for endowing us "with certain unalienable [sic] rights" with life, liberty and the pursuit of happiness.

For rooting those rights deep within our own nature as an immortal soul with an eternal destiny and a value unmeasured as a Child of God Our Father.

For enabling us to live for over one hundred seventy-five years under a government founded upon these rights irradicable rights given us by You in the very nature by which You have made us human beings.

For letting us realize that we are all brothers because we of all this world are members of Your one human family despite our variety of race and color and appearance.

For giving to our men past and present the heroic courage to leave home and family and to battle and suffer and die on distant shores, so great is our yearning for peace and security for dear ones.

For letting us live together in these United States of America Father, we thank You.

## VI. THE JOY AND LOVE OF FAMILY AND HOME
(Boy and girl enter bearing wedding rings, with altar boy bearing marriage ritual and holy sprinkler.)

We thank You, Lord Our Father—For the bond of love which unites our family and home. For the Sacrament of Matrimony by which man and wife become one in Christ. For the awesome power you the

Author of all Life share with Father and Mother—by entrusting to us the seed of life and allowing us to become co-creators with You the Creator of all.

For the joy of embracing our children the fruit of our love. For the joy of beholding our children grow and develop from helpless infanthood into the full perfection of mind and body soul and character potentialities with which you have endowed them.

For enabling us to share one another's happiness and sorrow, laughter and tears in the sanctuary of our well-blessed homes.

For giving us our friends far and near with whom we "share one another's burdens."

For the unit of brotherliness which pervades our community and neighborhood.

For all these gifts Father of Our Human Family, we thank you.

VII. GIFTS OF REDEMPTION
(Men enter bearing image of Divine Infant, Crucifix, Missal, Bible; two men servers carrying hosts for the sacrifice, wine and water; boy servers carrying six candles for the altar; Father Scherer carrying chalice and ciborium.)

Kneeling before you O Christ Our King, Redeemer and Savior, we thank you.

For coming down to our earth as a baby joining your divine nature to the human nature your One Person as Jesus Christ, the God-Man.

For living with us, for sharing our human experiences, for eating like us bread and meat, sharing our joys and tears, for working as a carpenter and sweating and sleeping like the rest of us humans.

For showing us the Way, the Truth and the Life. For carrying our Cross, for dying on the Cross that we "might live." For establishing your Church, for preserving us from error and for your own words in Holy Scripture. For the gift of sanctifying grace, for the forgiveness of our sins in the Sacraments of Baptism and Penance.

For giving us your own living self, Body and Blood, humanity and divinity as food for our souls in the Holy Eucharist. For becoming our Offering and Victim in the Sacrifice of the altar. For remaining here in the tabernacle as our Friend and Consoler in this home which we have with your help built for you in our neighborhood.

For the promise of everlasting happiness and for the grace and strength you give us daily to take up our crosses and follow in your footsteps. For all these Lord, we thank you.

We now present this bread and wine and we now offer the Sacrifice of your body and blood as a living memorial of your Great Sacrifice on the cross a memorial offering of praise and thanksgiving to God Our Father.

THE SACRIFICE OF THE MASS
All the congregation participating in "Dialogue" or "Community" form.

AFTER THE SACRIFICE
Recessional (All stand and sing; allow main participants who were seated in front pews to go out first via center aisle. Gifts and offerings remain through day on table in or near Sanctuary.)

All sing "Holy God, We Praise Thy Name"


## Appendix IV. Lectures Given at the Institutes for Social Study Program, 1935–36

*All lecturers were Benedictines unless otherwise noted.

October 26-27, 1935
Economic Principles: Capitalism

> Lecture 1: Historical Development, Walter Reger
> Lecture 2: Nature and Meaning of Culture, Dunstan Tucker
> Lecture 3: The Mystical Body of Christ, Edward Benning
> Lecture 4: Nature of Capitalism, Virgil Michel
> Lecture 5: Benefits of Capitalism, Mr. Arthur Farley

November 16–17, 1935
Economic Principles: Critique of Capitalism

> Lecture 1: Capitalism, Ownership and Finance, Virgil Michel
> Lecture 2: Characteristics of Culture, Dunstan Tucker

Lecture 3: Spiritual Intercommunication in the Mystical Body,
     Philibert Harrer
Lecture 4: Capitalism and Human Personality, Virgil Michel
Lecture 5: The Age of Plenty and Economic Planning, Mr. James
     Dincolo

December 14–15, 1935
Economic Principles: Reconstruction

Lecture 1: Socialism and *Quadragesimo Anno*, Augustine Osgniach
Lecture 2: Modern Culture, Dunstan Tucker
Lecture 3: The Mystical Body and Catholic Action, Boniface Axtman
Lecture 4: Labor Unions and *Quadragesimo Anno*, Virgil Michel
Lecture 5: Distributism by Ernest Kilzer

January 11–12, 1936
Economic Principles: The Question of Money

Lecture 1: Nature and Purpose of Money, Virgil Michel
Lecture 2: Christian Cultural Ideals, Dunstan Tucker
Lecture 3: The Mystical Body and Economic *Injustice*,
     Vincent Tegeder[1]
Lecture 4: Credit, Mr. James Dincolo
Lecture 5: Money—New Trends, Theodore Krebsbach

February 8–9, 1936
Political Principles: Nature of the State

Lecture 1: Need and Purpose of Civil Society, Ernest Kilzer
Lecture 2: Culture and the Liturgy, Dunstan Tucker
Lecture 3: The Mystical Body and Dissensions, Cosmas Dahlheimer
Lecture 4: Origin and Basis of Civil Order, Virgil Michel
Lecture 5: Totalitarian State, Dominic Keller

March 7–8, 1936
Political Principles: Questions of Jurisdiction

Lecture 1: Government Regulation of Business, Virgil Michel
Lecture 2: Culture and the Material, Dunstan Tucker

---

[1] In the collected version this lecture was not used; rather, Virgil Michel's "The Mystical Body and Economic Justice" was selected for that volume.

Lecture 3: The Mystical Body and Works of Mercy, Cassian
      Osendorf
Lecture 4: State and Individual, Ernest Kilzer
Lecture 5: State and Education, Augustine Osgniach

March 28–29, 1936
Political Principles: Forms of Government

Lecture 1: Democracy, Ernest Kilzer
Lecture 2: Culture and Religion, Dunstan Tucker
Lecture 3: The Mystical Body and Race Prejudice, Otto Eisenzimme
Lecture 4: Fascism and Communism, Dominic Keller
Lecture 5: The Corporative Order, Virgil Michel

April 25–26, 1936
Political Principles: Internationalism

Lecture 1: International Society, Virgil Michel
Lecture 2: Culture and Social Values, Dunstan Tucker
Lecture 3: The Mystical Body and War, Benjamin Stein
Lecture 4: Place of Nationalism, Dominic Keller
Lecture 5: Ethics of War, Ernest Kilzer

## Appendix V. Summary of *Blessing of Seeds and Soil for the Feast of St. Isidore*

Summary of *Blessing of Seeds and Soil for the Feast of St. Isidore*

In a procession (with singing), the children and adults brought forward soil and seeds in decorated baskets and placed them at the communion rail to be blessed. Even "city people" were encouraged to bring seed and soil for their lawn or garden.

The priest recites the antiphon: "And other seeds fell upon good ground, and yielded good fruit, / some a hundred-fold, some sixty-fold, some thirty-fold." The people followed in unison and recited Psalm 65:10-14: "You have visited the land and watered it . . ." This was followed by a "Glory be . . ." which the priest concluded by repeating the antiphon "And other seed fell on good ground . . ." All sung the hymn *Come Holy Ghost*.

The introductory dialogue "Our help is in the name of the Lord . . ." began the blessing of seed. The blessing was recited by the people: "To Thee, O Lord, we cry and pray; bless this sprouting seed, strengthen it in the gentle movement of soft winds, refresh it with the dew of heaven, and let it grow to full maturity for the good of body and soul." However, immediately following this English text one found the same blessing in Latin: "Adjutórium nostrum in nomine Dómini . . ." The seed was then sprinkled with holy water.

The blessing of soil followed. The introductory dialogue began as above: "Our help. . . . And with thy spirit." However, the dialogue was expanded to include: "Send forth Thy spirit and they shall be created / And Thou shalt renew the face of the earth / For the Lord will give goodness / And our earth shall yield her fruit."

Blessing (all): We humbly beseech Thy clemency, O Lord, that Thou wouldst render this soil fertile with rains in due season, and Thou would fill it with Thy blessing, and do grant Thy people may be ever thankful for Thy gifts. Take infertility from the earth, and fill the hungry with Thy gifts, which the fruitful earth will yield in fullness, that the poor and needy may praise the name of Thy glory forever and ever. Amen. (Repeated in Latin)

The soil was sprinkled with holy water and they concluded the ceremony by singing the *Hymn to St. Isidore* [composed by Clifford Bennett].

This led into the celebration of the feast day Eucharistic liturgy, for which the Mass parts were provided in order to foster participation.

# Bibliography

**Manuscript Sources**

The Archdiocese of St. Louis Archives. St. Louis, Missouri.

The Diocese of Covington, Kentucky Archives. Covington, Kentucky.

The Diocese of Springfield, Illinois Archives. Springfield, Illinois.

The Frederick P. Kenkel Papers. University of Notre Dame Archives. Notre Dame, Indiana.

The John L. LaFarge, SJ, Papers. Georgetown University Archives. Washington, District of Columbia.

The Joseph Gremillion Papers. University of Notre Dame Archives. Notre Dame, Indiana.

The Midwest Jesuit Archives. St. Louis, Missouri.

The Monsignor Luigi G. Ligutti Papers. Marquette University Archives. Milwaukee, Wisconsin.

The National Catholic Rural Life Conference Records. Marquette University Archives. Milwaukee, Wisconsin.

The National Catholic Welfare Conference/United States Catholic Conference, Social Action Department. The Catholic University of America Archives. Washington, District of Columbia.

The Rural Life Collection. St. John's University Archives. Collegeville, Minnesota.

The Seminarians' Catholic Action Collection. Marquette University Archives. Milwaukee, Wisconsin.

The Virgil Michel Papers. St. John's Abbey Archives. Collegeville, Minnesota.

**Unpublished Sources**

Bovée, David. "The Church and the Land: the National Catholic Rural Life Conference and American Society, 1923–1985." PhD dissertation. University of Chicago, 1986.

Henry, Miranda Gail. "Between Two Cultures: Fr. Hermann Joseph Untraut (1854–1941) and His Pioneering Efforts in the Liturgical Movement in Wisconsin." PhD dissertation. University of Virginia, 2003.


**Primary Published Sources**

Adam, Adolf. *The Liturgical Year: Its History and Meaning after the Reform of the Liturgy*. New York: Pueblo, 1981.

Adam, Karl. "The Assumption of Our Lady." *Orate Fratres* 3 (1928–29): 289–291.

Adams, Anthony. "God's Gift." *Land and Home* 8 (December 1945): 33.

Agrari-Ann, (An). "Catholic Rural Artists." *Land and Home* 10 (March 1947): 3–4.

———. "Catholic Rural Artists." *Land and Home* 10 (June 1947): 42–43.

———. "Catholic Rural Artists." *Land and Home* 10 (September 1947): 70–71.

Allen, Thomas. "Ember Days and the Land." *Land and Home* 6 (September 1943): 76–77.

———. "The Land and Sacramentals." *Land and Home* 5 (September 1942): 2–3.

———. "The Liturgical Week." *Land and Home* 5 (December 1942): 20.

Anderson, E. Byron. *Worship and Christian Identity: Practicing Ourselves*. Collegeville, MN: Liturgical Press, 2003.

Andrieu, Michel. *Les Ordines Romani Du Haut Moyen Age*. Vol. IV. Louvain: Spicilegium Sacrum Lovaniense, 1971.

Aune, Michael B. "Liturgy and Theology: Rethinking the Relationship." *Worship* 81 (January 2007): 46–68.

———. "Liturgy and Theology: Rethinking the Relationship Part II." *Worship* 81 (March 2007): 141–170.

Barry, Colman. *Worship and Work: Saint John's Abbey and University, 1856–1992*. Collegeville, MN: Liturgical Press, 1993.

Bartholome, Peter W. *The Land and The Spirit*. Des Moines: National Catholic Rural Life Conference, 1947.

Baxter, Michael. "Reintroducing Virgil Michel: Towards a Counter-Tradition of Catholic Social Ethics in the United States." *Communio* 24 (Fall 1997): 499–528.

266

Benedict XVI. Encyclical Letter *Caritas in Veritate* of the Supreme Pontiff Benedict XVI *On Integral Human Development in Charity and Truth.* Rome: Libreria Editrice Vaticana, June 29, 2009.

Bergant, Diane. *The Earth Is the Lord's: The Bible, Ecology and Worship.* American Essays in Liturgy. Collegeville, MN: Liturgical Press, 1998.

Berger, Florence E. *Cooking for Christ: The Liturgical Year in the Kitchen.* Des Moines, IA: National Catholic Rural Life Conference, 1949.

Bernstein, Eleanor, ed. *Liturgy and Spirituality in Context.* Collegeville: Liturgical Press, 1990.

Berry, Wendell. "Higher Education and Home Defense." In *Home Economics.* San Francisco, CA: North Point Press, 1987.

———. "Property, Patriotism, and Nation Defense." In *Home Economics.* Chap. 7, 98–111. San Francisco, CA: North Point Press, 1987.

———. "The Loss of the University." In *Home Economics.* San Francisco: North Point Press, 1987.

———. *The Hidden Wound.* San Francisco: North Point Press, 1989.

———. "The Pleasures of Eating." In *What Are People For?* 45–52. New York: Northpoint Press, 1990.

———. "The Agricultural Crisis As a Crisis of Culture." In *The Unsettling of America: Culture and Agriculture.* Chap. 4, 39–50. San Francisco, CA: Sierra Club Books, 1996.

———. *The Unsettling of America: Culture & Agriculture.* San Francisco: Sierra Club Book, 1996.

———. "The Whole Horse." In Wirzba, Norman, ed. *The Art of the Commonplace: The Agrarian Essays of Wendell Berry.* Washington, DC: Counterpoint, 2002.

———. "Thoughts in the Presence of Fear." In *Citizenship Papers.* Chap. 2, 17–22. Washington, DC: Shoemaker & Hoard, 2003.

———. "A Native Hill." In *The Long-Legged House.* Washington, DC: Shoemaker & Ward, 1969, 2004.

———. "Going to Work." In *The Essential Agrarian Reader: The Future of Culture, Community and the Land,* edited by Norman Wirzba. Chap. 15, 259–266. Washington, DC: Shoemaker and Hoard, 2004.

———. "The Way of Ignorance." In *The Way of Ignorance and Other Essays by Wendell Berry.* Part II, 53–68. Berkeley, CA: Counterpoint Press, 2005.

Bovée, David. *The Church and the Land: The National Catholic Rural Life Conference and American Society, 1923–2007.* Washington, DC: The Catholic University of America Press, 2009.

Bowen, Lee. "Symbolic Plowing." *Land and Home* 5 (December 1942): 5.

Brown, Alden. *The Grail Movement and American Catholicism, 1940–1975.* Notre Dame, IN: University of Notre Dame Press, 1989.

Brueggemann, Walter. *The Land: Place as Gift, Promise, and Challenge in Biblical Faith,* 2nd ed. Minneapolis: Fortress, 2002.

Bularzik, Rembert, OSB. "The Mind of the Church after Easter and Whitsuntide: Participation Outlines." *Orate Fratres* 9 (1934–35): 289–299.

Busch, William. "Liturgy and Farm Relief." *Catholic Rural Life* 8 (April 1930): 2–3.

Carlen, Claudia, IHM, ed. *The Papal Encyclicals: 1903–1939.* Wilmington, NC: McGrath Publishing, 1981.

Carlson, Allan. *The New Agrarian Mind: The Movement Toward Decentralist Thought in Twentieth-Century America.* New Brunswick, NJ: Transaction Publishers, 2000.

Chinnici, Joseph P. *Living Stones: The History and Structure of Catholic Spiritual Life in the United States.* New York and London: Collier Macmillan Publishers, 1989.

Chinnici, Joseph P., and Angelyn Dries, eds. *Prayer and Practice in the American Catholic Community.* Maryknoll, NY: Orbis Books, 2000.

Corpus Christi Sister, A. "A Corner of Our Lord's Vineyard." *Catholic Rural Life* 6 (February 1928): 10–11.

———. "The Corpus Christi Sisters." *Catholic Rural Life* 6 (November 1927): 13–14.

———. "Two Mission Sketches." *Catholic Rural Life* 6 (March 1928): 12.

———. "What in Life Is Most Worth While?" *Catholic Rural Life* 7 (January 1929): 8.

Cousins, Joseph A. *The Golden Secret of Green Acres.* Somerset, OH: Rosary Press, 1950.

Cram, Ralph Adams. "The Status of Church Art and Architecture." *Catholic Rural Life Bulletin* 1 (May 1938): 7–9.

———. "Strength from the Good Earth." *Catholic Rural Life Bulletin* 3 (May 1940): 1–3.

Cromartie, John, and Shawn Bucholtz. "Defining the 'Rural' in Rural America." *Amber Waves* 6, no. 3 (June 2008).

Curran, Charles E. *American Catholic Social Ethics: Twentieth-century Approaches*. Notre Dame, IN: University of Notre Dame Press, 1982.

Dachauer, Alban J. *The Rural Life Prayerbook*. Compiled by Alban Dachauer, SJ. Des Moines, IA: National Catholic Rural Life Conference, 1956.

Danbom, David B. *Born in the Country: A History of Rural America*, 2nd ed. Baltimore, MD: John's Hopkins Press, 2006.

Davis, Ellen. *Scripture, Culture, and Agriculture: An Agrarian Readings of the Bible*. New York: Cambridge University Press, 2009.

Day, Dorothy. *The Long Loneliness*. New York: Harper, 1952.

Day, Victor. "Catechism by Mail." *Catholic Rural Life* 4 (November 1925): 6.

Dickey, Susan Karina, OP. "Father George Nell, the Farmer's Friend in Jasper County." Paper delivered at the Conference on Illinois History, October 9, 2003.

Dolan, Jay P. *The American Catholic Experience: A History from Colonial Times to the Present*. New York: Doubleday, 1985.

Dolan, Timothy. *Some Seed Fell on Good Ground: The Life of Edwin V. O'Hara*. Washington, DC: The Catholic University of America Press, 1992.

———. "The Rural Ideology of Edwin O'Hara." *U.S. Catholic Historian* 8 (Fall 1989): 117–129.

Drabek, Josephine. *Love Made Visible*. Des Moines, IA: NCRLC, 1946.

———. *Rogation Days at Maranatha*. Des Moines, IA: NCRLC, 1951.

Editor. "Coops Again." *Catholic Rural Life Bulletin* 3 (February 1940): 9.

———. "Immediate Steps in Catholic Rural Life." *Catholic Rural Life* 5 (December 1926): 1–2.

———. "It Can Be Done." *Worship* 29 (1954–55): 485–486.

———. "Land Policy." *Land and Home* 8 (September 1945): 61–62.

———. "Rural Life Summer School." *Catholic Rural Life Bulletin* 3 (May 1940): 3.

———. "The Apostolate." *Orate Fratres* 8 (1934): 226–231.

———. "The Apostolate." *Orate Fratres* 10 (1936): 10–13.

———. "The Apostolate." *Orate Fratres* 14 (1939–40): 475–476.

———. "The Apostolate." *Orate Fratres* 14 (1940): 558–562.

———. "The Apostolate." *Orate Fratres* 18 (1943–44): 564–68.

Egan, John. "Liturgy and Justice: The Unfinished Agenda." *Origins* (September 22, 1983): 245–253.

Ehmann, Benedict. "Gather Ye into My Barns." *Land and Home* 9 (September 1946): 66–68.

Ellard, Gerald. "A Papal Motto and Its Meaning." *Orate Fratres* 1 (1927): 141–145.

———. "Liturgy for the Common Man in Austria." *Orate Fratres* 3 (1928-29): 7–9.

Empereur, James, and Christopher Kiesling. *The Liturgy That Does Justice: A New Approach to Liturgical Praxis*. Collegeville, MN: Liturgical Press, 1991.

Esser, Ignatius. "Farm Home—Kingdom and Sanctuary." *Land and Home* 7 (June 1944): 34–36.

Evenou, Jean. "Processions, Pilgrimages, Popular Religion." In *The Church at Prayer: The Sacraments*, edited by A. G. Martimort, and translated by Matthew J. O'Connell. One-volume edition. Collegeville, MN: Liturgical Press, 1992.

Farmer, David Hugh, general ed. "Isidore the Husbandman (Farmer)." In *Butler's Lives of the Saints*. Tunbridge Wells, Kent: Burns & Oates; Collegeville, MN: Liturgical Press, 1995.

Flannery, Austin, ed. *Vatican II: The Conciliar and Post Conciliar Documents*. Northport, NY: Costello Publishing, 1992.

Francis, Mark. "Announcing God's Reign: Liturgy, Life, and Justice." In *Finding Voice to Give God Praise*, edited by Kathleen Hughes. Collegeville, MN: Liturgical Press, 1998.

Freyfogel, Eric T., ed. "A Durable Scale." In *The New Agrarianism: Land, Culture, and the Community Life*. Washington, DC: Island Press, 2001.

Gardener, Bruce L. *American Agriculture in the Twentieth Century: How It Flourished and What It Cost*. Cambridge, MA: Harvard University Press, 2002.

Gauchat, William. "Cult, Culture, and Cultivation." *Catholic Rural Life Bulletin* 4 (August 1941): 64–66.

Gleason, Philip. *The Conservative Reformers: German-American Catholics and the Social Order*. Notre Dame, IN: University of Notre Dame Press, 1968.

Gremillion, Joseph. *The Journal of a Southern Pastor*. Chicago: Fides Publishers Association, 1957.

Groome, Thomas H. "Total Catechesis/Religious Education: A Vision for Now and Always." In *Horizons and Hopes: The Future of Religious Education*, edited by Thomas H. Groome and Harold D. Horell. New York: Paulist, 2003.

Haering, Dom Otto. "The Assumption of Our Lady." *Orate Fratres* 3 (1928–29): 289–291.

Hall, Jeremy. *The Full Stature of Christ: The Ecclesiology of Virgil Michel, O.S.B.* Collegeville, MN: Liturgical Press, 1976.

Hayne, Donald. "Westphalia: Pattern and Promise." *Catholic Rural Life Bulletin* 2 (August 1939): 18–19, 28.

Hellriegel, Martin. "A Pastor's Description of Liturgical Participation in His Parish." *National Liturgical Week, 1941.* Newark, NJ: The Benedictine Liturgical Conference, 1942.

———. "Archbishop Schlarman." *Worship* 26 (1951–52): 82–83.

———. "Brief Meditations on the Church Year: Fifth Sunday after Easter." *Orate Fratres* 18 (1943–44): 291–308.

———. "Family Life, the Liturgical Year and the Sacramentals." *National Liturgical Week* 1946. Elsberry, MO: The Liturgical Conference, 1947.

———. "Merely Suggesting I: Sprung from the Seed of Abraham." *Orate Fratres* 15 (1940–41): 442–443.

———. "Seasonal Suggestions." *Orate Fratres* 30 (1955–56): 374–390.

———. "Towards a Living Parish." *Worship* 30 (1955–56): 458–470.

Hennig, John. "Prayers for Farmers." *Orate Fratres* 18 (1943–44): 494–502.

Hesburgh, Theodore. "Theology of Catholic Action." In *The Lay Apostolate and the Priest: Talks Given at the Fifth Annual Week of Catholic Action Study for Priests, University of Notre Dame, August 4 to 8, 1947.* South Bend, IN: Fides Press, 1947.

Heschel, Abraham. *The Sabbath.* New York, NY: Harper Torchbooks, 1966.

Himes, Kenneth. "Eucharist and Justice: Assessing the Legacy of Virgil Michel." *Worship* 62 (May 1988): 201–224.

Hughes, Kathleen. *The Monk's Tale: A Biography of Godfrey Diekmann, O.S.B.* Collegeville, MN: Liturgical Press, 1991.

_____, ed. *Finding Voice to Give God Praise: Essays in the Many Languages of the Liturgy.* Collegeville, MN: Liturgical Press, 1998.

_____, ed. *How Firm a Foundation: Voices of the Early Liturgical Movement.* Chicago, IL: Liturgy Training Publications, 1990.

Hughes, Kathleen, and Mark R. Francis, eds. *Living No Longer for Ourselves: Liturgy and Justice in the Nineties.* Collegeville, MN: Liturgical Press, 1991.

Hurt, R. Douglas. *American Agriculture: A Brief History*, rev. ed. West Lafayette, IN: Purdue University Press, 2002.

Hynes, Emerson. "Before All Else." *Orate Fratres* 17 (1942–43): 204–208.

———. "Consider the Person." *Catholic Rural Life Bulletin* 2 (May 1939): 9–11, 28–29.

———. "Land and Liturgy I." *Orate Fratres* 13 (1938–39): 540–544.

———. "Land and Liturgy II." *Orate Fratres* 14 (1939–40): 14–18.

———. *Sacramental Protection of the Family*. Des Moines, IA: National Catholic Rural Life Conference, 1945.

———. "The Joy and Dignity of Work." *Catholic Rural Life Bulletin* 1 (November 1938): 16–18, 24–25.

Irwin, Kevin W. *Context and Text: Method in Liturgical Theology*. Collegeville, MN: Liturgical Press (Pueblo), 1994.

———. *Liturgical Theology: a Primer*. In American Essays in Liturgy. Collegeville, MN: Liturgical Press, 1990.

———. *Models of the Eucharist*. Mahwah, NJ: Paulist Press, 2005.

———. "Sacramentality and the Theology of Creation: A Recovered Paradigm for Sacramental Theology." *Louvain Studies* 23 (1998): 159–179.

John Paul II. *The Ecological Crisis: A Common Responsibility*, Message of His Holiness John Paul II for the Celebration of the World Day of Peace, January 1, 1990, Vatican City. In *And God Saw That It Was Good: Catholic Theology and the Environment*, edited by Drew Christiansen and Walter Grazer. Washington, DC: United States Catholic Conference, 1996.

Jounel, Paul. "Blessings." In *The Church at Prayer: The Sacraments*, edited by A. G. Martimort, and translated by Matthew J. O'Connell. One-volume edition. Collegeville, MN: Liturgical Press, 1992.

———. "Sunday and the Week." In *The Church at Prayer: The Liturgy and Time*, edited by A. G. Martimort, and translated by Matthew J. O'Connell. One-volume edition. Collegeville, MN: Liturgical Press, 1992.

Kalven, Janet. *Women Breaking Boundaries: A Grail Journey, 1940–1995*. Albany: State University of New York Press, 1999.

Kavanagh, Aidan. "Liturgical Business Unfinished and Unbegun." *Worship* 50 (1976) 354-364.

Kavanaugh, John. *Following Christ in a Consumer Society: The Spirituality of Cultural Resistance*. Maryknoll, NY: Orbis Books, 2006.

Kauffman, Christopher J. *Mission to Rural America: The Story of W. Howard Bishop, Founder of Glenmary.* New York: Paulist Press, 1991.

Kelleher, Margaret Mary. "Liturgy and Social Transformation: Exploring the Relationship." *U.S. Catholic Historian* 16 (Fall 1998): 58–70.

Ketter, Francis. "Psalms in Liturgical Processions." *Orate Fratres* 6 (1931–32): 502–505.

Kilmartin, Edward. *Christian Liturgy: Theology and Practice.* Kansas City, MO: Sheed and Ward, 1988.

Koester, Anne Y., ed. *Liturgy and Justice: To Worship God in Spirit and Truth.* Collegeville, MN: Liturgical Press, 2002.

LaFarge, John. "Land, the Hope of the Future." In *Catholic Rural Life Conference Proceedings.* NCRLC, 1933.

———. "Religion, the Groundwork of True American Culture." *Landward* 5 (Spring 1937): 1, 8–10.

———. "Returning Veterans to the Land." *Land and Home* 8 (March 1945): 16–17.

———. "Rural Racial Problems." *Land and Home* 7 (September 1944): 66–67.

———. "The Jacistes and Four-H." *Catholic Rural Life Bulletin* 2 (May 1939): 3.

———. *The Manner Is Ordinary.* New York: Harcourt Brace, 1954.

Leo the Great. *Sermons.* In *Fathers of the Church*, translated by Jane Patricia Freeland, CSJB, and Agnes Josephine Conway, SSJ. Washington, DC: The Catholic University of America Press, 1996.

Ligutti, Luigi. "Communism Goes to Mass." *Land and Home* 7 (June 1944): 32–33.

———. "Rural Recreation." *Orate Fratres* 21 (1946–47): 330.

———. "Sacrifice and Society: The Rural Problem." In *The National Liturgical Week*, 1943. Ferdinand, IN: The Liturgical Conference, 1944.

Ligutti, Luigi, G. and John C. Rawe, SJ. *Rural Roads to Security: America's Third Struggle for Freedom.* Milwaukee, WI: Bruce Publishing, 1940.

Liph, Samson. "Jewish Farm Settlements." *Land and Home* 7 (September 1944): 62–63.

Lowdermilk, Walter C. "The 11th Commandment." *American Forests* 46 (January 1940), 12–15.

Madeleva, Sr. M., CSC. "Limitations." *Land and Home* 3 (May 1940): 10.

———. "The Pepper Tree." *Land and Home* 3 (May 1940): 26.

Mannion, M. Francis. "Liturgy and the Present Crisis of Culture." In *Liturgy and Spirituality in Context*, edited by Eleanor Bernstein, CSJ. Collegeville, MN: Liturgical Press, 1990.

Marlett, Jeffrey D. *Saving the Heartland: Catholic Missionaries in Rural America, 1920–1960*. DeKalb: Northern Illinois University Press, 2002.

———. "Harvesting an Overlooked Freedom: The Anti-Urban Vision of American Catholic Agrarianism." *U.S. Catholic Historian* 16, no. 4 (1998): 88–108.

Martimort, Aimé Georges, and Robert Cabié, Irénée Henri Dalmais, Pierre Jounel, eds. *The Church at Prayer*, translated by Matthew J. O'Connell. One-volume edition. Collegeville, MN: Liturgical Press, 1992.

Marx, Paul. *Virgil Michel and the Liturgical Movement*. Collegeville, MN: Liturgical Press, 1957.

McBrien, Richard. *Catholicism*. New York: HarperCollins, 1994.

———, ed. *The HarperCollins Encyclopedia of Catholicism*. San Francisco, CA: HarperCollins, 1995.

McCarraher, Eugene. "American Gothic: Sacramental Radicalism and the Neo-Medievalist Cultural Gospel, 1928–48." *Records of American Catholic Historical Society Philadelphia* 106, nos. 1–2 (Spring–Summer 1995): 3–23.

———. "The Church Irrelevant: Paul Hanley Furfey and the Fortunes of American Catholic Radicalism." *Religion and American Culture* 7 (Summer 1997): 163–194.

McKibben, Bill. *Deep Economy: The Wealth of Communities and the Durable Future*. New York, NY: Times Books, 2007.

Michel, Virgil. "Agriculture and Reconstruction." *Commonweal* 29 (January 13, 1939): 317–318.

———. "A Religious Need of the Day." *Catholic Educational Review* 23 (1925): 449–456.

———. "Christian Education for Rural Living." *Catholic Rural Life Bulletin* 1 (August 1938): 19–21.

———. *Christian Social Reconstruction: Some Fundamentals of Quadragesimo Anno*. Milwaukee, New York: Bruce Publishing Co., 1937.

———. "City or Farm." *Orate Fratres* 12 (1937–38): 367–369.

———. "Liturgy: The Basis of Social Regeneration." *Orate Fratres* 9 (1935): 536–545.

———. "Natural and Supernatural Society: I. The Sacramental Principle As Guide." *Orate Fratres* 10 (1936): 243–247.

———. "Natural and Supernatural Society: II. Spiritual Communion of Goods." *Orate Fratres* 10 (1936): 293–296.

———. "Natural and Supernatural Society: III. Material Goods and the Supernatural Life." *Orate Fratres* 10 (1936): 338–342.

———. "Natural and Supernatural Society: IV. Early Christian Communism." *Orate Fratres* 10 (1936): 394–398.

———. "Natural and Supernatural Society: V. The Christian Possession of Goods." *Orate Fratres* 10 (1936): 434–438.

———. No title. *Catholic Rural Life Bulletin* 1 (August 1938): 3.

———. *Our Life in Christ*. Collegeville, MN: Liturgical Press, 1939.

———. "Participation in the Mass." *Orate Fratres* 1 (1926–27): 17–20.

———. "Pig to End Depression." *Indian Sentinel* 13 (1932–33): 30.

———. "The Cooperative Movement and the Liturgical Movement." *Orate Fratres* 14 (1939–40): 152–160.

———. "The Liturgical Movement and the Future." *America* 54 (October 12, 1935): 6–7.

———. *The Liturgy and Catholic Life*. 1936.

———. *The Liturgy of the Church According to the Roman Rite*. New York: Macmillan, 1937.

———. "The Scope of the Liturgical Movement." *Orate Fratres* 10 (1936): 485–490.

_____, ed. *The Social Problem II: Economics and Finance*. St. Paul, MN: Wanderer Printing Co., 1936.

_____, ed. *The Social Problem III—Political Theories and Forms*. St. Paul, MN: Wanderer Printing Co., 1936.

_____, ed. *The Social Problem IV: The Mystical Body and Social Justice*. Collegeville, MN: St. John's Abbey, 1938.

———. "Timely Tracts: City or Farm?" *Orate Fratres* 12 (1937–38): 367–369.

Mikolasek, V. M. "Bohemian Catholic Rural Activities." *Catholic Rural Life* 3 (July 1925): 6, 8.

Miller, Raymond W. *Monsignor Ligutti: The Pope's County Agent*. Washington, DC: University Press of America, 1981.

Miller, Vincent, J. *Consuming Religion: Christian Faith and Practice in a Consumer Culture.* New York: Continuum, 2004.

Miss Mary. "A Year with the Rural Parish Workers." *Review for Religious* 12 (September 1953): 242–248.

Moore, Ruth Craig. "Holy Mass of the Harvest." *The Louisville Courier-Journal.* December 27, 1953, 7–9.

Morrison, Joseph. "Using Sacramentals." *Orate Fratres* 24 (1950–51): 128–132.

Muench, Aloisius. "A Friend of Rural Life." *Orate Fratres* 13 (1938–39): 130–134.

———. *Partnership with God.* Des Moines, IA: National Catholic Rural Life Conference, 1941.

Murnion, Philip. "A Sacramental Church in the Modern World." *Origins* 14 (June 21, 1984): 81–90.

National Catholic Rural Life Conference. *A Program for the Family Farm.* Des Moines, IA: NCRLC, ca. 1956.

———. *Blessing and Prayers for the Feast of the Assumption in Honor of Our Lady of the Fields.* Des Moines, IA: NCRLC, 1955.

———. *Catholic Rural Life Objectives: A Series of Discussions on Some Elements of Major Importance in the Philosophy of Agrarianism.* St. Paul, MN: National Catholic Rural Life Conference, 1936.

———. *Christianity and the Land.* Des Moines, IA: NCRLC, 1951.

———. *Manifesto on Rural Life.* Milwaukee: Bruce Publishing, 1939.

———. *Manual for Rural Retreats and Family Meditation.* Des Moines, IA: NCRLC, n.d.

———. *Novena in Honor of St. Isidore.* Des Moines, IA: NCRLC, 1954.

———. *The Family, Church and Environment.* Des Moines, IA: NCRLC, 1947.

———. *The Land: God's Gift to Man.* Des Moines, IA: NCRLC, 1952.

Nutting, Willis. "Foundations of a Rural Christian Culture." *Catholic Rural Life Bulletin* 2 (February 1939): 1–2, 26–28.

———. "Pattern for a Native Rural Culture." *Catholic Rural Life Bulletin* 3 (May 1940): 9–11, 28–29.

O'Hara, Edwin V. "Catholic Vacation Schools." *St. Isidore's Plow* 7 (May 1923): 1.

———. "Missionary Work in Rural Parishes." *Catholic Rural Life* 3 (May 1925): 5.

———. "Religious Vacation Schools." *Catholic Rural Life* 8 (March 1930): 2–4.

———. "Sixty Hours of Religious Instruction." *NCWC Bulletin* 11 (July 1929): 6–7.

———. *The Church and the Country Community*. New York: MacMillan, 1927.

———. "The Clergy and Rural Life." *St. Isidore's Plow* 2 (October 1923): 3.

———. "The Great Problem of the Rural Pastor." *St. Isidore's Plow* 2 (October 1923): 2.

O'Mahony, James E., OFM Cap. "Joy in Praise." *Orate Fratres* 2 (1927–28): 76–79.

———. "Liturgy and Life." *Orate Fratres* 11 (1936–37): 290–294.

———. "Nature and the Liturgy: St. Francis." *Orate Fratres* 1 (1926–27): 301–304.

———. "The Sacramental Principle." *Orate Fratres* 3 (1928–29): 7–9.

———. "The Sacramental Principle: Its Source." *Orate Fratres* 3 (1928–29): 178–180.

———. "The Voice of Nature: The Voice of the Church." *Orate Fratres* 1 (1926–27): 167–71.

O'Rourke, Edward. "Sermon Outline: A Valiant Woman." *Land and Home* 8 (June 1945): 47–48.

———. "Soil Saving—A Plan." *Land and Home* 9 (March 1947): 22–23.

Pecklers, Keith. *The Unread Vision: The Liturgical Movement in the United States of America, 1926–1955*. Collegeville, MN: Liturgical Press, 1998.

Pius X. *E Supremi*. October 4, 1903. In *The Papal Encyclicals: 1903–1939*, Claudia Carlen, IHM., ed. Wilmington, NC: McGrath Publishing, 1981.

Pius XII. "The Pope Speaks on Rural Life." Speech delivered by His Holiness, Pope Pius XII to the delegates at the Convention of the National Confederation of Farm Owner-Operators. Rome, November 15, 1946.

Pollan, Michael. *The Omnivore's Dilemma: A Natural History of Four Meals*. New York: Penguin Press, 2006.

Power, David N. *Unsearchable Riches: The Symbolic Nature of Liturgy*. Collegeville, MN: Liturgical Press/Pueblo, 1984.

Quinlan, Patrick. "Rural Migrants on the March." *Catholic Rural Life Bulletin* 2 (May 1939): 12–13, 25–26.

Raphael, Sr. M., BVM. "En Route." *Land and Home* 7 (June 1944): 39.

Rawe, John. "Biodynamics." *Land and Home* 6 (September 1943): 67.

Reinhold, Hans Ansgar. "Secular and Religious Civilization." *Orate Fratres* 14 (1939–40): 558–561.

———. "Timely Tracks: Back to What?" *Worship* 26 (1951–52): 248–256.

———. "Timely Tracks: Rural Liturgy." *Orate Fratres* 18 (1943–44): 364–368.

Reynolds, Pauline. "Live Nobly and Well." *Catholic Rural Life Bulletin* 2 (February 1939): 8–10.

———. "Rural Dramatics in North Dakota." *Catholic Rural Life Bulletin* 2 (August 1939): 12–13, 16–17.

Roberts, John. "Harvest Thanksgiving." *Land and Home* 7 (December 1944): 98.

Roney, H. F. "A Thanksgiving Mass." *Catholic Rural Life* 3 (November 1925): 6.

Ross, Eva J. "Rural Priest Leads the Way." *Columbia* (October 1942): 9, 18–19.

———. "School for Living." *Columbia* (September 1941): 7, 24.

Ross, Susan A. *Extravagant Affections: A Feminist Sacramental Theology*. New York: Continuum, 1998.

Sacco, Paul. "Soil Reconstruction." *Land and Home* 9 (December 1947): 91–93.

Schirber, Martin E., OSB. "Catholic Rural Life." In *The American Apostolate*. Leo R. Ward, ed. Westminster, MD: Newman Press, 1952.

———. "Review of Manifesto on Rural Life." *Orate Fratres* 14 (1939–40): 93–94.

Schlarman, (Bishop) Joseph. *Catechetical Sermon-Aids*. St. Louis, MO / London: B. Herder Book Co., 1942.

———. "The Liturgy and the Parish." *Orate Fratres* 9 (1934): 10–13.

———. *With the Blessing of the Church*. Translated by Most Rev. Joseph H. Schlarman, Bishop of Peoria, IL. Des Moines, IA: NCRLC, 1947.

Schmiedeler, Edgar, OSB. "Art in the Countryside." *Catholic Rural Life Bulletin* 1 (November 1938): 7.

———. *Why Rural Life?* Washington, DC: National Catholic Welfare Conference, 1933.

Scholtz, Bede, OSB. "Family Sacramentals." *Orate Fratres* 5 (1930–31): 115–118.

———. "Religious Sacramentals." *Orate Fratres* 5 (1930–31): 400–405.

———. "Sacramentals: A General Idea." *Orate Fratres* 4 (1929–30): 545–549.

———. "Sacramentals and the Sick." *Orate Fratres* 5 (1930–31): 158–162.

———. "Sacramentals in Industry." *Orate Fratres* 5 (1930–31): 268–271.

————. "Sacramentals: The Sacramentals and Agriculture." *Orate Fratres* 5 (1930–31): 323–326.

Searle, Mark. "Serving the Lord with Justice." In *Liturgy and Social Justice*. Edited by Mark Searle. Collegeville, MN: Liturgical Press, 1980.

————. "The Liturgy and Catholic Social Doctrine." In *The Future of the Catholic Church in America: Major Papers of the Virgil Michel Symposium*, edited by John Roach, et al. Collegeville, MN: Liturgical Press, 1991.

Sengupta, Somini. "On India's Farms, a Plague of Suicide." *New York Times*, September 19, 2006.

Shapiro, Edward. "Catholic Agrarian Thought and the New Deal." *Catholic Historical Review* 65 (October 1979): 583–599.

————. "The Catholic Rural Life Movement and the New Deal Farm Program." *American Benedictine Review* 28 (September 1977): 307–322.

Sister Mary Charity, OP. "Thanking for the Harvests." *Orate Fratres* 23 (1948–49): 538–541.

Sister of the Most Precious Blood, A. "Ascension Week in the Classroom." *Orate Fratres* 19 (1944–45): 279–281.

Society of Jesus. "We Live in a Broken World: Reflections on Ecology." *Promotio Iustitiae* 70 (1999).

Stritch, Samuel. *A Christian Day*. Des Moines, IA: National Catholic Rural Life Conference, 1942.

Sullivan, John. "Co-op Worship to Co-op Work." *Orate Fratres* 19 (1944–45): 320–324.

Sullivan, John P. *Forward on the Land: Benedictines Set Pace in Complete Rural Life*. Kingston, Jamaica: The Social Action Department, St. George's College Extension School, ca. 1944.

Talley, Thomas. *Origins of the Liturgical Year*. Collegeville, MN: Liturgical Press/Pueblo, 1986.

Tuzik, Robert L., ed. *How Firm a Foundation: Leaders of the Liturgical Movement*. Chicago: Liturgy Training Publications, 1990.

Urbain, Joseph. "How We Observed the Easter Vigil." *Orate Fratres* 27 (1952–53): 191–195.

————. "The Easter Nightwatch." *Orate Fratres* 27 (1952–53): 215–216.

Vogel, Cyrille. *Medieval Liturgy: An Introduction to the Sources*. Translated by William G. Storey and Niels Krogh Rasmussen. Washington, DC: Pastoral Press, 1981.

Walsh, John J. "Wheat." *Catholic Rural Life Bulletin* 1 (August 1938): 8.

Walsh, Michael, and Brian Davies, eds. *Proclaiming Justice and Peace: Papal Documents from* Rerum Novarum *through* Centesimus Annus. Mystic, CT: Twenty-Third Publications, 1994.

Ward, Leo, ed. *The American Apostolate; American Catholics in the Twentieth Century*. Westminster, MD: Newman Press, 1952.

Weaver, Mary Jo. "Still Feisty at Fifty: The Grailville Lay Apostolate for Women." *U.S. Catholic Historian* 11 (Fall 1993): 3–12.

Weiser, Francis X., *The Easter Book*. Illustrated by Robert Frankenberg. New York: Harcourt, Brace, 1954.

Weller, Philip T. "The Liturgy in Rural Parish Life." In *National Liturgical Week, 1945*. Peotone, IL: The Liturgical Conference, Inc., 1946.

———. *The Roman Ritual: The Blessings in Latin and English with Rubrics and Plainchant Notation*. Translated and edited by Philip T. Weller. Volume 3. Milwaukee: Bruce, 1946.

Wickes, Mariette. "A Family Celebration of the Ember Days." *Land and Home* (December 1946): 100–102.

Willette, Florence Hynes, *A Handful of Straw*. Des Moines, IA: NCRLC, 1958.

———. "New Church." *Catholic Rural Life Bulletin* 3 (February 1940): 21.

Wirzba, Norman, ed. *The Art of the Commonplace: The Agrarian Essays of Wendell Berry*. Washington, DC: Counterpoint, 2002.

_____, ed. "The Challenge of Berry's Agrarian Vision." In *The Art of the Commonplace: The Agrarian Essays of Wendell Berry*. Washington, DC: Counterpoint, 2002.

———. *The Paradise of God: Renewing Religion in an Ecological Age*. New York: Oxford University Press, 2003.

Witte, Raymond P. *Twenty-Five Years of Crusading: A History of the National Catholic Rural Life Conference*. Des Moines, IA: National Catholic Rural Life Conference, 1948.

Yzermans, Vincent A. *The People I Love: A Biography of Luigi G. Ligutti*. Collegeville, MN: Liturgical Press, 1976.

Zwick, Mark and Louise. *The Catholic Worker Movement: Intellectual and Spiritual Origins*. New York: Paulist Press, 2005.

## Related Works

Bellah, Robert, Richard Madsen, William M. Sullivan, et. al. *Habits of the Heart: Individualism and Commitment in American Life*. Berkeley: University of California Press, 1985.

Boff, Leonardo. *Sacraments of Life: Life of Sacraments*. Translated by John Drury. Washington, DC: Pastoral Press, 1987.

Burke, Mary Gabriel. *Liturgy at Holy Cross in Church and School*. St. Louis: Pio Decimo Press, 1952.

Busch, William. "The Liturgy: A School of Social Action." *Orate Fratres* 7 (1933): 6–12.

Cooke, Bernard. *Sacraments and Sacramentality*. Mystic, CT: Twenty-Third Publications, 1994.

Dries, Angelyn. *The Missionary Movement in American Catholic History*. Maryknoll, NY: Orbis Books, 1998.

Duffy, Regis, Kevin W. Irwin, and David N. Power. "Sacramental Theology: A Review of the Literature." *Theological Studies* 55 (1994): 657–606.

Ellard, Gerald. *Men at Work at Worship: America Joins the Liturgical Movement*. New York, Longmans, Green, 1940.

———. *Participation of the Faithful in the Priesthood*. Milwaukee: Bruce, 1955.

Evans, Bernard F., and Gregory D. Cusack, eds. *Theology of the Land*. Collegeville, MN: Liturgical Press, 1987.

Franklin, R. W., and Robert L. Spaeth. *Virgil Michel: American Catholic*. Collegeville, MN: Liturgical Press, 1988.

Irwin, Kevin. "A Spirited Community Encounters Christ: Liturgical and Sacramental Theology and Practice." In *Catholic Theology Facing the Future*, edited by Dermot Lane. New York: Paulist Press, 2003.

———. "Recent Sacramental Theology." *The Thomist* 47 (1983): 592–608.

———. "Recent Sacramental Theology." *The Thomist* 52 (1988): 124–147.

———. "Recent Sacramental Theology III." *The Thomist* 53 (1989): 281–313.

Jasper, Anthony, and Martin B. Hellriegel. "*Der Schluessel zur Loesung der sozial Frage*." St. Louis: Central Blatt, 1925.

———. *The True Basis of Christian Solidarity*. Translated by William Busch. St. Louis: Central Bureau of the Central Verein, 1938.

Kiesling, Christopher. "Paradigms of Sacramentality." *Worship* 44 (1970): 422–432.

Kuntzler, James Howard. *The Geography of Nowhere: The Rise and Decline of America's Man-Made Landscape*. New York: Touchstone, 1993.

Martindale, Cyril Charlie. *The Mind of the Missal*. New York: Macmillan, 1929.

Martínez, Anne M. "From the Halls of Montezuma: Seminary in Exile or Pan-American Project." *U.S. Catholic Historian* 20 (Fall 2002): 35–51.

McNabb, Vincent Joseph. *The Church and the Land*. London: Burns, Oates & Washbourne, Ltd., 1926.

Mounier, Emmanuel. *Personalist Manifesto*. Translated by the Monks of St. John's Abbey. London, New York, Longmans, Green, 1938.

O'Hara, Edwin V. *A Pioneer Catholic History of Oregon*. Portland, OR: Press of Glass and Prudhomme, 1911.

Parsch, Pius. *The Church's Year of Grace*. Translated by William G. Heidt. Collegeville, MN: Liturgical Press, 1959.

Peters, Jason, ed. *Wendell Berry: Life and Work*. Lexington: University of Kentucky Press, 2007.

Pius X. *Tre le Sollicitudini*. Vatican City: Acta Sanctae Sedis, 1903.

Pinches, Charles. *A Gathering of Memories; Family, Nation, and Church in a Forgetful World*. Grand Rapids, MI: Brazos Press, 2006.

Putnam, Robert. *Bowling Alone: America's Declining Social Capital*. Thousand Oaks, CA: Sage Publications, 2001.

Ross, Eva J. *Belgian Rural Cooperation: A Study in Social Adjustment*. Milwaukee: Bruce Publishing, 1940.

Ross, Susan A. *For the Beauty of the Earth: Women, Sacramentality, and Justice*. Mahwah, NJ: Paulist Press, 2006.

Schmiedeler, Edgar, OSB. *A Better Rural Life*. New York: J. F. Wagner, 1938.

Shaw, J. G. *Edwin Vincent O'Hara: American Prelate*. New York: Farrar, Straus, and Cudahy, 1957.

Shorto, Russell. "The Anti-Secularist." *The New York Times Magazine*, April 8, 2007.

Smith, Kimberly K. *Wendell Berry and the Agrarian Tradition: A Common Grace*. Lawrence: University of Kansas Press, 2003.

Spaeth, Robert L., ed. *The Social Question: Essays on Capitalism and Christianity by Father Virgil Michel*. Collegeville, MN: St. John's University, Office of Academic Affairs, 1987.

Stamps, Mary, ed. *To Do Justice and Right Upon the Earth*. Collegeville, MN: Liturgical Press, 1993.

Sullivan, John Francis. *The Visible Church: Her Government, Ceremonies, Sacramentals, Festivals and Devotions*. A Compendium of the Externals of the Catholic Church. 4th ed. New York: P. Kennedy Pub., 1922.

Twelve Southerners. *I'll Take My Stand: The South and the Agrarian Tradition*, With a New Introduction by Susan V. Donaldson, 75th Anniversary Edition. Baton Rouge: Louisiana State University Press, 2006.

Twelve Southerners. *I'll Take My Stand*. New York: Harpers, 1930.

Vaillancourt, Raymond. *Toward a Renewal of Sacramental Theology*. Translated by Matthew J. O'Connell. Collegeville, MN: Liturgical Press, 1979.

Vorgrimler, Herbert. *Sacramental Theology*. Translated by Linda M. Maloney. Collegeville, MN: Liturgical Press, 1992.

# Index